shaping
neighbourhoods

ONE WE

What they say about the second edition ...

This compact, constructive and holistic handbook provides practitioners and students with an action checklist for the conception and design of major regeneration areas, sustainable urban extensions, and small new towns. The checklist is substantiated by chapters giving summary data, case study references, and an outline of controversial issues (e.g. densification) about which - because there is no universal design formula - place-specific judgements must be made. The fresh emphasis on health and wellbeing gets right to the heart of the matter: healthy places are successful, creative and sustainable. This handbook is attractive, accessible and indispensible.

David Lock CBE MRTPI Chair of planning and urban design consultancy David Lock Associates (Milton Keynes and Melbourne); Vice President Town and Country Planning Association, and former Chief Planning Adviser to the UK Government.

Shaping Neighbourhoods is all about building and rebuilding communities from the inside out. Neighourhoods are all about a sense of belonging to a community, to a locality and, beyond that, to our home planet. This book is a remarkable achievement, telling us how to re-inhabit local environments whilst also keeping an eye on the global context and impacts of human settlements. I strongly recommend this beautifully presented book to all who want new tools to create a sustainable world.

Prof. Herbert Girardet, Co-founder and Director of Programmes, World Future Council

What they said about the first edition ...

Neighbourhoods can have an enormous influence on our health, well-being and quality of life. *Shaping Neighbourhoods* builds on the concepts and principles previously explored in the WHO handbook *Healthy Urban Planning*, providing a comprehensive and practical guide to creating local environments which respond to our daily demands. It should prove an invaluable resource for city practitioners and communities everywhere.

Agis Tsouros, Director, WHO Europe Non-communicatable Disease and Healthy Cities

CABE welcomes this publication for the helpful guidance it provides to everyone involved in neighbourhood planning. We are particularly pleased that it underlines the Government's emphasis on the importance of strategic spatial design and masterplanning.

Stuart Lipton, Chairman, CABE

There are very few texts that bridge the gap between community planning and spatial planning. *Shaping Neighbourhoods* is the exception, and is essential reading for communities seeking to influence the planning process.

Alison West, Director, CDF (Community Development Foundation)

shaping
neighbourhoods

for local health and global sustainability

Second edition

**Hugh Barton, Marcus Grant
and Richard Guise**

Routledge
Taylor & Francis Group

LONDON AND NEW YORK

First edition published 2003
by Routledge
This edition published 2010 by Routledge
2 Park Square, Milton Park, Abingdon, Oxon, OX14 4RN

Simultaneously published in the USA and Canada
by Routledge
270 Madison Avenue, New York, NY10016

Routledge is an imprint of the Taylor & Francis Group, an informa
business

Typeset in Linotype Ergo 9.25pt on 12pt
First edition designed by Joan Roskelly, Bookcraft Ltd, Stroud,
Gloucestershire based on a concept from the authors
Second edition designed by the authors and typeset by Jamie Roxburgh
Printed and bound in Great Britain
by Bell & Bain Ltd, Glasgow

British Library Cataloguing in Publication Data
A catalogue record for this book is available from the British Library

Library of Congress Cataloging in Publication Data
Barton, Hugh.
Shaping neighbourhoods : for local health and global sustainability /
Hugh Barton, Marcus Grant & Richard Guise. -- 2nd ed.
p.cm.
1. City planning--Environmental aspects. 2. Neighborhoods. 3.
Sustainable development. 4. Community development, Urban. I. Grant,
Marcus, 1958- II. Guise, Richard. III. Title.
HT166.B38653 2010
307.1'416--dc22
2009037316

ISBN10: 0–415–49548–2 (hbk)
ISBN10: 0–415–49549–0 (pbk)

ISBN13: 978–0–415–49548–6 (hbk)
ISBN13: 978–0–415–49549–3 (pbk)

Mixed Sources
Product group from well-managed
forests and other controlled sources
www.fsc.org Cert no. SGS-COC-004704
© 1996 Forest Stewardship Council

the authors

Hugh Barton conceived and led the original *Shaping Neighbourhoods* project. He is a town planner and Professor of Sustainability, Health and Planning at the University of the West of England. In the early eighties he founded the Urban Centre for Appropriate Technology – now the Centre for Sustainable Energy. He is Director of the WHO Collaborating Centre for Health Urban Environments at UWE. His books include *Sustainable Settlements, a Guide to Local Authority Auditing, Sustainable Communities and Healthy Urban Planning*. Research focuses on sustainable urban form, the way people behave in neighbourhoods, and inclusive, rational decision processes.

Marcus Grant is a landscape architect and, with a first degree in ecology, he has been examining issues of sustainable development and health for over twenty years in both consultancy and academia. He is an honorary member of the Faculty of Public Health and is currently deputy director of the WHO Collaborating Centre for Healthy Cities and Urban Policy. He specialises in stakeholder working and knowledge exchange for sustainability through a consensus building and participatory processes. He is programme leader for the MA Spatial Planning at UWE.

Richard Guise is an architect and town planner, and director of his urban design consultancy, Context4D. He was formerly Course Leader of the MA Urban Design programme at the University of the West of England, where he is Visiting Research Fellow. Richard's clients are mainly local authorities, for whom he provides design advice, in-house training, produces design guides, urban design studies and conservation area appraisals. He was co-author of Sustainable Settlements and the South East and South West volumes of Streets for All, for English Heritage.

contents

Chapter 1

ORIENTATION AND PRINCIPLES

'Neighbourhood' is a contested concept. This chapter draws critical distinctions and sets out the planning principles that are used throughout the guide, linking them to wider policy debates.

Chapter 2

A NEIGHBOURHOOD PLANNING PROCESS

This chapter is about the process of creating neighbourhood-level spatial plans. It tells you how to go about collaborative decision-making, and how to ensure that policies are properly aimed at sustainable development.

Chapter 3

PROVIDING FOR LOCAL NEED

Here the emphasis is on spatial policies that promote health, equity and accessibility. The chapter explores who lives in a locality, and how to increase the level of local choice in housing, jobs, services, open space and movement.

Chapter 4

WORKING WITH NATURAL SYSTEMS

This chapter deals with policies and design for environmental sustainability at the local level. It covers the key resources of energy, water, food, materials and wildlife.

Chapter 5

NEIGHBOURHOOD DESIGN

While the two previous chapters are topic-based, this one provides integrated guidance for the physical development of neighbourhoods in terms of density, shape, use-mixing, and community.

Chapter 6

NEIGHBOURHOOD CHECKLISTS

Some users of the guide will be concerned with producing an integrated community plan, but many will be concerned with specific newbuild or regeneration projects that affect a locality. This chapter gives sustainability checklists for both. It also acts as a summary of the guide.

acknowledgements

Very many thanks are due to …

WHO Healthy Cities
Agis Tsouros and Claire Mitcham

Participants of the reference group

Philip Bisatt (Advisor RTPI Transport Panel and City and County of Swansea)
Amanda Brookman (The Recycling Consortium)
Robert Brown (North Hertfordshire District Council)
Caroline Brown (SPECTRA at UWE)
James Bruges (The Southern Trust)
Barbara Carroll (Enfusion Ltd)
Gillian Clark (Bath & North East Somerset Council)
Richard Copas (Environment Agency)
Patrick Devine-Wright (Institute of Energy and Sustainable Development)
Linda Ewles (Avon Health Authority)
Martin Fodor (Local Government Association & Bristol City Council)
Andy Fudge (Prowting Homes South West)
Oona Goldsworthy (Bristol City Council)
Adrian Gurney (Ove Arup & Partners)
Jo Hanslip (House Builders Federation)
Christine Hine (Avon Health Authority)
Janine Michael (Centre for Sustainable Energy)
Philip Smith (Land Use Consultants)
Mark Southgate (Royal Society for the Protection of Birds)

Staff from the Faculty of the Built Environment at the University of the West of England (UWE)

Caroline Brown, Jim Claydon, Isobel Daniels, Colin Fudge, Paul Revel, Vincent Nadin, Kim Seaton, Julie Triggle, Gillian Weadon

Others that helped
through correspondence, discussion and debate, both at the University of the West of England and in the wider world, including many staff and students at UWE, short course attendees, and in particular Matthew Frith (English Nature), Mike King (Energy Services Association), Robin Wiltshire (BRESCU)

For the second edition the authors would like to thank:

Jamie Roxburgh at UWE – for his commitment and creativity in laying out the pages for the whole text, including remarkable tolerance as ongoing changes and design tweaks were made; also assisting in the background at UWE; Louis Rice, Nada Brkljac, Tom Calvert, Chris Wade, Paul Revell, Caroline Graham and Elizabeth Smith .

Additional, and often last minute high resolution images, thanks to; Alison Bowyer, strategic GIS specialist at Stafford County Council; Alan Pearce, partner at AlderKing; Rebecca Sturge, senior project manager at Red Tree; Michael Ward

senior planning officer at Glasgow City Council and Martin Caraher, professor of food and health policy at City University.

Assistance with case studies; Ben Cave from Ben Cave Associates; Russell Jones from the Glasgow Centre for Population Health; Ove Mørck, director of Cenergia Energy Consultants, Denmark and Wulf Daseking, Director of City Planning, Freiburg, Germany

Additional help sourcing images and content from: Veronica Barry, Development Manager for Health and Well-Being at Ideal for All and Tim Jones, Campaigns Policy Officer at the World Development Movement; and UWE students Tom Albery and Emma Southward.

We would also like to thank a series of commissioning and production editors at Routledge for their patience; Caroline Malinder, Katherine Morton and Jodie Tierney.

Origins and funding

Shaping Neighbourhoods is in direct line of descent from the acclaimed guide to *Sustainable Settlements* (Barton, Davis and Guise 1995) which was jointly published by the University of the West of England and the Local Government Management Board.

The new manual has been produced by the WHO (World Health Organisation) Collaborating Centre for Healthy Cities and Urban Policy – based in the Faculty of the Built Environment at UWE – and under the auspices of the European region of the WHO Healthy Cities movement.

We are very grateful to the Southern Trust, Marks and Spencer and UWE itself for providing the resources which allowed this project to come to fruition.

foreword to the second edition

by Mike Kelly

Professor Mike Kelly is Director of the Centre for Public Health Excellence at the National Institute for Health and Clinical Excellence (NICE).

The relationship between place and health has been observed since public health first developed as a science in the nineteenth century. Yet notwithstanding the fact that the relationship between epidemic prevalence and the physical environment is well known, definitive understanding of how to develop and plan environments in such a way that they both maximise health gain and minimise the negative effects on people's lives of the physical spaces that they inhabit, has been surprisingly elusive.

Neighbourhoods and communities are the building blocks of people's lives. In a very real sense the immediate physical space we live in is the bridge between the social and biological dimensions of our lives. The impacts of the material and social world directly on our physical and mental health are profound. Planning is one of the mechanisms which can help to shape the nature of localities. However, this is a complex and demanding process and one where the importance of taking an evidence based approach is paramount.

This authoritative and comprehensive text provides helpful guidance on this very important public health issue. Its careful outline of the key areas and concepts as well as its very practical orientation and informative maps, plans and illustrations will provide a framework for the consideration of the factors involved in development and planning of the physical and social places in which we live and work for years to come. It's a great piece of work.

foreword to the first edition

by Jonathon Porritt

Jonathon Porritt is Director of Forum for the Future and former Chairman of the UK Sustainable Development Commission.

More and more, we're urged to celebrate the fact that we live in a more 'connected world'. Telecommunications, the internet, cheap air travel, increased car ownership: we certainly don't lack the means when it comes to staying in touch. Yet at the same time, there's growing evidence that people feel less connected to their local community or neighbourhood, less tied into that network of relationships and responsibilities that secure the 'social capital' on which we depend.

That loss of connection with locality can impoverish our lives and prejudice the integrity of local and global ecosystems. Urban problems of traffic congestion, pollution and health are in no small part due to the breakdown of neighbourhoods. Whilst many people feel little connection with their immediate locality (relying on work, leisure activities and social contacts far from home), others have little choice but to depend on declining local services, trapped in unsupportive, ill-served communities with little prospect of 'escape'.

Both planning and design are critical elements in addressing such dilemmas, as is powerfully reaffirmed in *Shaping Neighbourhoods*. Hugh Barton's text is very much 'of the moment', ensuring that the issues of health, social inclusion, economic vitality and sustainable use of resources are fully integrated. As such, it is likely to be an indispensable guide for students of and professionals in local planning. It should be required reading for all public sector investors, private developers and councillors whose decisions affect the future of neighbourhoods.

All across the world, innovative projects are now clearly demonstrating the huge potential for neighbourhood sustainability strategies that encompass housing, local facilities, rewarding livelihoods, green spaces, community development, food, energy, water and biodiversity. Such strategies can reinvigorate local communities whilst simultaneously playing a part in reducing the threat of global climate change and other pressing environmental and social concerns. All this is exactly in line with government aspirations: here in the UK, national policies for health, regeneration, transport energy and town planning all emphasise the importance of getting things right at the neighbourhood level.

Shaping Neighbourhoods manages to set a lot of important technical material in the context of an inclusive collaborative process, and provides clear signposts to involving local partners and people in the development of neighbourhood sustainability strategies. In that respect, it has the potential to make a profoundly empowering contribution to this critical debate by helping community groups to become even more focused and effective in their campaigns for better places to live, work and play.

how to use this manual

ITS PURPOSE AND SCOPE

This neighbourhood guide is designed as a desktop manual for planners, designers, developers and community groups. It provides an integrated picture of sustainable, healthy neighbourhoods, with a wealth of specific detail that can help local decision-makers, and people who are concerned about those decisions, get to grips with the issues.

The guide is radical, in that it tries to take the principle of sustainable development seriously, recognising the profound shift in practice that needs to occur. But it is not a utopian tract. It suggests policy options that are potentially implementable now – practical idealism.

The focus is on the physical fabric of neighbourhoods

The guide is concerned with how the planning, design and management of the physical environment can enhance quality of life, promote social inclusion and husband natural resources.

Two themes run through this guide:

- the neighbourhood as the local human habitat, providing a healthy, sustainable, convivial living environment
- the management of that habitat by voluntary co-operation between the various public, private and community stakeholders that affect it

It is not about social programmes (health, education etc.) or economic regeneration policy as such, but does deal with their implications for and interactions with space and place. It thus epitomises the integrated approach to town planning advocated by the EU and UK government, known as 'spatial planning'.

Converting rhetoric to reality

There is rarely one best answer for sustainability. The guide represents a staging post in a learning process. It cannot provide you with everything you need to know and makes no claim to infallibility. It tries to set out clearly the direction of change that is desirable, and the choices open to achieve it, allowing users to reach their own conclusions.

Equally, however, the guide attempts to distil the best knowledge and experience – from Europe and elsewhere, as well as the UK – and to synthesise diverse perspectives into coherent, integrated strategies for planning and design.

Its advice is generally consistent with UK government policy and has been prepared in consultation with a wide range of environmental, community and development agencies. If there is to be more than mere lip service paid to the goals of sustainable development and healthy communities, then this guide provides a challenge and a test.

Scope of the guide	Chapters	1	2	3	4	5	6
Theory	Neighbourhood planning principles	■				□	
	Ecosystem approach	■			□		
Processes	Collaborative decision-making	□	■				□
	Spatial planning frameworks	□	□	□		■	□
	Design briefs and masterplans		■			□	□
	Sustainability project appraisal		□	□	□	□	■
	Urban potential studies					■	□
Policies	Housing and community issues			■		□	□
	Local work and facilities			■		□	□
	Planning for movement			■		□	□
	Energy, water and other resources				■	□	□
	Biodiversity				■	□	□
	Mixed use and density			□		■	□
	Green space and recreation			□	■	□	□
	Detailed urban design			□		■	□

■ prime topic location   □ other locations

Pathways to follow through the guide

- **The contents pages** are designed for quick but precise pathfinding

- **The index** at the end of the book provides a finer topic net

- **The community checklist** in Chapter 6 gives a summary of the contents and an entry point for neighbourhood planning

- **The development checklist** in Chapter 6 gives a summary of the contents and entry point project design and appraisal

- **Cross-referencing** is given linking one topic to another

- **Page layout** assists quick flicking through to find a section

- **Follow-up reading** is suggested in the side column, with an extensive bibliography at the end

The guide is relevant to …

- existing urban neighbourhoods
- market towns
- urban regeneration projects
- new urban extensions
- new settlements
- town and district centres

It is useful to …

- local authority planners and designers
- public and private sector service providers (e.g. health, education, energy, water)
- commercial developers, house builders and housing associations
- planning, environmental and design consultants
- district, parish and town councillors
- community and environmental groups

It can help you with …

- defining what neighbourhoods are, or could be
- clarifying the full health and sustainability agenda
- working out a collaborative process for a Community Strategy
- preparing a spatial plan for an urban district or country town
- preparing development briefs and masterplans
- appraising the sustainability of development projects
- planning the natural ecology of settlements, coping with climate change
- tackling problems of social exclusion, unhealthy lifestyles and mental illness

orientation and principles | chapter 1

introduction

1.1 LOCAL GLOBAL PLANNING

Neighbourhoods are the localities in which people live. They imply a sense of belonging and community, grounding our lives in a specific place. But for many people the significance of their own local neighbourhood or town has declined as affluence, car-reliance and the internet have grown. This has coincided with broader trends which threaten personal and global health. Increasing problems of obesity, mental illness and social exclusion are all linked to the loss of neighbourhood. So too is the global crisis of climate change, as households use unsustainable levels of carbon-based fuels and export problems to other neighbourhoods across the world.

We see that microcosm and macrocosm are interdependent. Individual lifestyle and well-being are connected to earth ecology. Spatial planning, and in particular the integrated planning of neighbourhoods, is one of the critical intervening variables. It can exacerbate current trends or counteract them. This book offers the insight, knowledge and skills to support strategies for healthy, sustainable neighbourhoods: local global planning.

No magic wand, but clarity, co-operation, integration

It is vital to recognise that we cannot achieve local global planning of healthy neighbourhoods by simple bolt-on measures – such as wind turbines or 20mph zones – useful as they may be. The changes needed are much more fundamental. They relate to all policy areas and all levels of decision-making. The case study of Freiburg at the end of this chapter illustrates the point. Freiburg's planning of neighbourhoods works because broad strategy and local tactics reinforce one another; and because the key policy makers, the local communities themselves and the investors who implement development are all pulling together. This guide is therefore concerned with process as well as policy and design. Our hope is to inspire a collaborative and integrated approach.

CONTENTS

1.1

People can be supported to live in new ways, Freiburg, Germany.

A strong pedestrian-dominated town centre: Cheltenham, England.

THE IMAGE OF A SUSTAINABLE NEIGHBOURHOOD

Aspirations for neighbourhoods are surprisingly consistent amongst people with very different lifestyles. We want neighbourhoods that are attractive, safe, healthy and unpolluted, with high-quality local facilities, access to green spaces, and excellent connections to other areas. We would like the opportunity for convivial social activity and friendship. There is recognition that for some people – particularly the old and young, and those who are home-based throughout the day – the neighbourhood is vitally important for health and well-being.

This guide is about enhancing the quality of neighbourhoods as places to live, work and play. It advocates an inclusive, environmentally responsible model of neighbourhoods:

- a socially balanced population, and varied housing opportunities which are suited to a range of incomes and types of household;

- diversity of use – housing, business, shopping, social, cultural and health facilities, offering easy accessibility, opportunity and choice for all;

- pedestrian, bicycle, public transport and road networks within the neighbourhood, linking to the wider city and region, creating a permeable and connected environment with real transport choice;

- a pedestrian-dominated public realm to facilitate healthy social life and provide an attractive, safe, human-scaled environment;

- ecologically responsive development principles consistent with social inclusion and cutting resource use and pollution;

- a greenspace network that provides accessible open space, with effective water, energy, wildlife and climate management;

- aesthetic identity that is rooted in the collective identity of the region, reflecting characteristics valued by the local community;

- a fine-grained neighbourhood, structured around public transport accessibility, with varied densities, providing opportunity for gradual renewal and adaptation to new needs;

- the opportunity for active and frequent participation of all sectors of the population, commercial interests and voluntary groups in the planning and design of the area.

Health and quality of life

Health in this context is a state of complete physical, mental and social well-being and not merely absense of disease or infirmity. The physical environment of neighbourhoods affects health and well-being both directly, through the quality of housing and public space, and indirectly, through impact on behaviour and the sense of community. A key theme is the degree to which neighbourhoods provide for all groups – young and old, rich and poor.

Environmental sustainability

The ecological footprint of settlements in terms of resource use and pollution is great, continues to grow in certain respects, and ought to be greatly diminished. We advocate local, neighbourhood, responsibility for the health of the global commons – climate, land, biodiversity. Planning sustainable neighbourhoods means reworking the development conventions of the recent past.

Economic and civic vitality

Localities should not be mere dormitories. Their rejuvenation as healthy and sustainable neighbourhoods can only be achieved if there is the local will and energy. Part of the energy comes from the vitality of the local economy, investing in people and places; part comes from local political commitment, and effective partnerships between community, voluntary, public and private sectors.

1.2 RE-INVENTING NEIGHBOURHOODS

RECOGNISING THE DIFFICULTIES

The reality is often rather different, and there is widespread concern about the future of neighbourhoods. High mobility and economic change have undermined the significance of locality in people's lives. Where once children played on the street and there was a close local community, people now travel out by car to disparate activities or rely on virtual connections. As a result, local shops and facilities cease to be viable. While the changes represent greater choice and opportunity for some, others find their lives impoverished. Our lifestyles have become less healthy at the same time as we are using resources in unsustainable ways and threatening the stability of global ecology.

Public policy: sometimes part of the problem

These trends are in part the response of the market to perceived consumer preferences, but they have been reinforced by official policies for schools, hospitals and post offices that demote the significance of local accessibility. In addition, planning authorities in alliance with developers have been promoting single-use

---

The role of this guide

This guide is designed to bridge the gap between rhetoric and action.

It adopts a radical and challenging stance in terms of the search for effective neighbourhood strategies,

- *taking health, sustainability and vitality as the touchstone of success, in terms of local decision-making the guide takes an inclusive approach,*

- *recognising that neighbourhood initiatives may stem from a range of sources including community groups, private investors and the local authority.*

Collaboration between local partners, leading to synergy in the design and management of the built environment, is a hallmark of sustainable development.

The guide is concerned with reality, not vain hopes. It is about socially and economically feasible policies for commonplace, everyday neighbourhoods.

1.2

Neighbourhood rennaissance begins when people take over the street. Margaret Bond, the oldest resident in this Bristol street, only became visible once the cars were cleared out and street parties happened. Her wealth of stories became part of the oral history of the street.

residential estates and business parks, at relatively low densities, which are innately car-dependent, land-hungry and polluting. The trends not only affect the quality of the environment, but also exacerbate problems of social exclusion, discourage exercise and restrict the potential for local economic activity. A linked problem is the sense people can have, particularly in run-down areas, of powerlessness to influence the decisions that are progressively degrading their own environment.

Signs of hope

Suggestions of the death of neighbourhoods, however, are premature. Despite rising car dependence, 30 per cent of trips are still less than 1 mile, and most of those by foot. Even in outlying suburban estates with very high car ownership there is a perhaps surprising level of use of local facilities where they exist. And in some urban neighbourhoods the fabric of local community networks remains strong (Gilchrist 2000). In many areas, therefore, it is not a matter of recreating neighbourhoods from scratch, but reinforcing and building on current patterns of activity.

NEIGHBOURHOOD RENAISSANCE

In this context, the shift in European and UK policy towards a more sustainable and locally responsive approach is welcome. The planning of safe, convenient and attractive neighbourhoods is an essential part of a sustainable development strategy, and key to urban renaissance. It is also advocated as part of the UK public health strategy and the WHO Healthy Cities movement.

Yet local authorities (and the development industry) are finding it difficult to change tack. Change is hampered, particularly at the neighbourhood level, by the absence of integrated and coherent policy guidance, by the diverse perspectives of different stakeholders, including the local communities themselves, and by the dearth of local authority resources available for local planning.

The neighbourhoods of the future need to reflect cultural shifts and new technology. We cannot return to the (supposedly) cosy localism of the past. Rather, neighbourhoods will be open, varied, egalitarian and connected places – providing more choice, opportunity and beauty but without undesirable impacts on health and ecology.

The neighbourhood is not an island

Except for isolated settlements, far from the influence of major cities, neither country towns nor urban neighbourhoods, are islands of potential self-sufficiency. Inhabitants are dependent on the city or town region of which they are a part. Job markets and the catchments of higher level services, and also social networks, link between places. Roads, cycleways and public transport services are the web of connectivity that enable social and economic development. The location of the neighbourhood in relation to that web is therefore critically important. Only if the strategic planning of transport, land use and economic development are correctly aligned can a place hope to become 'sustainable'.

Neighbourhoods as testbeds

Neighbourhoods can be cast as a pivotal spatial scale for change. Neighbourhoods have a special role in a transition to sustainable settlements. Their unique scale in human habitation makes them small enough to reflect the personal; lifestyles, social networks and quality of life, yet they are also of sufficient size for their nature to affect the environmental impacts and economic function of districts, towns and cities. Whether in their mangement, renewal or construction, they are a vital element in a bottom-up approach to sustainable development. They can be seen both as *'troublemakers which inflitrate the whole unsustainable system and act as cells of development'* (p.1763 Wallner et al.1996) and as vital testbeds for innovaton to support healthier lifestyles.

Bottom-up creativity can be a valuable resource in change and renewal.

Official advocacy for neighbourhoods

DETR 1998c: Planning for Sustainable Development
- *Promoting urban villages*
- *Pedestrian-based neighbourhoods*
- *Mixed use and mixed tenure*
- *Density sufficient to support local facilities*
- *Community involvement*
- *A strong sense of place*

Urban Task Force DETR 1999i: Towards an Urban Renaissance
- *Promotes neighbourhoods 5,000–10,000 population*
- *District local catchment areas 400/500 m radius*
- *Gross densities of 150 people per ha*

English Partnerships and Housing Corporation 2000: Urban Design Compendium
- *Walkable neighbourhood units*
- *Distinctive local identities*
- *Permeable grid-based layouts*
- *Perimeter block development*
- *Graded densities*

The Brundtland definition of sustainable development

'Sustainable development is development which meets the needs of the present generation without compromising the ability of future generations to meet their own needs.' (WCED 1987)

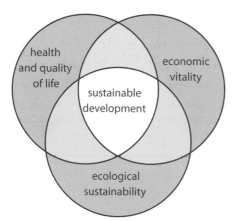

Figure 1.1
Searching for sustainable development

The trefoil diagram does not imply a weak trade-off between social, economic and environmental priorities, but the need to find solutions that marry all three

policies and agendas

1.3   PROMOTING SUSTAINABLE DEVELOPMENT

DEFINING SUSTAINABLE DEVELOPMENT

Despite over-exposure, and the consequent danger of the phrase losing any resonance it might once have had, sustainable development remains a valid and challenging goal for planning. It is often, wrongly, pigeonholed as a purely environmental goal, and therefore sidelined by those who have an economic or social agenda. But the classic Brundtland definition (see side column) makes clear that the focus is on people – on equity for current and for future generations. In this context 'development' is concerned not only with economic success but also health, social inclusion, quality of life, quality of environment.

Sustainable development is therefore about maintaining and enhancing the quality of human life – social, economic and environmental – while living within the carrying capacity of supporting eco-systems and the resource base. The trefoil diagram makes the point that that it is not a question of choosing one of the three aspects of sustainability over the others, but searching for solutions that marry all three. We need to win socially, economically and environmentally.

UK policy context

The principle of sustainable development is in theory at the heart of UK planning policy. The National Sustainability Strategy (DETR 1998b) paved the way for a strengthening of commitment through the Local Government act of 2000, and the Planning and Compensation Act of 2004. The former gave local authorities explicit power to promote economic, social and environmental well-being, and required them to co-ordinate 'local strategic partnerships' and 'Community Strategies' (see below). The latter established the new regime of 'spatial planning', replacing 'town and country planning'. Note that Scotland, Wales and Northern Ireland all have some devolved powers, and separate statements of intent though all moving in the same direction.

The UK model of sustainable development distinguishes between final goals and supporting objectives, and at the same time could make it easier for different sectors to understand the part they play in the integrated activity needed to meet sustainable development goals: 'We want to live within environmental limits and achieve a just society, and we will do so by means of sustainable economy, good governance and sound science' (DEFRA 2009).

All departments of state are supposed to be active in implementing sustainable development. But at present (2009) only two seem to have a clear idea of what this means in practice: The Department for Communities and Local Government

has produced a series of planning guidance statements which
together give a strong steer for local policy and decision-making.
It has also broadened the way in which plans and policies are
assessed: rather than simply following the European Directive
and requiring Strategic Environmental Assessment (SEA), it
has enlarged the agenda to include social and economic criteria
– 'sustainability appraisal'.

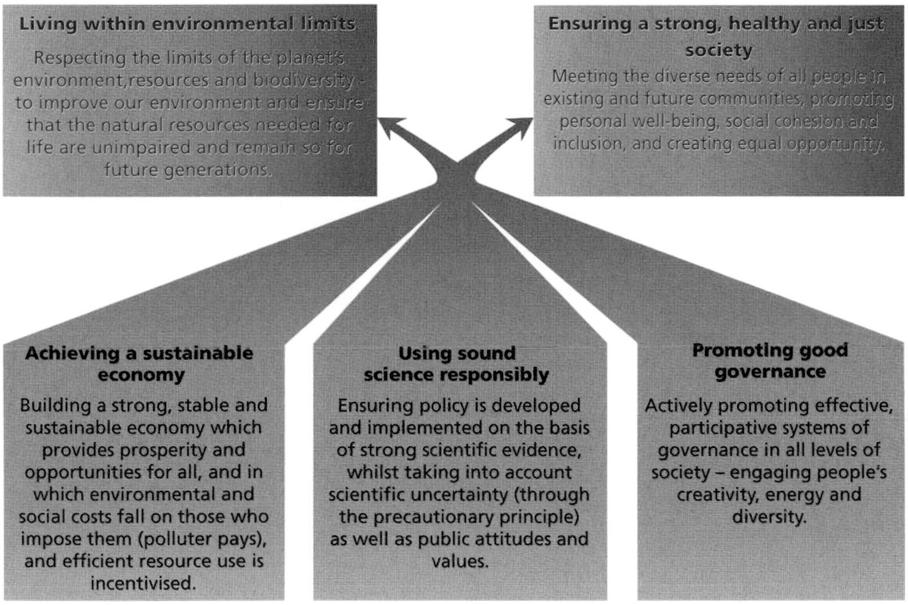

Living within environmental limits

Respecting the limits of the planet's
environment, resources and biodiversity –
to improve our environment and ensure
that the natural resources needed for
life are unimpaired and remain so for
future generations.

**Ensuring a strong, healthy and just
society**

Meeting the diverse needs of all people in
existing and future communities, promoting
personal well-being, social cohesion and
inclusion, and creating equal opportunity.

**Achieving a sustainable
economy**

Building a strong, stable and
sustainable economy which
provides prosperity and
opportunities for all, and in
which environmental and
social costs fall on those who
impose them (polluter pays),
and efficient resource use is
incentivised.

**Using sound
science responsibly**

Ensuring policy is developed
and implemented on the basis
of strong scientific evidence,
whilst taking into account
scientific uncertainty (through
the precautionary principle)
as well as public attitudes and
values.

**Promoting good
governance**

Actively promoting effective,
participative systems of
governance in all levels of
society – engaging people's
creativity, energy and
diversity.

Figure 1.2
**Shared UK principles of
sustainable development**

*These principles form the basis of
national sustainable development
strategies and action plans across
the UK. Two core principles and
three supporting principles – all
goals in themselves.*

The Department for Environment, Food and Rural Affairs takes
the lead on 'sustainability'. It has important arms-length
operational bodies – the Environment Agency and Natural England
– which strongly promote responsible long-term thinking on the
environment. In addition the Royal Commission on Environmental
Pollution has produced a series of reports, seeking to expand
understanding of sustainable development; and the Sustainable
Development Commission (SDC) acts as a watchdog, charged with
scrutinising the Government's progress on implementing the UK
Sustainable Development Strategy: Securing the Future (2005).

The need for a more thorough-going approach

The problems, though, are profound. The language of government
policy is general and establishes broad aspirations, often in
apparent conflict with each other, which planning authorities are
obliged to reconcile in practice. At the level of local planning the
preconceptions of councillors, the vested interests of residents,
businesses and institutions, skill gaps amongst professionals
and the perceived arbitrariness of some higher level decisions
on housing numbers, transport and economy, all mean that the
quality of decisions is highly compromised.

If we look to mainland Europe there are signs of hope, at least in
specific cities such as Freiburg (featured as a case study at the

**Sustainable Development responses in the
UK devolved administrations**

*Scotland: Choosing our future: Scotland's
Sustainable Development Strategy, 2005*

*Northern Ireland: 'First Steps towards
sustainability', 2006*

*Wales: Sustainable Development Action Plan',
2004*

**The Royal Commission on Environmental
Pollution** *has produced a number of key
reports for Sustainable Development*

Adapting the UK to climate change, 2008

The urban environment, 2007

Environmental Planning, 2002

Energy - the changing climate, 2000

Transport and the Environment, 1993, 1997

1.3

An example of the aims of a Community Strategy from Havant Borough Council:

Overiding aim: 'to improve the quality of life now and for the future in ways that do not cause irreversible harm to the environment'

- *making a safer community*
- *strengthening our economy*
- *improving educational attainment and lifelong learning*
- *enhancing our environment*
- *promoting a healthier community*
- *promoting social well-being*
- *working to engage young people.*

end of this chapter). But the lesson of such places is not easy: if we are to achieve more sustainable settlements, then local authorities need more power: specifically power over budgeting and land (PRP et al. 2008).

LA21, COMMUNITY AND SPATIAL STRATEGIES

The Local Agenda 21 initiative has been running since 1993 and seeks to encourage local authorities to develop collaborative programmes for sustainable development involving stakeholders from the voluntary and private sectors. For some local authorities the emphasis has been on the neighbourhood or local community level, but often without effective participation by the agencies (such as the education department, the housing department, large local employers) who have a major influence on the locality.

Local Strategic Partnerships

The UK obligation – under the Local Government Act 2000 (England and Wales) – to form Local Strategic Partnerships (LSPs), is set to replace or transform LA21 and should make co-ordination much more effective. LSPs bring together at local level the various parts of the public sector as well as private, voluntary and community sectors so that diverse initiatives and services can be designed to support rather than contradict each other.

Each LSP has to produce a Community Strategy. This establishes a long-term vision for the area, specific goals/priorities and an agreed action plan. The Department for Communities and Local Government (CLG) sees the active involvement of neighbourhood and community groups as vital to ensure that diverse local needs and aspirations are recognised. Community strategies can thus provide a very helpful integrated policy framework for neighbourhood initiatives.

Local development documents

The development plan is, of course, the key document setting local authority policy for the physical evolution of settlements. The Community Strategy and the development plan have to be consistent with each other. The idea of 'spatial planning' is to broaden local planning policy to incorporate transport, health and education agencies and work holistically towards sustainable development (Local Government Association 2000b). It thus could provide the physical dimension of the Community Strategy.

Neighbourhood level spatial frameworks could rest within the local authority-wide strategy. The critical context is set by the *core strategy*. It determines the housing, employment, transport, retail and greenspace policies that shape the possible future of every locality. Neighbourhood-level plans – which might be *action plans* if there is major change – will have to be in conformity with the core strategy and formally adopted by the local authority if they are to be effective.

1.4 CLIMATE STABILITY

KEY MESSAGE

Global climate change is a profoundly important issue for neighbourhood planning. The microcosm and the macrocosm are interdependent. Localities need to evolve coping mechanisms to deal with the predicted impacts of climate change. At the same time the form and organisation of localities needs to be such as to permit and encourage low-carbon lifestyles. Global problems can be in part tackled by local neighbourhood action: local global planning.

The problem of climate change

The Intergovernmental Panel on Climate Change (IPCC) – the most authoritative source around – revised its predictions in 2007, mostly in an upward (i.e. worsening) direction. It pointed out that atmospheric carbon levels are at their highest for three million years, and global temperatures have increased by 0.6°C in the last 150 years. It is convinced that human activity is causing the emission of higher levels of greenhouse gases than can be absorbed by Earth's metabolic processes, and thus is contributing to observed and predicted climate change. The median predictions are:

- 3–4° temperature rise by 2100

- an increase in extreme weather events, including storm surges, very heavy rain, high winds, periods of drought

- warmer, drier summers; warmer wetter winters (in the UK)

- sea level rise of 0.4 metres, on average, by 2100

However, the uncertainties of the predictive techniques, reflecting uncertainties in our understanding of global ecology, mean that there are risks of much more severe impacts – particularly on sea levels. The recent observations of melting glaciers on Greenland and the reduction of the north polar sea ice give added cause for concern.

Adaptive measures

In the face of climate change, it is vital to increase the resilience of neighbourhoods. According to Rob Shaw (2008) the key risks are higher temperatures, increased run-off and flooding, water availability (in S.E. England) and ground conditions (drying out in hotter, dryer summers). By way of example, the ASCCVE study of Manchester, using modelling techniques, found that there is likely to be a wide variation in maximum temperatures between high density, hard surface parts of the city and major green spaces, with suburbs somewhere in-between. It also predicted that water run-off in winter will be at least 50% higher than at present.

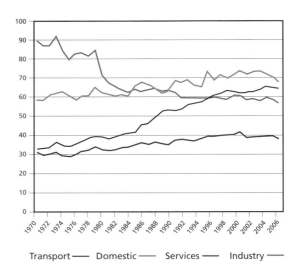

Transport —— Domestic —— Services —— Industry ——

Figure 1.3
Energy consumption by sector, UK

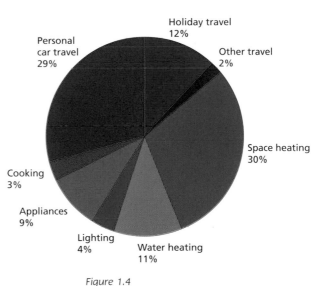

Figure 1.4
National per capita annual emmisions from different personal activities in 2005

Total per person: 1.16 tonnes of carbon per year

SOURCE: Energy White Paper (DTI2007)

Carbon emission figures for 2004

The following countries emissions (US Energy Information Administration, 2006)	million tonnes of carbon dioxide a year
Kenya	8.5
Uganda	1.6
Tanzania	3.5
Malawi	0.8
Zambia	2.3
Mozambique	1.9
Total	**18.6**
Drax power station emissions (Drax, 2005)	20.5

Figure 1.5
Carbon emmissions: Drax v Africa

SOURCE: World Development Movement, 2007

NB. The UK in total emits 580 million tonnes a year, so Drax accounts for 3.5 per cent of our emissions. The figures for both Drax and the countries are for 2004.

Zero Carbon Britain

Taking the imperative that the world now needs to move to net zero emissions as quickly as possible the study Zero Carbon Britain presents an emergency action plan that could achieve this globally within 20 years. They argue that Britain, as part of this process, has the capacity to take a leading role. The study explores a scenario in which Britain becomes self-reliant in energy. This is a plausible outcome based on the likely responses to Tradable Energy Quotas and feed-in tariffs. It demostartes that zero carbon emissions can be acheived even under the strictest conditions, with no energy imports and without resorting to 'silver bullet' technologies such as carbon capture and storage.

SOURCE: Zero Carbon Britain, Larsen and Bull 2007

Coping mechanisms could include:

- planning major connected urban greenspace to break up urban heat islands

- increasing the amount of green throughout the town by parks, gardens, green roofs, roof gardens, hedges, trees

- permeable hard surfaces for on-site surface water percolation into the ground to reduce flood risk, recharge aquifers, and sustain evapo-transpiration (as a cooling device)

- ample provision of holding ponds, swales etc. and protection of flood plains as part of a sustainable drainage system (SUDS) aimed at controlling flood risk

Mitigation measures

Carbon is the prime global warming gas. In the UK energy used in housing accounts for about half of total carbon emissions, transport for a quarter and industry/services for the remainder. What happens in neighbourhoods therefore had the potential to affect a substantial proportion of the total. Measures to reduce carbon emissions include:

- heavily insulated, draught-proofed buildings, orientated so as to make good use of passive solar gain, photovoltaics and solar hot water

- a neighbourhood energy strategy maximising the potential for renewables and combined-heat-and-power (CHP) schemes while minimising heat loss in winter and overheating in summer (e.g. through tree planting)

- a local food strategy encouraging local organic production and composting of organic waste matter

- a transport strategy which favours walking, cycling and outdoor play/socialising over motor vehicles

- a land use strategy which gives the opportunity and incentive for local facilities and local use, including local/home-based work

Contraction and convergence

A number of strategies for stabilising the climate have been proposed. Not just carbon dioxide but all anthropogenic emissions of climate changing gases need to be covered in terms of reduction targets. The net result has a huge impact on economies and technologies. Industrialised countries will need to reduce emissions though cultural and technological change; advanced developing countries will need to change the trajectory of their cultural, technical and economic development; and the least developed countries will need to adjust their long term vision of what development may look like and will need assistance in meeting development aims but hopefully side-stepping the 'advanced' cultures and technologies which have proved most harmful. This process is referred to as contraction and convergence, and the intention is for per capita harmful emissions to be capped for all countries at a level that can sustain human life on the planet.

This guidance shows what needs to be done in terms of planning and design to allow existing and new neighbourhoods to play their part in this global agenda.

1.5 PROMOTING HEALTHY COMMUNITIES

KEY MESSAGE

All decision criteria in neighbourhood planning and renewal must relate back to support for the health of individuals, communities and the planet. With a creative approach and skilful stakeholder team, outcomes which support health can be found which align well with other objectives such as economic resilience even within funding constraints. Building neighbourhoods to support health is an economic imperative as it reduces costs of illness associated with health services and lost productivity and is part of providing a fairer society though reducing inequalities in health.

HEALTH IS NOT ABOUT JUST HEALTH SERVICES

Health Authorities are increasingly working in partnership with local authorities, both in service delivery and health promotion. But the broader view of health promulgated by the World Health Organization (WHO), and by the UK Government in Our Healthier Nation (DoH 1998), emphasises that public health is not just a matter of hospitals and health centres: amongst other influences, the planning/design of neighbourhoods has a vital role. Combating a range of diseases such as heart disease, respiratory problems, obesity, type 2 diabetes and even some forms of cancer and mental illness relies on factors mediated by local urban design; factors such as healthy exercise, air quality, fresh food and local social networks, all of which are influenced by the physical nature of localities.

The neighbourhood as the basic setting for health

The neighbourhood is the basic setting for our lives from infants through to old age, the place communities we find ourselves in, the local services we use and the lifestyles we lead. In a critical literature review of 65 cross-sectional studies, the Glasgow Centre for Population Health found evidence that consistently indicated an association between the built environment; and health and well-being (Croucher et al. 2007).

Defining health

'Health is not only the absence of disease but a state of complete physical, mental and social well-being. The enjoyment of the highest attainable standard of health is one of the fundamental rights of every human being, without distinction of race, religion, political belief, or economic and social conditions.' (WHO 1946)

Wider determinants of health – some examples

Social and economic	Environmental	Lifestyle	Access to services
Employment	Air quality	Physical activity	Education
Social inclusion	Housing	Diet	Health services
Social capital	Water quality		Leisure facilities
	Urban form		Transport

Figure 1.6
The influence of the spatial environment on health

SOURCE: Based on DHSS 1999

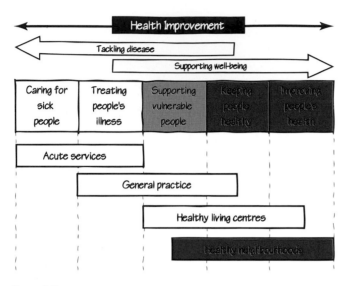

Figure 1.7
The neighbourhoods role in health

Life expectancy at birth (men)	Years
Glasgow, Scotland (deprived suburb)	**54**
India	**61**
Philippines	**65**
Korea	**65**
Lithuania	**66**
Poland	**71**
Mexico	**72**
Cuba	**75**
US	**75**
UK	**76**
Glasgow, Scotland (affluent suburb)	**82**

Fig. 1.8
WHO World Health Report 2006 and Hanlon et al. 2006

In the same year, an article in the Lancet (Rao et al. 2007) stated that 'To make a difference, public-health and built-environment professionals need "to learn from each other how best to address the needs of the communities they serve, to determine what answers each has that the other needs, to create a common language, and to initiate the opportunities to use it"' (quoted from Jackson and Kochitzky, 2001). That year the Royal Commission on Environmental Pollution's report 'The Urban Environment' (RCEP 2007) came to similar conclusions noting that factors in the urban environment affect health and well-being, in particular citing impacts on mental health, obesity and premature death. The report called for 'knowledge, capacity and skills to promote health and well being' to be increased.

Without a concerted focus by all built environment professionals on the impacts they are having on health, supported by the public health movement, the costs of running a health service will spiral out of affordability. Such a focus is part of the 'fully engaged' scenario developed in a report for the Treasury in the UK looking at different scenarios for future health funding up to 2050 (DH 2002 and Wanless 2004).

HEALTH ISSUES IN NEIGHBOURHOOOD PLANNING

Health inequalities

Inequalities in health are becoming a major concern for many governments. The typical situation, as represented by the UK, is a year-on-year improvement in life expectancy but in tandem an increasing widening of the gap between the most disadvantaged and the better off. These differences are often avoidable and always unjust. In England, to tackle health inequalities, the govenment is focusing on three areas for action;

- The conditions people live in

- The lives people lead

- The services people use

Planning and design at the scales focused on in *Shaping Neighbourhoods*, the living zone, the neighbourhood and the district/town, is highly relevant to action in each of these three areas.

In Bristol, a fairly prosperous city with a population of about 400,000 in the south west of England, there is a 9 year difference in male life expectancy between the most and least deprived neighbourhoods. Going from east to west London, following patterns in deprivation, average life expectancy increases by one year for each station on the tube line.

Inequalites are not unique to disparities in wealth. A report from Cambridge University's Centre for Housing and Planning research

(Burgess 2008) found gender inequalites arising from land use policy. It discovered that policies which separate residential areas from where peoeple work can have a disproportionate effect on women's employment prospects, unless schools and shops are within easy reach of jobs.

Healthy ageing

Global ageing is too often posed in the popular press as a demographic time bomb. Indeed by 2030 almost one in three Europeans will be older than 60 years with many years of life still ahead of them (Ritsatakis 2008). However many myths have developed around the ageing agenda with an adverse impact on the debate and policy development (see sidebox). To promote healthy communities, the EU Healthy City programme has adopted a life-course approach (Green and Tsouros, 2008) with the physical environment seen as an essential enabler of healthy and independent life. The social environment is also important and getting these both right can assist in reducing support though service delivery. Loneliness and isolation are key issues (Owen 2001). Lonely older people are at greater risk of physical and mental health problems (Victor et al. 2002). Indeed better social connectivity is associated with improved health and well-being (Dean 2003). With generally restricted mobility in terms of range and ability, this places the neighbourhood as the key environment for support of healthy ageing. Some of the particular issues raised for neighbourhood planning and design are: availability and accessibility of local facilities with special attention to distance requirements; safe and convivial public realm supporting inclusive pedestrian footfall; provision of a variety of housing tenures which encourage the development of supporting networks including co-housing options, sheltered housing and mixed schemes; provision of allotments.

Obesity

In most European countries, the prevalence of obesity is estimated to have increased by 10–40% from the late 1980s to the early 2000s (Butland et al. 2007). This pattern is repeated in other countries across the globe with a western development pattern. Physical inactivity is now the second most important risk factor for poor health after tobacco smoking in industrialised countries. See section 1.6 for further details.

Mental well-being

The main causes of depression and mental illness are to do with personal life crises (such as unemployment) or family stress. But increasingly it is being recognised that the place where you live can have a profound influence too. This happens in several ways:

- through the over-concentration of deprived households, experiencing relative poverty, unemployment, crime and social security dependence is rife, reinforcing a downward spiral

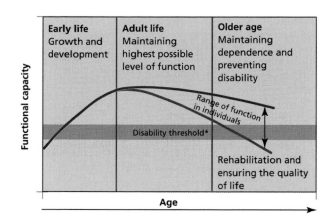

Figure 1.9
Disability threshold and environment after Kalache and Kickbusch 1997

The WHO Healthy Cities approach uses a life course approach to ageing. At a senior age, individuals show a range of functions, whether this leads to disability is dependent on the local environment.

* Dwellings and neighbourhoods which lower the 'disability threshold' will lead to a decrease in the number of disabled people in a given community.

The 12 myths of an ageing population

All 12 are debunked in Demystifying the myths of ageing (Ritsatakis 2008) a WHO report.

1. People should expect to deteriorate mentally and physically.

2. Most older people have similar needs.

3. Creativity and making a contribution is the province of young people.

4. The experience of older people has little relevance in modern society.

5. Many older people want to be left in peace and quiet.

6. Hospital beds and nurses are the main issue.

7. Providing for older people takes away resources from young people.

8. Spending on older people is a waste of resources.

9. Older people are not suited to modern workplaces.

10. You can't teach an old dog new tricks.

11. Older people expect to move aside.

12. Things will work out for themselves.

*Designing health into local environments
and local neighbourhoods*

*In a critical literature review of 65 cross-
sectional studies, the Glasgow Centre for
Population Health found evidence that
consistently indicated an association between
the built environment and health and well-
being (Croucher et al. 2007).*

*The Royal Commission on Environmental
Pollution's report 'The Urban Environment'
(RCEP 2007) noted that factors in the urban
environment affect health and well-being, in
particular citing impacts on mental health,
obesity and premature death. The report
goes on to call for 'knowledge, capacity and
skills to promote health and well being' to be
increased.*

*An article in the Lancet (Rao et al. 2007)
stated that 'To make a difference, public-
health and built-environment professionals
need "to learn from each other how best to
address the needs of the communities they
serve, to determine what answers each has
that the other needs, to create a common
language, and to initiate the opportunities to
use it"' (quote from Jackson and Kochitzky,
2001).*

3.4 Social capital

- through the feeling of isolation and lack of social support where there are few local facilities and little opportunity for planned or casual meetings and social contact.

- through the sense of separation from nature in places which lack parks, street trees, green gardens and spaces

Policies for mental well-being therefore involve promoting socially mixed areas, not ghettos; accessible, walkable neighbourhoods, not car-dependent estates; and accessible greenspace, not unrelieved tarmac, brick and concrete.

INTEGRATING HEALTH AND URBAN PLANNING

The UK's commitment to local sustainable development is reinforced internationally by a wide range of UN and EU policies and programmes. One of particular relevance to this guide is the WHO Healthy Cities programme, which provides a model for an integrated approach to neighbourhoods.

The WHO Healthy Cities Programme

Launched in 1988, the programme has grown from a handful of cities to a movement of over 1,000 cities and towns in 29 European countries (and more globally). The concept of 'healthy urban planning' is being promoted by WHO to draw attention to the need for planners, public health professionals and others to work together to plan places that foster health and well-being. The Healthy Cities principles of equity, intersectoral co-operation, community involvement and sustainability underpin the idea of healthy urban planning.

The initiative is gaining momentum in Europe. In 2000 a book entitled Healthy Urban Planning was published on behalf of WHO, and provides an introduction to many of the issues explored in this guide. Subsequently a group of twelve cities across Europe has formed to elaborate the concept in terms of practical programmes at the neighbourhood and city-wide levels.

Healthy Cities is about changing the ways in which individuals, communities, private and voluntary organisations and local authorities think about and make decisions about health. It seeks to improve the physical, mental, social and environmental well-being of people living in urban areas.

Top-down and bottom-up processes

Healthy Cities emphasises the need to take a strategic approach, with explicit political commitment at the highest level of the municipality, and co-ordinated programmes across different departments and agencies. But there is also the understanding that 'top-down' commitment must be matched by the active involvement of local groups in decision-making and implementation if the initiatives are to be productive. Neighbourhood-level projects are central to Healthy City programmes and demonstrate the potential of the integrated community approach.

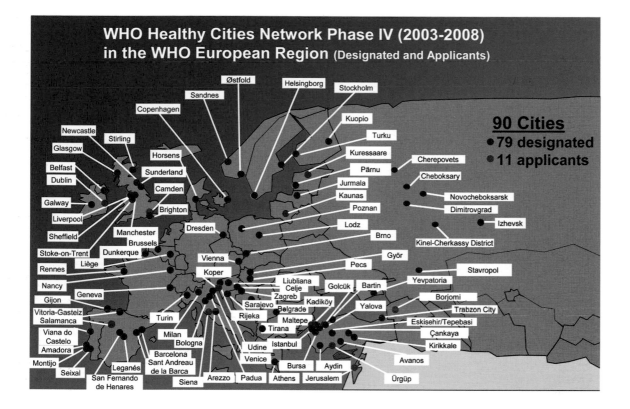

WHO Healthy Cities Network Phase IV (2003-2008) in the WHO European Region (Designated and Applicants)

HEALTH AS THE TOUCHSTONE FOR SUSTAINABILITY

The principle of health can provide common ground, to draw different interests into support for sustainable development at the neighbourhood level – a core value everyone can 'buy into'. It also helps tie the human purpose of neighbourhoods with the ecosystem approach:

- the health and well-being of individuals
- the health of the local community
- the health of the local economy
- the health of the local environment
- the health of the bioregion
- the health impact of the neighbourhood on the wider world.

A healthy neighbourhood, with equity of access to housing, work, local facilities, good food, green environment, safe streets, exercise and diverse social opportunities, together with a concern for the well-being of future generations, is likely to be a sustainable neighbourhood.

CHECKLIST

The 12 Healthy Urban Planning Objectives

Do planning policies and proposals promote and encourage:

1 *Healthy lifestyles?*
2 *Social cohesion?*
3 *Housing quality and access?*
4 *Access to work, hence income?*
5 *Access to local facilities?*
6 *Local food production and access?*
7 *A sense of safety and security?*
8 *Social inclusion?*
9 *Local environmental quality?*
10 *Healthy water supply/treatment?*
11 *Clean air and uncontaminated soils?*
12 *Climate stability?*

SOURCE: Barton and Tsourou 2000

1.6

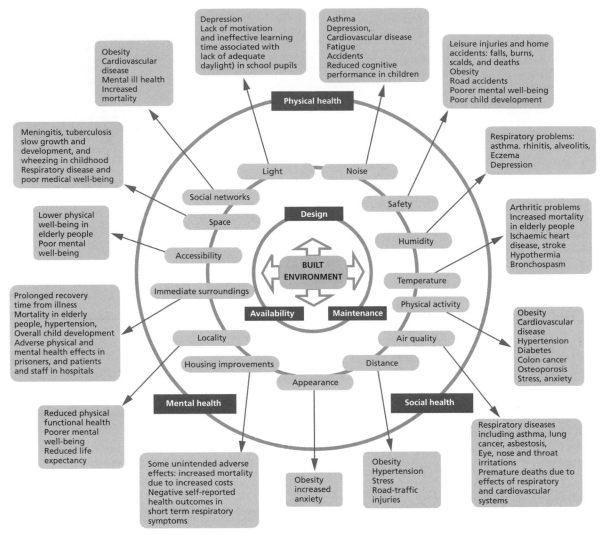

Figure 1.10

**Health problems
with potential
links to the built
environment**

SOURCE: Rao et al, 2007

Obesity
Cardiovascular
disease
Mental ill health
Increased
mortality

Depression
Lack of motivation
and ineffective learning
time associated with
lack of adequate
daylight) in school pupils

Asthma
Depression,
Cardiovascular disease
Fatigue
Accidents
Reduced cognitive
performance in children

Leisure injuries and home
accidents: falls, burns,
scalds, and deaths
Obesity
Road accidents
Poorer mental well-being
Poor child development

Meningitis, tuberculosis
slow growth and
development, and
wheezing in childhood
Respiratory disease and
poor medical well-being

Respiratory problems:
asthma. rhinitis, alveolitis,
Eczema
Depression

Lower physical
well-being in
elderly people
Poor mental
well-being

Arthritic problems
Increased mortality
in elderly people
Ischaemic heart
disease, stroke
Hypothermia
Bronchospasm

Prolonged recovery
time from illness
Mortality in elderly
people, hypertension,
Overall child development
Adverse physical and
mental health effects in
prisoners, and patients
and staff in hospitals

Obesity
Cardiovascular
disease
Hypertension
Diabetes
Colon cancer
Osteoporosis
Stress, anxiety

Reduced physical
functional health
Poorer mental
well-being
Reduced life
expectancy

Respiratory diseases
including asthma, lung
cancer, asbestosis,
Eye, nose and throat
irritations
Premature deaths due to
effects of respiratory
and cardiovascular
systems

Some unintended adverse
effects: increased mortality
due to increased costs
Negative self-reported
health outcomes in
short term respiratory
symptoms

Obesity
increased
anxiety

Obesity
Hypertension
Stress
Road-traffic
injuries

Physical health

Light | Noise

Social networks

Space

Design

Safety

Humidity

BUILT
ENVIRONMENT

Accessibility

Temperature

Immediate surroundings

Physical activity

Availability | **Maintenance**

Locality

Air quality

Housing improvements

Distance

Appearance

Mental health

Social health

1.6 THE OBESITY ISSUE

Weight gain is prevalent across the whole population, as a result
the number of people clinically overweight and obese is rising.
This places people at risk of a large number of other diseases
which reduce both quality of life and longevity. Neighbourhood
planning has a key role to play in tackling epidemic at both 'ends'
– creating environments which support more everyday energy
expenditure and support better quality energy intake. Activity,
such as walking and cycling, needs to be (re)built into the lives
people lead through placing the places people need to go in
locations, and at the distances, which encourage active travel.
Access to good quality food and reduced access to junk food is
important especially around schools. Some local solutions such
as food growing on allotments tick both boxes.

SICK SETTLEMENTS: AND THE NEW LIFESTYLE DISEASES

In 2003, an article in the Lancet medical journal drew attention to urban environments from a health point of view (Larkin 2003). The article titled 'Can cities be designed to fight obesity?' argued that we have created settlements that were causing ill-health, the disease was obesity, the term obesogenic urban environments was coined.

The incidence of obesity in the general population is rising worldwide and at such a rate that the trend has become the focus of national governments. In the UK, the authoritative Foresight 'Tackling Obesities' report (Butland et al. 2007) highlighted both the systemic nature of the increasing health issue of obesity and the role of the built environment as a key element in this system. In the UK, over half the adult population could be obese by 2050 with the costs attributable to overweight and obesity being £10 billion in the National Health Service and almost £50 billion in wider society and business. In England, 2008, nearly 25% of adults and 10% of children are obese with another 20% of children overweight. Statistics and trends for other countries in the UK and worldwide are similarly worrying.

Poor health for all!

Vital for those wanting to shape neighbourhoods for health is the realisation that obesity is not only an issue of individual willpower to eat less and to exercise more. The trend to increase in weight is spread across the whole population. The cause is a combination of more opportunity to eat a poor (fast food) diet and less opportunity for activity to be built into everyday lifestyles. Environmental causes pinpointed by research are changes in food production, the degree of motorised transport and work/home lifestyle patterns. In tandem with the rise in access to cheap personal motorised transport, settlements have been re-modelled to facilitate and prioritise such 'access' at the expense of access involving physical activity.

A pointed indicator of the dire medical consequences is the fact that the National Institute for Public Health and Clinical Excellence has now published public health guidance (NICE 2008) on how to promote and create built or natural environments that encourage physical activity. Cheap personal motorised transport is not universally available and the lack of locally accessible facilities entrenches other health disadvantages for certain groups such as the elderly, those caring for young children, children themselves and those with disabilities. In most neighbourhoods built since the 1970s people without cars may find themselves living in areas where there just are no useful destinations within walking distance anyway.

Unhealthy neighbourhoods, unhealthy lives: Obesity

Obesity reduces life expectancy by an average of 9 years. Trends show a worrying increase in all age groups in most countries.

Over 7% of the disease burden in developed countries and up to 50% of heart disease is due to obesity and overweight.

Obesity and overweight:

- *increases the risk of heart disease, cancer, type 2 diabetes and high blood pressure*

- *may account for 14% of male and 20% of female cancer deaths*

Lifestyle risk factors include:

- *lack of physical activity*

- *poor diets, low in fresh fruit and vegetables*

SOURCE: Crowther et al. 2004

Defining obesity

Obesity is usefully measured as Body Mass Index (BMI). This is a person's weight (kg) divided by their height (m).

Classification	BMI
Underweight	*<20*
Normal	*20-25*
Overweight	*25-30*
Obese	*30-40*
Morbidly obese	*>40*

1.6

Obesity increases the risk of these nine diseases

Type 2 diabetes
90% of Type 2 diabetics have a body mass index (BMI) above 23 kg/m2.

Cancers
10% of all cancer deaths among non-smokers are related to obesity (30% for endometrial cancer of the womb).

Respiratory effects
Neck circumference of greater than 43 cm in men, and 40.5 cm in women is associated with obstructive sleep apnoea, daytime somnolence and development of pulmonary hypertension.

Reproductive function
6% of primary infertility in women is attributable to obesity. Impotency and infertility are frequently associated with obesity in men.

Coronary artery disease and stroke
2.4 times risk in obese women and 2 times risk in obese men under the age of 50 years. Obesity is a contributing factor to cardiac failure in more than 10% of patients. Overweight/obesity plus hypertension is associated with increased risk of the most common kind of stroke.

Osteoarthritis
Frequent association in the elderly with increasing body weight – risk of disability attributable to osteoarthritis equal to heart disease and greater than any other medical disorder of the elderly.

Hypertension
Five times higher risk if obese. 66% of hypertension is linked to excess weight and 85% of hypertension is associated with a BMI above 25 kg/m2.

Dyslipidaemia
This condition is one of abnormal blood fat levels. It progressively develops as BMI increases above 21 kg/m2.

Liver and gall bladder disease
Overweight and obesity associated with non-alcoholic fatty inflammation and disease of the liver, 40% of such patients are obese. Three times risk of gall bladder disease in women with a BMI of over 32 kg/m2 (seven times if BMI of over 45 kg/m2).

SOURCE: Foresight Report – Tackling Obesities, 2007

The weight gain game

Obesity occurs from an imbalance in the body's energy account, an imbalance between energy intake (food energy then converted and stored as fat in the body) and energy expended (the body using its resources, including stored fat, to do work). The importance of neighbourhood design is highlighted by the fact that, for most obese adults, weight gain has been accumulated over a number of years. A small daily or weekly imbalance in this energy account over a decade can lead to major weight gain. The Institute for European Environmental Policy (Davis et al. 2007) has calculated that the decline in walking in itself is enough to account for much, if not all, of the recently observed upsurge in obesity. Not only is energy expended during activity itself but increased levels of physical activity have a positive effect on the metabolic rate of an active person even at rest (Rippe and Hess 1998).

The body weight consequences of car dependency

■ Each additional hour a day spent in a car is associated with a 6% increase in the likelihood of obesity. Each additional kilometre walked a day (12 minutes) is associated with a 4.8% reduction in the likelihood of obesity. (Frank et al 2004 in Croucher et al. 2007).

■ The main car driver walks for half the distance and time of an adult in a non-car owning household. This equates to a deficit of 56 minutes walking a week. This could lead to a weight gain of over 2 stones in a decade (*Davis et al. 2007*).

TACKLING OBESITY

To tackle population level obesity, whilst taking into account health inequalities and promotion of communities, the first urban agenda is to build activity back into every day lifestyles and movement patterns. The promotion of gyms and organised sports may be effective for some individuals, in some socio-economic groups, for a limited period of time, but as a response to population level obesity, is not an adequate or effective strategy. The second urban agenda must be to ensure access to good quality fresh food including food growing opportunities at the local level.

The Foresight 'Tackling Obesities' report suggested addressing obesity through the urban environment is more likely to be effective since it affects multiple pathways within the obesity system in a sustainable way. Moreover, many of the objectives for neighbourhoods arising from environmental and economic drivers align perfectly with reducing obesity. Urban policy objectives such as reducing energy consumption, air pollution, traffic congestion, and crime rates and increasing social capital, densities and access to local facilities and opportunities for local food growing can all be implemented in ways that will create less obesogenic environments.

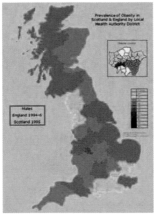
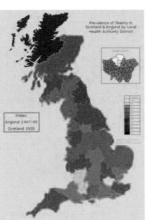

1994-1996   1997-1999   2000-2002

Figure 1.11
Trends in levels of obesity in England and Scotland from 1994–2002 (males)

SOURCE: Butland et al. 2007

1.7 THE GREAT URBAN FORM DEBATE

The future of neighbourhoods and small towns cannot be divorced from broad questions of strategic planning. No place is an island. The pattern of life and the size of the eco-footprint is influenced by location, density and transport networks as well as by culture, income and social position. Below are set out briefly five linked areas of strategic policy debate. The position taken in this guide is made clear in each case, cross-referenced to material in subsequent chapters. Hovering behind each of the spatial polarities is a bigger question still: to plan or not to plan? This is about the degree of choice open to the market and the role of the state in planning settlements.

Compact city versus dispersal

The question here is whether urban activity should be concentrated within well-defined major settlements, at relatively high densities, or dispersed (following market tendencies) across the countryside and/or smaller settlements. The presumed benefits of compaction are improved accessibility, lower car dependence, greater vitality and community, lower carbon emissions. The presumed benefits of dispersal are cheaper land, more space, green surroundings and the potential for home-self-efficiency. The pros and cons have been researched in depth but firm conclusions are difficult because of the range of variables involved and the divergence between theory and reality.

This divergence needs recognising. The theory requires concentration but even where the urban core is compact and intensifying, the reality for most cities is also of an expanding suburban penumbra, either widely dispersed or in the form of satellite towns. Modelling studies show that without huge increases in the friction of distance (the cost of travel) or draconian limits on market freedom, such trends will persist (Blackledge et al. 2007).

1.7

The Proximity Principle
why we are living too far apart

The Council for the Preservation of Rural England has been looking at the role of density in supporting the quality and sustainability of rural lives.

Based on detailed qualitative research with householders in four towns and villages, the report says that a new focus on proximity could bring both social and environmental rewards:

- *living closer together encourages more community interaction, and reduces isolation for vulnerable social groups, such as young families;*

- *compact settlements require less transport, and reduce car use, with health and environmental benefits;*

- *higher density development is environmentally beneficial, resulting in lower carbon emissions;*

- *in rural areas, more compact villages could help to stem the decline in rural services such as shops, post offices and bus services.*

Recommendations to encourage proximity include:

- *tax incentives for refurbishment and reuse of land and buildings within existing settlements;*

- *ambitious design standards for new homes: internal 'space standards' should specify generous living space within homes, while minimum density levels should ensure compact, walkable settlements;*

- *new settlements such as eco-towns should only be considered when there is clear demand for additional housing that cannot be provided within existing settlements.*

SOURCE: Willis, 2008

In this context decisions about new and renewed neighbourhoods need to be much more sophisticated than the polarised debate of brownfield versus greenfield, urban extensions versus new settlements, higher density versus lower density.

Brownfield regeneration versus greenfield cleanslate

While developers often prefer the simplicity and lower costs of developing the open fields, governments favour reuse of previously developed land where possible. The UK government has a particularly strong angle on this (PPS3). There are powerful arguments in favour:

- reclaiming land that would otherwise lie derelict, and decontaminating land that has been polluted

- putting new life into decaying urban neighbourhoods where population is falling and poverty is concentrated

- locating new commercial developments where there are existing pools of potential employees and accessible markets

- locating new housing where there is a wide range of jobs and services accessible by public transport, foot and pedal (in line with compact city theory)

- protecting valued greenspaces and countryside from development.

The problem comes when these valid reasons for supporting brownfield development are crudely equated with a 'brownfield good, greenfield bad' stance. This can lead to the over-exploitation of urban sites where the conditions above do not apply: development on playing fields and allotments; higher densities at locations lacking any prospect of good public transport services. It can also lead to 'sporadic' development on isolated rural sites (dead industries or old airfields) which would be much better returned to agriculture or nature.

If neighbourhoods are to be sustainable, then each existing and potential location must be assessed on its real merits. Greenfields may sometimes be preferable to brownfield.

Urban extensions versus new settlements

Exactly the same arguments apply to this other hotly debated issue. There is no simple answer. In principle, where new development is necessary, then it is logical to place it as close to existing concentrations of jobs and services as possible in order to minimise travel distances and maximise choice. But it depends entirely how it is done. Recent evidence from four city regions in England suggest that satellite settlements if well planned are less car dependent than new suburbs (Barton and Horswell 2009).

Conversely, where commuter settlements lack their own job-base or local facilities, then car dependence can be very high indeed, and the level of active travel very low, with consequences for greenhouse emissions, obesity levels and life-chanCES.

There is therefore no honest alternative to comparing the potential of different locations on a systematic basis, and then planning any new development to maximise the opportunity for people and business to choose healthy behaviours.

To densify or not to densify?

Within urban areas the pursuit of compact city principles, and the favouring of brownfield development has led to densification wherever the market can support it. The progressive reduction in household size has also an influential motive. Without the provision for extra households then the falling population progressively undermines the viability of local services. In extreme cases once vibrant neighbourhoods become moribund, with empty shops, closed schools and a rising tide of hard-to-let or unmarketable properties.

5.4 Graded densities

It is essential to have a strategy of intensification and diversification to counteract such decline before it reaches crisis pitch. However, the blanket adoption of high density on any urban redevelopment site is storing up problems for the future. As set out in Chapter 5 in much more detail the key factors are:

5.13 Change and renewal

5.14 Intensification

- densify where public transport accessibility is high, not where it is low

- densify within the pedshed of district centres offering a good range of services and jobs

A *pedshed* is a pedestrian catchment area around a local facility: see p.29 local catchments.

- avoid loss of open space – densification demands more open space, not less

- plan for diversity of housing stock and population, which may mean flats in some areas but 'executive' houses in others

- maintain a variety of densities within any particular neighbourhood

1.8

the neighbourhood as habitat

Advocates of the ecosystem approach to settlements

McLoughlin (1968) Urban and Regional Planning: A Systems Approach

Odum (1971) Environment, Power and Society

Barton, Davis and Guise (1995) Sustainable Settlements

EU Expert Group on the Urban Environment (1995) European Sustainable Cities

Hough (1995) Cities and Natural Processes

Tjallingii (1995) Ecopolis: Strategies for Ecologically Sound Urban Development

1.8 THE ECOSYSTEM APPROACH

The ecosystem approach provides a coherent philosophy to underpin the principle of planning for health and sustainability. The neighbourhood is an ecosystem in the sense that it is the essential local habitat for humans, providing not only shelter but also a network of social support and opportunities for a wide range of leisure, cultural and economic activities. It is also a natural habitat, where humans and other species live in a symbiotic relationship. Physical systems – part natural, part constructed – control energy and water flows, affect soil and air quality, and influence climate.

The idea of the settlement as ecosystem has a long heredity. Plato used the idea (if not the phrase) with remarkable insight when describing the decline of Greek settlements in the fourth century BC (Critias). In the modern era, Ebenezer Howard's Garden City of Tomorrow was essentially based on an ecosystem model, relating the town to the land.

Figure 1.12
The settlement as an ecosystem

SOURCE: Forest of Dean 1998

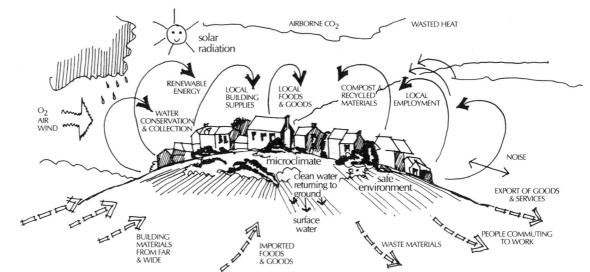

ECOSYSTEM CONCEPTS

The central insight of the ecosystem approach is to see the settlement as a system. As the picture above illustrates, there are synergies and feedback loops within the settlement, and inputs from and outputs to the wider world. This applies to the activities and relationships of people as much to the natural assets of air, water, soils, materials and climate. The object of sustainable settlements is to progressively increase healthy synergy within the settlement while minimising the contamination of, or over-reliance on, the wider environment.

Ecological niche and rent level

The neighbourhood can function as a complex ecosystem in supporting a diversity of ecological niches within the locality for different groups and activities that are living more or less in harmony with each other.

It is important to recognise the diverse needs in a locality – different ages and life stages, different income levels, varied ethnic, household and family groupings, different cultures, lifestyles and levels of mobility – and to encompass not only the needs of residents but workers, providers, visitors, those running businesses and those just passing through. There is no such person as an 'average' neighbourhood user. Rather, there are many people with specific demands: the kids playing on the waste ground, the people drinking in their local, the elderly couple next door.

People are responsible for satisfying their own needs, but the spatial design of the neighbourhood can either support this self-reliance or restrict and frustrate it. So a key principle of neighbourhood planning is to open up choice, providing a congenial and sustainable habitat for everyone, while protecting it from destructive forces.

Rent levels is a handy tool for analysing the opportunities in a neighbourhood. This not only applies in the housing field, where the need for social inclusion dictates varied rent levels, but also in the commercial field. Superstores and offices can normally afford high rents (or land price) because they need and justify highly accessible locations. But most service industries and small

3.2 A diverse population

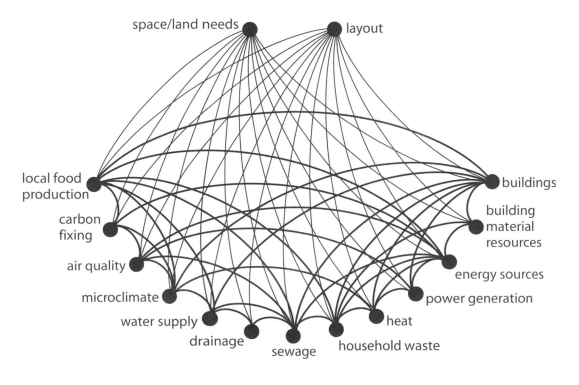

Figure 1.13
The interplay of ecological management and spatial planning

SOURCE: Barton et al. 2000

workshops cannot compete. It is therefore vital to have zones set aside, protected by the planning authority, where small-scale industry can flourish without fear or temptation of selling up-market.

Invasion and succession

Neighbourhoods are dynamic places. Households, businesses, activities evolve, and the physical form needs to be able to adapt. In some localities new social groups start buying up property and gradually taking over from an older population – as in gentrification or ethnic change. In urban ecology this is called invasion and succession. Many villages have experienced this to an extreme degree, with rich commuters or retired households effectively pushing poorer local households out, with unfortunate social impacts and the decline of village facilities. Such processes need managing to avoid social dislocation and social monoculture.

Symbiosis and climate

In natural ecology habitats such as tropical rainforests, or the oak woodlands in the English Lake District, represent the climax vegetation. This is the most complex, diverse and rich ecology possible in that landscape and climate, relying on symbiotic relationships between species, every niche filled.

The neighbourhood can be looked at in the same way. The principles of diversity and symbiosis work in many situations to the general good. There is small-scale dynamic change but large-scale relative stability.

1.9   THE SETTLEMENT HEALTH MAP

The Settlement Health Map is a way of organising our thoughts about, and our analysis of, the human habitat. It integrates the ecosystem approach (with its emphasis on the bio-physical environment) with analysis of the social determinants of health and well-being. It embraces therefore everything from the personal to the planet. The settlement health map has been widely welcomed as a means of linking spatial planning, public health and environmental sustainability. We advocate it as a means of grappling with policy impacts and the complex interactions within settlements.

The map puts **people** at the heart. It is the health and well-being of people, now and in the future, that we are concerned with. The global environment goes right round, enfolding the settlement, providing the critical ecological life-support functions, but also ultimately placing limits on growth. The sequence of spheres between is carefully arranged to mirror the sequential impacts (or knock-on effects) of change within any particular sphere.

The determinants of
health and well-being
in our neighbourhoods

Figure 1.14
The Settlement Health Map

SOURCE: Barton and Grant 2007

VARIED USES OF THE MAP

The model can be used for quite specific processes of analysis or evaluation. Different spheres can be taken as the starting point depending on the issue being examined. Including the two purposes illustrated it can:

Analyse health impact

In line with Brundtland's definition of sustainable development (see p.6), the model has people at its heart. Each of the outer layers has an impact on people's health and well-being. The model helps to structure the analysis and ensure a consistent approach.

Analyse factors affecting 'social capital'

A later chapter discusses the important of community networks and local social groups (see Section 3.4). Whether or not a local community can be said to exist depends not only on individual and household choices but the degree to which people meet in local schools, shops, pubs and clubs, enjoy chatting on the street, feel at home in the neighbourhood.

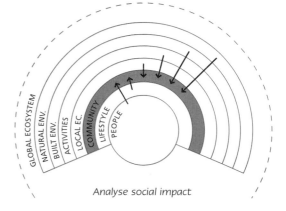

Analyse health impact

Analyse social impact

1.9

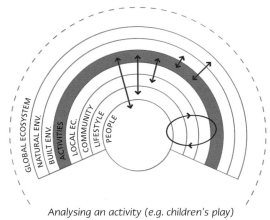

Analysing an activity (e.g. children's play)

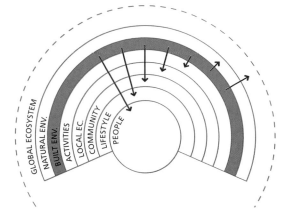

Analysing the impact of a development project

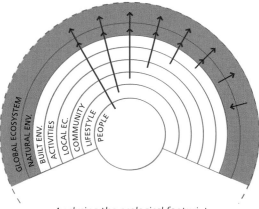

Analysing the ecological footprint

Analyse the needs of an activity

Local activities (or the absence of activity in a dormitory settlement) help define the nature of a neighbourhood. It is instructive to take an activity defined as a problem (such as young people loafing about) and assess what kinds of places can provide for it most appropriately; or to take an activity conspicuous by its absence (children cycling to school, for example) and assess the social, educational and physical changes that might be needed to effect change.

Analyse the impact of development projects

This is the most important use of the model in the context of this guide. The model gives a clear agenda for evaluating planning policies and specific development projects:

- What natural resources (energy, land, water, materials) does it use, and what resources (such as air quality and biodiversity) does it impact on?

- How will it directly or indirectly affect the character and function of the place?

- What local activities will it provide for or affect (including its impact on transport)?

- How is it likely to affect community groups/networks by either direct physical change or by impact on activities?

- How, in the light of these other impacts, is it likely to affect the health and quality of life of people?

Analyse the ecological footprint of a neighbourhood

The outermost spheres constitutes the natural environment, which provides essential life-support functions for the people of the neighbourhood. It is not so much the number of people, but the activities they indulge in and the character of the buildings and streets that impact on the sustainability of those life-support systems. For example, local air quality is affected by traffic, heating systems and industrial activity. The model reminds us of our dependence on the biophysical environment.

IN SUMMARY

The health of the neighbourhood as ecosystem is measured by the degree to which it sustains:

- a good quality of life and environment for everyone

- vital and viable services and economic processes

- the carrying capacity of the supporting natural systems and resources.

The model of the settlement/neighbourhood as habitat can help establish common ground, a context within which specific interests can be placed, and assess the overall health of the neighbourhood.

Objectives	Policy directions
Lifestyle	• facilitate active travel
	• encourage recreational physical activity
1. to promote healthy lifestyles	• encourage local food production and access to fresh food
Community	• create opportunities for local social groups and networks
	• promote mental health through supportive social environments
2. to enhance local community	• strengthen social and cultural life
	• build local social capital through the participatory process
	• create local partnerships and trusts
3. to increase local community	• increase local user control
Economy	• diversify local entrepreneurial opportunities
	• recycle financial resources locally
4. to promote enterprise	• promote urban regeneration and renewal
	• ensure diverse local employment opportunities
	• enhance further education and training opportunities
5. to promote employment	• ensure good public transport, walking and cycling connections to the wider area
Activities	• diversify housing opportunities and affordability
	• promote accessible local facilities
6. to increase equity	• enhance movement options – especially walking, cycling and public transport
	• diversify opportunities for local facilities, work and social contact
7. to enhance freedom of choice	• open up lifestyle and movement options
Built environment	• reduce the chance of accidents
	• reduce the likelihood (and fear) of street violence
8. to improve safety and security	• encourage a sense of ownership and belonging
	• create an attractive public realm
	• promote local distinctiveness and value local heritage
	• reduce noise and vandalism
9. to enhance environmental quality	• create robust, adaptable and high-quality buildings
Natural environment	• manage water resources sustainably
	• reduce demand for non-renewable resources
	• close local resource loops (re-use and recycling)
10. to safeguard natural resources	• ensure good air quality
	• enhance habitat diversity within the neighbourhood
11. to promote wildlife and open country	• realise urban 'brownfield' potential thus reducing countryside loss
Global ecology	• increase energy-efficiency of buildings
	• promote renewables and combined heat and power
12. to cut greenhouse gas emissions	• reduce car reliance and the need to travel

1.10

It is sometimes difficult to see where neighbourhoods start and stop.

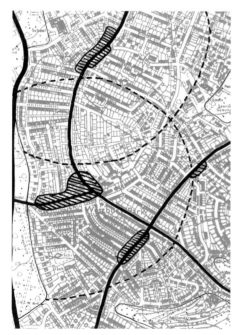

Local centres and their catchment areas help articulate form.

Figure 1.15
Defining neighbourhoods

the neighbourhood in focus

1.10 DEFINING NEIGHBOURHOODS

NO EASY ANSWER

There is no generally accepted basis for defining neighbourhoods. If a local authority or a community forum wishes to identify different urban localities for purposes of public debate and planning then they will first need to agree the criteria.

Neighbourhoods may be defined:

- **administratively**: by ward or parish boundaries

- **aesthetically**: by distinctive character or age of development

- **socially**: by the perceptions of local residents

- **functionally**: by catchment areas for local services; and/or

- **environmentally**: as traffic-calmed areas where through traffic is excluded and the quality/safety of the living environment is paramount.

Given these varied interpretations, it is vital for stakeholders to agree the main purposes of the neighbourhood exercise before defining areas on the ground. At the end of this chapter we suggest a consistent categorisation, which is then used in the rest of the guide.

CRITERIA DISCUSSED

1 Administrative convenience

Using existing ward or parish boundaries is a pragmatic, simple way of defining localities. It has the advantage of tying into local democratic processes and thereby clarifying political responsibility. The local ward councillors, the parish or town councils are given clear obligations and added legitimacy.

Wards and parishes are also the units for census analysis and 'state-of-the-environment' or 'quality-of-life' reports. Assessing problems, measuring progress and comparing different areas thus becomes relatively straightforward.

The major disadvantage with reliance on administrative boundaries is that they may be historical accidents unrelated to people's own perceptions, functional linkages or aesthetic character. If so, then reliance on them can compromise both the level of public involvement and practical value.

2 Areas of distinctive character

These may be defined by analysis of maps and aerial photographs supplemented by personal knowledge. Typically age and dominant building form give the distinctive character: for example, Edwardian terraces or late-twentieth-century estates. Such areas may not conform at all to social or functional definition of neighbourhoods – in smaller settlements and inner cities they may be quite small – but they can be valuable for analysis of physical change and urban capacity (see Chapter 6).

3 Residents' perceptions

Social surveys and/or community workshops can be used to find out what the people living in an area perceive as their own neighbourhood. The Ipswich study shown here (undertaken as part of the city expansion project) illustrates a surprising degree of resident consensus. While residents had varying views about neighbourhood size, the boundaries they chose provide a strong pattern, often following barriers formed by rivers, railways, main roads and open space. For the most part the perceived neighbourhoods were not centred on local shops and facilities. Rather they were bounded by them, because retailing was concentrated along main roads. Local centres can thus be the place where people from different neighbourhoods mingle.

4 Local catchments

The conventional image of a neighbourhood – derived from many new estates and new towns – is that of a local catchment area, with residential areas grouped around a local service centre or primary school. The Harlow plans illustrate this principle at the township scale, shaping the pattern of the settlement.

Catchments may be identified empirically by pedestrian surveys and time/distance mapping. One study has coined the term 'ped-shed' (like 'watershed') for the area within a 5- or 10-minute walk of the local centre (Llewelyn Davies 1998). Such ped-sheds are not normally the same as perceptual neighbourhoods. But they do offer a useful analysis, and a prompt for action where barriers or cul-de-sac layouts impede accessibility.

5 Traffic-calmed areas

These are areas where the local quality of environment takes precedence over the needs of traffic – similar to Buchanan's 'environmental' areas. According to Buchanan et al. (1963) traffic flows in such areas should not exceed 300 passenger car units an hour. Government advises maximum traffic speeds of 20 mph. These targets can be achieved by the careful planning of road hierarchies and traffic management. Traffic-calmed areas may approximate to perceived neighbourhoods, but not normally to catchments. The Ipswich planners used the residents' views of neighbourhood boundaries, which often followed main roads, to define environmental neighbourhoods used in traffic planning.

In this guide we adopt criterion 3 (i.e. neighbourhoods defined primarily by the perceptions of residents), but complement that with larger catchment neighbourhoods which we call districts or small towns (see next sections).

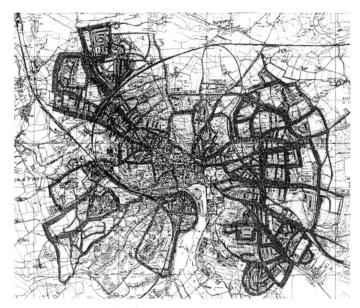

Figure 1.16
Ipswich: Residents' perceived neighbourhoods

Note: thickness of line denotes the frequency of mention by residents

SOURCE: Shankland, Cox and Associates 1968

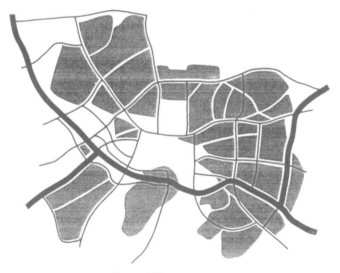

Figure 1.17
Ipswich: Neighbourhoods delineated by planners on the basis of the survey of residents

SOURCE: Shankland, Cox and Associates 1968

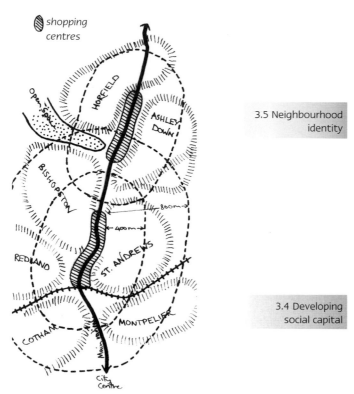

shopping
centres

Figure 1.18
Named city neighbourhoods are not always the same as catchment areas

CHECKLIST

The key variables which enable us to describe the spatial character of localities are:

- *the population and social mix and how these are evolving*
- *social networks and the distinctive local culture/spatial character*
- *the level of economic activity and facilities available locally*
- *movement networks especially for walking, cycling and public transport*
- *the pattern of land use – the degree of clustering*
- *density patterns, including intensity of use, footfall etc.*
- *the relationship of open/greenspace and outdoor recreational activity*
- *the ecology of the settlement: water, energy, wildlife, food supply etc.*

All these are explored in detail in subsequent chapters.

3.5 Neighbourhood identity

3.4 Developing social capital

5.9 Form and function

5.11 Neighbourhood cells

NEIGHBOURHOOD AND COMMUNITY

There are seeds of confusion in the way these two terms are used: they are not interchangeable, as neighbourhood is about place while community is about people. The neighbourhood, in terms of its streets, houses, facilities and greenspaces, may be consciously planned. Communities – in the sense of networks of mutual support and friendship – cannot be planned in the same way, but occur through people's choices and actions. Most communities are based around shared interest or identity rather than closeness. Many communities of interest (to do with work, education, leisure pursuits or politics) are spatially wide-flung, though most still have a specific local base somewhere. With high mobility, individual lifestyle choice and 'virtual' meetings, propinquity is not a prerequisite for community.

None the less, the locality still provides the focus for a number of overlapping interest communities and activities – children in school, scouts and guides, baby-sitting circles, surgeries, local shops, pubs, allotments, churches. Together with casual meetings in the street, these create the sense of a diverse, evolving local community. The opportunity for such communities to flourish is profoundly affected by public policy and design – for example through the provision of local facilities and the perceived safety of the streets. The existence of such communities is important for health and well-being, particularly amongst young families, retired people, and those out of work (for full discussion see Barton et al. 2000, particularly Chapters 1 and 9).

NEIGHBOURHOOD FORM

A clear and realistic view of neighbourhood form and function is a prerequisite for the effective planning of development so as to promote health, equity and sustainability. Central to such a view is the recognition that neighbourhoods are not separate units but interconnected parts of the urban continuum.

Neighbourhoods come in many shapes and sizes. There is an illuminating distinction to be drawn between old and new settlements. In some ways, traditional town patterns are working better than more recent models; the key variable is the degree of separation or integration.

Traditional 'fuzzy' neighbourhoods

Neighbourhoods merge into each other and often do not coincide with the main retail catchment areas (as in the Gloucester Road area of Bristol, Figure 1.18), which act like urban townships, linking several neighbourhoods together.

Planned neighbourhood units

The dominant neighbourhood model in the British new towns, exported to the world, treats the neighbourhood as a cell, with a nucleus or centre, and distinct boundaries.

Planned urban townships

Groups of neighbourhoods cluster together in compact or linear form to create larger urban districts or townships.

5.12 Linear districts

Suburban 'campus' development

Low density single use car-based enclaves in the form of cul-de-sac housing estates, business parks, superstores, campus-style educational/health facilities.

1.11 DISTRICT/TOWN, NEIGHBOURHOOD AND HOME PLACE

The need for a consistent approach

Towns and cities vary tremendously in size, form, density and character. There is no universally applicable template for neighbourhoods. But some variables of identity, catchment and accessibility are sufficiently predictable to offer a basis for planning practice (Barton et al. 2000). This guide structures policy at three distinct levels.

1 DISTRICT AND SMALL TOWN

A small town or a district of a city should be large enough to support in principle a full range of local facilities and a good level of employment opportunities. The median population is about 25,000. Facilities could include a district or town centre, one or more superstores, several secondary schools and, depending on local authority policy, a library, leisure centre and technical college. The figure of 25,000 is the population recommended by one UK report as the minimum viable size for a free-standing new settlement (Breheny et al. 1993). In practice, the population may vary widely, from, say 12,000 to 40,000.

The bustling heart of a small town on market day

This scale is equivalent to many rural or market towns, especially if the dependent hinterland population is taken into account. Many of the principles applicable to the urban district are also relevant to these small towns. Indeed, the principles are often clearer for the towns because of their physical detachment from other settlements.

Within urban areas, districts are rarely so distinct. But the essential goal of providing accessible jobs and facilities to every part of a city is articulated by this principle.

2 NEIGHBOURHOOD

The definition of 'neighbourhoods' adopted in this guide is one based on resident perceptions. As such they are normally residential areas of distinctive identity, often distinguished by name, and bounded by recognisable barriers or transition areas such as railway lines, main roads, parks, and the age or character of buildings (often associated with social or land-use differences).

1.11

These two terms used in the first edition have been replaced. 'Township' has been dropped because unwanted associations (with huge South African townships, for example) can confuse the issue - though it is still useful on occasion and equates with a well-defined urban district. 'Homepatch' has been dropped altogether because we consider 'home place' has greater resonance.

5.16 Home place

Neighbourhoods thus defined vary in size very widely according to local circumstances, but a typical size might be 4,000–5,000. They are often large enough to include a primary school and some local shops. However, as noted in Ipswich, they may not coincide at all with local catchment areas. The local high street with its wider range of township facilities will sometimes be at the edge of the neighbourhood.

3   HOME PLACES

The living zone is the individual streets, squares, blocks or cul-de-sacs that make up the patchwork of the neighbourhood. The livng zone is critically important in residents' feelings of security or insecurity. Increasingly, the scale of the living zone is seen as a useful unit for urban design – offering the potential for Dutch-style 'Woonerfs' or British 'homezones', where the safety of the streets for play and social exchange is paramount, and traffic is calmed to 5 or 10 mph.

Figure 1.19
Defining terms

The three levels		Typical population
District/Small town	A sector or district of a town large enough to support a good range of job opportunities and local facilities including secondary school(s), large supermarket and leisure centre.	15,000–40,000
Neighbourhood	A mainly residential area of distinctive identity, sometimes named, which may coincide with either a local catchment area or an environmental area, and is geared to pedestrian/cyclist access.	2,000–10,000
Home place	A cluster of dwellings often developed at the same time, with shared identity or character, grouped round a common access (e.g. square, street, cul-de-sac or shared semi-private space), and ideally enjoying pedestrian priority.	20–200

Other useful terms	
Local catchment area	Zone of good pedestrian accessibility to local services such as primary school and shops, normally defined by threshold walking times (5 or 10 minutes) or distance (400–800 m). Note that catchment areas for different facilities will vary widely, according to their nature and location.
Environmental area	Zone where through traffic is excluded and the quality of the local environment takes precedence. Routinely achieved in new development though careful planning of road hierarchies.
Local community	A network of overlapping and interacting communities of interest and identity at the local level, providing mutual recognition, support and opportunities for friendship and co-operation.
Urban village	A medium- to high-density neighbourhood with a core of mixed uses and bustling pedestrian character. Normally applied to new development.
Urban quarter	A neighbourhood or district where uses are of a particular complementary character, such as the jewellery quarter in Birmingham. But also used more generally.
Homezone	Official UK term for a home-place where special traffic management and environmental improvement policies are pursued to give residents a safe and pleasant environment, especially for children's play.

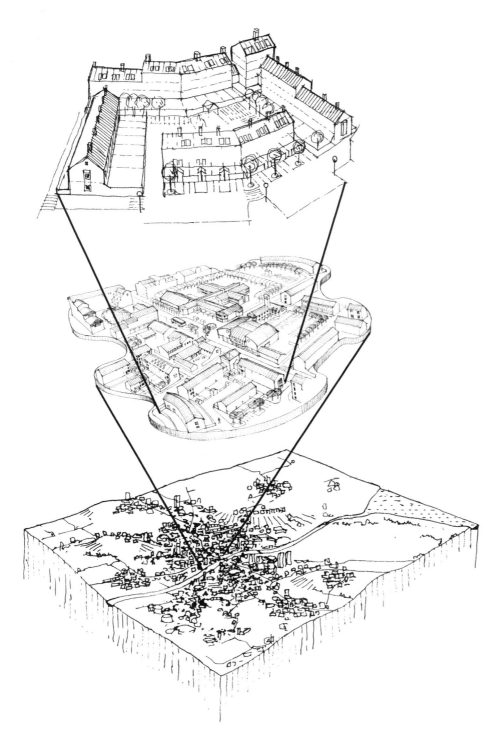

Figure 1.20
Nested scales: district/small town, neighbourhood and home place

Building scale
Dwelling, office, shop

Key sustainability and health issues
Flexibility of design for entire life course, for changing lifestyles and for diversity. Reductions in embodied energy and energy in use.

Home place scale
Street, home zone, Woonerf, block

Key sustainability and health issues
Active street life and support for community interaction.
Design to support low carbon living and local nature.

Neighbourhood scale
Local area, locality, village

Key sustainability and health issues
Plan for local facilities with attractive walking routes. Local hubs to support healthy lifestyles.
Develop local food, waste, water and energy capture systems.

District/ Small town scale
Town, quarter

Key sustainability and health issues
Good public transport and cycling access to centres.
Biodiversity, energy distribution and the water management need to be planned as critical network infrastructure.

City scale
City region, functional bioregion

Key sustainability and health issues
Active and public transport must have good linkage within the city and beyond the city.
Conurbation and hinterland need to be approached as a single system.

1.12

THE NEED FOR ROBUST PRINCIPLES

The neighbourhood objectives presented earlier in this chapter (1.2) set up formidable aspirations for neighbourhood planning and design. In themselves, the objectives are difficult to argue with, but many people would see great tension between them – they would seem to be difficult or impossible to achieve all at the same time.

Equivalently, the ecosystem philosophy presented above (1.8) may seem admirable in theory, providing a holistic and integrated approach, but difficult to interpret in practice. Some would even question its relevance.

It is for these reasons that we believe it is important to try to identify robust principles of spatial planning and design that cut right across the divergent objectives and demonstrate the practicality of the ecosystem approach. We have identified six such principles that seem to stand every test we have subjected them to. They underpin the detailed advice given in the guide.

Figure 1.21

12 health objectives matched with 6 design principles.

OBJECTIVES		Stakeholder involvement	Increase local autonomy	Connectivity	Diversity	Response to place	Adaptability
Lifestyle and community							
1.	Healthy lifestyles	○	●	●	○		
2.	Enhance community	●	●	○	○	○	○
3.	Local decision making	●	●	○		●	○
Economic							
4.	Promote enterprise	●	○	●	○		○
5.	Promote employment	○	●	●	○		○
Activities							
6.	Equitable access	○	●	●	●		
7.	Freedom of choice	○	○	●	●	○	○
Built environment							
8.	Safety and security	○		●	○		○
9.	Environmental quality	○			●	●	○
Natural environment							
10.	Safeguard assets	○	●			●	●
11.	Promote biodiversity	○		○	●	●	
12.	Combat climate change	○	●	○			○

● Critical relationships

○ Other important relationships

1   STAKEHOLDER INVOLVEMENT

The active involvement of all the locally relevant interests in the process of decision-making is widely recognised as essential if sustainable development is to be achieved in a pluralist society. One objective is to gain the backing of all stakeholders for a consistent and integrated programme; another is to build the capacity of the community (particularly less vocal segments) to take action.

Mechanisms need to be developed which ensure that all the main stakeholders (public, private and community sectors) are consulted and involved when their interests are at stake. Inclusive processes aim to achieve mutual knowledge and understanding along with opportunities for collaboration and joint projects. These mechanisms have to be adaptable to different circumstances, such as community-led initiatives, major development projects, and the preparation of local plans.

2   INCREASING LOCAL AUTONOMY

The principle of increasing the degree to which localities provide for themselves runs counter to powerful trends but is key to the achievement of many of the objectives – supporting accessible employment, choice of local facilities, the opportunity for healthy exercise and the development of local community networks. At the same time, it can lead to reduced pollution and reduced need for the import of energy, water and materials.

The basic principle is that services/activities should be managed at the lowest feasible level. In some spheres that may mean changed practices at the level of the individual building – for example, in relation to energy efficiency. In others the home-place or housing cluster is a practical level – say for toddler playspace, or water-demand management. The neighbourhood provides the appropriate level for primary schooling, local park, shops and pubs, while the township can satisfy services requiring higher population thresholds – such as library and leisure centre.

3   CONNECTIVITY

Supporting greater local autonomy does not imply isolation of one neighbourhood from another. On the contrary, connectedness between as well as within localities is essential for vitality, viability and choice. Rather than a fragmented, agency-by-agency pattern of provision it is the links between activities and between places that help ensure their success.

The principle of connectivity applies across many areas of policy:

- the management of resources (see Figures 4.1 and 4.2)
- the provision of retail, social and leisure facilities
- the permeability of the street network

2.3 Collaborative communities

3.8 Planning local accessibility

4.1 The local global system

5.2 The spatial framework

4.2 Integrated resource strategy

'Local authorities should develop a shared vision with their local communities'

SOURCE: PPG3 (DETR 2000g)

1.12

- the interdependence of adjacent neighbourhoods
- the network of wildlife and water corridors.

4   DIVERSITY

3.2 A diverse population

The principle of diversity is in response to the failures of conformity. The tendency has been to seek economies of scale in the process of urban development, and segregate uses to safeguard environmental quality. The result has been zoning strategies that create huge single-use, single-class estates, with local employment opportunities squeezed out, social polarisation and exclusion rife, and visual monotony.

The solution is to value diversity over conformity – and apply the principle of reasonable diversity to most aspects of neighbourhood planning:

3.3 Housing for all

- diversity of housing type and tenure (social inclusion)

3.7 Resilient economies

- diversity of local work and service opportunities

- diversity of modes of movement (choice)

4.18 Wildlife

- wildlife habitat diversity

5.3 A mix of uses

- variety of aesthetic character.

Reasonable diversity across a neighbourhood does not exclude small-scale homogeneity or imply that 'bad neighbour' uses should be allowed.

5   RESPONSE TO PLACE

3.5 Neighbourhood identity

5.15 Designing places

A central facet of connectivity is connection to place. The ecosystem approach requires recognition of, and response to, the unique heritage of each locality: its location, resource base and cultural landscape. But what we have had too often has been the application of standard development solutions irrespective of the ecological and cultural characteristics of the place concerned. This can lead to resource inefficiency, characterlessness and functional isolation. Rather, we should:

- capitalise on the specific environmental resources (e.g. streams, woods, slopes)

- build new developments to reflect the best of what is already there, cultivating 'local distinctiveness'

- judge development policy according to the area's location, links and character.

6   ADAPTABILITY: THE LIFE-TIME NEIGHBOURHOOD

5.13 Change and renewal

Neighbourhoods, like wildlife habitats, are not fixed and unchanging. People come and go; initiatives are born, grow, mature, and die; buildings are extended, used for different purposes, redeveloped. The human habitat has to adapt to changing conditions or decay. The aspiration for every neighbourhood is that it should evolve steadily and 'naturally', at an unforced rate, providing a healthy, convivial environment for residents and users at all stages. In terms of planning and design this means:

- adaptable building forms (designed for varied uses)
- extendable buildings, adaptable streets
- encouraging gradual renewal
- evolving heritage, not mothballing it
- keeping transport options open
- making space available for next-generation households and businesses
- avoiding fixed edges and barriers.

The comprehensive approach

- the historic core of mixed uses and close-knit streets fully pedestrianised
- the integrated transport system of rail, tram and bus reaching all parts of the city and the hinterland settlements
- all new development closely tied to existing or programmed tram routes
- economic development based on new technology (especially solar) and knowledge industries
- buildings very energy efficient and many relying on solar electricity, locally managed
- a very green environment promoting biodiversity, local food production, and both combating and coping with climate change
- a decentralised model of retail and social facilities, with early provision in new development
- pedestrian and bike friendly streets, encouraging social interaction and children's play.

For more information on Freiburg, see the reports of the study on the website: www.bne.uwe.ac.uk/who

The historic city of Freiburg in Bresgau, at the edge of the Rhine rift valley and the Schwarzwald, has become a place of pilgrimage for British planners. It exemplifies an integrated approach to spatial planning that UK cities can only dream about. The Freiburg achievement encompasses land use, transport, economic development, green infrastructure, social cohesion and environmental quality. It has been driven by a political consensus that values sustainability and quality of life. New neighbourhoods such as Vauban and Reiselfeld are planned as integral to the city, but also offering excellent opportunity for local living.

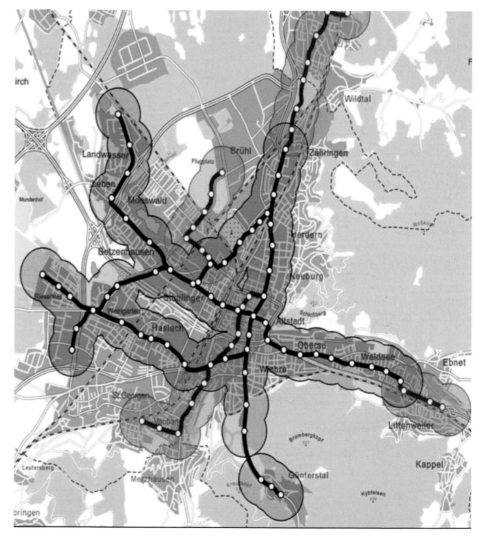

The expanding tram network of Freiburg now means that 80% of the population is within 500 metres of high quality public transport.

Reiselfeld

The new suburb of Reiselfeld will eventually cater for 12,000 people. It is being constructed on brownfield land (an old sewage works) as a large unified neighbourhood with one dominant centre. It is structured around an extension to the tram system that gives a reliable 5-10 minute service to the rest of the city. The pattern of densities and streets ensures everyone has good accessibility.

Reiselfeld caters for all segments of the population: a balance of self-build, market sale, private rented and social housing; a diversity of building types for varied household sizes and needs. The tram system and essential services were there from the outset. Now the neighbourhood includes primary and secondary provision, a medical centre doubling as a library and community/ social centre, recreation facilities, a multi-faith centre acting as a venue, parks and playgrounds, and a range of shops with a superstore imminent.

How do they do it?

- a significant level of local authority autonomy
- purchase of development land by the city, which then lays down infrastructure and sells plots on at a profit which pays for the outlay
- clarity over goals, and over the essential mechanism and design policies needed to achieve them
- in that context, extensive and ongoing public involvement in the detailed planning and management
- effective partnerships between diverse commercial and institutional interests
- strong leadership and continuity of key personnel

The city centre: no traffic, and somehow trams, cyclists and pedestrians get along together.

The neighbourhood planned around the tram line extension - which was constructed in advance of occupation to establish good habits from the outset.

Local facilities, centrally located and sharing space to encourage use: library, gym, cafe...

39

1.b

East End development
Glasgow, Scotland
Making the health and ecosystem principles integral to the spatial framework

The Council's vision for the East End is, to create a vibrant, new city district, through a regeneration process based on reinvention and reconnection. Existing and new communities will benefit from a new approach to living in cities, as regeneration in the East End will be a model of sustainable development addressing issues of population quality and meeting people's needs.

Glasgow City Council has been leading a collaborative stakeholder process to provide a strong long term strategy for 626 hectares of land lying to the east of the city centre. This main focus of the work is the East End which itself is part of a wider Clyde Gateway strategic zone. Clyde Gateway is a 25 year project to create 10,000 new jobs, 10,000 new homes and bring in some 20,000 new residents. This is securing major investment in new trunk roads, a new National Indoor Sports Arena and the Commonwealth Games Athlete's Village for 2014.

The work is ongoing, with many contributory stages, the East End Local Development Strategy (GCC 2008) marks a milestone. Under a banner of 'Changing places – Changing lives', the strategy demonstrated how the wider determinants of health can be addressed in a spatial framework. An ecosystem approach is also very evident in this work and underpins the design at every scale from strategic down to neighbourhood and street level place making.

In this ambitious, but carefully developed programme, the Council is seeking to transform one of the city's former industrial heartlands, now a patchwork of vacant sites, transport corridors and rundown housing and industrial estates into a modern city district. The vision is to develop a new district for people to live and work, which meet their needs, including the need for health and well-being.

Integrated infrastructure approach

Through early work involving partnerships with relevant sectoral agencies audits and strategies were commissioned for the green network, the movement network and surface water. This work indicated that not only is there considerable scope to deliver each of these different infrastructure networks, but that was the 'potential for integrating infrastructure into a multi-functional network combining water management with green spaces and with walking/cycling routes'. This potential for multi-function solutions led to the development of what was termed an Integrated Infrastructure Policy Framework. Wherever appropriate this addressed issues relating both to the quality of the physical environment, and to its wider socio-economic objectives such as to population health. As such delivering better quality open spaces and choices relating to movement, by providing quality walking and cycling and public transport infrastructure, became central to the concept of Integrated Infrastructure and the achievement of the core regeneration objectives.

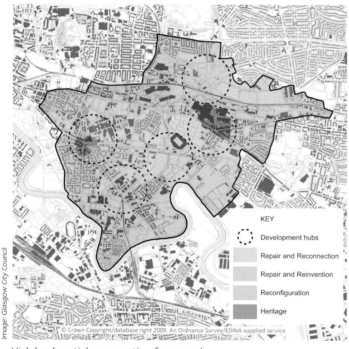

Image: Glasgow City Council

KEY

⭕ Development hubs

Repair and Reconnection

Repair and Reinvention

Reconfiguration

Heritage

© Crown Copyright/database right 2009. An Ordnance Survey/EDINA supplied service

High level spatial regeneration framework.

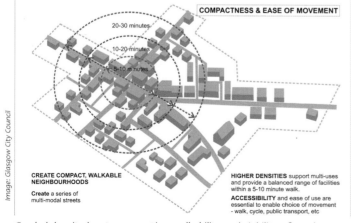

Image: Glasgow City Council

COMPACTNESS & EASE OF MOVEMENT

20-30 minutes

10-20 minutes

5-10 minutes

CREATE COMPACT, WALKABLE NEIGHBOURHOODS

Create a series of multi-modal streets

HIGHER DENSITIES support multi-uses and provide a balanced range of facilities within a 5-10 minute walk.

ACCESSIBILITY and ease of use are essential to enable choice of movement - walk, cycle, public transport, etc

Graded density key to supporting walkability and viability of services.

The heath impact assessment

Glasgow is a member of the WHO Healthy City Network and city planners and public health are developing close working relationships. In July 2007, as part of the development of the East End spatial framework, the Glasgow Centre for Population Health carried out a health impact assessment of an early draft strategy (Ison 2007). A main driver for this work was the commitment by Glasgow City Council to integrate health into the strategic planning process, especially important as the health of the East End population is amongst the poorest in the UK.

The health impact assessment used a rapid appraisal technique and combined results from two participatory stakeholder workshops, a half-day site visit and expert assessors' reflections. The strategy was tested against the healthy urban planning determinants of health (Barton et al. 2003) supported by evidence from various sources.

This process resulted in highlighting a number of concerns with the draft plan. These were also expressed as a series of both strategic and detailed recommendations to be taken on board in subsequent plan development. In subsequent iterations, the outcomes from the health impact assessment helped knit even more closely the integrated approach, already established, with the potential health outcomes.

Design and invent

The underlying ethos in the East End Development Strategy has been to set sights high; not to be comfortable with a 'predict and provide' approach but to adopt an 'imagine and invent' philosophy (Ravetz 2000). This philosophy runs through the whole project including the economic and urban design approaches. Key messages that the development team are pursuing and testing are:

1. Investment in good urban design can add financial value to a place.

2. Well-designed places deliver environmental and social benefits.

3. Poorly designed places are likely to incur higher costs to individuals and society in the long run.

As a testament to the joining-up of human habitat and health and environment, the East End Local Development Strategy is being seen as a nationally important example of how to tackle health inequalities in urban areas by the Scottish Government.

Key integrated infrastructure policy

POLICY 16. Developers will be expected to work with the Council to deliver its Integrated Infrastructure Framework. Developers will be expected to bring forward Masterplans and other development proposals which contribute to this framework by:

- *establishing a green network of quality open spaces and quality paths*
- *establishing an integrated network for walking and cycling paths linked to the use of public transport*
- *creating a regional Sustainable Urban Drainage scheme (SUDs) scheme and strategic conveyance routes*
- *upgrading existing road and path network*

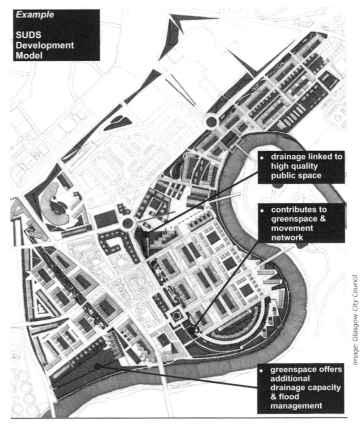

Example
SUDS Development Model

- drainage linked to high quality public space
- contributes to greenspace & movement network
- greenspace offers additional drainage capacity & flood management

Image: Glasgow City Council

Green infrastructure planning underpins quality of life and environmental fit.

a
neighbourhood
planning chapter 2
process

overview

2.2 PURPOSE AND SCOPE

This chapter is about how to consult, collaborate, analyse and take effective decisions at the neighbourhood or township level. It is therefore not so much about what to do but how to do it. It encompasses both the political and technical processes:

- a collaborative process of decision-making and implementation;
- an integrated and systematic appraisal of problems, policy and development opportunities.

These two processes are entwined but distinct. Effective collaboration between planners, investors and the local communities is indispensable to the implementation of co-ordinated strategies. But collaborative processes without dispassionate analysis can lead simply to negotiated agreements between established and vested interests. If the needs of under-represented groups and future generations are to be recognised, then political expediency must be married to inclusive rationality.

Clearly in some areas there will be no or little impetus for an integrated neighbourhood strategy. Even in relatively stable areas, however, each modest incremental change affects the trajectory towards or away from sustainability. A strong spatially specific strategy, backed by the significant local players and the community, is desirable.

WHOSE PROCESS?

The process described here is for a neighbourhood-level community strategy or spatial framework. The focus is on the physical development of the area.

The impetus for some kind of neighbourhood plan may come from public, private, voluntary or community sectors. Whatever the trigger, however, the decision process needs to follow the same basic pathway if it is to gain the support of the local partners and have a chance of promoting healthy development. This section shows some of sources of initiative and the mechanisms involved.

2.1

There is a lovely tradition of community involvement in regeneration.

Power to the people

The Local Government Association (2000c) is calling for neighbourhood plans where local communities are empowered to take responsibility for a range of service delivery, detailed land use and development control. One model they refer to is the Village Design Statement. Transferring that idea to the much larger scale of market towns and urban townships would depend on resources, legitimacy and capacity-building.

Cautionary tale

A community forum decided to create a plan for a declining town centre. Almost everybody joined in – except for the local authority planning committee. Visions and strategies were produced, enthusiasm was high, but five years later nothing had happened.

Clearly something went wrong early on. Without a key partner on board the initiative was still-born.

Investor-led community consultation at Street, Somerset

COMMUNITY-LED PROCESSES

Community campaigns may be triggered by frustration at the lack of local facilities, by economic decline, social crisis or environmental degradation. The main purpose of such campaigning is to influence the authorities. Credibility depends heavily on the network of contacts and the level of demonstrable community support.

Community groups, voluntary organisations and small businesses are vulnerable to higher powers, but they are also able to innovate and experiment with a flexibility that big business and big government cannot match. Many of the most exciting examples of sustainable development have been launched and managed by local groups (Barton and Kleiner 1998). Often innovations are born in the localities where the key people live, but they can only flourish with public- and private-sector support.

Winning friends and influencing people

The starting point for such a campaign is making alliances. The ambition is to form partnerships that enable effective and implementable decisions. To achieve that the community initiative group needs to:

- articulate the aims and character of the initiative clearly

- attract attention by appropriate publicity

- build grassroots membership to help with the work and increase credibility with local authority/funding organisations

- develop a pilot project (if appropriate) to demonstrate the group's capability and prepare the ground for more ambitious schemes

- build a constituency of support among local politicians, the local press, local groups and the community at large

- form partnerships with private and public sectors to undertake the project.

INVESTOR-LED PROCESSES

Where a development site is large enough to have a significant impact on the future of a neighbourhood then the investor has a responsibility to promote a collaborative decision-making process. This is not only a question of sustainability ethics; it is also enlightened self-interest.

The major investor can, and should, follow the same set of planning steps as the planning authorities. This includes working with local stakeholders to consider problems, needs and opportunities, and preparing a spatial framework that knits the new development into the old. The planning authority is key partner in this process.

LOCAL AUTHORITY-LED PROCESSES

The local authority should work towards adopting an integrated approach to spatial policy in every urban township, rural town or parish, so that local plan review, LA21, economic development and regeneration projects all have a clear relationship to service department programmes, and support from local stakeholders.

There is a profusion of official initiatives affecting neighbourhoods: health action zones, housing actions zones, safe communities, traffic schemes, regeneration partnerships, development plans, etc. The risk of conflict, duplication and ineffectiveness is high. Co-ordination can occur via a number of mechanisms:

Neighbourhood community strategies

Town or locality-based community strategies provide an opportunity for integration at the local level. Such plans are intended to promote social, economic and environmental well-being. They should include service provision, land-use and development policies.

Neighbourhood spatial frameworks

Changes to strategic (e.g. city-wide) plans give an opportunity for neighbourhood partnerships with the parish/town councils, service providers (education, health), and the community. The locality-based spatial frameworks could give detail to strategic policies in areas of significant change.

Development briefs

The preparation of development briefs for major redevelopment or town expansion schemes requires partnership with service providers, land and development interests, and local people.

2.2 THE SEVEN-STAGE PROCESS

BASIC PRINCIPLES

Any process of spatial policy-making or major development affecting a locality needs to be RITE:

- Rational, in the sense that there is a real attempt to understand the nature of the problems, to analyse the merits of different solutions, and learn from the process of implementation.
- Inclusive, in the sense that important stakeholders – whether they be local people, voluntary associations, private- or public-sector agencies – are actively involved.
- Transparent, in that information is readily available and verifiable and the sources of power and influence visible and open to challenge.
- Effective, in that decisions, once taken, are capable of being acted on – that responsibilities are clear, the programme realistic and co-ordinated.

The potential benefits to the investor include:

- *Reducing conflict by listening to local people's concerns and responding to them appropriately*

- *Improving the function of the scheme by early discussion with relevant transport, education, health, etc. agencies*

- *Reaching an acceptable scheme more quickly, avoiding costly redesign*

- *Reducing the risk of planning application refusal, and increasing the strength of any subsequent appeal if it were to be refused*

- *Positive publicity and improved profile*

Examples of investors who should initiate collaborative processes

- *A house builder with an option on urban fringe land.*

- *A hospital trust selling off a redundant facility.*

- *A housing association developing a major regeneration scheme.*

- *Railtrack selling unwanted sidings in the inner city.*

2.2

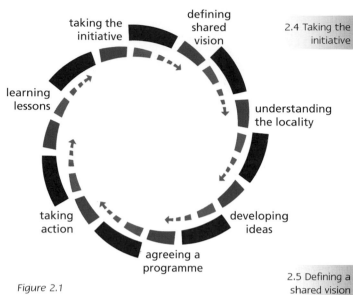

Figure 2.1
The seven-stage process - *The seven stages, starting with **taking the initiative**, structure the rest of this chapter*

**Appraisal and evaluation:
the SPECTRUM approach**

It is important to ensure consistency of approach at all stages of the process, and in an inclusive, collaborative way. SPECTRUM is just such an approach. It offers an open and holistic way of tying together all the strings of evaluation. The Spectrum sign shows where it is described in the seven-stage process.

For an overview of SPECTRUM see the Houndwood case study at the end of this chapter.

THE PROCESS IN OUTLINE

1. Taking the initiative

The initiative for a neighbourhood-wide project may come from the local authority, a major investing organisation or the local community. Effective and sustained leadership by the initiator is very important, but equivalently it is vital to recognise fully the other interests involved. Early and open consultation may well reveal opportunities or problems that lead to redefinition of the project. 'Scoping' should aim to answer these questions:

- What is the purpose and scope of the project?

- Is the initiating organisation capable of pursuing it?

- What stakeholders should be involved?

- Is the project consistent with broader goals and strategies?

2. Defining a shared vision

The first milestone in a collaborative neighbourhood planning exercise is the development of a shared vision. The vision must be both highly motivating and practical, so that potential partners want to 'buy into' it. The vision should then be reflected in a project brief which sets out:

- the aims, scope and hoped-for outcome

- the way the project will be managed

- the collaborative and consultative process; and

- the process of appraisal and policy-making.

3. Understanding the locality

A careful appraisal of the neighbourhood (or the project) and its context is essential before fixing on specific policies or proposals. This is to avoid blinkered solutions and open up the possibility of synergy/collaboration. A neighbourhood appraisal should if possible:

- be undertaken with other key stakeholders, to broaden the base of understanding and engender a sense of shared ownership of the initiative, using the appraisal to build community capacity

- involve a quick but systematic scan of all the levels of analysis in the neighbourhood model: people, community, activities, place, resources and the wider context

- link into and contribute to monitoring of the quality of life

- focus attention where there are real difficulties, tensions or uncertainties, bringing on board others who are involved, looking for opportunities as well as assessing problems.

2.4 Taking the initiative

2.5 Defining a shared vision

2.7 Understanding the locality

4. Developing ideas

It is important not to lurch prematurely into supposed 'solutions' to local problems. The established policies of service providers, developers and planning authorities have often failed (or not attempted) to deliver sustainable development. It is therefore vital to examine radically different options. Ideas may be triggered simply by the process of inter-agency collaboration, but also by a deliberate search for best practice in the field, learning from experience elsewhere. Techniques of visioning and brainstorming can help in the right context.

2.8 Developing ideas

In some situations a formal evaluation process may be required. The purposes of such evaluation, and who should do it, are key issues for discussion. The process of evaluation should be seen as part of a creative process, pushing ideas forward, not an end in itself.

5. Agreeing a co-ordinated programme

A local neighbourhood plan – whatever form it takes – serves not only to identify policies but also to win commitment from the key implementing organisations. The process of gaining political support and influencing investors is critical. Without backing the plan will flounder.

2.9 Agreeing a co-ordinated programme

The core document is therefore a programme rather than a plan. It needs to be explicit about the agreed vision for the area, the development priorities, and the way in which the often-unpredictable process of implementation is to be handled. The roles and tasks of contributing agencies need to be spelt out and agreed, with staging posts for co-ordinated review. Desired outcomes should be stated.

In the context of such a programme individual agencies produce their own policy documents. Specifically the Planning Authority should produce the spatial framework which will shape the physical evolution of the area.

6   Taking action

The best-laid plans can fail. Implementation is an incremental and often disjointed process over an extended timespan. Effectiveness depends on:

2.10 Taking action

■   long-term consistency of vision and strategy

■   a creative, pro-active stance from the planning authority setting the objectives and parameters for the development of specific sites (with development briefs, for example)

■   seizing opportunities when they emerge, for example when land ownership changes bring forward sites unexpectedly

■   responding to concerns and sharing problems by flexibility in design solutions, and networking with other stakeholders

■   maintaining the sense of shared ownership and decision-taking, through regular information exchange and meetings

2.3

Ineffective partnerships

'Partnerships (may) represent little more than the key players suppressing mutual loathing in the interests of mutual greed' (Rowe and Davanne 2003, p.375)

In their study on regeneration partnerships and governance, the authors go on to say that to release the potential in partnership working there is a need to:

- *challenge the existing way of delivering services*

- *engage different voices in decision making*

- *acknowledge that just putting different people around a table, without acknowledging the domination of existing hierarchies and markets, does not necessarily constitute a new way of working.*

It follows that meeting the training and capacity building needs essential for partnership working should be identified as an early key activity in shaping healthy neighbourhoods.

A model to learn from

The WHO Healthy Cities movement has since 1987 provided a model for inclusive, collaborative working at the levels of both the neighbourhood and the municipality. See Green (2009) for an analysis of the Healthy Cities programme.

Bringing stakeholders together around health and sustainability

- cultivating community and councillor support.

Effectiveness also depends on subsequent management. It needs to be crystal clear in the neighbourhood plan: who is going to manage any community facilities? Is the local authority able to pick up the tab? If not, does a Community Trust or residents' management committee exist which could manage on behalf of users?

2.12 Learning lessons

7   Learning lessons

On-going monitoring and review works on three levels:

1   Assessing policy impact – i.e. how far have policies been implemented and with what success? If there are undesirable side effects, or hiccups in delivering the policy, then what can be done?

2   Assessing health and sustainability outcomes – i.e. what are the trends in quality of life for residents/workers in the area? How is the neighbourhood changing? Has the plan as a whole addressed the issues?

3   Assessing the effectiveness of the process – have the collaborative and policy-making processes worked? Could they be fairer, more inclusive, more efficient? What lessons for elsewhere, or next time round?

2.3 COLLABORATIVE COMMUNITIES

THE CO-OPERATIVE PRINCIPLE

The creation of sustainable neighbourhoods depends on the active commitment of local stakeholders. Public, private and community sectors need to pursue common purposes. This co-operative principle is not about romantic community idealism; it is about co-ordination. It may mean working in partnership with other bodies, sharing ownership of a neighbourhood project, or it may simply mean open/effective information exchange and consultation.

Reasons

- *Health and sustainable development*

Collaboration is necessary in order to understand problems and to promote effective solutions. For example, a sustainable energy project, a regeneration scheme or a local healthy food strategy will rely on co-operation between many interests.

- *Human rights*

There are legal rights for households and businesses to be consulted about planning policies and decisions that affect them. These rights are being progressively extended into other spheres, for example council housing and education. In the context of the Human Rights Act it is arguable that obligatory consultation should also be extended to health services and leisure management.

■ *Shifting attitudes*

Social and environmental objectives are promoted by the mutual education and consciousness-raising which can occur when different interests engage in dialogue. For example, a local wildlife trust or a black women's group can affect local authority attitudes and priorities.

■ *Taking control locally, changing behaviour*

Businesses and households become more aware of shared communities of interest, and may be willing to alter their behaviour, when sustained public debate occurs – say in relation to safety on the streets or supporting the local post office or primary school. A collaborative community provides channels and forums where such concerns can be highlighted and joint action considered. It helps to establish new social norms of behaviour and foster individual behavioural change.

■ *Strengthening local community networks*

The collaborative processes no doubt only involve a small minority of people in the neighbourhood, but the people drawn in will be reinforcing their commitment to the locality and to local community networks. New and often serendipitous local initiatives will be born. Stronger community networks will help support vulnerable people, reduce anomie and depression (Gilchrist 2000).

WHO IS INVOLVED

A realistic map of local partners in neighbourhood/township development provides a means of assessing the appropriateness of any consultation or decision process. The simple map given here and elaborated later (Section 2.5) is specific to the spatial planning of an area, and distinguishes four groupings:

The planning authority and statutory bodies

The planners are charged with guiding the spatial evolution of an area towards sustainable development. They produce the plans and policies but have little direct power of implementation, relying on the other partners, including service departments of the local authority (housing or education, for example) to play the game. In many situations statutory bodies such as (in England) the Environment Agency, Natural England or a Regional Development Agency may be involved.

Investors and providers

These are the private-, public- and voluntary-sector organisations who are the main agencies of change. This sector includes the major employers, the private developers, the non-profit developers (such as housing associations), and varied transport, health, education and social service providers. These agencies normally have quite specific remits, which they often pursue completely independently of neighbourhood participatory processes.

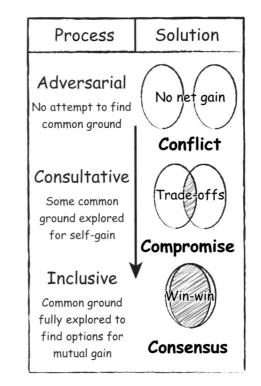

Figure 2.2 **Build on common ground**

Adversarial approaches to development decisions can be counter-productive

Figure 2.3

Stakeholder groups in neighbourhood planning

This simple map of the stakeholders forms the basis for subsequent guidance

Going local?

Guidance on area and neighbourhood governance is given in Hoggart and Kimberlee (2001)

The community groups

Local voluntary organisations include campaigning groups (such as civic societies), service-providers (the Citizens Advice Bureaux, for example) and a host of social, religious and recreational clubs and associations. Certain groups may see participation in community development projects as central to their mission, but most will not. Many will have a remit and catchment much broader than any specific neighbourhood. Politically active local groups are central to the development of a neighbourhood strategy. However, they do not necessarily provide an adequate proxy for the views/needs of the whole population.

The people of the area

These are the users of the neighbourhood – the real owners. They include all the residents, together with local business people, workers, and those dependent on local leisure/retail/education/ health facilities but who live outside the area. Typically, about 10 per cent of local residents are members of organised groups – so 90% are unrepresented except through the ballot box. Consultation processes often fail to reach (or motivate) the most vulnerable or marginalised groups.

NEIGHBOURHOOD GOVERNANCE

The section above assumes there is the political and institutional will to achieve effective collaboration between local partners. This guide does not attempt to deal with the more formal methods of neighbourhood governance, but it is important to note the mechanisms, appropriate in different situations and with varying degrees of local democratic control, for example:

- Parish and town councils, directly elected, with powers delegated by the local authority.

- Area or neighbourhood committees, responsible for the co-ordinated delivery of local authority services.

- Neighbourhood forums, with cross-sectoral membership, creating potentially good conditions for partnership working.

- Community Development Trusts, with strong community representation, able to undertake development projects.

TOP DOWN OR BOTTOM UP?

2.6 Working with local people

Attitudes to local government are shifting, with the growing interest in decentralised models of decision-making. Yet much community involvement in the planning of neighbourhoods is well-meaning tokenism that fails to deliver what people are led to expect, or is overtly placatory, 'managing' public opinion. Equivalently much community activism is misdirected, and fails to hit its target. Community initiatives are misconceived, because of lack of analysis about where power lies.

The 'ladder of citizen participation' analyses the relationship between the local authority and local people. It does not necessarily imply that the top rung of the ladder is 'best'. Rungs four and five – 'Genuine consultation' and 'Partnership' – may be more realistic aspirations in many situations.

Figure 2.4
A *ladder of citizen participation*

SOURCE: Freely adapted from Burns, Hambleton and Hoggett 1994, itself based on Arnstein 1969

Rungs of the ladder	Neighbourhood-level characteristics	Attitude of the local authority	Comments
7 Autonomous powers	An elected neighbourhood government with substantial powers, legally and financially independent from local authorities.	Confrontational	This is the ideal of social anarchism, and would require new legislation. Reality might fall rather short of the ideal, and be prone to NIMBYism.
6 Delegated powers	Community Development Trust or parish/town council with substantial responsibilities delegated by the local authority.	Collaborative	Achievable without major legislation; can be innovative and radical.
5 Partnership	Neighbourhood Forum or Management Company with power sharing between local authority, business and citizens' groups.	Collaborative	Widely practised. Relies on shared ownership and effective leadership.
4 Genuine consultation	Public meetings, stakeholder groups, web votes, citizens' focus groups, planning for real, etc. – a real attempt to encourage local debate and respond to it.	Enabling	Widely practised. Local authority positive attitudes and skills are critical.
3 Two-way information	Good-quality information from authority to citizens and from citizens to authority via community newspapers, local social surveys.	Technical	This is not adequate in itself, but it is a vital part of an inclusive strategy, reaching the non-joiners.
2 Tokenism	Consultation too little, too late, going through the motions.	Manipulative	
1 Spin and bluster	No attempt at consultation considered necessary.	Autocratic	

getting going

2.4 STAGE 1 – TAKING THE INITIATIVE

KEY PRINCIPLE
Whether the process is initiated by the local authority, a major developer or a community alliance the same principle applies: the goal is not narrow and self-interested but holistic – in the interests of the long-term health and well-being of the whole community. So there is a moral obligation to identify, and where appropriate work with, the various local stakeholders.

Who is taking the initiative?

Any new neighbourhood plan needs a driving force and champions if it is to succeed. As noted in section 2.1, the motivation may come from resident concerns/aspirations, or commercial profit, or statutory obligation and political vision. Whatever the context there needs to be a critical number of core actors, willing to carry the initiative through.

In situations where consultants are employed, or a planning team is set up within the local authority, it must be clear what their remit is, to whom they are directly responsible. Who is in charge? Who will back them when the chips are down?

SCOPING

The purpose of 'scoping' is to set the initiative in context and review its purpose and scope before formal commitments are entered into. Effective scoping by the initiating organisation safeguards against false perceptions, blind alleys and blinkered vision. It can save time and energy, and help ensure that appropriate partners and stakeholders are identified early. Scoping typically involves

Using the health map in a scoping workshop. Just how will the new policies and proposals affect peoples health?

- round-table discussion/brainstorm/visioning

- informal discussion with key organisations and opinion-formers

- quick review of relevant legislation, policy documents or guidelines; and/or

- a dispassionate visual appraisal of the area involved.

Scoping seeks to answer these questions:

What is the purpose and scope of the project?

Clarity about aims is half the battle! Scoping should identify connections with other issues, the spatial area that could be affected and the range of possible means of implementation.

What is the organisation's capacity?

Capacity to pursue the initiative depends on commitment, time and skill. If the organisation does not have the capacity, then what key partnerships could be forged to enable effective progress?

The scoping process should identify:

- *Potential partners, needed to achieve a co-ordinated plan.*

- *Relevant regulatory bodies and potential sources of funds.*

- *Representatives of groups who stand to benefit.*

- *Representatives of groups who might feel threatened.*

Is the initiative consistent with broader aims?

The original idea of the project needs to evolve in such a way that it has the potential to fit into the broad goals and strategies of the development plan and/or the Community Strategy, and also to satisfy the three criteria of sustainable development: economic viability, health/social justice and environmental sustainability. There may be links or symbiosis with other projects that can help.

WHAT STAKEHOLDERS SHOULD BE INVOLVED?

Whichever organisation is the initiator, it is vital to draw in other stakeholders as soon as possible. The potential value of a plan is as much in the process as in the product. If some of the major players are not on board then the effectiveness of any output in shaping policy will be severely hampered. Indeed it is quite possible for a LA21 or community-initiated process to sink without trace. At the outset, therefore, the strategy should be devised to reach out to sympathetic people within other groups and organisations. The intention should be to build a constituency of support, and share ownership of the project so that effective collaboration is possible.

Why should they be involved?

Participatory processes are sometimes seen by local authority officials – and even more by local business leaders – as a time-consuming deflection from the main task of getting things done. But principles of community collaboration and partnership are nothing to do with political correctness or cosy utopianism. They are everything to do with effectiveness and ownership. One organisation by itself has neither the power nor the authority to deliver sustainable development. Working with stakeholders is necessary to ensure that:

■ local expertise is tapped and local demands understood;

■ a co-ordinated strategy is possible and implementable;

■ important interests are not excluded from consideration;

■ creative, integrated solutions are devised;

■ decisions are reasonably transparent and have legitimacy;

■ trust between people and local capacity are built up; and

■ people's quality of life is improved through empowerment.

Partners, participants and consultees

The scoping exercise should endeavour to identify who needs to participate and in what way. It is useful to distinguish between three levels of potential involvement:

Partners – who share the decision-making and accept responsibility for making things happen. Partnerships may involve formal contractual agreements and the dovetailing of investment programmes.

CHECKLIST

Golden rules

There are at least five golden rules for initiating organisations to follow in formulating a clear participation strategy:

1 Clarity of purpose

– What are you trying to achieve?

– Why is consultation or collaboration needed?

– Who are you targeting?

2 Fitness for purpose

– What are the participating approaches suited to the task?

– Will the approaches help deliver a co-ordinated plan?

– Does the approach fulfil statutory requirements?

– Have you got the capacity to see it through?

– Have the other participants got the capacity to see it through?

3 Avoiding false expectations

– Are you clear about your 'bottom line'?

– Are the project boundaries explicit?

– Have you got something of value to offer the participants?

– Have you got on board the key agencies that can deliver improvements?

4 An open, inclusive process

– Can you give leadership without patronising participants?

– Can you share ownership of the process with the other stakeholders?

– Are the channels for involvement clear and inviting?

– Is information about the process as it evolves available for scrutiny?

5 A positive process

– Have you a programme for developing a shared vision?

– Can you orientate the process towards problem solving and win–win solutions?

– Can you avoid the dangers of polarisation and entrenched views?

2.5

CHECKLIST

Visioning stages ... in outline

1 Imagine the kind of neighbourhood you would like in twenty years' time.

2 Identify the features of the present that are unsatisfactory.

3 Work out barriers that make it difficult to get from the unsatisfactory present to the idealised future.

4 Explore the levers that could enable some of the barriers to be overcome.

5 Develop a strategy (or alternative strategies) for making progress.

6 Identify first steps on the path, and who will help take them.

Neighbourhood organisations can take control and communicate directly with local people

Community initiatives

Where a community group is promoting the ideas of a neighbourhood plan it is obviously not possible to move straight to a draft brief. Instead, getting to the point where a brief can be drafted becomes a prime goal. The drafting must involve the main agency (the local authority, for example) that has the power to deliver.

Participants – who actively participate in the decision-making process, but are not prime movers. Participants are likely to be involved in consensus-building processes in the context of stakeholder forums, focus groups, citizens' juries, etc.

Consultees – who are formally asked for their views about current problems and possible solutions but do not engage in the collaborative forums. Consultation implies the opportunity for two-way flows of information but maybe only limited dialogue. Typically all local private and public organisations would have this opportunity, plus all local people.

COMMUNITY VISIONING

One way of broadening the community base and sharing ownership at an early stage is the community visioning event. A joint visioning exercise between initiators and the wider community can be a means of welding disparate interests into a team. A shared vision however, does not mean an idle dream. It is about gathering insight and momentum, leading to a clearer plan of campaign.

Participation in a visioning exercise should be as open as possible. The process needs to be managed by a skilled facilitator, preferably independent of any of the main organisations. It can take a day or more. One purpose of visioning is to find and enlarge the common ground between participants; another is to get to know people; a third is to develop new, creative ideas together. All this can help engender mutual understanding, trust and enthusiasm.

2.5 STAGE 2 – DEFINING A SHARED VISION

KEY PRINCIPLE

An effective neighbourhood plan depends on developing a common view about its aims, scope and the process of getting there. This takes time and effort. Somehow disparate interests have to be welded into a collaborative team. It is vital the initiating group devises a participatory process that is focused, transparent and deliverable. A shared vision does not mean an idle dream. It is about a practical plan of campaign that can be encapsulated in a formal project brief.

THE PROJECT BRIEF

Agreement on the project brief is a pivotal milestone in any neighbourhood planning exercise. The purpose of the brief is to set out clearly the aims and scope of the project, the process of appraisal and decision-making, and the way stakeholders and the public will be involved in that process. Joint ownership of the brief is key to partnership. Transparency of the process is key to legitimacy.

Preparing the brief

If there has been a community visioning exercise then the participants may have allocated the task of preparing the brief. However, it is essential that the key initiating (or lead) organisation keeps a tight rein at this stage to maintain momentum. The lead organisation may prepare a first draft of the project brief on the basis of the scoping exercise and/or the visioning process. The draft should take into account the views expressed informally by potential partners. It can be used to draw other parties into engagement with the project by showing how their interests might be affected and how they could become creatively involved.

Clarity of aims is critical. The lead organisation needs to be honest and explicit about its own motives and aspirations. Fudge and waffle have no place: they can lead to misunderstanding and store up problems for later. Conversely, premature prescription must be avoided. The first draft is just that, a draft, for consultation. It is not the final version. It can therefore be short. If appropriate it may be brought back to the neighbourhood 'visioning' group for further joint work. The final brief, once agreed, is the basis for collaboration. If there are to be partners in the project, then the brief acts as part of the formal agreement. It is also the basis for initial publicity, and available for public scrutiny.

STAKEHOLDERS' GROUP

For neighbourhood projects the stakeholders' group or forum is a central part of the planning process. Its role, membership and modus operandi should be set out and agreed in the project brief. The group meets on a regular basis (once a month, for example) and exists to:

- share ownership and engender commitment

- exchange information and contacts

- sort problems and develop project ideas collaboratively

- participate in health and sustainability impact assesment

- help build a wider constituency of support; and

- facilitate co-ordination and implementation.

The stakeholder group needs to involve all potential *partners* and those *participants* who are able and willing to give regular commitment. It may be used as a way of building towards partnership. To be effective the group needs reasonably stable membership, able to develop common understanding and momentum. Do not be tempted to use it as a catch-all for transient interests or debates.

Invite people to join in a stakeholders' group as soon as possible after the scoping exercise, with clear guidance as to the essential purpose and rationale for the plan or project. Hopefully a number

---

CHECKLIST
What should the brief include?

The final version of the brief should be explicit about:

- the broad policy context

- the purpose and scope of the exercise, with explanation

- the sustainability and health objectives

- how the project will be managed: leadership, resources, timescale

- the agreed roles of other stakeholders

- the process of public consultation

- the scope of the appraisal

- the process of policy-making

- expected outputs.

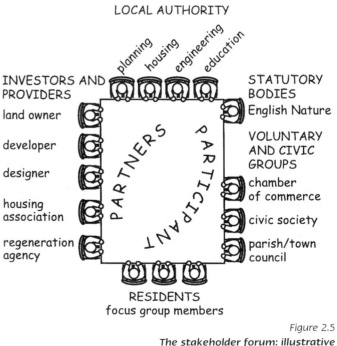

Figure 2.5
The stakeholder forum: illustrative membership

A shared vision expressed as a newspaper front page

One way to get the stakeholder forum off the ground, and give participants a feeling of empowerment, is to use the first (or an early) meeting to agree sustainability objectives.

This is the first stage of the Spectrum approach. The objectives are subsequently used to evaluate the current situation and future plans.

Stakeholders using simple images to start to discuss their different objectives and visions for future development.

of the members will have been informally consulted already, and have made their conditions for membership known. Membership is not casual but a negotiated agreement where both parties have something to gain.

Avoid premature forming of a group, except on a purely consultative basis. If the context is not clear people will come with very varied agendas and the initiative may well get derailed or meander off down a branch line.

Conversely, it is vital that the partners/participants join in soon enough to influence the shape of the project – both to engage their interest and to give the opportunity for better (more integrated) strategies to emerge. If possible the stakeholders should make an important input to the project brief.

Agreeing objectives

It is vital to agree objectives, so that all the members of the stakeholder group recognise the range of interests involved. Given the often conflicting starting points, this may seem a tall order! The objectives need to be devised by a skilled professional so that they include all the legitimate interests and are clear and concise. They are then subject to debate and revision as necessary. Individual agencies are happy so long as they can see their interests properly represented in the list. The process of discussion helps build mutual understanding and (hopefully) trust. Developers discover what is really important for residents. Residents appreciate the realities of market pressures. Both learn about statutory obligations from local authority representatives and official bodies. Those representatives get a much more rounded understanding.

The need of future generations

Sustainable development is about intra-generational and inter-generational equity. When decisions are being made by people with quite specific interests and concerns in the present day, it is all too easy to discount future generations, or under-represented groups in the current generation. National and international guidelines for assessment encourage proper recognition of both. It is the job of professionals involved in the process to ensure this happens. From experience, local people and businesses will normally recognise this broader picture as valid.

HORSES FOR COURSES

The participation map shows the four local partners – planning authority, investors and providers, community groups and the people – interlinked by varied participatory processes. Most neighbourhood planning exercises will need a range of participatory processes at different levels.

There is no one right way to work with local partners. Each process has specific benefits and limitations. Normally several complementary processes should be running in tandem. e.g:

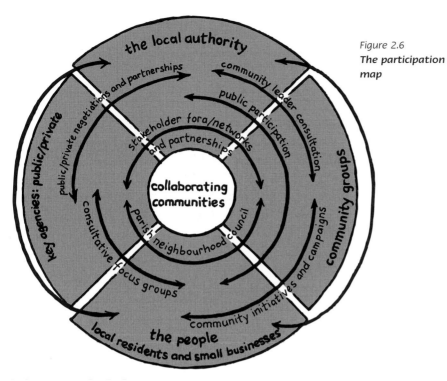

Figure 2.6
The participation map

Participation map

The participation map illustrates the diversity of participatory processes on offer, from formal democratic procedures to informal consultation and focus groups. No one technique reaches all the community partners. It is vital to be clear about the participation objectives and then select the techniques that are most likely to deliver.

- A *neighbourhood community plan*, led by the local authority, might focus on a stakeholder forum involving public-, private- and voluntary-sector membership; served by a cross-departmental officer group; with a social survey of a cross-section of residents, information to all residents at regular intervals via the local paper, and the invitation to participate in public meetings.

- A *major renewal project*, led by the land owners, might involve a public sector/private sector co-ordinating group at officer level, occasional public meetings with local politicians invited, and a residents' focus group meeting regularly throughout the process.

- A *neighbourhood action campaign*, led by a consortium of community groups, might use a public conference as a launchpad to draw in the powers that be to a stakeholder forum, and develop their popular base through direct action to improve the environment.

BUILDING ALLIANCES

Many neighbourhood planning exercises founder because of lack of clarity about who should be actively involved: false expectations raised; key players ignored. Others founder because key agencies are unwilling or unable to participate. A central part of the participation strategy (whoever is the initiator) is therefore about trying to ensure that the appropriate partnership is brought together. The art is to woo potential collaborators successfully, and build alliances that have the practical and political clout to carry projects through.

CHECKLIST

Forging partnerships

The experience of the Healthy Cities Movement suggests that success in collaborative, cross-sectoral projects relies on four ways of working:

1 Explicit political commitment at the highest level to the principles and strategies of the project. (Without backing from key committee chairs or the mayor of the town, ambitious schemes may be stillborn.)

2 Establishment of new organisational structures to manage change. (Formal partnerships or a Community Development Trust can help break down barriers.)

3 Commitment to developing a shared vision and plan. (Effective collaboration depends on shared ownership and consistency of purpose.)

4 Investment in formal and informal networking and co-operation, not just locally (deepening understanding and building capacity for co-operation).

For further information on the Healthy Cities approach see:

• City Planning for Health and Sustainable Development – www.euro.who.int

• Twenty steps for developing a healthy cities project – www.euro.who.int

• Healthy Urban Planning (Barton and Tsourou 2000).

2.6

Housing renewal – Doesn't it make you sick?

Some tenants can obviously find the process of housing renewal itself deeply stressful and damaging, while others find it enjoyable and rewarding. A study by Allen (2000) revealed a complex web of factors influencing an individual's quality of experience. However, the predominant and most influential factor was individual control, its degree of importance to the individual and its negotiability.

Table talk at a community and stakeholder forum

A worthwhile investment?

Collaboration costs time and effort. It needs to be undertaken with commitment. But the investment can reap rewards later in the process if it results in barriers being lowered which allow quicker and more effective implementation.

2.6 WORKING WITH LOCAL PEOPLE

Local residents, business people and other users are the real owners of a locality. They have a right (sometimes statutory) to be involved in major decisions that affect their environment or livelihood. But effective, inclusive participation is notoriously difficult to achieve. This section briefly sets out a range of techniques available, with special emphasis on the 'focus group'.

AVOIDING THE PITFALLS

Sometimes participation is perceived by local people as having only marginal influence on events, so involvement is desultory, and the instigators (even if initially enthusiastic) reduce their efforts next time round. Or participation may be vociferous as people react strongly to a perceived threat, and cultured debate is squashed. Either way there is a risk of discussion being dominated by articulate minorities who are not necessarily representative. Therefore:

- Don't undertake consultation as a cynical exercise in public relations.
- Value and respect the views of others.
- Raise awareness through use of the local media.
- Don't rely just on public meetings, which can be too easily hijacked.
- Engage with opponents, creating opportunities for real debate (and discovery), not rhetorical confrontation.
- Seek out and represent the views of non-joiners (both the silent majority and specific relevant minorities).

Match purpose and method

It is all too easy to use inappropriate participatory methods. To check against this, specify the purpose of participation clearly, then match the method to the purpose. If, for example, the purpose is to find out the general attitudes of residents, then while a public meeting may be important to give people a chance of dialogue, it is not sufficient. Particular interests will be well represented but others will not. So a sample social survey should be considered as well. If the purpose is to raise public consciousness about sustainability issues, then information sheets, meetings or focus group activity will have very limited impact. Much better to work with local groups, schools or the health authority to promote a media event or competition around a highly motivating issue such as safe routes to school.

FOCUS GROUPS

A focus group is a discussion group that meets regularly throughout the plan-making processes. It acts as a proxy for the local people, hopefully reflecting their consensus. It may be joined by volunteering or invitation. It should if possible include people from the diverse elements within the community.

■ Continuity of membership is important to allow understanding and expertise to grow. At the same time open access is important to avoid the suspicion of exclusivity.

■ The ideal number of people is 8–12. The group must be attended by key professionals involved in the whole process, who are able to speak with authority about the attitudes of the major players and fully understand the context. The professionals are there to support and enable the group, not to dominate it.

■ The focus group serves to raise and debate issues, respond to proposals as they emerge, and generate new ideas for testing by the main agencies. While it is not a decision-making arena, the group's views need to be taken seriously by other stakeholders. If there is a positive, creative attitude by participants then innovative solutions can emerge which help to shape the final plan.

■ The focus group process may involve a series of more specific exercises such as story-telling, visioning, or planning for real.

Setting up a focus group

A land owner, developer or regeneration partnership could approach this task as follows:

1 Hold an initial public meeting (widely advertised) to raise the key issues before the detailed development proposals have gelled or an architect been briefed.

2 Ask for people at the meeting to volunteer themselves to be involved in on-going discussions, giving their specific interests and skills.

3 Form a residents' focus group (preferably without pre-selection) to meet regularly and represent the local community interests. It is vital that key professionals working for the development company give this process their time and treat it seriously, without manipulation.

4 Hold subsequent public meetings as appropriate – at which focus-group members report back to the wider community on the discussions held and any solutions proposed.

5 When the plan or planning application is submitted, include a report of the focus group and public meetings, and action taken to recognise and deal with the concerns raised.

THE NEIGHBOURHOOD MOOT

This is an informal meeting of residents and community representatives to discuss the planning issues and respond to emerging plans and proposals.

• it meets regularly, in an accessible venue, well advertised

• it is voluntary and open to anyone, designed not to be a clique

• it is preferably supported by community enablers who chair meetings so as to ensure everyone can have their say

• discussion is encouraged, consensus is sought, but minority views respected

• it can delegate members to a more formal focus group or to the stakeholder forum

• it helps to organise and publicise bigger consultation events

• it may be attached to a community council and on occasion may develop its own community plan

SOURCE: adapted from Pearce 2007

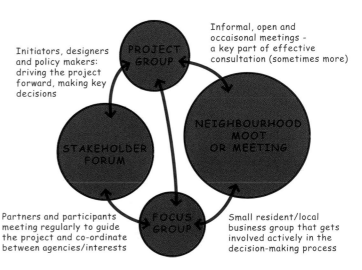

Figure 2.7

Participating groups and linkages

Getting going

2.6

Figure 2.8

PUBLIC PARTICIPATION TOOLKIT

A selection of techniques useful for development decisions and spatial strategy.
See websites cited for other methods and tools.

Technique	Use	Seven stages	Description and contacts
World Cafe and round table discussions	To discuss ideas and perspectives, establish common ground and define areas of conflict for future consideration.	1,2,7	Workshops bringing people from a range of sectors, organisation and power bases together. Ideally providing a non-hierarchical format in which all contributions can be heard and valued. Can be one-off workshops or linked to a series. FFI The World Cafe www.theworldcafe.com
Planning for real	Identifying issues and priorities, producing options and helping to select the best scheme.	1,2,3,5	Simple models of the proposed development are used as a centre of focus. Participants are invited to be involved in design decisions by interacting with the model. This may take the form of placing stickers to indicate like/dislike/options. FFI Neighbourhoods Initiative Foundation www.nif.co.uk
Local design statement	To help define and protect what is particular and distinctive in an area.	2,3,5,6	A way for local people to help produce guidance for future development. Can be adopted as supplementary planning guidance. FFI The Community Planning website www.communityplanning.net
Local mapping	To reveal and record the local impression of an area by the people who live there. Also helps groups see the local area from different perspectives.	2,3	An event is organised supporting local people to map the area. Discussions led to help compare the maps and learn more about the area, the interests of the residents in the area. Both problems and opportunities can be looked at. Can be used to map specific issues such as safety/crime or mobility/access. FFI See 'Parish' maps; Common Ground www.commonground.org.uk
Enquiry by design	To produce a masterplan framework for a new development with multi-disiplinary professional groups.	3,5,6	An intensive design process usually run as workshops over a few weeks. Involves key stakeholders such as the developer, land owner and local authority as well as representatives of interest groups, and statutory consultees. With the assistance of facilitators and specialists, options and approaches to the proposed development emerge having a high degree of consensus. Immediate output is a masterplan framework. FFI The Prince's Foundation www.princes-foundation.org
Roadshow	To collect comments on proposals or options.	5,6,7	Travelling exhibition with provision for people to record comments and participate. Allows the exercise to be re-run in several locations convenient for local people. Comments then compiled and used as basis of a report. Variations include recording comments by video or staging events and entertainment at each location. FFI Architecture Foundation www.architecturefoundation.org.uk Or the Community Planning website www.communityplanning.net
Spectrum	To produce a masterplan framework for a new development with multi-disiplinary professional groups.	1,2,3,4,5,6,7	A participatory and open sustainability and health impact appraisal process. Global and local criteria are created and used during the design development to help a better scheme emerge. FFI WHO Collaborating Centre for Healthy Cities www.bne.ac.uk/who

creating a strategy

2.7 STAGE 3 – UNDERSTANDING THE LOCALITY

BASIC PRINCIPLES

Neighbourhood appraisal is a systematic review of the attributes, problems and potential of an area, undertaken as an essential part of neighbourhood plan-making or a major development proposal. Detailed information on every issue is not so important as awareness of the whole sustainability agenda. Appraisal can proceed hand in hand with stage 4, 'developing ideas', as part of a progressive and collaborative learning process.

The neighbourhood appraisal ...

- may be tackled at different levels of sophistication depending on specific needs and resources but must encompass all the spheres of the neighbourhood model. Where time pressures and lack of resources dictate, it can take the form of a quick but comprehensive scan of all the issues, drawing on the knowledge of stakeholders. Part of the purpose of the scan is to identify where detailed research is needed.

- should build upon, and contribute to, wider review processes such as quality-of-life reports, urban capacity studies, community health profiles and local plan review.

- involves collaboration between stakeholders and this can be as important to effective action as the product itself.

- rarely occurs in a policy vacuum. Often there are already specific ideas and proposals. But it is vital to suspend judgement on those proposals and open the mind to other possibilities. The appraisal becomes, effectively, part of the evaluation process, tying in with any SEA or EIA.

SHARING OWNERSHIP AND DEFINING SCOPE

A neighbourhood appraisal needs to be co-ordinated by one organisation (the local planning department, for example). But it should not be owned by only that organisation. Rather, the appraisal can be seen as a way of forging working relationships between a range of stakeholders. The scope of the appraisal should be defined by the stakeholder group and benefit from the specialist input they can make. For example the health authority, and the housing and education departments can each supply part of the picture. Local voluntary groups can get involved in specific surveys (such as pedestrian counts or open space surveys).

Looking at the wider area

Neighbourhoods cannot be treated as isolated. It is vital that the appraisal encompass the areas adjacent to the neighbourhood that are locally connected, including local high streets, industrial areas, secondary schools, parks and adjacent areas of open or greenfield land. At the same time the area has to be meaningful in terms of local identity and allegiance. This broader area may be equated with the urban district or the country town and its immediate setting.

5.7 The scope of neighbourhood appraisal

Community health profiles

Every designated healthy city in the WHO network has produced a 'city health profile' often with an explicit neighbourhood dimension. They include the full range of social, economic and environmental factors that affect health, and involve collaboration between health and local authorities.

Guidance is available from www.euro.who.int City health profiles: how to report the health of your city.

Spectrum appraisal

The spectrum approach requires a baseline sustainability appraisal of the area (akin to that needed in a formal SEA process). The Stakeholder Forum assists in this process, agreeing the objectives and identifying issues. There is huge benefit in pooling the knowledge of the members. They can pinpoint aspects of the locality that need to be investigated and understood more deeply.

The Spectrum Process

- *Agree objectives*
- *Baseline appraisal*
- *Outline or option appraisal*
- *Final scheme appraisal*

The Stakeholder Forum is involved at each stage of the process. The project team are part of the Forum and learn from it.

Forms of assessment

Strategic Environmental Assessment - SEA

Environmental Impact Assessment - EIA

Health Impact Assessment - HIA

Social Impact Assessment - SIA

Sustainability Appraisal - SA

2.7

Making sense of statistics

If possible, make the area of study coincide with one or more wards or parishes. This greatly simplifies the analysis of data and links with quality-of-life indicators. It also makes clear which local councillors, parish or community councils should be involved.

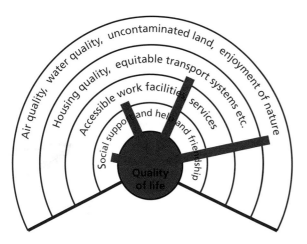

Figure 2.9
Linking with quality-of-life indicators

Much of the neighbourhood level information should not require special surveys but be collected regularly as part of district-wide quality-of-life monitoring (often in the form of 'state-of-the-environment' reports or 'city health profiles' or 'joint strategic needs').

BASELINE APPRAISAL

The purpose of the baseline appraisal is two fold:

- to understand the character of the area and the way it works

- to identify issues and concerns relevant to the main project

The objectives agreed at the outset of the exercise (in the project brief) help to give the scope of the appraisal. So too does the Settlement Health Map.

- **People**
  basic population information
  quality-of-life indicators
  health and deprivation status

- **Lifestyle**
  qualitative information about how people behave
  levels of physical activity: walking, cycling, play, recreation

- **Community**
  stock-take of community groups, activities and participation
  community engagement

- **Economy**
  local entrepreneurial activity, work opportunities, training
  access to wider job markets

- **Facilities**
  housing stress, housing availability and quality
  local retail, social, cultural, recreational opportunities
  educational health, police and social services

- **Land use and movement**
  the pattern and condition of land use and buildings,
  the street pattern, movement and accessibility
  neighbourhood potential and regeneration

- **Aesthetics and 'meetingness'**
  aesthetic audit of spaces and places
  social interaction and safety in the public realm

- **The resource base**
  energy and water services and sustainability
  local food production and recycling
  biodiversity and wildlife habitats

- **Global ecology**
  buildings and energy supply carbon footprint
  transport carbon emissions

THE USE OF AN APPRAISAL

Neighbourhood appraisal is needed when the area is likely to experience considerable change. The change might be the result of regeneration policies, new housing/commercial allocations, or progressive restructuring over a considerable period.

The appraisal is designed to assist and validate policy formulation. Its purpose is to show:

- what the current problems are and how serious they are

- how effective current policies are at tackling those problems

- what the local significance is of broader trends/pressures

- how the various issues and policies are interconnected

- what the capacity or potential for change is

- who needs to be involved in policy-making.

The political dimension

The process is far from being value-free. The questions above imply a set of objectives and criteria. The appraisal is a means of articulating local and societal values, hopefully consistent with sustainable development. It is therefore highly politically charged. The involvement of councillors at an early stage is critical. The help of community leaders and the local press/media should be actively sought. From the outset the process needs to be seen as an opportunity not a threat.

A holistic approach

The typical approach to appraisal at present is based on narrowly defined problem solving. For example, there is pressure to find more housing land: so sites are identified and assessed against specific criteria. This is not adequate. The appraisal should be used to give a rounded view of the dynamics of a settlement so that individual sites are seen in context.

Map-based systems and GIS

The approach needs to be accessible, policy-orientated, adaptable and cheap. Much of the information can be recorded on a series of appraisal maps and commentaries which can be manually or electronically cross-referenced. This allows the incorporation of specific data on land, building, activities, social and environmental capital in a context which assists forward planning. The approach can be adopted at different levels of sophistication. It is ideally suited for Geographical Information Systems (GIS) manipulation, and consistent with both urban capacity techniques and the environmental capital approach.

5.7 The scope of neighbourhood appraisal

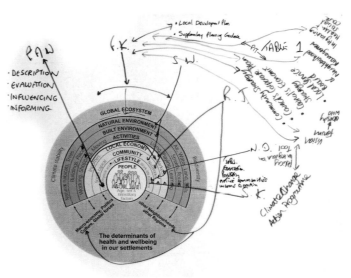

The health map being used as a tool for appraising how policies (and in this case also council and public health officers) are interconnected.

5.9 Analyzing form and function

Creating a strategy

2.8

BASIC PRINCIPLES

Policy ideas and specific development proposals may be put forward by a wide range of organisations at any stage in the process. It is likely that some proposals will proceed at a different rate to others, and with different (sometimes conflicting) objectives. This is not in itself a problem. But it lends weight to the need to agree a common approach to policy-making. There are three essential principles:

■ Search for the best options. Do not rely just on the first or most strongly suggested ideas, but examine other options that might do better.

■ Evaluate alternatives systematically. It is not only a matter of reaching agreement between key players, but also ensuring fundamental social and environmental goals are achieved.

■ Ensure consistency. Make sure that different policies and proposals harmonise and reinforce each other. In particular work towards an agreed spatial framework.

Avoiding premature conclusions

It is all too easy for a particular agency or a key individual to present a proposal in answer to recognised problems without adequate analysis of the situation. For example, a self-evident solution to a congested shopping street might be to ban traffic, or the answer to the question of a derelict industrial site might be a brand new business park, but such decisions need cool, dispassionate evaluation, separated from the particular financial or political issues at stake. Such evaluation relies on greater understanding through a neighbourhood (or township) appraisal, and a willingness to compare alternative solutions.

Avoiding prevarication and delay

At the same time as avoiding premature judgements it is also important to make progress. There is a balance to be struck between knowledge and speed. Events (including political/market pressures) often require decisions in the teeth of uncertainty. So all technical and collaborative processes need to be pragmatic, while avoiding superficiality.

■ How much do we need to know to make progress?

■ What decisions can be taken now without foreclosing desirable longer-term options?

■ What specific studies can be done to reduce key uncertainties?

How is this problem related to others?

What theoretical options are there?

What has worked elsewhere?

The problem

Can the problem be redefined as an opportunity?

What range of ideas do stakeholders have?

Figure 2.10
There are always choices. Make sure you look at the problems in the round

EXPLORE AND TEST OPTIONS

It is important to present real options to local people and decision-makers. This is just as vital when the options are basic ('do nothing' versus 'do something', for example) as when they are complex. Options should be compared for their likely effects using some form of sustainability assessment (see below), and testing

- desirability – fulfilling aspirations for health, sustainability and vitality

- feasibility – ensuring the mechanisms, land, finance and expertise is there to make things happen.

Win-win-win

Policies and proposals do not normally spring from nowhere; they evolve, they respond to new pressures or opportunities. As they are doing so, it is easy to lose the sustainability focus (or miss it from the start).

The normal confrontational approach to policy debate, where one interest is pitted against another (jobs versus the environment, greenfields versus brownfields) is unlikely to lead to sustainable development. So the questions are:

- How can the different interests be successfully reconciled?

- How can we devise creative policies that fulfil social, economic and environmental priorities?

It is not a matter of either/or but of both/and.

The process therefore needs to be inclusive, drawing different (sometimes competing) interests into mutual engagement, forming alliances, negotiating collaborative programmes, tackling problems in the round. A committed search for solutions, together with a willingness to challenge vested interest, can lead to success. One example, in relation to transport, is the promotion of walking: creating a safe, convenient and attractive pedestrian environment is at the heart of neighbourhood planning, and has clear health, community, environmental and local economic benefits.

The real problem is not necessarily *finding* win–win–win policies, as in implementing them with sufficient coherence and dynamism to make them work. That coherence and dynamism will only happen if a common philosophy is accepted by the key interests involved: i.e. an acceptance of key goals and willingness to work together to achieve them.

Synergy

Policy failure, from the sustainable development viewpoint, often occurs because *implementing* agencies are hamstrung by their institutional or financial conventions. Conversely, when agencies

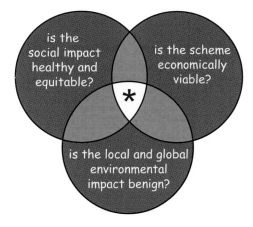

Figure 2.11
Use the trefoil symbol of sustainable development as a 'quick and dirty' analytical tool. *All three criteria need to be achieved. If they are not, then search for another solution that could perform better.*

Examples of synergy later in the guide

3.13 Community health

3.16 Pedestrian planning

4.2 Integrating natural systems

5.3 A mix of uses

5.6 Green infrastructure

5.16 Home-place

CHECKLIST

CATEGORIES AND CRITERIA

Health and well-being

- *Healthy lifestyle*
- *Social cohesion*
- *Social inclusion*
- *Community safety*

Economic vitality

- *Local work opportunities*
- *Good local facilities*
- *Market buoyancy*

Social need

- *Housing availability*
- *Quality of built space*
- *Open space*
- *Pedestrian accessibility*
- *Public transport accessibility*

Environmental quality

- *Aesthetic quality*
- *Cultural heritage*
- *Biodiversity*

Resources and climate

- *Food*
- *Water*
- *Air quality*
- *Energy efficiency*
- *Carbon-fixing*
- *Land and soils*
- *Minerals*

Sustainability appraisal

SOURCE: This list is derived from DOE 1993, and Barton and Tsourou 2000.

This appraisal list is not too different from lists produced by many local authorities.

---

collaborate for mutual benefit, new doors are opened. For example, joint recreational provision by Education Authorities and Leisure or Parks Departments ('dual use') can benefit everyone and cut costs; energy-efficiency measures reduce pollution, combat fuel poverty, and create local jobs.

EVALUATE THROUGHOUT THE PROCESS

Key principle

Evaluation is not just an end-point test of a scheme, when the big decisions have often already been taken. It should be part of the process of developing and improving the proposal, policy or programme. It is a learning exercise. Evaluation is therefore not something to hand over to some external consultancy or sideline by giving it to a junior member of staff. Its value will only be realised if:

- key decision-makers are actively involved in the process

- other stakeholders assist in 'scoping' – identifying problematic impacts and proposing solutions

- experts/specialists are used with discretion to explore those problematic impacts

- evaluation occurs as part of a cyclic process of policy development

- the evaluation takes an holistic, integrated viewpoint

Integrated versus specialist evaluation

It is vital that the testing of policy/proposals does not get pre-empted by partial evaluations. These partial evaluations are often demanded by statute (e.g. Environmental Impact Analysis, Habitat Directives) or by particular concerns (e.g. Cost-benefit analysis, Health Impact Assessment). In some situations they are necessary and/or appropriate. But they must be seen in context of an holistic understanding of the locality/town, and an integrated process of defining (scoping) priorities.

The objectives agreed in the project brief (or equivalent), and used to assess the current state of the neighbourhood, should also be employed to scope the issues raised by policy/spatial options. See the Spectrum case study at the chapter end as an illustration.

CONSISTENCY AND SYNERGY

Major development projects cannot be considered in isolation. They always have knock-on effects. Equivalently the elements of a town or neighbourhood plan are part of the complex social/economic/spatial/ecological system of the settlement. Developing an understanding of synergistic effects is essential. This can be approached in a number of ways.

Consistency workshop

This is an essential part of sustainability appraisal. It is particularly important in relation to the spatial framework. The purpose is to establish the degree of consistency between the spatial policies being pursued by different organisations or different sections of the local authority.

The analysis can be undertaken as a stakeholder workshop, with representatives from relevant agencies. The sustainability checklist provides the context against which policy combinations are evaluated. A matrix provides the agenda and mean of summarising results. The workshop is a scoping process, identifying the awkward or problematic policy interactions for subsequent work.

Using the Settlement Health Map

Another approach is to use the Settlement Health Map to analyse primary, secondary, tertiary and quaternary impacts. This is appropriate when there is one big proposal, and the impacts can be followed through systematically. It may not be possible or appropriate to give quantitative forecasts, but it does greatly increase understanding and, through testing discussion, help estimate the relative scale of positive and negative impacts.

The example used here is the proposal for a new bypass around a market town of 50,000 people. The assessment of impacts (summarised below) is based on an actual case.

■	EXCELLENT	The criterion is fully satisfied
■	GOOD	The criterion is generally satisfied
■	NEGOTIABLE	Success depends on further work and negotiation
■	PROBLEMATICAL	Not likely to be satisfactorily fulfilled without major reassessment
■	UNACCEPTABLE	The criterion cannot be satisfied

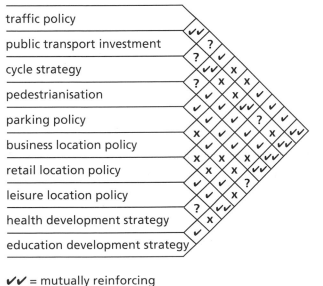

traffic policy
public transport investment
cycle strategy
pedestrianisation
parking policy
business location policy
retail location policy
leisure location policy
health development strategy
education development strategy

✔✔ = mutually reinforcing
✔ = compatable
? = uncertain
X = contradictory
XX = unworkable

Figure 2.12
Compatibility matrix

2.8

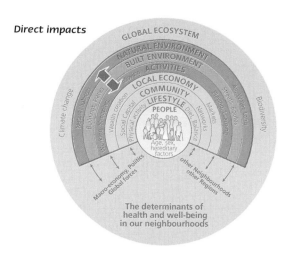

Direct impacts

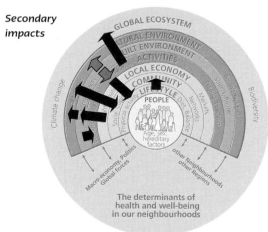

Secondary impacts

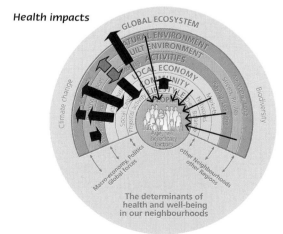

Health impacts

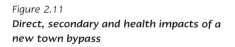

Figure 2.11
Direct, secondary and health impacts of a new town bypass

Direct impacts

- On the landscape, farmland and habitats through which the bypass goes

- On the pattern of accessibility and therefore on travel patterns: some rerouting of vehicle movements; some transfer to car from other modes; some newly generated trips.

Secondary impacts

As a consequence of changed travel patterns and accessibility there are a series of impacts:

- increased carbon emissions

- increased air pollution near the bypass junctions, possibly reduced air pollution in the town centre

- improved economic prospects near bypass junctions, uncertain impacts on the town centre

- reduced active travel as people switch to car and use more distant facilities that are now accessible round the bypass.

Tertiary impacts

Note that the analysis of impacts can extend into tertiary and quaternary stages, but for simplicity these are not included here.

HEALTH IMPACTS

Once the likely effects have been assessed, including the degree of confidence or uncertainly in the assessment, then the health map can be used to assess the impacts on human health. In this case changes in every sphere could potentially have an impact on health, from increasing the threat of climate change to reducing active travel.

Some impacts could be positive: the economic/employment impacts; some could be negative: the predicted loss of local shops and town centre shops as new larger retail outlets are attracted to the bypass; some are uncertain: the net effect on air quality.

DECISION TIME

In this case many of the impacts were negative because the bypass was proposed in isolation from any overall transport and sustainability strategy. The red gradings in relation to global economy and lifestyle meant a different approach was needed. That should be a comprehensive land use/movement strategy, including plans for enhancing walking/cycling and town centre environment and creating economic opportunities on sites which are not inherently car-dependant. The bypass might or might not form part of such a plan.

2.9 STAGE 5 - AGREEING A CO-ORDINATED PROGRAMME

The partners should, after due consultation, aim to agree a package of commitments that encompass not only broad aims and policies but also specific mechanisms for implementing and co-ordinating change, and for subsequent management. As part of this, an agreed spatial framework working towards sustainable development is essential.

The commitment package described below could be appropriate for an area of major change: a regeneration area or urban extension. But many of the elements would be necessary, at some level, in an area of only modest change, or an evolving market town.

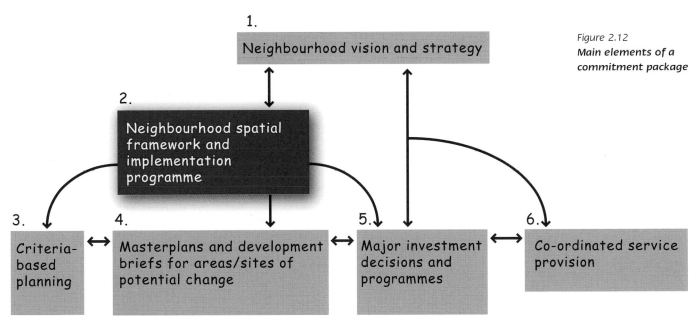

Figure 2.12
Main elements of a commitment package

1. Neighbourhood vision and strategy
2. Neighbourhood spatial framework and implementation programme
3. Criteria-based planning
4. Masterplans and development briefs for areas/sites of potential change
5. Major investment decisions and programmes
6. Co-ordinated service provision

1 AGREED VISION AND STRATEGY

The starting point for the plan should be an agreed vision for the future of the area, with a clear overall strategy on how it might be implemented. The vision and strategy should have been subject to extensive consultation. It should be accepted in principle by all the major players represented on the Stakeholder Forum, including major potential investors, service providers and the various policy-making bodies. Broad public and political support is essential, to avoid subsequent derailing. The strategy also needs to be in accord with wider policy statements for the whole city or sub-region.

2.9

Figure 2.13
Spatial framework for a major urban extension

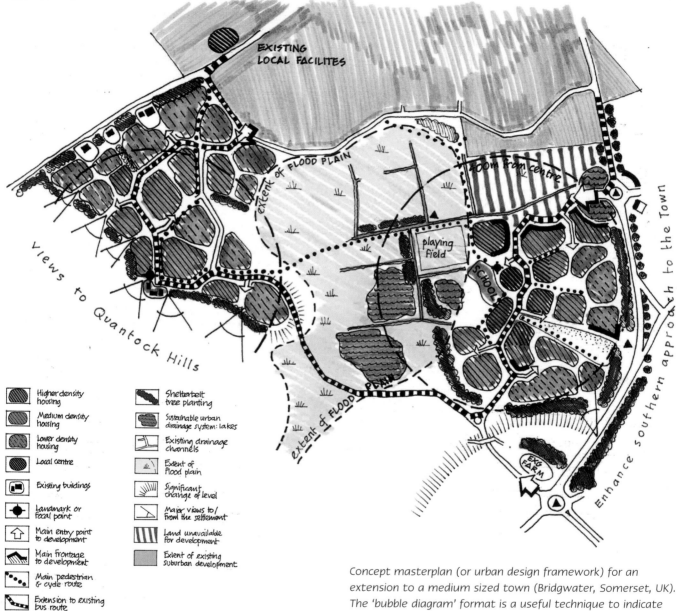

Higher density housing

Medium density housing

Lower density housing

Local centre

Existing buildings

Landmark or focal point

Main entry point to development

Main frontage to development

Main pedestrian & cycle route

Extension to existing bus route

Larger scale public art

Shelterbelt tree planting

Sustainable urban drainage system: lakes

Existing drainage channels

Extent of flood plain

Significant change of level

Major views to/ from the settlement

Land unavailable for development

Extent of existing suburban development

Concept masterplan (or urban design framework) for an extension to a medium sized town (Bridgwater, Somerset, UK). The 'bubble diagram' format is a useful technique to indicate the strategic layout principles of a scheme prior to the detailed design of buildings and spaces. Premature depiction of detailed built form can suggest that all decisions have been finalised and that there is only one solution, therefore discouraging debate. The 'bubble diagram' approach shown here, it is hoped, is perhaps more likely to focus on larger scale issues.

2. THE SPATIAL FRAMEWORK

This is the crucial tool for planning sustainable towns and neighbourhoods. It is a land use/movement strategy which specifies the big picture, working to create a coherent, spatial pattern for healthy, low-carbon settlements. Its basis is the logic of spatial relationships set out in the following three chapters. It therefore needs to have the robustness and clarity associated with Dutch urban extensions or British new towns.

The need for a good spatial framework applies equally to regeneration as to greenfield development. Indeed, it could be argued that it is most neccessary in situations of gradual renewal (i.e. many parts of all settlements) where incremental decision making can all-too-easily distort the best-laid plans of well intentioned planners, undermining health and sustainability.

Thus the spatial framework plugs the gap between policy and design. It is a vital co-ordinating mechanism that gives a clear spatial context for more detailed development decisions. Without such a plan it is difficult, in a democratic market-based society, to achieve inclusive, carbon-efficient, healthy environments.

The area for a spatial framework should encompass the whole of a small town, and at least an urban district or township within a city. It is, in other words, bigger than most neighbourhoods in order to ensure that median-level services such as leisure centres, superstores, comparison shops, secondary schools and major parks, are considered as well as very local facilities.

It is not, however, a precise land use guide. Rather, it is a broad co-ordinating mechanism, to be used in concert with criteria-based policies (see below). The degree of site specificity depends on levels of certainty. Firm commitments (for example an agreed site for a new health centre, or a firm reservation for a new tram route) can be shown precisely. But less certain proposals should not be prematurely identified. The framework should provide the context within which future decisions can be taken, allowing for the fact that development needs and opportunities cannot be entirely foreseen. It provides the setting for design frameworks, detailed masterplans (areas of major change) and site development briefs.

The illustration opposite shows a spatial framework for an urban extension. Chapter 5 provides in-depth guidance for both regeneration and greenfield contexts.

3. CRITERIA-BASED PLANNING

While future development proposals may be unpredictable, the criteria by which they will be judged should be as explicit as possible. This helps to reduce uncertainty for those making proposals, as well as for those evaluating them. Criteria can be devised for all facets of development, from location to design.

5.2 Devising the spatial framework

The Spatial Framework

What it is not:

- a superficial sketch
- subject to the vagaries of land owner or political whim
- a detailed site guide
- prematurely certain about investments which are uncertain
- a fixed blueprint

What it should do:

- articulate the 'most sustainable' pattern of land use and movement
- specify main public transport, walking/cycling and vehicle networks
- specify landscape, ecological and resource assets
- identify zones for different land uses, sometimes mixed
- determine the pattern of density
- provide a route map for investment in new/renewed infrastructure
- guide new residential commercial and institutional investment
- assist the long-term planning of service providers
- specify the main design and planning criteria which underpin the spatial proposals
- give clear guidelines for community development
- provide residents/users/local politicians a defensible plan

Chapters 3 and 4 provide specific criteria in relation to most aspects of local planning.

Avoid weak criteria

For example, the statement 'Health centres should be accessible by public transport' is open to a wide range of responses. The underlying principle should lead to a more pointed statement of criteria, such as: 'Health centres should normally be within 200 m of a regular (minimum half-hourly) public transport service giving access to nearby residential areas'.

2.9

They should encompass housing, commerce, open space, energy, water, biodiversity, etc. Higher level city or sub-regional plans may provide generic criteria which can be refined to reflect the specific vision and strategy of the township/town.

To be useful, the criteria should be pointed and precise. For example, the 'development code' devised for Ashton Green by Leicester City Council (1998) included the following in relation to accessibility and transport choice:

- A comprehensive network of safe, direct and attractive facilities for cyclists including cycle park provision must be provided.

- Easy access for cycle storage shall be provided for every household.

- All pedestrian routes must be well lit and overlooked by adjoining developments.

- As a minimum, public transport routes should aim to achieve accessibility standards not in excess of 250 m from trip origins to either a 'hail and ride' or formal bus stop for at least 75 per cent of the site. 250 m shall be measured 'as you walk'.

4. THE DESIGN FRAMEWORK

We use the term 'design framework' to encompass both development briefs and detailed masterplans. These are applicable to specific development sites or a regeneration area where a specific agency has a dominant say over what happens. They are therefore part of the process of implementation, converting broad policy and the spatial framework into practical schemes. How they are used depends heavily on context. Typically, where the local authority has taken the initiative, then development briefs should be prepared by the authority for each site, and the investor (from whatever sector) produces a detailed masterplan which fulfils the requirements of the brief.

Clearly there is likely to be a process of negotiation between policy-makers and investors. The principle of the 'commitment package' is that where possible initial discussions have been held, and mutual understanding established – so that the development briefs, emerging masterplans and the spatial framework itself are fully tuned to the sustainable neighbourhood agenda and realistic in terms of what can be achieved.

2.10 Taking action

Section 2.10 presents more detailed ideas on development briefs and detailed masterplans.

5 MAJOR INVESTMENT DECISIONS: STAKEHOLDER COMMITMENT

A plan has little value if the means of implementation are not clear. Realisation may depend on major investment decisions. An obvious example is a new tramway, without which proposals for higher density and commercial use may be invalid. The plan should be specific about commitments entered into by public, private and voluntary organisations, or, if that is premature, the process by which commitments will be made.

The importance of this is difficult to exaggerate. The concept of integrated spatial planning means the important agencies buying into the plan. If it is to work it must become *their plan*.

6 CO-ORDINATED SERVICE PROVISION

Local authorities conventionally have separate departments and separate plans or programmes, for land use and for municipal services such as education and open space provision. But people in general do not think in silos. They see the neighbourhood more holistically. So the town or neighbourhood strategy needs to encompass the provision and quality of services, with commitments from providers, taking concerns on board and using land use decisions to trigger change. Secondary schools, for example, may link with community sports, swimming pool and library provision; a joint local centre for decentralised local authority services might need office/retail space; sharing of church facilities between different denominations and community groups might result in redundant buildings. The plan can facilitate and help manage such changes.

The commitment package can provide the context for reaching agreement between providers, and help to tie in investment decisions.

TAKING THE LONG VIEW

Contingency plans and uncertainty

The one certain thing about the future is that it is filled with uncertainty. Predictions will go awry. Uncertainty comes in three forms: uncertainty of the environment (e.g. the speed of climate change); uncertainty of values and related behaviour (e.g. the desire to eat organic or local food); and uncertainty of related decisions that are outside the control of the stakeholders involved (e.g. the decision of a multinational company to close a branch factory). Understanding which form uncertainty takes in each case is a major step in starting to manage the uncertainty and address contingency. Any plan therefore needs to be robust. Understanding what aspects of uncertainty are likely to affect any particular case is a major step in starting to manage uncertainty and prepare contingencies. The decisions the plan embodies

---

CHECKLIST

The usual suspects

Commitments may be needed from:

- the Planning Department
- the Transport/Engineering Department
- the main public transport operator(s)
- the Health Authority
- the Education Authority
- the parks/leisure department;

plus, depending on context

- community groups and Community Development Trusts
- major employers/chamber of trade/house-builders
- the housing department and/or housing association

Two specific concerns

- *Uncertainty of the financial environment – the state of the housing market, the level of interest rates*

- *Uncertainty of political values – when a project extends beyond a key election, or media hype distorts the agenda*

2.9

should not be dependent on one scenario of the future, but be capable of adapting to a range of critical scenarios.

Conversely the plan itself is part of the system of reducing uncertainty. It sets the scene for decisions by firms, agencies and households. It needs to have a sure sense of its remit – its area of responsibility. It needs to state the values and clarify the policies/decisions of the partners, so that others can make their decisions with sure footing.

So the commitment package should:

- provide as much clarity about future direction as possible

- be robust in the face of uncertainty – e.g. will the oil price be as now, or much higher?

- provide contingency plans to cope with major known unknowns – such as whether funding is forthcoming for a big infrastructure project.

On-going management

It is all too easy to produce impressive schemes and policies which subsequently fail because nobody is clear how they will be implemented or managed. For example, the re-use of upper storeys above shops will often require specific grants. Similarly, the management of communal open spaces, reed-bed sewage schemes and community energy schemes is likely to require a special board or residents' management committee. The agreed programme has to anticipate these problems and be realistic in its expectations. The design framework should not therefore, be simply about design, but a practical plan for implementation and management-in-use. The 'survival' of a long-term, larger scale project can be assisted by its subdivision into relatively short-term phases which are comparatively autonomous. This can also ensure a 'quick win', which can help to engender confidence and commitment to the project.

Monitoring and review

A plan is not a blueprint, set in aspic and guaranteed to deliver. Rather, it is part of a continuous, evolving process – hence the circularity of the summary diagram in 2.2. Yet frequently decisions, once implemented, are not reviewed to establish whether they are 'working', or what can be learnt from them. It is therefore vital to establish how monitoring and review will occur – who will do what – as part of the overall package.

making it happen

2.10   STAGE 6 – TAKING ACTION

The process of implementation tends to be disjointed and incremental, as opposed to the neat world of analysis and strategy. Proposals may come forward from a wide range of interests, reacting to circumstances that are often unpredictable. The task is to match this bottom-up process of implementation with the top-down principles embodied in plans. The planning authority need to ensure that it is ahead of the game, not just reacting to events. Within the context of spatial framework and criteria-based plans, there are a series of tools available for site-by-site co-ordination: these include development briefs, design codes, detailed materplans and planning application requirements.

THE DESIGN AND IMPLEMENTATION FRAMEWORK

The purpose of the design framwork provided by the planning authority for large and small developments is to realise the health and sustainability ambitions of the community and put the spatial framework into practice. The central principle is *place-making*. All new developments should contribute to the creation of places that satisfy needs, encourage healthy and sustainable lifestyles, and can be efficiently constructed and managed. The three tools of design co-ordination outlined below may be appropriate seperately or together, depending on the context. Further detail, with examples, is provided in Chapter 5.

5.17 Urban design framework

Development briefs: being ahead of the game

Briefs for development on specific sites should be produced by planning authorities or development companies within the context of a spatial strategy or masterplan. The main purpose of the brief is to trigger an appropriate development response. Timing is everything. The brief can invite competition in areas of high demand, or offer development incentives where demand is low.

Normally sites will be owned or available for sale as one unit. The brief sets the context for any subsequent development proposal. It interprets policy at the site level, and affects site value.

Briefs are most useful where they co-ordinate the policy and advice from various interested departments and agencies: planning, highways, utility companies, conservation agencies, for example. Objectives, site and context appraisal may be accompanied by an indicative layout and built form guidance – especially on access, desire lines across site, mix of uses, density, key building heights, views, trees, management of communal space, and so on. However, the brief should not be used as an aesthetic control tool. It is important to give freedom of interpretation to the architect/designer.

CHECKLIST

The development brief

Typically, contents of a brief relating to a major development site might consist of:

- a statement of the rationale of the brief

- status of the brief (is it adopted local authority policy or advisory?)

- identification of the site

- preferred uses and mix of uses, density, etc.

- context and site appraisal

- requirements: access, wildlife corridors, etc.

- urban design objectives, connections, frontages, etc.

- Section 106 requirements

- submission of information for planning application

- criteria for sustainability appraisal required by the local authorities; and

- contacts.

Elements of a design code

- *Plot size and shape (width, depth and general 'grain').*
- *Amount of building footprint on the plot.*
- *Placing of footprint on the plot (for example, terracing or distance of space between buildings, orientation for maximum solar gain, depth of front garden or yard, dependent on whether house has sunny front or not).*
- *Position of garage, car hardstanding or car court and relationship to layout.*
- *Width of pavement, verge and carriageway.*
- *Provision for cycle parking.*
- *Internal and external provision for recycling.*
- *Treatment of front and back boundaries, and front and rear access, planting.*
- *Number of storeys related to importance or width of street.*
- *Roof pitch related to optimum pitch of solar panels and/or achieving headroom for storage and extension.*
- *Placement of any projections in front or behind the main building lines, including potential for later extensions, conservatories.*
- *Range of building and surface materials.*
- *Proportion of windows to wall in relation to solar aspect.*

Note that national design assessments - such as the Code for Sustainable Homes, Greenprint BREEAM and 'Building for Life' standards - will affect the content of codes.

It is essential that briefs are compiled early in the development process, before sites are purchased or as a condition of purchase. At this stage the developer can assess the value of land in relation to the requirements of the brief.

A vital part of the requirements will be a legal planning agreement, setting out expectations for contribution to public transport infrastructure, schools, parkland, off-site road junctions, etc.

Design codes

Design codes can be used in the context of a city plan, a spatial framework or a specific masterplan. They are a method of street-making: that is a creation of coherent set of design rules which address the character of the street, the buildings on either side, and the plots on which the buildings sit. The code aims to deliver:

- a locally distinctive and attractive environment
- low crime levels and a sense of safety
- a convivial, pedestrian-orientated public space
- a good orientation and aspect for home and garden
- satisfactory and secure parking arrangements; and
- an appropriate plot-planting and biodiversity regime.

Design codes can be a huge assistance when many small developments are involved. The case study of Vauban on pages 154-5 illustrates its use in co-ordinating residents' co-operatives, small builders and individual households to create a convivial, low carbon living environment.

Detailed masterplans or design frameworks

The term 'masterplan' is used rather confusingly in many different situations. Here we restrict its use to what are sometimes called 'detailed masterplans'. Such a masterplan establishes a three-dimensional framework for buildings and public spaces. It is needed for any area of major change – such as an urban extension or a regeneration area. The masterplan is more detailed and prescriptive than the spatial framework or old-fashioned zoning plan. It is a tool of urban design and implementation.

The masterplan should be prepared for or by the agency which has the power to deliver. This normally means the prime land-owning or funding organisation. However, it is essential that other stakeholders are involved and preparation is seen as a collaborative exercise, with shared ownership and commitment. There is also much more chance of a masterplan being grounded in the realities of neighbourhood planning if it is developed with the continuous involvement of the local community.

The masterplan for a regeneration area or new urban extension is likely to be a package rather than a single plan, and acts to draw together all the strands which guide and control development. It should consist of four main parts: the appraisal, the design strategy, the design code, and the implementation plan.

The planning authority should be involved in drawing up the scope of the masterplan, in its final approval and monitoring its implementation. The vision and quality of many masterplans can be eroded in the implementation, without effective development management.

THE LIMITS OF MASTERPLANNING

The Taskforce report suggests masterplans should be both visionary and deliverable. Beware of glossy images where they have no clear means of realisation. Implementation relies on a supportive planning and neighbourhood context, the ownership of land and the availability of capital.

In areas of modest or unpredictable change, masterplans are not the answer. Rather it is better to rely on the spatial framework and design guidance (adopted by the local authority as supplementary planning guidance). These can provide a good basis for negotiations with developers but are intentionally robust and flexible enough to survive the extingencies of the development process. Such guidelines should identify the 'bottom line' and articulate the opportunities without being prematurely prescriptive. The process can move straight to development briefs for specific sites.

Figure 2.14
Masterplan for a greenfield site

Image courtesy of Powell-Dobson Urbanists, Cardiff

2.11

Proposals for development come from a wide range of sources:

- *The investment programmes of public bodies – transport, schools, health, water, leisure, etc.*

- *Planning applications from local households and businesses – mainly small scale but adding up to significant change over time.*

- *Major development proposals – from house-builders, housing associations, commercial developers.*

- *Projects put together by Community Development Trusts or other special voluntary sector bodies, with cross-sectoral partnerships and often local leadership.*

Design and access

The D & A statement is intended to 'tell the story' of the development of the design, from an analysis of the context and site, the lessons learned from consultations with the local community and the local authority, and the justification of the design response. The foregoing consultation methods outlined in this chapter and the appraisal maps fig. 2.15 and 2.16 and concept plan 2.17 would be key components of a design and access statement.

Implementing masterplans

- Phasing strategy – shows the sequence of building and the allocation of development sites or parcels. It should also include a strategy regarding short-term use of 'fallow' sites for future development.

- Ownership and tenure statements – shows the projected residential tenure distribution (owner-occupied, self-build, housing association, shared equity, private rented, etc.), and the land owned by major developers/financial institutions, public ownership, and so on.

- Management plans – these could include
  – waste management plan
  – biodiversity strategy
  – water management plan
  – energy strategy
  – areas likely to be covered by covenants/restrictions.

- Development briefs – the masterplan creates a framework in which the need for more detailed guidance is identified. It is likely that the guidance will be required for the more complex or environmentally sensitive areas.

- Design codes – as described previously, these can be key to achieving a high quality streetscape sympathetic to pedestrians, cyclists, children playing and people talking.

2.11 MAKING A DEVELOPMENT PROPOSAL

One acid test of the spatial planning process is the quality of planning applications. In the context of a collaborative approach the onus is on the prospective investors – households, firms or institutions – to come forward with appropriate schemes. The planning regime should encourage and facilitate this by requiring appraisal information and impact statements with applications above a certain size.

The applicant can demonstrate the logic of the proposal in its context by providing the following information in a clear and helpful way. This should apply to all applications over a certain size.

Application form and Design and Access Statement

- Describe what is proposed and the types of users/residents provided for.

- Specify the precise numbers of different types and sizes of dwellings. Give the gross site area and net and gross housing density figures.

- Specify by built area all the non-housing uses.

- State the NHER (energy-efficiency) levels achieved.

Context map

To cover an area of at least 800 m radius from the site boundary.

■ Show the location of nearby shops, schools, open spaces and public transport routes/stops.

■ Identify the main potential pedestrian and cycle routes from the site to local facilities such as those above, and to the town or district centre.

■ Indicate the walking distance in metres from key facilities to the site boundary.

■ Mark older buildings in the vicinity which help define the distinctive character of the area.

■ Identify nearby natural and wildlife features (such as streams, woods, railway cuttings).

Site appraisal map

To cover the area of the development site and its immediate neighbouring sites.

■ Show all adjacent development, as it is now.

■ Show the form of the land (perhaps with a cross-section) and hatch any areas of north-facing slope (NW–NE) over 1:15.

■ Show water courses and any particular ground water conditions.

■ Mark woodlands, mature trees, hedgerows and any other specific wildlife feature.

■ Identify all existing structures, buildings (current use and condition) and boundaries (materials, height, condition).

■ Show potential pedestrian access points (related to routes shown on the location map) and diagrammatically indicate any likely pedestrian/cycling movement across the site.

■ Mark existing utility routes and possible connection points.

Site layout

To cover the same area as the appraisal map.

■ Identify the different housing types, tenures and sizes clearly.

■ Show plots and curtilages clearly, distinguishing private, semi-private, semi-public and public spaces.

■ Identify any work, educational or social uses (including reservations) and buildings where use flexibility would be built in.

■ Highlight the pedestrian routes, any 'nodes' or concentrations of pedestrian activity, and any special public spaces.

■ Identify any specific cycling facilities (other than normal access roads).

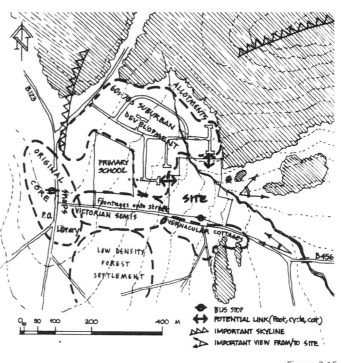

Figure 2.15
Context map

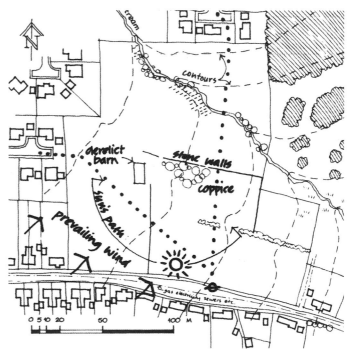

Figure 2.16
Site appraisal map

79

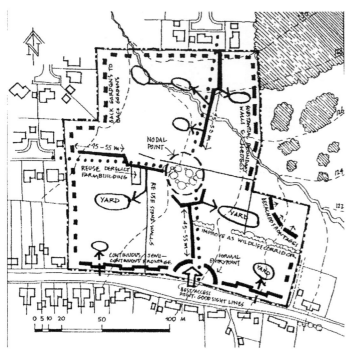

Figure 2.17
Concept plan – a useful intermediary stage between site appraisal and layout

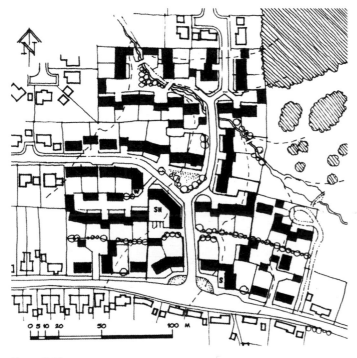

Figure 2.18
Site layout

- Distinguish buildings which are oriented and designed to maximise passive solar gain.

- Show areas set aside for on-site water treatment and management.

- Show tree and shrub planting, identifying any planting intended to create a shelter belt.

- Demonstrate which structures are retained and re-used or adapted.

MINI SUSTAINABILITY IMPACT ASSESSMENT (SIA)

All applications over a certain size (for example, 1,000 m² of built space) could be accompanied by a short 'mini-SIA' report. This would use the same checklist as the Local Plan or neighbourhood plan. It should be scoped initially by a consultation process with other stakeholders (including, of course, the planning authority), and then focus on the key issues. It should show how problems have been avoided or mitigated.

2.12 STAGE 7 – LEARNING LESSONS

BASIC PRINCIPLE

Monitoring is not an optional extra. It is fundamental to the whole process – the basis on which success or failure is assessed and policy is revised. The monitoring and review process should be:

- *broad ranging* – covering local quality of life, policy impacts and the effectiveness of the decision process

- *practical* – simple enough to be handled for each neighbourhood, ward or parish despite very limited resources

- *motivating* – examining the factors that matter to people with the involvement, as appropriate, of local stakeholders and decision-makers.

Monitoring occurs not only through formalised data collection by local authority officials, but also through the awareness and alertness of local community groups, and parish/town/district councillors. Local planning officers have a particular responsibility to be sensitive to the way neighbourhoods are changing physically. Effective channels of communication between local people, elected representatives and relevant agencies are vital.

ASSESSING POLICY IMPACT

The main responsibility for assessing the direct impact of policies and development schemes rests with those who are implementing them – though others, particularly those directly affected, should be involved in the process. The key questions are:

1   *How far have policies or proposals been implemented?* For example, if the township strategy proposed new bikeways,

how many have been constructed or firmly programmed? Are there mechanisms in place to ensure future progress?

2 *Have policies delivered the expected or desired results?* For example, where new bikeways have been realised, are they being used as intended? Have they led to increased cycling and less car travel? Have they proved safe? Are they approved of by residents? Have they resulted in any unintended consequences?

3 *If there are problems with implementation, what are the causes?* For example, is there a lack of money or key personnel? Has the policy been deflected or highjacked by events? How could the barriers be overcome?

4 *If the results are disappointing where things **have** happened, then why?* For example, if the cyclists are not choosing to use the bikeways, or there has been no increase in cycling or transfer from car, then is this because of poor choice of route? Poor design? Perceived dangers? Lack of knowledge? Lack of reinforcement by other policies?

ASSESSING HEALTH AND SUSTAINABILITY OUTCOMES

The monitoring agenda is essentially about updating and reviewing the neighbourhood appraisal on a regular basis. It is concerned with the full range of topics listed in Section 2.7: people, community, activities, place and resources. The purposes of assessment are the same.

Practicality

While during the initial preparation of a neighbourhood strategy there may be extra resources and money to undertake detailed appraisal work, on-going monitoring is more difficult to resource. It is essential to put clear, simple mechanisms in place that are both practical and effective. For example:

Neighbourhood quality of life indicators

Social, economic and environmental variables are routinely collected and publicised by the local authority. This menu of indicators should be designed by the local authority to be relevant to the neighbourhood level – allowing comparison between neighbourhoods and facilitating prioritisation for action. For this purpose it is normally necessary to rely on ward-based data.

Neighbourhood groups, parish and town councils can then extract the data for their own wards and see their area in context.

Social survey

While much quality of life information is already collected by official agencies and may already be collated by local authorities and published annually, it is recommended that local authorities supplement such statistics with a sample survey of households every two or three years.

5.7 The scope of neighbourhood appraisal

Indicators of policy impact

- *Citizen's satisfaction with the local community*

- *Local contribution to global climate change*

- *Local mobility and passenger transportation*

- *Availability of local public open areas and services*

- *Quality of the air*

- *Children's journeys to and from school*

- *Sustainable management of the local authority and local enterprises*

- *Levels of noise pollution*

- *Sustainable land use*

- *Products promoting sustainability*

Examples of other possible indicators

- *Health: mortality rates, by ward*

SOURCE: Register of births, marriages and deaths; health authority; census. (core national indicator F1)

- *Housing: homes judged unfit to live in*

SOURCE: Housing departments. (national headline indicator H7)

- *Movement: mode and distance of children travelling to school, by ward*

SOURCE: Special school or household surveys. (similar to core national indicators J1 and J2)

- *Environment: number of days of air pollution*

SOURCE: Environmental health departments. (national headline indicator H10)

Social and environmental landlords: Vale Housing

In addition to neighbourhood level monitoring, individual stakeholders need to also conduct regular assessments against health and sustainability objectives. Vale recognise they have both direct and indirect effects, and have chosen initially to concentrate on those areas where their impact is greatest. An independent organisation carries out six monthly checks to monitor commitments to environmental targets.

Tenants' Energy Consumption – the amount of carbon dioxide produced as a result of tenants heating their 6,000 of our properties is critical. By carrying out energy efficient improvements Vale have minimised this impact and reduced the costs of tenants' fuel bills.

Association's Energy Consumption – heating the space occupied by office based staff results in the emission of approximately 0.5 tonnes of CO2 per person a year.

Tenant Use of Transport – Nearly 39% of their tenants don't own a car and rely on bus services, cycling or walking.

Staff Use of Transport – The Association's staff travelled nearly 750,000 miles during the course of their work in 2007/08.

Tenants' Water Consumption – Vale's householders use on average 155 litres of water per person a day.

Built Environment – In 2007–08, Vale built 59 new properties, many will still be standing in 100 years or more.

Natural Environment – As a major builder, Vale recognise that their activities should not affect sensitive local wildlife habitats.

Waste – Vale produce at least 1 skip full of waste each day. Approximately 30% at present is sent to a local landfill site.

Purchasing – Vale's operations recognise that it is important not only to recycle, but also to buy recycled products and help close the recycling loop.

Importantly for a neighbourhood focused organisation, Vale understands the systemic impact of their activities and have put in place an effective strategy to monitor and reduce their impact and that of their tenants.

FFI: www.vale-housing.co.uk

The household survey can identify trends in travel behaviour, use of local facilities, levels of satisfaction, changing attitudes and specific concerns. It acts as an objective record of actual behaviour and residents' views. It thus offers an invaluable cross-check on the views expressed by local community groups, businesses and councillors, and will in turn influence those views.

There should be at least 50 households surveyed per ward in order to provide a significant sample. Where there are very different socio-economic, ethnic or cultural groups there may be justification for sampling 50 of each group – though this may be averaged over a number of comparable wards.

Physical trends

It is also important to monitor physical change within the neighbourhood: renewal processes (or their absence), densities, land uses, routeways, aesthetic character. Increasingly, this information will be held on GIS software and collated as part of urban capacity or potential studies by the local planning authority. The planning officer responsible for a particular neighbourhood, town or township, working with local groups and councillors, should have a specific remit to review the evolving pattern of the area against sustainable development criteria (see Sections 6.10, 6.11 and 6.12).

Monitoring by individual agencies

In addition to neighbourhood level monitoring, individual agencies (such as major investors or management companies in the area) should as a matter of course conduct regular assessments against sustainability objectives. Vale housing, a registered social landlord, were the first Housing Association in the UK to achieve ISO14001 accreditation in 1998.

ASSESSING THE EFFECTIVENESS OF THE PROCESS

It is important to observe and learn from the experience of a particular neighbourhood initiative both to improve that initiative itself and to pass on lessons to subsequent projects elsewhere.

Has the process been effective in:

■ clarifying the best way forward towards sustainable development?

■ reaching decisions and taking timely action?

■ involving all relevant stakeholders, including the population at large?

■ sorting problems and overcoming barriers?

■ enhancing the social capital and capacity of the neighbourhood?

Much more information about masterplanning is provided in Chapter 5. Here we just note its significance as a tool of implementation.

Houndwood site criteria

University of the West of England

Spectrum sustainability appraisal
WHO Healthy Cities at UWE

Criteria					
1. **Carbon emissions in buildings** — energy efficiency of buildings; layout for solar access and shelter; renewable energy supply. Notes:	—	—	3	6 (HP)	9 (actual)
2. **Carbon emissions by transport** — predicted level of car use; measures to reduce car reliance. Notes:	—	1	5	9 (some)	—
3. **Wildlife habitats** — retention/enhancement of existing valued habitats; creation of new habitats; tree planting. Notes:			1	17	1
4. **Land and food** — efficient use of urban land; soil retention/enhancement; local food growing opportunities. Notes: Land / Food				5	12 / 18
5. **Water** — reduced water demand; greyrain water use; sustainable urban drainage systems. Notes:				19	
6. **Construction materials** — low embodied energy; local sourcing; long life and reusability; healthy materials. Notes:				2	16
7. **Materials in use** — reuse/recycling encouragement; organic material composting. Notes:				8	8
8. **Housing stock** — provision responding to local needs in terms of range of price, size and form. Adaptability. Notes:				6	11	—
9. **Housing affordability** — appropriate provision and access - social housing, shared-ownership and co-housing. Notes:				4	13
10. **Social facilities** — provision of on- &/or off- site facilities & formal/informal meeting places. Notes:				12	3
11. **Open space** — open space recreational provision; green space provision; children's play opportunities. Notes:				4	12
12. **Accessibility** — to a good range of jobs and facilities, especially by foot/pedal/public transport. Notes:			4	7	5
13. **Pedestrian/cycling routes** — a permeable pedestrian/cycling network with direct, convenient and attractive routes for internal and external trips. Notes:				6	11
14. **Vehicle movement/parking** — safe, convenient and adequate provision for motor vehicles; secure, convenient and adequate parking. Notes:	3	2	2	6	4
15. **Air quality and noise** — protection from noise sources; air pollution minimised. Notes:			1	14	
16. **Local heritage/values** — enhancement of valued local features and distinctive character, minimising disturbance to local residents' lifestyles. Notes:				2	16
17. **Safety and privacy** — a design that reduces risk of crime, gives the sense of safe streets, and allows privacy to dwellings. Notes:				2	13
18. **Quality of the public realm** — layout and townscape that is functionally efficient, visually attractive and creates a good sense of place. Notes: VISUAL IMPACT → LANDMARK			11	5 / 7	2
19. **Project viability** — the whole scheme generating a reasonable level of profit for the owners/developers. Notes:				5	12
20. **Local job creation** — construction maximising local labour; development enhancing opportunities for local business creation & home working. Notes:					
21. **Stakeholder involvement** — effective involvement of public, private and community sector interests in decision-making processes. Notes: S106 - revisit — TO RATE FUTURE					
22. **On-going management** — planning & maintenance of communal services and spaces on a sustainable basis, sensitive to evolving community needs. Notes:					

Grading sheets

In the plenary, grades were recorded as 'blobs' from the relevant break-out group, and then after discussion, by number of individual votes.

The small Somerset town of Street, near Glastonbury, remains something of a company town, with the fortunes of Clarks shoes exerting a strong influence on the fortunes of the town as a whole. Clarks own a major site close to the town centre which was in the past occupied by factories and warehouses. In 2003 it gained outline planning approval for 400 new homes and associated open space. Houndwood, as it was named, is now by far the biggest new housing development in Street, destined to influence the feel and even the population structure of this town significantly, as it provides types of dwellings – in a convenient location – not previously available.

The process

The process involved a series of workshops at particular stages of design development and led eventually to a sustainability report evaluating the qualities of the emerging scheme. The sequence of actions and events is shown in the diagram.

A complete spectrum of stakeholders, representing all the main interests in the development, was considered essential:

- the owners of the site and the prospective developers
- the planning consultants and the design team
- the local planning authority, housing and transport authorities
- the Parish council and influential civic/environment groups
- the residents of the surrounding areas

Building mutual trust and understanding

The early stages of the process are all about shared experience and building mutual understanding between the disparate groups. The values inherent in the idea of sustainable development were the starting point, specified by Clarks. The trips out to exemplary projects allowed shared learning. The initial list of 22 objectives, proposed by the WHO Centre and then adjusted through workshop discussion, were comprehensive in scope, including economic viability as well as social and environmental criteria. The essential principle was that all interests could clearly identify where their own aspirations or concerns were represented in the list, and at the same time accept the legitimacy of the other interests, even where these might conflict with their own.

Achieving consensus on the objectives – which are then used to evaluate schemes and structure the sustainability appraisal, is critical. The objectives are not weighted. Each is valued for itself, and all need to be achieved to a reasonable degree.

Triggering new ideas through the appraisal process

The evaluation workshops were structured so as to ensure everyone could participate effectively, with a combination of small group discussions around subsets of the objectives (with an obligation to reach consensual recommendations) and plenaries where each individual had a vote in relation to all objectives. This resulted in a rich diet of information which then went to inform the technical report. The aims of the discussions were not only evaluation but also shared learning and creativity. The spectrum grades identified which objectives were not being achieved and therefore needed further work or a design review. The investors and their professional team learnt from the insights and ideas of the other stakeholders. Because the discussions were about levels of impact on a given objective, not about relative importance, it was also surprising how far agreement was possible.

Sustainability appraisal

The preferred scheme, having been subject to a stakeholder appraisal workshop, was then evaluated by the UWE team. This evaluation drew on three elements: specialist reports commissioned by the developers (e.g. on transport, the housing market, wildlife and landscape); the consensual and individual arguments/votes of the stakeholders; and the 'best practice' expertise of the team. The report was presented to the design/development group, and formed part of the supporting documentation given to the local authority.

Early table top site planning workshop.

Shared visit to Bedzed; building understanding and capacity amongst the participants.

Photographs provided courtesy of Alder King Planning Consultants, Clarks' planning consultant responsible for co-ordinating the Houndwood project

Figure 2.19

The six-stages of the Spectrum process at Houndwood

(Barton and Grant, 2008)

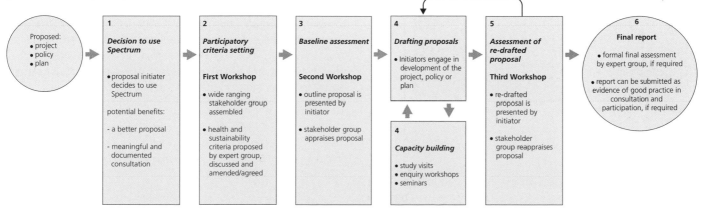

2.b A new community at Sherford
Devon
Health impact assessment influencing spatial development

Some of the key strategic requirements:

- *Detailed involvement of key stakeholders leading to the early approval and implementation of an appropriately phased comprehensive development.*

- *Provide a town centre and three neighbourhood centres to create a clearly structured development. These centres are located to maximise access to a centre for all Sherford's residents, with at least 80% of all dwellings to be within a 5 minute walk of a centre.*

- *Achieve, at each phase of development, a high degree of self-sufficiency for the community (including early provision of soft and hard infrastructure) and a mix of uses avoiding the segregation of land uses.*

- *Be well related to Plymouth and other nearby settlements, with good sustainable transport links and a mutually supportive range of services and facilities, whilst retaining its own identity and not coalescing with adjacent development.*

- *Create and sustain a high quality of community life within Sherford whilst not undermining the quality of community life in neighbouring communities.*

Adopted Sherford New Community Area Action Plan, August 2007, South Hams District Council

Photo: Red Tree LLP

The disused Sherford Quarry will be retained as a key recreation and wildlife area within the town

The site at Sherford, at present farmed pasture and arable land in a wide river valley, is proposed for a major mixed-use development. The site comprises some 415 hectares of land, half of which is dedicated to a country park. The agreed plan is for approximately 4,000 new dwellings by 2016, increasing to 5,500 by 2026 with the potential for further growth to the north. This site will also provide an economic land use mix of retail (about 16,800 m² gross) and commercial and employment uses (about 67,000 m² gross).

An important objective in process terms is also to deliver a body to manage the community assets for the benefit of the community, promote sustainable living and support social networks. This development plan needs to secure sufficient sources of funding for the long term management and development of the community and its assets.

Process

Driven by national housing allocations, regional spatial policy started to focus on Sherford as an area to accommodate a new community as early as 2001. With a development on this large scale there have been a number of studies, reports and consultations all feeding into the development of the scheme through the statutory planning process. Autumn 2004 saw an 'Enquiry by Design' workshop led by The Prince's Foundation. This process engaged with a very wide range of sectoral actors and the general public. Through option testing and creative design, several basic element of the proposed spatial framework arose during these workshops.

Key regional and sub-regional consultations concluded in 2005, confirming many of the strategic elements of the planning to date and the role of the new development within the sub-region.

A more detailed planning process at Sherford continued culminating in an examination and the adoption of a schematic spatial framework in summer 2007. While this work was being completed the County Council, along with the Devon Primary Care Trust and South Hams District Council commissioned a full Health Impact Assessment of these proposals. This was finalised by the winter of 2007.

The role and impact of the Health Impact Assessment

The HIA was conducted in the knowledge that health and wellbeing are central to sustainability and that an holistic approach would assist in delivering the exemplar sustainable community all stakeholders wished to see.

The HIA examined the negative and positive health impacts of the development proposals and conducted surveys and interviews with a wide range of stakeholders, community representatives and interest groups. Approached as an integrative and inclusive process the HIA was used to develop a series of practical recommendations and actions for stakeholders to implement. It influenced both the policy framework and the subsequent development of the planning application.

A series of recommendations in the form of topic based Health Codes was used to inform the masterplanning, design coding, strategy development, Section 106 negotiations and development control procedures. The codes suggested ways in which public health issues could be addressed and managed at various planning and development stages from strategic principles, through design and management requirements to monitoring and review.

Many of the Health Codes' requirements were encapsulated in the evolving Section 106 requirements for the development, in particular where they relate to developer contributions and management.

Figure 2.20   **The HIA process**

HIA is a combination of procedures, methods and tools that systematically judges the potential, and sometimes unintended, effects of a policy, programme or project on both the health of a population and the distribution of those effects within the population. HIA identifies appropriate actions to manage those effects. (IAIA and Quigley et al. 2006)

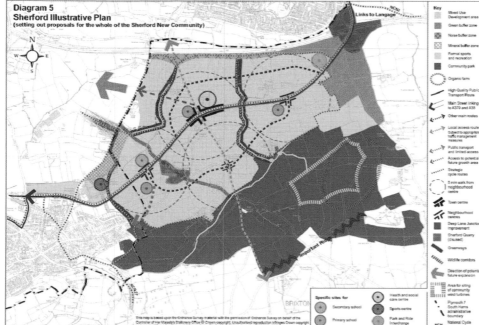

Sherford Area Action Plan (adopted August 2007).

Examples of how the health codes were used to inform different aspects of the Sherford plan are shown below:

- *Strategic Principle* – The entire community should be highly accessible with each dwelling no further than 400 m from a bus stop.

- *Developer Contribution* – Funding for community travel plan officer and community travel plan.

- *Design Requirement* – Distance of houses from public transport modes or playspace.

- *Management Requirement* – Personalised Travel Planning.

- *Monitoring and Review* – Modal shift targets, accessibility targets and public transport use.

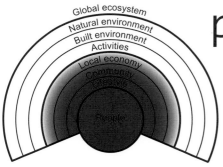

Global ecosystem
Natural environment
Built environment
Activities
Local economy
Community
lifestyle
People

providing for local need | chapter 3

3.1 PURPOSE AND SCOPE

The essence of sustainable development is providing for people's needs, now and in the future. This chapter takes the people of the neighbourhood as the starting point. It gives guidance on the way to approach questions of new housing provision and social mix. It looks at ways in which local community networks are undermined or promoted. It examines the way decisions about land use and location affect the access people have to local jobs, shops, schools and open spaces. And it introduces the planning of local movement and the public realm.

In terms of the Settlement Health Map, the chapter covers a huge range of concerns, from the core of people and their lifestyle out to the structure of the built environment. It is ultimately about the social and economic factors that need to be recognised when shaping healthy neighbourhoods, towns and cities.

GENERAL PRINCIPLES

The over-arching goals are health, equity and quality of life, now and for future generations. In these respects there is one vital key that opens the door to understanding what is needed in terms of spatial planning – and that is walkability. If we can create neighbourhoods where people have the option, and will often choose, to live more of their lives locally, getting around by foot and bike, then health and well-being, social inclusion and low carbon lifestyles are all much more likely to be achieved. Local needs can be met locally. The 'neighbourhood design principles' set out in Chapter 1 are developed here from this viewpoint.

■ **Stakeholder involvement**

The surest way to understand different needs and aspirations is to ask the people involved. The obligation to try to understand and then take account of different interests rests with all stakeholders – public, private and voluntary sectors. Note that the principles of participation have been elaborated in Chapter 2.

■ **Increased local autonomy**

Neighbourhoods cannot be – and should not attempt to be – self-sufficient in work and services. But there is tremendous value in increasing the proportion of daily and weekly needs that can be satisfied locally. Surveys find that the availability or otherwise of local facilities is a key issue for residents. Where local facilities are available then people generally choose to use them, even in areas

3.1

Unhealthy neighbourhoods, unhealthy lives

In providing for local need the imperative for health is to support local people in choosing and leading healthy lifestyles. Chapters 3, 4 and 5 all contain the basic elements for building neighbourhoods that can achieve this goal. This publication outlines many health impacts of poor urban design (see Sections 1.5 and 1.6).

Physical activity and health

Physically active people have half the risk of heart disease than those with a sedentary lifestyle, and 33-50% lower risk of type 2 diabetes and obesity. Physically active people (30 mins walking a day) have:

- *up to 50% lower risk of colon cancer*
- *up to 30% lower risk of breast cancer*
- *reduced risk of prostate, uterine and lung cancers*
- *fewer falls and fractures in older age groups*

SOURCE: Crowther et al. 2004

The dimensions of difference are many, but six of the most significant in the context of local planning are:

- *different age groups*
- *varied household sizes/types*
- *different ethnic groupings*
- *different income levels*
- *different levels of personal mobility*
- *diverse lifestyle choices*

of high car ownership. Local use has benefits in terms of health, social inclusion, economic vitality and environmental sustainability; but local provision will only work if the preconditions of quality, accessibility and viability are right.

■ Social stability and choice
In the face of increasing fear of violence, people are retreating behind locked doors. The goal of sustainable development is to create opportunities for social contact, social stability and 'community', which depends in part on shared local activities and life on the street. The object is to open up choice in every field: choice of housing type, tenure and location, options locally for entrepreneurs and shopkeepers, choice of means of movement. Satisfying varied needs increases the likelihood of social stability.

■ Connectivity
A connected, integrated approach to provision means agencies working together to deliver shared facilities: for example, the education and leisure departments working with community groups to provide a better hall or library or hard pitch than they could separately; or small businesses and volunteer organisations sharing a serviced office space and café. Connectivity also applies to the pattern of streets: creating a permeable environment that increases accessibility, especially by foot and pedal.

■ Diversity
Within a neighbourhood, and even more a town or urban district, choice and opportunity can be increased by achieving requisite variety: a 'balanced' population in terms of age, family status and wealth; a wide variety of housing stock; a diversity of economic niches and type of service provision. The object is to achieve and maintain what ecologists might call a 'climax culture', with maximum diversity and opportunity within a stable overall pattern. Neighbourhood decision-makers should recognise the specific social needs relevant to any particular issue.

■ Response to place
Place is not only important in terms of function and connectivity but also in terms of people's perceptions: the local cultural landscape. Places are valued for their history and associations, their smell, touch, sound and visual quality. As much care needs to be taken in aesthetically mundane or tawdry environments as in Conservation Areas. Each new project should make a positive contribution to the identity and quality of place.

■ Adaptability
The idea of the 'life-time neighbourhood' means adaptability to changing needs through an individual's life and to changing social/economic patterns. It means overt consideration for future generations – for example, options for second generations' homes. It means recognising the neighbourhood as providing for a dynamic community, avoiding unnecessary constraints on market and lifestyle innovation.

people and community

3.2 A DIVERSE POPULATION

BASIC PRINCIPLES

At the scale of the urban district or small town, and where possible in every neighbourhood, there should be a long-term, carefully monitored strategy to achieve a diverse, balanced community. This diversity should be in relation to two main variables:

■ Types of household: young single people, young families, mature families, middle-aged and retired singles/couples, the elderly infirm and institutional/community groupings.

■ Income levels and socio-economic groups: low income households, including those reliant on state support, middle income groups (with a particular concern for 'key workers' such as nurses, plumbers and policemen), and higher income groups, including entrepreneurs and managers.

In many places the diversity strategy also needs to explicitly recognise the needs of different ethnic and cultural groups, and varied lifestyle choices. These needs and pressures will evolve with time, especially if rising sea levels lead to mass migrations from low-lying parts of the world. The diversity strategy will need to be responsive to change.

Reasons

■ *Social inclusion*: the opportunity for people, whatever their income, to find accommodation in every town or part of the city, according to their specific needs.

■ *Life-time neighbourhoods*: providing for people at every stage of their lives, so that if they want to stay within the same community, they can, and the community benefits from social continuity and living history.

■ *Economic provision of services*: avoiding the 'leads and lags' of social provision which occur with unbalanced populations – where, for example, on a new estate there is initially a dearth of primary school places, then a lack of secondary places, and then a long-term under-provision for the elderly.

■ *Tolerance and appreciation of difference*: ensuring that children, in particular, have the chance to experience a varied, well-rounded community, not a one-class ghetto or dormitory suburb, and have the opportunity to see different kinds of people at work and play

■ *Less need to travel*: increasing the likelihood that people can find local jobs, local services, specific activities, and thus reduce the need to travel.

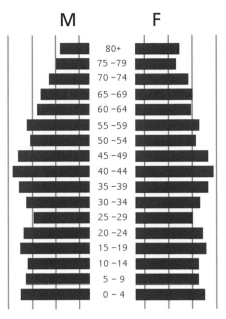

A balanced age profile, signifying continuous, even population renewal

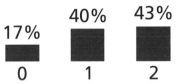

Car ownership: cars per household

Housing mix: tenure

Figure 3.1
Analysis of an urban ward

This well-established neighbourhood shows a reasonably balanced age/sex profile, signifying a steady process of population renewal. But the patterns of both car ownership and housing tenure suggest a skewed social mix, with lower-income groups experiencing a degree of exclusion.

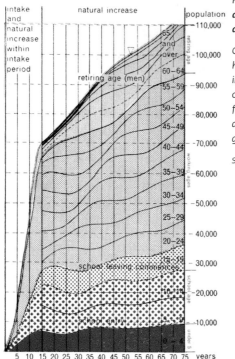

Figure 3.2 **Peaks and troughs of demand**

Graph showing how an unbalanced incoming population causes successive fluctuations in each age group during the growth of a town

SOURCE: GLC 1965

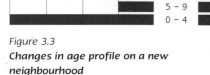

Figure 3.3

Changes in age profile on a new neighbourhood

An unbalanced profile from a new growth area, leading to peaks and troughs of demand for local facilities. Over the next decades the peaks and troughs move up the age profile, only being slightly diluted by further migrations.

BUCKING THE MARKET

In large cities market trends, often reinforced by official housing and planning policies, have tended to differentiate whole parts of the city by class and age. Very high land/property values in one locality ensure exclusivity, while in another market demand is notable by its absence. Young adults and some retired people may be attracted by flats in the inner area, while families occupy houses in the outer suburbs. Achieving diverse township populations in this context relies on sustained commitment and inter-sectoral co-operation. Regeneration of low-prestige zones, for example, depends on integrated strategies that tackle existing problems and create the right conditions for a change in market attitudes.

INTER-GENERATIONAL PLANNING

The time-scale for planning balanced communities is long. In areas of major change (brownfield regeneration, urban extension or new town) the minimum time period should be a generation (about 25–30 years): that is, the period needed to even out peaks and troughs of demand for local facilities such as schools. Any such new development should be seen, of course, in the context of potential sharing with adjacent neighbourhoods, which itself can help even out demand cycles if each area is following different trajectories. But if one locality depends on another for its local facilities, it is important to consider whether those facilities still remain local. Are they still accessible by foot, within acceptable distance thresholds?

Building adaptability into the physical fabric

The neighbourhood can also be future-proofed by building adaptability into the physical fabric so that buildings and spaces can be easily reused in new ways. This could facilitate young adults leaving home that want to stay locally, or 'empty nesters' wanting to downsize, houses becoming shops, or shops becoming houses, parking areas being converted into parks, and so on. Examples of adaptability include:

- Building types capable of adapting to new needs: houses that can be turned into flats (or vice versa), the ground floor of buildings on main streets having high ceilings so they can be shops, offices, workshops or homes.

- Gaps in the urban framework available for eventual development if the need arises, but meanwhile occupied by, for instance, short-term storage sheds, car parking (pending public transport improvements) or simply lawn.

- Design main routeways generously to permit later changes (such as the insertion of a tram system, wider bike lanes or unloading bays outside future shops).

CREATING THE RIGHT CONDITIONS

Each locality – especially at the scale of a small town, urban district or township – needs to be carefully planned in relation to the whole range of community functions. The sub-headings below provide a brief agenda which is expanded in subsequent sections of this chapter:

• Housing: a balance of different types, sizes, tenures and affordability which provides opportunities for all types of households and flexibility over time. A central issue is the degree to which under-represented groups – such as families with children in the inner city, young single people in the outer suburbs or affluent households in peripheral council estates – can be attracted to the area.

• Jobs and workspace: diverse local opportunities which provide openings for new small scale businesses, encourage home-based work, provide employment especially for young people and part-time workers, and support local services.

• Retailing: viable retail and social facilities that recycle financial resources locally and give life and vitality to the township core.

• Quality: an aesthetically pleasing, safe and friendly environment that attracts all sectors of the population to the area and encourages them to stay.

• Accessibility: a place that is not only easy to get around internally but is externally well connected by main roads and public transport services. This factor is absolutely key to the success of the township: good accessibility is a driver for the local economy, viable facilities and private housing development. These in turn attract and help retain diverse populations.

3.3 HOUSING FOR ALL

BASIC PRINCIPLE: BALANCING SOCIAL NICHE WITH SOCIAL DIVERSITY

In every part of a town or city there should be a broad balance of different housing opportunities in terms of tenure, size and affordability, while at the same time safeguarding local social identity and sense of security. The strategy to achieve this needs to be agreed by the housing authority and the planning authority and fully understood by councillors.
• At the level of the home-place or street, housing mix is possible but not normally essential.
• At the level of the neighbourhood it is important, but there will be differences between neighbourhoods depending on their location and density.
• At the level of the small town or urban district housing mix is critical, and within the town there should be the full range of housing options.

Teenage capital of Europe

A full-page article in a national paper announced that Milton Keynes had the largest proportion (21.8 per cent) of under-14s in Europe per head of population. It continued that one in three people were aged under 20 and that schools couldn't be built fast enough (Daily Telegraph, 14 October 2000).

The demographic trends underlying this article have come about from building a new town that was mainly geared to a narrow age band of the population.

As the population matures Milton Keynes could expect a wave of derelict schools and mounting pressures for employment opportunities. Later still, it may see a peak in demand for care and retirement facilities that will be difficult to meet.

UK Government guidance

Planning Policy Statement 3 on housing (PPS3) suggests that affordable housing can be provided where there are 15 or more dwellings proposed. Affordable housing is defined as including social housing (such as council housing) and intermediate housing (such as shared ownership, part supported rent, part buy). PPS3 allows considerable flexibility to local planning authorities to define the particular threshold of dwelling numbers that triggers affordable housing provision, according to context.

3.3

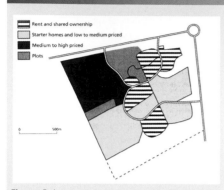

A patchwork of housing sites

Rent and shared ownership
Starter homes and low to medium priced
Medium to high priced
Plots

Figure 3.4

The patchwork of housing sites in Chepstow Drive grid square, Milton Keynes

SOURCE: Barton et al. 2000, Figure 8.1, adapted from MKDC 1992

'Every grid square neighbourhood of 2000–4000 people [in Milton Keynes] has a mix of housing. The home-zones were developed by different agencies or house-builders and in the example they range from 9–130 units. The pattern of housing within the grid squares is designed to ensure that the elderly, disabled and those least likely to have cars are conveniently located at or near a local centre. To attract the more affluent residents the high-priced dwellings are located to ensure an attractive approach and the opportunity for larger gardens'. (Barton et al. 2000: 128)

	Shenly Church End	Crown Hill
Rent/shared ownership	388 (28%)	383 (39%)
Lower priced	484 (35%)	370 (38%)
Higher priced	422 (30%)	139 (14%)
Plots (very expensive)	93 (7%)	90 (9%)
Total (100%)	1,387 (100%)	982

SOURCE: Milton Keynes 1992

Reasons

- To free up the various housing markets (social housing/rental/first-time buyers/mid-range/'executive' housing, etc.) and allow households of all kinds the maximum opportunity to select locations convenient to their needs, which can reduce their total travel cost/distance and consequent pollution.
- To assist equity and social inclusion: normally poorer groups are particularly constrained in their search for appropriate homes; conversely, some places (certain Welsh Valleys, for example) have fewer up-market homes available.
- To avoid peaks and troughs of demand for local facilities (especially in relation to different age groups), which lead to alternating problems of shortage and surplus, with consequent extra public or private costs.
- To maintain a balance of rich and poor, growing households and shrinking households, over time – so that local shops and businesses remain viable and bus services are supported.
- To maintain or increase population levels at a time when average household size is falling, in order to bulwark local service viability, and reduce average trip length.
- To increase the potential for mutual support, surveillance, and learning between age groups – for example, real or acting grannies assisting young families; informal surveillance of streets, imparting a sense of safety; teenage role-models for younger children; young working adult role-models for teenagers.
- To ensure the local availability of a wide range of skills and professions, easing job-filling and job-search problems, and reducing the need to travel. This is particularly important for part-time workers and carers (see Barton et al. 2000: 90–2 for a fuller discussion).

WORKING OUT LOCAL HOUSING NEEDS

2.7 Understanding the locality

Regular reviews of housing need and provision in each town or township should involve partnership between the Parish or Town Council, the Local Authority, and house builders/providers. Each partner brings distinctive understanding to the table. The review should input to the development plan and the overall city or municipal strategy.

Parish/Town Council

A bottom-up appraisal of local housing needs should be instituted by the parish, town or neighbourhood council. This appraisal should encompass not only the need for social housing but identify other needs as well, as perceived by residents and local community organisations. From time to time it may justify a local household suvey.

The Local Authority

The bottom-up appraisal is not, however, the whole story, but has to be married with a top-down appraisal undertaken by the local authority. This will identify needs over a wider area which are not necessarily expressed or visible locally. It will take account of regional trends, including migration patterns, birth and death rates which are beyond the control of the community.

House builders and providers

The housing developers (building firms and housing associations) and estate agents have knowledge of local demands and also of the degree to which specific sites are developable and marketable. As with housing land availability or urban capacity studies it is important at the town or parish level to consult the potential investors.

RECOGNISING DIVERSE NEEDS

Local housing policy is not only a matter of the proportions of affordable homes and market homes. Each area should ideally provide for all legitimate local needs. Below are some of the important questions:

Variety of housing type/size/price

- Can single people (young or old) find accommodation to suit their needs and pocket – particularly are there enough flats (some with gardens/patios)?

- Can large families find large homes (not necessarily with a high price tag) to match their needs?

- Can founding families who wish to stay in the area find appropriate 'first-time' properties? Starter homes? Shared equity?

- Can successful business people/executives who want to remain in the area, or others who have work/local connections, find accommodation to match their aspirations?

- Is there a potential local demand for car-free development or for co-housing schemes, and are there appropriate sites?

- Can keen gardeners of limited means access properties with large gardens, or live very close to allotments?

Eco-housing with a joint management committe of all households at Bedzed in South London.

Figure 3.5
Edinburgh car-free development

High density car-free development in Edinburgh, in an accessible inner-city location.

SOURCE: Canmore Housing Association

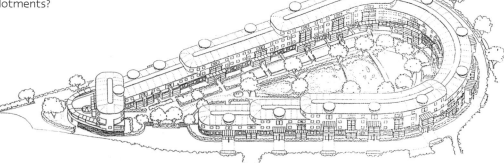

3.3

Allaying fears

The sense of threat sometimes felt by home owners in relation to social housing can be reduced by discussing the spatial scale for diversification: i.e. at the neighbourhood and township level, not necessarily in each home-patch.

Housing mix

Mixed income neighbourhoods have been suggested as being beneficial to health. A Canadian study found that in neighbourhoods of mixed income, the less affluent have better health and quality of life compared to those living in less affluent neighbourhoods (Hou and Myles 2004).

Conspicuous failure of the policy of social polarisation: the demolition of a 1960s social housing estate.

Social and affordable housing

•   Are there people living in the area currently sharing, or in poor housing conditions, who qualify for social housing or could benefit from shared equity homes?

•   Are there households and key workers who have been forced out of the area by high prices, or others who have a local connection but cannot move in?

•   Are there potentially sites available in convenient locations for households with limited car availability?

Special-needs housing

•   Can local infirm elderly people gain access to sheltered housing or nursing homes in the area if they want to?

•   Is there an unmet need for hostel accommodation, half-way houses or other special requirements?

•   Is housing for elderly or disabled people available within (say) 300 m of general store or supermarkets, local parks, pub, church, etc., and of a bus-stop giving good access to the town centre, with a near-level gradient on the approach?

DECONSTRUCTING THE GHETTO

Where long-established planning policies and house-price differentials are still reinforcing housing monocultures, it is important to develop an explicit strategy for diversification. Typically this is needed in affluent commuter exurbs/villages, poor inner areas, peripheral council estates, and middle-class suburbs of 'family' housing. The local authority can identify 'unbalanced' localities and set out a strategy and targets for diversification. The strategy could involve:

•   expressly outlawing the 'more of the same' convention, whereby social housing attracts more social housing, sheltered housing is unnaturally clustered, and up-market estates maintain exclusivity

•   using local-plan density guidelines to diversify housing opportunities rather than as a covert policy of social exclusion: note that density should if possible reflect different needs (e.g. family cf. single person households) not different levels of income

•   redefining 'maintaining the amenity' of an area in terms of variety and quality rather than similarity and not only in relation to affordable houses

•   requiring every application for over (say) three or more new units to contribute appropriately to the diversity targets: for example, if the town lacks flats, and some local demand is apparent or suspected, then sites in appropriate locations could be required to provide them.

Political dynamite

Achieving better community balance can run counter to established market practice, raise fears about lost local amenity and run the gauntlet of social prejudice. Top-down imposition of quotas may be political dynamite. A collaborative community strategy approach could involve working towards a general recognition that every 'community' has a responsibility for helping to tackle housing stress across a city region. This can then be complemented by neighbourhood- or town-level analysis of need by local stakeholders.

Market resistance

In areas of low market potential (e.g. hard-to-let council estates or inner-city under-occupied zero-value areas), private sector development may be unprofitable – i.e. the potential sale value may be less than the cost of rehabilitation/new build. Obviously, such areas are priority for regeneration funding, which can be used to pump-prime as well as directly improve the lot of existing residents. If such pump-priming of the market is to avoid sending good money after bad then it is likely to be part of a very radical reshaping of the area, sufficient to challenge public preconceptions and the assumptions of state and private investors, and perhaps enabling unconventional/marginal housing to find a niche.

5.14 Neighbourhood intensification

The redevelopment of Hulme in inner Manchester and of the Gorbals in Glasgow provide object lessons in comprehensive restructuring along neighbourhood lines.

3.4 DEVELOPING SOCIAL CAPITAL

BASIC PRINCIPLES

Investors and policy-makers have a responsibility to understand the importance of local community networks – including formal and informal social groups – and to work with local organisations to ensure that their decisions facilitate those networks. This social responsibility applies across the board – to the private sector as well as to the public and voluntary sectors. Planners have a particular responsibility to structure the public realm in such a way that social networks are supported and fostered, not undermined.

THE IMPORTANCE OF COMMUNITY

'Community' is generally perceived as a Good Thing, but the nature of community has changed dramatically since the mid-twentieth century. Communities of interest and identity (linked to work, hobbies, religious belief or political activity, etc.) have for many people replaced communities of place. Such interest communities may have a very wide geographical spread (facilitated by car, phone and internet), but most also have a

Caution: There is no magic wand that can create community

Local community links are forged by the people themselves and by the groups they form. Deterministic design solutions and governmental 'new deals' achieve little without the positive choice of residents. However, planners, developers and service deliverers have an obligation to ensure that they make it easy for people and that they remove barriers to local association, supporting the development of communities.

Aspects of social capital

- *informal networks of friends and neighbours*
- *local identity and sense of belonging*
- *norms of mutual trust and support*
- *community-level networks and pressure groups*
- *the level of civic engagement.*

(after Putman 1993, and Atkinson and Kintea 1998)

3.4

Social esteem and the urban environment

Townhill Neighbourhood, Swansea

Funded by URBAN (EU), this project is set within an area of acute social, physical and environmental deprivation.

A comprehensive package of projects is involved; priorities are employment, education, training, environment, crime detection and prevention, health and housing.

The poor conditions of the front gardens of tenanted properties was taken as an indication of lack of self-esteem in the community. The poor and drab environment also affects self-confidence and self-esteem, so negatively reinforcing the problems.

Environmental projects were aimed at tackling low pride, and encouraging participation and self-realisation. Social inclusion was promoted through involving those in need in environmental projects (including training and work).

The environmental projects involved improving safety, quality of life, enhancing wildlife and landscape, and traffic-calming measures.

The involvement of local people in the improvement of their local area has resulted in an improvement also in both social capacity and health.

Council funded notice boards if well managed can help connect people together.

specific locus as well – school, pub, club, office, place of worship – tying them to the locality. Poorer and less-mobile people often rely heavily on locally based networks – for example, young children in a playgroup, the elderly infirm in a day-care centre.

The existence of local networks of mutual support and trust is important for health and mental well-being. Conversely, the absence of such neighbourliness exacerbates problems of isolation and social exclusion; it also increases the need to travel (with consequent environmental damage) in order to satisfy social needs.

Social capital

This is a measure of the residents' sense of community and their ability to act together to pursue shared objectives. It is characterised by civic identity and engagement, trust and reciprocity of actions, and networking between individuals, groups and agencies. The approach taken by official, market and/or voluntary agencies impacts on social capital, affecting the level of engagement of local people with decision processes and their sense of power or powerlessness. According to some commentators these are significant determinants of health (Atkinson and Kintea 1998).

ACTION TO SUPPORT LOCAL COMMUNITY

Service delivery by public agencies

• Provision of accessible local educational facilities at primary, secondary and further-education levels. This is particularly important in smaller settlements where the primary school is a vital network-builder for both children and parents.

• Decentralised, visible provision of services, including health, housing, social services, police, job centre, library, etc.

• Co-ordinated provision across departments and agencies, for example in relation to school, library and recreational facilities.

• One-stop service provision for deprived and vulnerable groups.

Planning and design

• Density and land-use/movement pattern planned to increase the viability of local retail, leisure and public transport facilities, hence increasing the number of places people meet.

• A permeable, safe and attractive pedestrian environment which encourages people onto the streets; convivial meeting places at nodal points.

• Mixed-use development and regeneration programmes responding to the needs of existing/potential local businesses and facilitating home-based work.

• Varied housing provision responding to the needs of different household types and cultures, and of second-generation house holds; providing life-time homes, adapted to the full life span of the residents

- Focus on the sense of local identity and safety within each street or home-place – this is the scale that particularly matters for mental well-being.

- Availability of indoor and outdoor spaces for assembly: local halls/rooms for public meetings, clubs, courses, competitions; parks, commons, allotments for events, games, shared activity.

Capacity building

- A collaborative approach by the local authority to the community strategy and the local plan, encouraging effective participation by groups and individuals.

- In areas of urban regeneration, the appointment of a community development officer to connect with 'invisible' groups/ interests and ease their path to involvement and joint project working ('capacity building').

- A responsive, positive attitude by official agencies and major private/voluntary-sector organisations to grass-roots initiatives.

SENSE OF SECURITY AND HOUSING MIX

There is tension between the need to provide a mix of housing and the need to safeguard feelings of security. The social identity of a local area – in terms of the social class and ethnic group residents experience or the streets near home – help to determine feelings of security. People like to live next door to people like themselves. If they feel cut off from their own social group, that can increase anxiety and fear and mental illness, and fewer local people are in a position to be able to support them (Halpern 1995).

The patchwork neighbourhood

The important scale for this feeling of security is very local – not the neighbourhood as a whole but the street, the home-place. The home-place represents the safe territory or niche. There should be a limited range of housing diversity within it. This accords with the instincts of people in general and house-builders' marketing strategies in particular. Historic towns frequently exhibit a patchwork pattern which has survived for centuries and provides diversity with identity. More recent experience also suggests that income types can be mixed successfully in adjacent streets (Duany and Plater-Zyberg 1991; Milton Keynes 1992 – see side column).

Pepper-potting

UK Government guidance enabling local authorities to demand a proportion of affordable housing in every development over 15 or 25 units is desirable in that it leads to wider availability and dispersal of affordable homes. This implies a policy of pepper-

Community halls in accessible locations are essential if community activities are to flourish. They can be provided in many different ways:

- *local authority/parish council halls*
- *school halls*
- *church/faith halls*
- *pub function rooms*
- *shared club spaces*
- *leisure centre/library hall*

The ingredients of a good facility are appropriate size, pleasant outlook, kitchen, toilets, easy booking, cheapness and devoted caretaking.

2.3 Collaborative communities

2.6 Working with local people

potting. However, care should be taken to avoid haphazard sprinkling. Planned scatter in groups of three or four can work well (such as at the Bournville Village Trust), so long as the housing is of similar visual quality to its neighbours. Many social housing providers believe that rather larger groupings work better for both residents and mangers. However, over the whole neighbourhood there should be many kinds of housing opportunities. The mosaic of home-places, each with its particular character, go to make up a neighbourhood which is physically and socially diverse.

Figure 3.6

Community interaction on three Bristol streets: lines represent friendships or aquaintances, dots represent where people are said to gather and chat.

SOURCE: Hart 2008

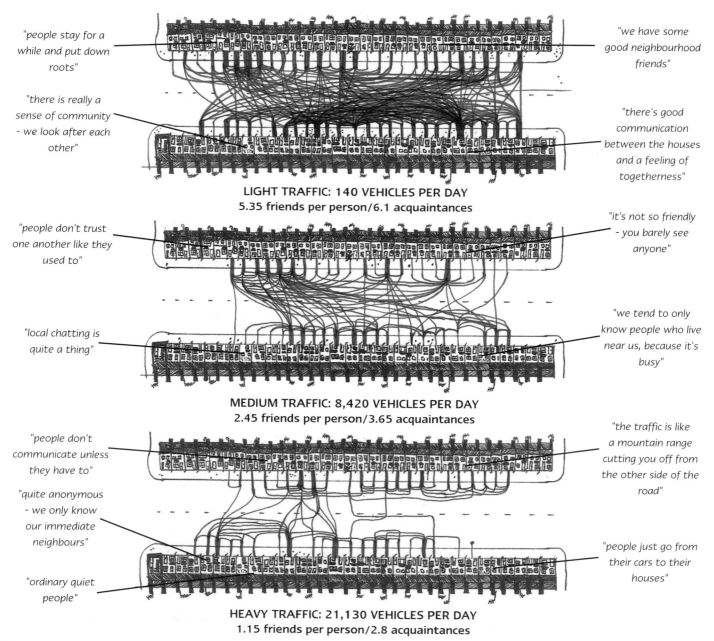

"people stay for a while and put down roots"

"there is really a sense of community - we look after each other"

"we have some good neighbourhood friends"

"there's good communication between the houses and a feeling of togetherness"

LIGHT TRAFFIC: 140 VEHICLES PER DAY
5.35 friends per person/6.1 acquaintances

"people don't trust one another like they used to"

"local chatting is quite a thing"

"it's not so friendly - you barely see anyone"

"we tend to only know people who live near us, because it's busy"

MEDIUM TRAFFIC: 8,420 VEHICLES PER DAY
2.45 friends per person/3.65 acquaintances

"people don't communicate unless they have to"

"quite anonymous - we only know our immediate neighbours"

"ordinary quiet people"

"the traffic is like a mountain range cutting you off from the other side of the road"

"people just go from their cars to their houses"

HEAVY TRAFFIC: 21,130 VEHICLES PER DAY
1.15 friends per person/2.8 acquaintances

TRAFFIC FLOWS AND SOCIAL NETWORKS

Studies in California and England have shown that there is a strong relationship between traffic levels and community. Where traffic flows are high, so as to make crossing the road awkward and normal conversation difficult, then the number of neighbours known by residents is low. Conversely a peaceful street, where children can play in reasonable safety and chatting is a pleasure, leads to many more residents knowing each other. This also relates to the sense of ownership of space. Where traffic dominates the street people feel their own territory is just the inside of their dwelling. But where people can flow out onto the street without intimidation, their sense of territory can include their street.

This does not have to mean that no housing should be constructed along main roads, or that houses should turn their backs to the main road in a protective gesture. That leads to 'dead' streets and a lack of eyes on the street, increasing risk. Rather it means:

• Keeping dwellings well back from main thoroughfares, where possible with trees along the street giving a sense of psychological and visual separation from traffic, and with wider pavements to give a sense of space and free movement.

• Placing family homes where possible on less-trafficked streets.

• Placing commercial properties and flats along the main route – the flats appropriate if likely to be occupied by young adults who typically rely largely on non-place based social networks.

3.15 Neighbourhood movement strategy

3.5 NEIGHBOURHOOD IDENTITY

KEY PRINCIPLE

The identity of residents, especially long-term residents, is tied up with the physical character of their neighbourhood. This character is about sights, sounds, smells and feel. It is also about personal and community history. It is an expression of culture and continuity. The evolution of the area needs to occur so that facets which are valued locally are enhanced, while aspects that detract are remedied. Planning for the enhancement of neighbourhood character should therefore be applied generally, not limited to special conservation areas.

INTRODUCTION

Experience has shown that the design of the built environment alone cannot create a neighbourhood in the sense of a fully functioning community. However, good urban design – in other words, responsiveness to the existing context, compatible mix of uses, appropriate buildings to accommodate activities at the right

Perceptions of neighbourhood

1 Mental maps

How do people define their neighbourhood? What are the key nodes, edges and centres of activity?

2 Access and safety

How safe does it feel to move about, for people of all ages and abilities?

3 Image

What images and associations do local people have of the neighbourhood; and why?

4 History

What features do people value as giving a sense of continuity with the past?

New houses and streets can be distinctive (albeit expensive too). Poundbury, Dorchester.

Figure 3.7
19th century former Corn Exchange converted to a library

Sudbury, Suffolk

An excellent example of a new use matching the characteristics of the building, ie: central location, easily identifiable building, top lit main space. The new work to accommodate the library reflects good practice in conservation in that it does not pretend to be 'olde' and is largely removable.

rent, appropriate location and levels of accessibility, all brought together in a place which is attractive and feels safe – can create the conditions where a sense of neighbourliness and belonging is more likely to develop.

This section deals with anchoring and structuring the neighbourhood. It starts from the assumption that a major new scheme (regeneration or urban extension) is to be developed within the neighbourhood. Localities need to be 'anchored' to a place or community if they are to feel like 'neighbourhoods'. This can only develop over time. It is essential to utilise all the possible anchoring devices to generate a sense of continuity and rootedness, which gives a place character and local distinctiveness, reducing criticisms of anonymity and alienation often levelled at and experienced in so many developments.

ANCHORING ELEMENTS IN THE EXISTING ENVIRONMENT

Involving the existing community

The more that the local community is involved in the design and development process of any major scheme affecting the neighbourhood, the greater likelihood there is of evolving a place that has local relevance, and where new proposals have a higher chance of acceptance through the approvals process. The process of involvement requires integrity and a continuing commitment by the design team, and inevitably points to different modes of working and communication. It is unlikely that everyone in the community will wish to be involved, but they will wish to be kept informed. It will be of great value in creating dialogue and reducing suspicion about remote professionals if the design team can locate themselves in a local shop front or office; this can also be used as a drop-in centre and meeting room.

Re-use of existing buildings and structures

Existing redundant or vacant buildings in the scheme area are a positive resource that will lend character to the development as well as, in many cases, valuable accommodation at affordable prices or rents. Existing buildings and structures represent resources in three ways (sometimes all in the same building):

- **Cultural value**: for example, buildings of special architectural or historic interest ('listed' buildings or ancient monuments in the UK). These may be of national or local importance. More mundanely existing names (of streets, areas, fields, farms) may have local resonance and associations.

- **Locally distinctive buildings**. Their former use or function based on the local economy, and/or building materials deriving from the local geology both testify to a sense of local identity (vernacular buildings).

- **Spatial resource**. Buildings provide forms of accommodation which are likely to be more expensive to build and rent as new, especially small shop or business units. It is important to match the spatial characteristics of buildings to their proposed new use in order to reduce wasteful conversion (for example, converting a multi-cellular building to a single-cell space).

Re-use of existing building materials or elements

If, after comprehensive appraisal of the existing buildings in the scheme area, it is proved that retention of some buildings would affect the viability of the scheme or that (exceptionally) a building is beyond repair, then the building could be dismantled carefully in order to re-use as much of the materials and other architectural features as possible. It is likely that in any building built prior to about 1920 the building materials are virtually irreplaceable as they may be 'natural' and may be from long-defunct local sources. Retention and incorporation of these into new buildings will help to reinforce local distinctiveness.

Use of the existing land form

The main criticism of so much contemporary volume housing is that it ignores its context: that standard building forms are designed to a standard layout of roads and plots; that the resultant development is so placeless it could be anywhere.

If we want development to incorporate local distinctiveness it has to be designed as if the site really matters, so that the features, orientation, topography and location of the site have a major influence on the layout of the site and the character of the built form.

Recovering lost but remembered patterns

There are many cases of redevelopment in the twentieth century where the original street pattern was destroyed. As those redevelopments themselves fall into disrepute (and maybe were never loved) there is the chance to recover some of the traditional streets, making connections which were lost, using original names which carry a memory of the history of the place. This can be particularly relevant if the first redevelopment resulted in a less permeable environment. The revived street pattern can promote an accessible, walkable neighbourhood.

LOCAL DISTINCTIVENESS

Neighbourhoods in towns and cities are organic, transforming entities; they are the expression of the interaction of a number of social, economic and physical factors:

- The people (past and present) who lived and/or worked there.
- The types and pattern of activities (past and present) carried out.

Local distinctiveness

The organisation Common Ground has been exploring and developing the concept of local distinctiveness since the 1980s. Below is what they see as the four key elements of the concept:

1 Detail

We need the nourishment of detail, in things as ordinary as rumples in a field, detail in doors and windows, dialect, local festival days, seasonal variation in the goods on sale in the market, to subtly stimulate our senses and sensibilities.

2 Authenticity

The real and the genuine hold a strength of meaning for us.

3 Particularity

The point here is not to be preoccupied by difference, but by appropriateness to and expressiveness of time and place.

4 Patina

Age has to be recognised as having been gathered, hence the paradoxical vitality of patina. Local distinctiveness must be about history continuing through the present (not about the past) and it is about creating the future.

For further information contact Common Ground: www.commonground.org.uk

- The type, size and value of the premises and their plots from where people live, work and spend leisure.
- The location of the neighbourhood in relation to the centre of the urban area.
- The topography of the area.
- The age and style of the buildings.
- The distribution and type of greenspace and streets.
- The materials, whether homogeneous or diverse.
- The condition of the area.
- Ownership patterns.
- The townscape of the area: compact/enclosed/spacious, formal/informal, repetitious, hard-edged/soft-edged.

5.15 Design of the public realm

Whatever the neighbourhood characteristics, there is a sense of local identity perceived by the residents. Perhaps it is a well-established district or quarter, or it was built all at one time, or is characterised by being of a particular architectural style or by using a local building material. The neighbourhood might be physically distinct from its surroundings or just a part of the urban continuum.

TYPES OF NEIGHBOURHOOD

5.9 Analysing form and function

Many established urban neighbourhoods are valued by their residents who wish to see that their qualities are maintained and protected against adverse development, traffic and environmental conditions. Conservation Areas provide this for certain areas but many neighbourhoods do not qualify. Below are some such typical neighbourhood categories:

- Residential villa suburbia: free-standing villas, detached or semi-detached, within relatively extensive plots and set back from the streets. Considerable vegetation (boundary hedges, trees, front gardens, etc.). Usually wide, tree-lined roads.
- Terrace housing in inner suburbia: shallower but well-tended front gardens. Usually some form of grid street pattern with corner shops.

- Inner-city mainly residential area, often identified by a name. Established small-scale mixed uses – workshops and local shopping street, interspersed with terrace housing. Housing often more varied in size and age than the types above

AREAS OF NEIGHBOURHOOD QUALITY

While conservation areas are distinguished by special (in other words outstanding or rare) historic or architectural merit, all communities have an equal right to expect that the aesthetic quality and cultural heritage of their locality is enhanced, not destroyed. The policy (possibly unintended) of allowing ugly neighbourhoods to absorb further ugly or discordant built elements, often compounded by lack of care and maintenance of open spaces as well, is clearly inequitable. It is also unwise, reinforcing a sense of exclusion.

The ideal is to care for every area, place a value on (and value the place of) every community. Given the variety of local environment, policies for neighbourhood quality might be classified under four heads:

- Conserve: enhance the existing neighbourhood quality, protecting and reinforcing local distinctiveness. This might apply to many stable, well-served residential areas as well as formally designated conservation areas.

- Enliven: promote more variety and contrast, and demand high standards, in areas which are perceived as dull or tawdry. This might apply to many commercial enclaves as well as extensive areas of similar housing character, lacking facilities.

- Promote coherence: require conformity to strict design principles to join up and coalesce a disjointed, disparate townscape. Typically this could apply in 'fracture zones' around city centres, or urban/rural fringe areas where there has been sporadic, car-based development.

- Deregulate: adopt a consciously laissez faire aesthetic stance to allow local taste and culture to be expressed. This could occur where the general character of the area reflects (or is beginning to reflect) ethnic diversity and the residents wish to allow individual creativity not conformity. It does not, however, imply a laissez faire attitude to the spatial fundamentals of use and density.

5.13 Change and renewal

Designation

Local neighbourhood or parish councils could take the initiative to promote a new area of neighbourhood quality – or it might come from the local authority. Either way designation would follow extensive public involvement to establish the qualities that are valued (or not), the threats and opportunities that affect those qualities, and also the appropriate boundaries of the neighbourhood. The experience of parish mapping, village design statements, and conservation area character appraisals should be drawn on for such appraisals.

Assessing neighbourhood quality

Parish mapping

A survey undertaken by the community in a parish to celebrate its locally distinctive character, history, culture and customs and its activities. Large-format maps often take the form of collages of detailed work contributed by individuals.

For further information, refer to Common Ground: www.commonground.org.uk

Village design statements (VDSs)

These are compiled with the aid of a local authority conservation officer or other facilitator. The aim is to set out the character of the local built environment and to establish guidelines for sensitive new development and alterations. VDSs can be adopted as Supplementary Planning Guidance.

For further information search for village design statements at the following websites: Campaign for the Protection of Rural England www.planninghelp.org.uk Resource for Urban Design Information www.rudi.net

Conservation Area character appraisals

These reports should be compiled for every Conservation Area, setting out the rationale for the designation of the Conservation Area, its character and appearance, its mix of uses, its evolution, a critique of the issues facing the Area and a programme for improvements. It is undertaken by the Local Authority in consultation with the local community.

For further information, refer to English Heritage guidelines on the appraisal and management of conservation areas available at www.english-heritage.org.uk

3.6

local enterprise

3.6 ACCESS TO JOBS

BASIC PRINCIPLES

Every town or urban township should offer a good range of job opportunities generally matching the character of the local work force. Equivalently, each town should offer a range of workspaces for small businesses, located so as to maximise non-car access by employees and minimise the environmental impact of freight movement. The possibility of home-working should be actively promoted by the planning system.

Reasons

- The possibility of local work opens up choices to residents. This is particularly important for those wanting part-time work – such as carers, house parents and teenagers – or those unable to afford travel.
- Local work allows people to choose to walk or cycle, with lifestyle and health benefits, and reduced emissions.
- Local workspace increases the practicality of setting up new businesses, avoiding the need for time-consuming and polluting car trips to reach suitable accommodation.
- Home-working is a growing trend in terms of both telecommuting and sole trading. It has the potential to reduce travel, support local services and enhance local social interaction.

OPENING UP THE JOB MARKET

There are two polarised myths about the local job market. One is that the creation of local jobs solves unemployment problems. This is an exaggeration. Employers will normally advertise vacant posts city-wide and get the best person for the job: hence the importance of training, and of public transport and road links between localities and main employment centres.

The other myth is that people do not like living near their work and that local job provision has no value. This is equally untrue. While many workers' job-search areas have increased dramatically since the 1970s, others are still very localised, for quite pragmatic reasons. There is a strong correlation between the availability of local jobs, the average length of the journey to work, and the proportion of people walking to work (Stead 1999).

The availability of local work and local workspace helps to support the viability of local shops, cafés and pubs. Many local jobs are related to local services. Local shops, schools, surgeries, pubs, police, social services, etc. provide diverse work opportunities, and can amount to 30 per cent of total demand.

Township job ratio

There is some evidence of a significant threshold in local job provision. The job ratio is defined as the number of job opportunities in an area divided by the number of people available for work. A ratio of 0.7 or more may be associated with shorter trips and more walking. This ratio could be a target for each town/township (Barton et al. 1995, p. 83).

Local jobs and health

If walking or cycling to work results in an increase in physical activity of just one or two hours a week, this can result in a measurable reduction in absenteeism and improvement in productivity (Davis et al. 2007).

THE RIGHT BUSINESS IN THE RIGHT PLACE

Promoting local employment does not justify a locational free-for-all. Location should be related to likely employee and customer catchments and the need for freight access. Businesses that draw on a city-wide or regional market, and/or rely on frequent inter-city trips, should be located centrally. This includes for example the head offices of major firms, universities, major shopping centres. Conversely some activities by their nature serve a more local clientele, and may draw on local workers. They should be located so that people can access them by foot, bike or local bus. For the sake of simplicity the chart below uses scale as a proxy for catchment size – though clearly that is over simplifying the situation – and later guidance in this chapter is much more specific.

Suburban business parks rely on very heavy car use (90–95 per cent) and profligate use of land. They should not be permitted.

Figure 3.8
Using scale as a proxy for catchment

Business	Locational criteria
Large offices (e.g. over 1,000 m²)	Locate only in town and township centres that have centrality in relation to public transport and good connections to intercity rail.
Medium offices (e.g. 100–1,000 m²)	Locate in neighbourhood and township centres, or along high streets, that have good public transport and good foot/pedal accessibility.
Small offices less than 100 m²)	Locate anywhere within the built-up area – typically as home- (e.g. based workplaces, subject to normal environmental safeguards.
Factories/ warehouses	Locate so as to avoid the need for lorries to go through residential and shopping areas, with good access to the national road network and to existing/potential rail or water freight possibilities.
Workshops and nursery units	Locate as for factories or in the higher intensity zones of townships where there is good access to a distributor road.
Backyard workshops	Locate anywhere within the built-up area, subject to the normal environmental and access safeguards.
Other facilities (e.g. retail, educational, leisure)	See in the relevant sections later in the chapter

3.18 Public transport operation: A, B and C locations

DIVERSITY OF ECONOMIC NICHE

Local economic activity creates wealth in the community. It also demonstrates the diversity and connectedness of life. The range of local activities experienced in some market towns and mixed-use inner-city districts can cause noise/disturbance problems but also delight. Progressively fewer small businesses are now real environmental hazards. For these reasons strict zoning policies should be eased. The chart above suggests a flexible approach to small offices and workshops in residential areas, while safeguarding good neighbourliness.

3.6

*Small workshops/offices can be combined with
housing in accessible locations.*

Within any town or urban district we need to ensure diversity
of economic and service opportunity. Replacing land-use zones
with sustainability criteria is part of this; so also is the intentional
planning of a range of economic niches (as in 'ecological niche'
for a particular kind of habitat and range of species). Examples of
niche uses:

- Small workshops caught in the interstices of residential
  streets.
- Double garages sold with ready-made change-of-use
  permission for working space.
- Ground floor space in three/four-storey terraces along
  neighbourhood spine roads designed for change-of-use
  to retail or office.
- Secondary and tertiary shopping areas (where lower
  rents permit more marginal businesses) allowed to
  switch between uses but protected from comprehensive
  redevelopment.
- In-town 'scruffy zones' where building re-use and
  temporary constructions are protected by zoning from
  comprehensive redevelopment (see
  service industry zones below)
- Seedbed business premises with small size-adjustable
  units for subsidised rent (often in railway arches, old
  mills or factories) and access to support services.
- Serviced community workspace for professional firms
  and sole traders, with shared reception/IT
  services/coffee room/van hire, etc.
- 'Solicitors' row': highly accessible on or adjacent to the
  main street, with attractive setting and buildings.
- Craft workshops in association with exhibition/meeting
  space and café, behind the main street frontage (rents
  being lower), in old school or mill building.

The suggestions here rely on local enterprise but may be
facilitated by positive, non-bureaucratic official attitudes plus
judicious financial support for start-ups and non-profit activities.
Community networking helps create the right environment for
initiative.

Creating low rent opportunities

Left to itself, the market for new development tends to create
a monochrome world of high rent uses such as business parks,
retail malls or housing for sale. By contrast most older towns
and inner city areas have areas – such as the 'lower' high street
and aging industrial estates – which provide opportunity for less
profitable (often very local) enterprises. Creating or maintaining
these economic niches in boom times relies on determined
community action. The survival of some of the uses above might
depend on planning permission being refused for change of use. It
may sometimes be better to have some temporary untidiness in
the environment rather than sacrifice any economic diversity.

5.10 Land needs

Scruffy zones

A basic principle is that every small town and every urban township should have one or more small scale industrial estates, or service zones. Such estates were common-place in earlier eras, but are rarely planned as part of a new urban extension. Given rigorous protection from higher rent paying activities, a laisser faire attitude to use and building quality can be allowed to prevail – scruffy zones. They can provide for a wide range of local services, workshops, recycling activities, builders merchants, small scale manufacturers, repairers, starter units and mucky/noisy uses. These estates should if possible be located so that commercial vehicles can access them without passing through residential areas. But they should be close enough into the town to permit easy access by non-motorised means, and to make necessary vehicle trips for collection of large or heavy items as short as possible. These scruffy zones provide for local economic vitality and the useful services without which any settlement is incomplete.

SEEDING LOCAL GROWTH

Local economic regeneration can be promoted in a number of ways: in brief ...

Local Agenda 21 or transition town meetings may draw together 'movers and shakers' – perhaps as part of a community planning exercise – and create opportunities for co-operation. Often people are meeting properly for the first time. They discover shared concerns and enthusiasms. Such meetings can provide fertile ground for seeding new ideas, often serendipitously.

Local employment policies may be promoted by business and the local authorities. Certain jobs can be specifically advertised very locally (not across the city or county), linked to training and regeneration initiatives. For example, a publicly funded neighbourhood nursery school could employ part-time untrained parent assistants to work with an experienced childcare person. The spin-offs in such situations can be many: income for families, socialisation and shared play for children, boosted confidence in childcare for the assistants (reflected then in their own homes), social contact and parental support networks.

Local training and adult education is demand-responsive and will not necessarily result in local work. But the localisation of basic skills training (provided by technical colleges or special-needs charities) increases accessibility for client groups (often unskilled and/or young) and boosts local social interaction. Local space may depend on collaboration between the service provider, the local authority and secondary school or local enterprise.

Advice and support on business planning, funding, management and accommodation may be provided by banks, local authorities, voluntary organisations or government. It should

Scruffy zones come in many forms.

Some homeworking facts

- *Over 25 per cent of the UK workforce carry out some of their work at home*

- *680,000 (in 1998) worked mainly from home, and this is increasing around 20 per cent per annum*

- *Women account for two-thirds of those working mainly from home*

- *60 per cent of those working at home part-time rely on telephone and computer*

- *1.5 million people telecommuted at least one day a week in 2000*

SOURCE: Dwelly 2000

'Zoning the rigid separation of residential, commercial and industrial areas – is a planning system completely at odds with the new ways people live and work. Applying land-use regulations to activities carried out in single rooms in buildings, in particular, now looks preposterous.' (Dwelly 2000).

be free, accessible and comprehensive – a one-stop shop at the centre of a district that can provide avenues to help on all fronts. This relies on co-ordination in terms both of space available and services offered.

WORKING FROM HOME

Home-based working is increasing rapidly and is a key part of any strategy for local economic diversification. It is being facilitated not only by the potential for telecommuting but also by smaller households and more space per household. The likely benefits of home-working are:

- it opens up work and lifestyle choice for individuals

- it creates extra patronage of local services and reinforcement of local social networks

- there may be a reduced need to travel for work purposes.

High speed internet access is progressively making home-working more viable and attractive. However, the outsourcing of work by firms can lead to worker isolation, and the overall travel benefits are unproven. The promotion of 'televillages' in small settlements may indeed be counterproductive if it encourages households to move there who were previously in more accessible locations (this is based on evidence from Crickhowell Televillage – Paternoster 2000).

Policies for homeworking

- Abolish tenancy, leasing, rating and zoning restrictions which deter homeworking.

- Promote homeworking as part of any regeneration or new development programme, incorporating high bandwidth infrastructure alongside water, gas and electricity.

- Estimate housing needs (in the context of development plans or social housing provision) on the assumption of providing most households with a spare room/flexible space.

- Encourage provision of live-work units as part of major development projects.

- Support local retail/community facilities and a pleasant pedestrian environment, which can help compensate homeworkers for their working isolation.

3.7 RESILIENT LOCAL ECONOMIES

KEY PRINCIPLE

Every city should identify an urban district, and every county a town, as beacons of economic sustainability, where a developing cluster of businesses trail blazes green management and environmentally sustainable processes. These green business zones rely on strong motivation of the participating businesses and support from the local authority. They are there to provide inspiration for the rest of the city or county, fostering an innovative and resilient economy

Explanation

Support for the scruffy end of town (as in the previous section) is part of a much bigger principle of working towards a sustainable economy, helping to transform economic priorities so that scarce resources are conserved, pollution is minimised, quality of work is valued and local economic diversity provides a hedge against global uncertainties. It has been argued that to achieve this in the current situation we need to create 'Islands of Sustainability' (Wallner, Narodoslawsky and Moser 1996): particular areas, with local business backing, can act as beacons, lighting the way to a healthy and sustainable future. They can be centres of innovation and experiment, hopefully showing by success that social and environmental responsibility can go hand in hand with wealth creation.

STRATEGY FOR A SUSTAINABLE ECONOMY

Inspiring action

There is a widespread lack of awareness or engagement with the idea of sustainable development in the small/medium businesses community. Apart from lack of incentive and lack of time the main perceived barriers are concerned with extra costs and bureaucratic procedures. This resistance can sometimes be overcome by a combination of carrots and sticks, some external to the local area:

- Inspirational examples pointing the way, making good business sense
- Easy-to-use tools or approaches made accessible
- Business survival threats – such as increasing cost of waste disposal
- New legislation forcing a rethink, creating new opportunities
- Local business networks sharing good practice
- Opportunities triggered by development plans and regeneration strategies

This civic tip in Leamington Spa, England, gives people the option of leaving unwanted items for re-sale instead of landfill. The project also repairs items and provides training and employment.

Green business development

Green and ethical business can take many forms, spanning all sectors of the economy, for example: renewable energy, low energy products, water management, low impact processing, reuse and recycling (including retail, wholesale, processing and manufacture), organic food production and distribution, crafts using locally available materials, environmental services, IT tools for sustainability, educational and charitable services, etc. In the industrial and commercial spheres the change to green approaches can result in improved brand value, access to new markets, and in some cases cost savings and better productivity.

The idea of a beacon of economic sustainability – an area or settlement defined as a 'green business zone', maybe as part of a regeneration strategy – can act as a catalyst for innovation. Its success will depend on more than just defining an area and hoping for the best:

- Are there a few existing green businesses that are interested in spearheading the green business zone, acting as flagships?

- Are the key local business networks on board, supporting the initiative and promoting sharing of learnt experience, maybe willing and able to broker deals?

- Have voluntary or business networks reviewed the inputs and outputs of local firms and bodies, analysing goods 'from cradle to grave to cradle', to establish how far the waste from one process can be used as raw material for another?

- Is the technical college actively developing green training programmes for potential entrepreneurs, workers, managers in a range of locally appropriate spheres?

- Are links established with the nearest university's research and technology institutes, with channels being opened for incubation units for creative business ideas?

- Are the local financial institutions supportive in principle, willing to devise risk-spreading funding arrangements? NB. There are national and international banks and institutions who specialise in sustainable and ethical business support.

- Is there a single point of contact to ease access to information and entry to the business networks.

Environmental auditing

Apart from the product or service on offer, which might be considered sustainable, there are issues about how the business's own activities impact on environmental capital, including climate change. Many enterprises that are not necessarily part of the emerging green economy should contribute to the overall reduction of pollution and resource use. The green business zone can act as a demonstration of what is possible. There are savings to be made through greater resource efficiency and better use of land. An environmental audit should encompass:

■ Energy efficiency and energy sourcing, for buildings and processes

■ Water sourcing, use-efficiency, reuse, treatment and drainage

■ Pollution controls; air, water and soil quality outcomes

■ Purchasing strategies and their environmental and ethical implications

■ Reuse and maintenance regimes, recycling and waste disposal strategies

■ Transport of raw materials and goods to and from the enterprise

■ Accessibility and transport energy efficiency for employees and clients

■ Biodiversity on site, and habitat implications of processes and purchasing

■ Cultural and aesthetic assets (buildings, spaces) – their quality and maintenance

■ The overall carbon and environmental footprint

Travel plans

A key part of the environmental strategy is the travel plan. For many organisations the biggest environmental impact is due to the way in which people access the business, as employees, clients or customers. It is vital that the green business zone has an integrated travel plan and monitors its implementation and efficacy. The zone should be an exemplar:

■ Choosing a location that maximises the potential for low energy transport modes while minimising the average distance to be travelled

■ Through its development triggering improvements in pedestrian and cycling networks and public transport services

■ Supporting active travel, and penalising car travel, by clear financial signals, including car park charging for employees, owners, and clients/customers as well if appropriate

Look after local shops and suppliers. They provide more local jobs per pound spent. St. Helens, Isle of Wight, England.

■ Ensuring excellent provision on site for cyclists and walkers, and including mixed use facilities for lunchtime and post work sustenance, socialising, recreation and shopping

■ Releasing land progressively from car parking to other, more productive and profitable uses as public transport services and cycling connectivity improves

THE LOCAL MULTIPLIER

The purpose of promoting a green business zone is to show the way forward towards a more sustainable and resilient local economy. Four key principles are:

■ Business diversity, avoiding over-dependence on a few major employers. This is especially important when the large employer is a branch of an international firm. Branch factories are more vulnerable to closure than indigenous firms. In addition where ownership of the firm is elsewhere profits are lost to the local community.

■ Local supply networks, which circulate the money locally between companies, reinforcing a virtuous cycle. This is the so-called multiplier effect. Much of the money is re-spent in the local area rather than leaking out to other places. According to one calculation the multiplier effect (and thus the local economic benefit for a given turnover) for an organic vegetable box company is twice that of a local supermarket which is part of a national chain (Ward and Lewis 2002).

■ Local employment: companies and institutions giving first preference to local applicants over more distant applicants, other things being equal, help strengthen this multiplier effect, because employees will spend some or all of their income locally. In addition employing locals reduces travel distance, carbon emissions, and travel time/stress for the employee.

■ Export or die! That is an exaggeration but highlights a basic reality, that it is vital that some of the people and businesses of a settlement sell their wares elsewhere, or to visitors, thus drawing finance into the community and helping to sustain it. The internal market by itself (i.e. full localisation) is not sufficient. The art is to export to the wider region and the world, then use the resulting surplus for *several* local transactions before resorting (perforce) to buying from the world. In buying from the world, preference should be given to closer sources where feasible: first the region, if not that the country, then further afield where necessary. (Ideally it is more sophisticated than this – working out the overall carbon and social costs of each good purchased, and making a choice on that basis).

Decaying communities

There are particular issues when developing a regeneration strategy for a deprived settlement or neighbourhood. Residents typically have low incomes and therefore little spending power. This can result in a chronic dependence on external supply. Any money (earned or from social security) is sucked out of the community because the retailers and other suppliers are based elsewhere. In this situation radical measures to change the population balance and introduce new impetus are essential.

But regeneration can also be fostered from within by mutual aid. For example, credit unions, community-based zero-interest banks, informal exchange mechanisms, can help. The attitude of businesses or public institutions based in the area is critical. If they give local people priority in employment they can assist their prospects by training them and raising confidence and aspirations. If some dynamism returns to the community then those businesses will be well placed to benefit.

THE INFORMAL ECONOMY

The economic wealth of an area is not measured purely in terms of monetary income, but in terms of actual goods and services. Mutual help, barter systems and volunteering create an informal economy, often breaking down barriers between social, recreational and economic activity, and benefiting local people in many ways.

Initiatives for informal economic activity come primarily from individuals and groups choosing to work together. However, local authorities and business can seek to support such initiative by grants, space and flexible interpretation of regulations. The essential attitude of officials is responsiveness – responding to requests for help, facilitating contact-making, co-ordinating the authority's stance.

Promoting the informal economy is a key part of any regeneration strategy. Consider:

■ The provision of, and multi-cultural access to, community halls and meeting rooms.

■ Free or cost-rent availability of small community offices in public buildings or by local enterprises.

■ Creating potential market space at the heart of every town or township.

■ Safeguarding some cheap storage and workshop space within each township from renewal – for community (or small business) use – see scruffy zones in 3.6.

■ Supporting the creation of LETS (Local Exchange and Trading Schemes) or time-banks which reinforce the local trading of services and are particularly relevant in areas of higher unemployment or low (formal) activity rates.

The informal economy takes many forms:

- *baby-sitting circles*
- *parent and toddler groups*
- *food co-ops*
- *community gardens*
- *allotments and home-growing*
- *Local Economic Trading Systems (LETS)*
- *Environmental Improvement Action Groups*
- *Credit Unions (though also part of the formal economy)*

3.8

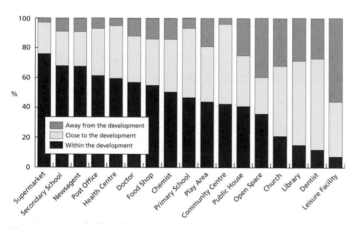

Figure 3.9

Percentage of trips made to services when they are provided locally

This chart is based on peripheral estates in the Bristol sub-region – often designed primarily for car use, not pedestrians, and having very high levels of car ownership. Taking the two categories 'within the development' and 'close to the development' together, the use of local facilities is surprisingly high – for example 93 per cent of primary schools trips, 95 per cent of health centre trips and 97 per cent of supermarket trips, where these facilities are locally available.

SOURCE: Barton et al. 2000, based on Winter and Farthing 1997

access to local facilities

What is 'local'?

Access to local facilities is fundamental to the concept of a neighbourhood. It is commonly said that for a village to be a village it needs a church, a shop, a pub and a primary school. A small town, or an urban district functioning as a 'township' within the city, needs more. It needs the full range of social, retail, educational, health and recreational facilities to allow people – especially those of limited means or mobility – to carry on daily life if they so choose. That means that the main food/convenience stores and durable goods (though not specialist) stores; banks and post offices; health centres, secondary school, library and leisure centre; playgrounds, parks and playing fields – should all be local. Accessibility is the central concept: accessibility by foot or bike, motorised wheelchair or local bus.

3.8 PLANNING LOCAL ACCESSIBILITY

BASIC PRINCIPLES

Localised provision of facilities to permit access by foot, bike and local bus should be fundamental to the planning of every neighbourhood, urban district or small town. This means having a sound understanding of the evolving needs of market and institutional service providers and investors. It also means knowing, through active public engagement and survey, how people currently behave, where they go, how they get there, what they feel is lacking locally. It is important to plan for viability through clustering of facilities, flexible catchment size and access by all modes. Specific standards of accessibility (detailed later) should be negotiated with service providers and, where possible, market interests. Where local facilities are missing or in decline, then strategies for neighbourhood revival (e.g. densification, social diversity, increased connectivity, social infrastructure investment, environmental improvement – all discussed elsewhere in this guide) are essential for health and sustainability.

Reasons for local provision

■ The availability of local services, including schools, health services, convenience stores and post-offices, is a continuing and sometimes vociferous concern of local people.

■ The exercise involved in local walking and cycling trips – particularly for children – is important for health and well-being.

■ The meetings (casual or planned) that occur at local facilities, or on the streets getting there, reinforce local networks of support and a sense of community, which are important for psychological health.

- Local facilities – especially retailing – are important providers of local jobs, and help recycle money locally.

- Local provision encourages local trips, with a significant proportion of those by foot (ECOTEC 1993; Winter and Farthing 1997; Barton et al. 2000: 60), thus reducing the need for car use and helping to achieve pollution/congestion-reduction targets.

The systematic approach

A proactive stance is needed by local communities and councils if the long-term trend in most areas towards increased car dependence and loss of local facilities is to be reversed. The overall planning of economic development, land use and transport within a town or city region is key – and largely beyond the scope of this book (though see Chapter 5). Local knowledge and political pressure is also vital. The main elements of a systematic neighbourhood or town assessment are listed below:

- Do a stock-take of all facilities locally available – their presence and quality – and identify

  - the gaps in provision

  - The competing or gap-plugging attractions

  - The approximate catchment population (size and nature) they might rely on

- Do a household survey (at least a hundred households) to establish how people currently behave: the facilities they use, the way they normally get to them, the amount of trip chaining (i.e. where people visit several facilities before returning home)

- Through a public meeting or focus group workshops (as well as the survey) discover what people think about their local facilities, what they consider most important functionally and socially, and what they feel about their accessibility – for example deterrents to walking or cycling

- Map all the facilities and the route network, working out how far people are travelling to access facilities, how far they are able or prepared to walk or cycle (this can be done by hand or by geographical information systems (GIS))

- Compare actual behaviour with the average accessibility criteria suggested in this chapter, and agree what standards should be applied in your area

- On the basis of all this, discuss options with service providers (private, state and voluntary), argue for change to strategic planning and transport policies if appropriate, prepare neighbourhood or town plans for longer term change, work with voluntary groups to achieve short-term benefits

5.7 The scope of neighbourhood appraisal

Recommendations

- *Undertake a study of local conditions and spatial patterns.*

- *Collaborate with stakeholders in agreeing the principle of equitable accessibility standards.*

- *Select accessibility standards that are viable with actual routes and catchment population, not theoretical.*

- *Seek to increase permeability and reduce barriers to movement by foot and bike, making routes more direct.*

- *Seek to ensure a reasonably even distribution of facilities and avoid isolated pockets of housing.*

- *Gradually increase dwelling densities, to increase local catchments, or at least to maintain population as household size declines.*

Comparing trip distance accross the twelve areas - Arranged by percentage of trips under 1600m

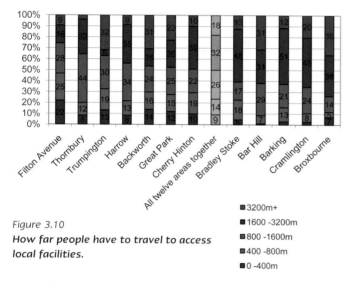

Figure 3.10

How far people have to travel to access local facilities.

3200m+
1600 -3200m
800 -1600m
400 -800m
0 -400m

Comparing modal split in twelve areas - Arranged by level of walking/cycling

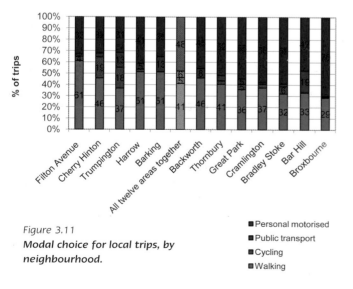

Figure 3.11

Modal choice for local trips, by neighbourhood.

Personal motorised
Public transport
Cycling
Walking

CONTRASTS IN EXISTING LOCALITIES

The significance of undertaking specific local studies can be appreciated if we study the huge discrepancies between different places. The charts in the side column are derived from a major study (2005–9) of suburban neighbourhoods and satellite settlements in four English city regions: London, Bristol, Newcastle and Cambridge. About 130 households responded in each area, on average a healthy 30% response rate. They were asked what local facilities they used and how they got there. The journeys included in the survey were for food shopping, other retail services, schools, inside and outdoor leisure activities. Reports on this work can be found on www.suburbansolutions.ac.uk.

How local is local?

Figure 3.10 illustrates the variation in the distance residents have to (or choose to) travel in order to access facilities. Taking the distance of 1600 metres or one mile as signifying 'local' the people of one neighbourhood satisfy 75% of their needs locally, while at the other extreme the figure is 26%. The average figure across all twelve localities was 50%. If we take 800 metres or half a mile as the critical distance, then the average local use is only 26%, and the range 9–47%. These figures show both the degree to which generalisations are dangerous, and also the conspicuous failure of many places to provide for local need.

Walking and cycling

The variation between communities is also marked in terms of modal choice (Figure 3.11). The range of car dependence is from 33% to 70%. Conversely the proportion of active travel (walking and cycling) is from 29% to 65%. It is noteworthy that two communities, both in Cambridge, have a much higher share for cycling. The difference in order between this and the previous chart is significant. For instance the households in the part of Barking (in East London) surveyed had relatively low levels of income and car ownership, and therefore high levels of walking, but had to travel considerable distances to access some essential facilities.

The third chart (Figure 3.12) shows the fall-off in active travel as distance increases. It also illustrates the perhaps surprising consistency of behaviour across the three Bristol study areas, despite contrasts in social and physical character. This was not the case across all twelve. People in Barking perforce walked longer distances. People in Broxbourne were not prepared to walk as far.

Cars, culture and form

There are three principle reasons for the difference between places. These are the level of car ownership (which itself is affected by income and location); the distinctive culture of the area; and the physical form and land use/movement pattern. In some situations culture (or attitude, or preference) can be very attitude to cycling from the British. Some Dutch towns have 60% of trips by bike. But within the majority of British neighbourhoods as indicated by this study, form is the critical factor. There is a reasonable consistency in terms of how far people are willing to walk. The difference between, say, Filton Avenue and Bradley Stoke is largely accounted for by the presence or absence of local facilities, together with the directness or otherwise of the route network. Density, incidentally, does not appear to be a key factor in these suburban locations.

Key thresholds of non-motorised accessibility

Accepting that particular places may well be different, and also that behaviour can change over time, the third chart does nevertheless begin to give a basis for selecting general accessibility standards based on walkability:

- 75%+ of trips by foot or pedal   up to 600 metres

- 50%+ of trips by foot or pedal   up to 1000 metres

Note, however, that different trip purposes are associated with different thresholds. People walk less far for food shopping at superstores, and further for school and outdoor recreation trips. The oft quoted 'pedshed' threshold of 800 metres equates to around 60% of trips on foot.

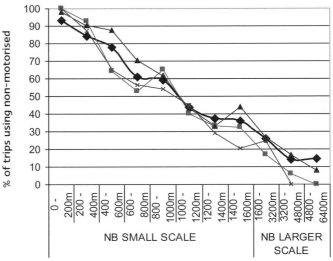

Figure 3.12

How the percentage of trips using non-motorised means varies for trips of different distance, differentiated by study area – Bristol.

—◆— All twelve areas together
—■— Bradley Stoke
—▲— Filton Ave
—✕— Thornbury

Catchment area radius										
	200 m		400 m		600 m		800 m		1,000 m	
Gross residential density	Direct routes	**Bendy routes**	Direct routes	**Bendy routes**	Direct routes	**Bendy routes**	Direct routes	**Bendy routes**	Direct routes	**Bendy routes**
30 ppha	375	**210**	1,500	**850**	3,400	**1,900**	6,100	**3,400**	9,600	**5,300**
40 ppha	520	**280**	2,000	**1,130**	4,600	**2,500**	8,200	**4,600**	12,000	**7,000**
60 ppha	780	**420**	3,000	**1,700**	6,900	**3,800**	12,000	**6,900**	19,000	**10,600**
80 ppha	1,000	**500**	4,000	**2,260**	9,000	**5,100**	16,000	**9,000**	25,000	**14,000**
100 ppha	1,300	**700**	5,000	**2,820**	11,300	**6,300**	20,000	**11,300**	31,000	**17,500**

ppha = persons per hectare

FLEXIBLE CATCHMENTS

In an increasingly privatised economy it is often not possible or appropriate to define specific catchments for specific services. The principles of consumer choice, and the fact of high mobility, means that local people may or may not choose to use local facilities. Some facilities, when available locally, are very heavily used – for example supermarkets and health centres (see Figure 3.9); others much less so – for example churches and dentists.

Figure 3.13

Catchment populations

NB: Bendy routes assume 75 per cent of the direct-line radius, giving around 55 per cent of the catchment population

5.11 Designing
neighbourhood cells

5.12 Linear districts
and towns

The pattern of catchment and movement must therefore be planned so as to permit ease of access between neighbourhoods as much as within them (this point is taken up in Chapter 5).

Changing patterns of service provision and of retailing also point to the need for a flexible and open system of land-use control. New commercial initiatives (e.g. 'one-stop' local shops, filling station shops, private nursery schools, local office services) which enhance provision need to be welcomed.

REVERSING DECLINE

The general long-term decline of local facilities – caused by falling population densities as well as consumer choice and car use – is matched by increasing unit size of facilities. The result is longer trips and poorer local accessibility. In some outlying estates and rural settlements this trend has effectively disenfranchised whole sections of the population who do not possess individual mobility, or who lose their mobility. It is therefore vital to have a clear and flexible strategy for reversing the trends and for taking best advantage of opportunities that present themselves. There are potentially some powerful levers: service providers – particularly education and health – need to adopt user accessibility as a key objective. Briefs for major brownfield or greenfield residential development should specify facility provision – with the principles written into the spatial plan.

MEASURING CATCHMENT POPULATIONS

Despite the fact that people sometimes choose not to use local facilities, it remains a vital planning goal to give everybody the option. Policy is likely to rely on assumptions about catchment populations and appropriate accessibility standards. The accompanying tables illustrate the degree of variation of catchment population with different assumptions about density, distance and route directness. Note that:

■ Catchment population varies directly in proportion to gross population density (i.e. including all the local land uses). Net density is not a good indicator.

■ Modest increases in access standard result in major changes of catchment (e.g. 600 m gives more than double 400 m).

■ Actual routes are not normally direct and this dramatically reduces the catchment population – if average distances are a third longer, then the catchment radius is 75 per cent of the direct-line radius, and the population is 56 per cent of the direct-line catchment.

■ In reality facilities are not evenly distributed across an urban area, and the urban area itself is varied in pattern and shape. Thus in some areas it may be impractical, for the moment at least, to set rigorous accessibility standards.

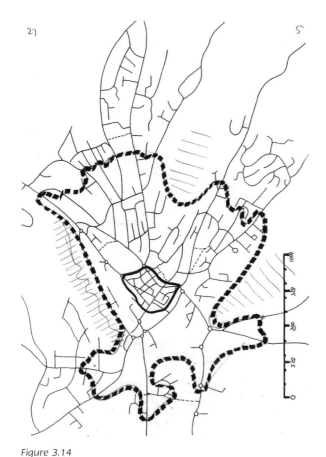

Figure 3.14
Catchment analysis

Stroud: 800 m
'Pedshed' measured along pedestrian routes from the edge of the town centre, revealing quirks in the access pattern.

3.9 ACCESSIBILITY CRITERIA

Accessibility standards are used to ensure facilities are as walkable as possible. The actual standard chosen, however, cannot just reflect the distance people are willing to walk. It also needs to recognise the scale of the facility, the number of people required to support it, the density of the area and the vagaries of geography. Standards for common facilities are given in the table below.

5.4 Graded density

Local facility	Illustrative catchment populations (to be adapted to local conditions and policies)	Minimum reasonable accessibility standards at different gross densities (assuming bendy routes)			
		40 ppha	60 ppha	80 ppha	100 ppha
Nursery/first school	2,000	600 m	500 m	400 m	400 m
Primary/middle school	4,000	800 m	700 m	600 m	500 m
Secondary school	8,000	1,200 m	1,000 m	700 m	700 m
Secondary school (large)	16,000	1,500 m	1,200 m	1,000 m	1,000 m
Health centre (4 doctors)	10,000	1,200 m	1,000 m	900 m	800 m
Local shop	1,500	500 m	400 m	400 m	300 m
Pub	6,000	1,000 m	800 m	700 m	600 m
Post office	5,000	800 m	700 m	600 m	600 m
Community centre	4,000	800 m	600 m	600 m	500 m
Local centre	6,000	1,000 m	800 m	700 m	600 m
District centre/superstore	24,000	1,900 m	1,500 m	1,300 m	1,200 m
Leisure centre	24,000	1,900 m	1,500 m	1,300 m	1,200 m

Figure 3.15
Minimum accessibility standards for compact settlements by density

Note: these thresholds are based purely on catchment populations needed to support the facility. Overleaf are more practical suggestions!

How to use accessibility criteria

In major urban extensions it is reasonable for the community to expect developers and service providers to achieve good standards of local facility accessibility. Appropriate standards can be agreed and incorporated into the spatial strategy and subsequent development briefs.

In fully built-up areas the ability to achieve any standards is highly constrained by existing morphology and ownership. This is particularly the case in hilly or poorly planned settlements. Standards cannot be mandatory, but may be a starting point for negotiation. Infill or redevelopment projects may be guided by accessibility standards. Service providers should identify gaps and seek to fill them.

ILLUSTRATIVE CRITERIA FOR A TOWN

Accessibility criteria need to reflect:

- the gross densities that are achievable

- the catchment populations of different facilities

- the degree of permeability/directness of pedestrian/cycling routes

- the general shape of the town

- the propensity of users to walk to specific facilities

- the siting requirements (some facilities require more land and are therefore less locationally flexible)

- the need for some standardisation, for ease of understanding/planning.

Figure 3.16
llustrative accessibility criteria

Adapted from Barton et al. 1995

These criteria are suggested merely as starting points for discussion. They are judgements based on the factors listed on the right. Most are explained more fully in subsequent sections. (Distance in kilometers)

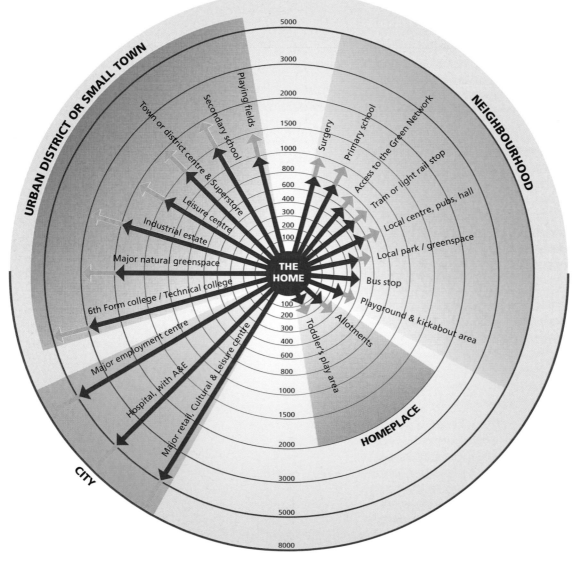

3.10 LOCAL SHOPS AND SERVICES

BASIC PRINCIPLES

Local retail and service facilities should be clustered together to reinforce their viability, provide choice and encourage trip chaining, at locations which are well served by pedestrian, bike, bus and general purpose routes. These local centres should be attractive and convivial places to spend time. They should be located to maximise both the local accessible catchment population, and potential customers from further afield – preferably in the form of a high street that offers variable catchments as businesses adapt to changing market conditions.

The potential benefits

- Local convenience and accessibility, especially through trip chaining.

- Reduced car travel and emissions – where local shopping facilities are good most people use them; and where they are close (<500 m) most people walk to them (Saye 1999).

- Local employment opportunities, and increased viability of both retail and social facilities.

- Opportunities for local fresh produce to be supplied.

- Informal social contact, building social capital and promoting a sense of belonging.

- Responsiveness to particular local needs/tastes.

- Awareness of elderly/frail shop or facility users and potential alertness to their health problems.

- Clustering also increases the proportion of people using public transport rather than the private car (Cervero 1993).

LOCATING LOCAL CENTRES

Local neighbourhood centres should be supported by a planning strategy aimed at maximising their accessibility and attractiveness:

1 Pedestrian flows

Local shopping centres flourish on streets with the greatest connectivity to surrounding areas, where the footfall is naturally highest. Policy should work to increase pedestrian and cycle connectivity further by creating new links and overcoming severance effects (e.g. severance by heavy traffic flows).

2 Public transport networks

Historic centres are normally at the hub of local bus routes. New or revitalised centres should be too, giving the option of bus

Proportion of walking / cycling trips to local food shops, by distance

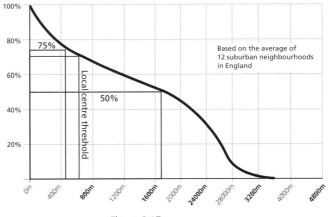

Figure 3.17

Accessibility thresholds

Local centres are valued if they are close. 600m is the best that can be achieved at 60 persons per hectare gross density and 6000 catchment population. At that distance on average 70% of trips are on foot.

Wherever possible new housing must be located within 600 m of an existing/proposed viable local centre.

travel to those travelling from further away. Bus stops should be located conveniently in front of the shops and facilities clustered so as to permit access (e.g. all parts of the centre within 300 m of regular service stops).

3   Visibility and passing trade

Shops should not be hidden away in inward-looking neighbourhoods (where they are likely to fail), but open to general view, particularly to passing car and bus travellers: easy advertising, extended market. Local shopping centres must be close to distributor roads serving the wider residential area to permit casual purchases on the way to and from home. (This is not a cop out! The alternative is for the purchase to be made elsewhere, sometimes involving special trips rather than en route, and significantly reducing local retail viability.)

4   Locational flexibility

Along with catchment flexibility goes a degree of locational flexibility for small shops and businesses. In the context of a main local distributor, with a 'high street' character and regular bus services, retailers should be able to choose their location. So housing along the distributor road should be capable of converting to retail, and vice versa. Location and catchment flexibility gives commerce more freedom to respond to changing conditions and seize opportunities. It helps ensure diversity of provision.

Figure 3.18
The quality of the shopping environment is key to success

This is an analysis of Coleford town centre by Roger Evans and Associates

SOURCE: Gloucestershire Market Towns 2000

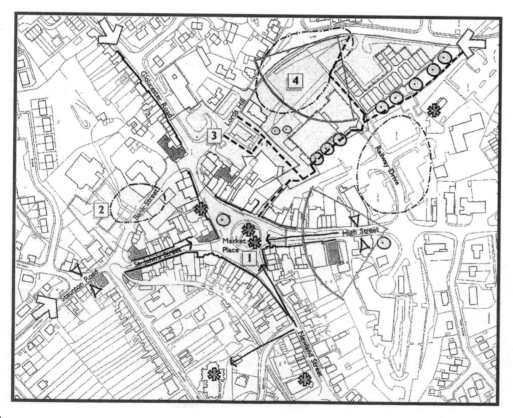

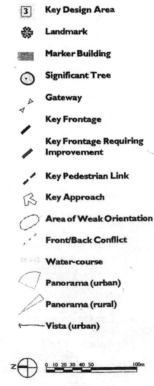

5   Core retail areas

The point when residents feel they have arrived in a local shopping centre is important in relation to footfall, turnover, and perceptions of distance walked to 'get to the shops'. If at all possible, maintain active retail frontage from that point on. Continuous frontage on one side of the street is better than the same number of outlets discontinuous on both sides.

6   Diversity

It is important to promote diversity of retail and non-retail uses within local and township centres, making use of side streets, squares, arcades, etc. to increase the compact capacity of the centre. The reasons for this are:

- the convenience of linked journeys: i.e. fulfilling several purposes in one trip

- evidence that such convenience is valued by consumers, enhances social opportunity and boosts vitality and viability

- the reduction of journeys (due to trip chaining) reduces energy use and CO_2 emissions

- the diversity allows mutual reinforcement between activities: for example, office workers can shop during the lunch hour and frequent the pub after work

- the spread of travel demand over a longer period of the day increases the viability of bus services, and the capacity of the road network.

SPECIFIC LOCAL FACILITIES

Village and corner shops

The village shop and the neighbourhood corner shop are important contributors to the social as well as the economic fabric. Strategies to support them should involve market, voluntary and local authority action.

- Retailing organisations (for example publicans, petrol companies and the post office) need to recognise a responsibility to be creative in building partnerships to maintain local viability.

- Community groups can support or run local outlets through consumer co-operatives, LETS schemes and voluntary clubs.

- Local authorities can offer rate rebates and a flexible attitude to local retail planning applications.

Small general stores (e.g. 50 or 100 m2), located in residential areas outside main shopping parades, have had their viability undermined by changing shopping habits and falling population densities. However, urban intensification and renaissance could create new opportunities at points of high localised pedestrian

Diversity helps vitality.

Local shops support social capital and community networks.

Decline of local shops in the UK

According to data from HM Revenue & Customs, 2,978 greengrocers closed between the 11 years from 1997 to 2008, a decline of more than 50%. In addition, 2,700 butchers and fishmongers closed between 2001 and 2008.

Reported in the Telegraph, 8th June 2008

3.10

Figure 3.19
The relative decline in local grocery shops
SOURCE: WHO (1999)

Village shop support scheme

The Village Shop Support project, a rural project in south Norfolk, involved a package of measures aimed at helping small village shops survive, thrive and improve the service they offer; and hence the health and quality of life for people in local communities. Can we offer something similar in urban neighbourhoods?

Objectives

* *To improve the shopping environment*
* *To attract more customers*
* *To improve accessibility*
* *To enhance the skills of shopkeepers*
* *To encourage the supply of more local produce*
* *To encourage greater use of shops by local people*

The partnership included Tesco Stores plc, Rural Development Commission, Norfolk and Waveney Training and Enterprise Council, Norwich Enterprise Agency Trust.

---

flow. If local initiatives bubble up, then local councils should support them, with easy change-of-use regulations and, if possible, rates reduction. In new-build areas, adaptable building types are required on street corners where pedestrian flows are likely to be high.

Public houses

Large pubs – normally part of regional or national chains – should be located in-centre, helping to bring vitality to township/neighbourhood centres, benefiting from workers' and shoppers' trade, and encouraging access by foot/pedal/public transport.

Small pubs are a dying breed. Many recent suburbs have none at all. The potential for new 'locals' is hampered by licensing and planning restrictions, but also by the absence of houses suitable for conversion into public houses.

An alternative approach would be to create opportunities for small-scale local provision by:

■ ensuring over time that every neighbourhood has properties where the ground floor can be converted to pub/café/office/retail use – typically larger terraced units fronting directly onto the street at a node of pedestrian activity

■ permitting small pubs/cafés (maximum customer space specified) to set up in such locations with zero parking requirements

■ easing the licensing regulations, especially where a voluntary group has set up a community-run pub in an area lacking such facilities.

Filling stations

In some smaller settlements filling stations can offer the best opportunity for a local convenience store. Their location in-settlement (not outside it) is important. The retail element should be planned for local non-car access as well as for car users.

Hairdressers

Single practitioners (often operating from one room in their own homes) are entirely appropriate in residential areas: they diversify household income and provide a valued service within easy walking distance of local clients, part of the indigenous neighbourhood economy. Conversely, larger establishments, with several employees, benefit from the visibility, trip-purpose sharing and social opportunities of an in-centre location where access by bus is possible.

Community halls

These are essential local facilities, helping to gel the community, and should be located close to the nucleus of the neighbourhood (see Section 3.4).

3.11 TOWN CENTRE VITALITY

HIGH STREETS IN CRISIS

Many town, district and local shopping centres are declining as a result of an increasingly mobile society, 'consolidation' of retail trade into fewer outlets, the growth of out-of-town retailing and internet shopping. The latest major threats to the high street are from the banks, which are 'rationalising', and superstore pharmacies, which may replace their high-street competitors. In some centres, however, there is a compensating trend towards a café culture: the role of high streets is becoming more explicitly social.

Arresting decline

The spiral of decline can only be arrested by a concerted effort on the part of all partners, not least the local residents themselves. In the case of smaller (neighbourhood) centres, community-planning exercises could provide the momentum towards a co-ordinated strategy. In larger (town/townships) centres there may need to be a formal public/private sector partnership, which would:

- Develop a shared vision in a strategy agreed by all stakeholders, based on an analysis of the competitive position, and a (usually) five-year rolling programme to secure vitality. This includes action through the Local Plan and transport investment programme.

- Appoint a dedicated town centre manager to co-ordinate and monitor the delivery of that programme and of services provided within the centre.

- Promote the centre with effective marketing to attract shoppers, visitors, tourists and new businesses; including the sponsorship of events and initiatives (farmers' markets, goodwill evenings, etc.).

TOWN CENTRE HEALTH CHECK

Various indicators can be used to provide an insight into the performance of a retail centre and offer a framework for assessing vitality and viability (based on Carley 1996):

- Footfall (pedestrian flow) – measures the number and movement of people on the streets. Footfall is a critical indicator for prospective retailers.

- Rental values –̈ provide a measure of the relative attractiveness of different locations in-centre and between centres. Often, however, rents reflect historic expectations (from a few years back) rather than current reality, so potentially excluding more marginal users and contributing to vacancy.

Vitality and viability

PPG6 on retailing defines vitality as a measure of how busy a centre is, and viability as a measure of its capacity to attract ongoing investment for maintenance, improvement and adaptation.

5.3 A mix of uses

Shops and well-being

'local retail services provide wider social and health benefits than simply the provision of goods'

SOURCE: Health Education Authority 1999a

Footfall measures social opportunity as well as retail viability.

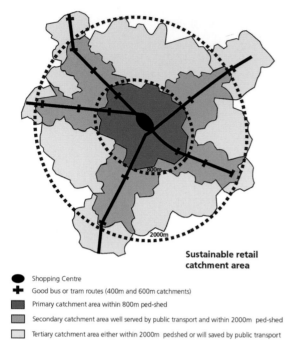

Sustainable retail
catchment area

● Shopping Centre

✛ Good bus or tram routes (400m and 600m catchments)

▓ Primary catchment area within 800m ped-shed

▒ Secondary catchment area well served by public transport and within 2000m ped-shed

░ Tertiary catchment area either within 2000m pedshed or will saved by public transport

Figure 3.20
Sustainable retail catchment area

Getting it wrong

*Research on market towns and district centres
shows that following the development of
large edge/out-of-town-centre foodstores,
the traditional convenience sector declines
21–75 per cent in market share.*

SOURCE: Hillier Parker 1998

*Note that where a supermarket is available
locally the majority of people choose it in
preference to travelling to reach other brands.
One study suggests up to 90 per cent of
people choose their local branch.*

■ Vacancy rates – particularly street-level vacancy in prime retail areas; and, related to that, rates of enterprise turnover.

■ Retailer representations and intentions, particularly as evidenced by actual investment in maintenance, window displays, refits, or redevelopment.

■ Commercial yield – generally, the lower the yield (reflecting high property value) the more confidence investors have in the long-term profitability of the centre.

■ Changing patterns of use – the number of units and area devoted to food and durable goods, charity shops, services, social/ leisure outlets, etc.

■ Survey of consumers – to assess their views, attitudes and priorities.

Working out town centre catchment areas

The principle of the 800 metre pedshed is a good starting point, but not the whole story. Low and medium density areas may not be able to support sufficient town or district centres to make 800 metres a reasonable criterion of success. As the earlier evidence (in 3.8) indicates, many people are prepared to walk further. Local bus services and cycling provide other options. The diagram (Figure 3.21) therefore distinguishes three grades of catchment: the primary area – within very easy walking distance; the secondary area – offering both a modest walk/cycle (<2 km) and a frequent, accessible bus/tram service; and the third zone – which has either a frequent bus service or a modest walk/cycle. The exact distances used will vary according to local circumstances.

In practice, rather than sustainability theory, there is of course a fourth and wider catchment, based on car access and longer distance cycling. This is particularly relevant in terms of town hinterlands. In some places the fourth catchment zone may currently provide for a majority of trade. But the object of good planning is to progressively extend the secondary zone, or to create the situation where a new centre is viable, so that fewer people have to depend on their vehicles.

SUPERSTORES

Large food stores are key generators of local activity in the UK. They increasingly provide a diversity of retail/service functions under one roof. They have an important social function for casual and planned meetings. Many shoppers currently visit them more than once a week. In the long term, with internet shopping, their role may change, but for the moment they are vital ingredients of local culture, and potentially by far the most important starting points for local food strategies. In this context any further development of supermarkets needs to be seen, not least by the retailers themselves, as an opportunity for more sustainable development in relation to organic and locally-produced food, mixed use centres and transport. In time they need to be a key part of a reduction in reliance on carbon intensive access.

When superstores are centrally located in neighbourhoods they encourage a substantial proportion of local access on foot or bike (contrary to the general impression). Within 1 kilometre 40% or more of trips on average are 'active' travel (see chart). Location and quality of access is critical. In time, with arm-twisting from consumers, government and local councils, superstore firms might be persuaded to rely on energy-efficient local delivery rotas, reduced car parking (releasing land) and active travel access from further afield.

Township stores

In that context, most towns, and every district within a city, should have one or more supermarkets embedded within it in order to increase local consumer choice, allow pedestrian/cycling access, reduce general trip lengths and cut retail/employment leakage out of the township. Total store size should roughly match a set proportion of the town/township catchment, and the range of goods on sale stipulated (see below). Large supermarkets poach custom from smaller shops and can kill them off. It is therefore vital that investment in new stores is used to bulwark the viability of existing/planned shopping centres.

Supermarkets should be located 'in centre', integrated with other retail/service facilities. Only when this is not physically possible can edge-of-centre locations be considered. Out-of-centre locations should only be contemplated as part of a planned new retail focus satisfying the essential criteria of pedestrian, bike and bus (as well as car) accessibility. Isolated stores should not be allowed.

Integration in-centre

This should be planned so as to foster use of other shops and facilities as well as the supermarket, and facilitate access by non-car-users.

- Site the supermarket as a key 'anchor store' within the centre, with a legal obligation to avoid trading in competition with specific locally strong retail trades.

- Integrate it into the active retailing frontage, not set back behind a car park.

- Ensure the car park is available for non-supermarket users, with pedestrian access in all directions.

- Plan excellent bike parking and bus-stops close to the main entrance.

- Create an attractive frontage, with a sense of place.

Proportion of walking / cycling trips to superstores and non-food services, by distance

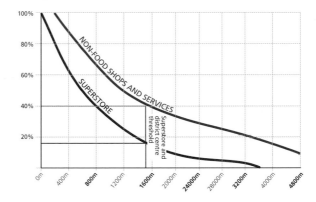

Figure 3.21

Accessibility thresholds

SOURCE: SOLUTIONS 2009

Superstore as part of the town centre:

Ideal = 1500 m

Bottom line = 2000 m

1500 metres is the best that can be achieved at 60 ppha gross and an assumed catchment population of 24,000. However, at that distance only a minority will walk or cycle at present-about 40% to access the town centre generally, and only 15% to the superstore.

3.12

The school trip

- *Only 2 per cent of children now cycle to school compared to 60 per cent in Denmark.*

- *Less than 10 per cent of 7–8-year-olds are allowed to walk to school, unaccompanied by a parent – down from 75 per cent in 1970.*

- *Half the car journeys to primary school serve no other function.*

- *20 per cent of peak-hour traffic is associated with school trips.*

- *The average distance to secondary school has increased by a third between 1985/86 and 1994/96.*

(Percentages apply to the UK.)

CHECKLIST

Education providers should

- agree the objectives of schools serving their local community and being locally accessible

- consider the appropriate balance between economies of scale and local accessibility

- avoid the 'school as fortress' mentality, instead enabling access from all directions

- promote safe routes to school (see Planning for the pedestrian, 3.16)

- look at ways of reducing land-take without compromising provision – to facilitate use of smaller, accessible urban sites (e.g. two- or three-storey buildings)

- promote dual use of facilities with the local community (e.g. hall, swimming pool, hard pitch, library/resource centre)

- promote the 'community school' principle, with schools seen as a focus for training, life-long learning, voluntary activities and social events

- consider the degree to which 16+ provision should be integrated with local economic/cultural activity, and colleges seen as 'permeable' on-street facilities.

BASIC PRINCIPLES

The provision of accessible local schools – primary and secondary – is central to the maintenance and revival of local community. Besides their prime educational functions, schools can:

- contribute to and instil appreciation of local culture(s)
- foster social inclusion and tolerance
- encourage healthy lifestyle habits
- shape children's travel behaviour
- create opportunities for a flourishing school community; and
- help generate long-term networks of mutual support.

The disposition of schools across a settlement (in extreme cases, the very existence of local schools) is a central issue. The education providers and the planning authority have a shared responsibility to maximise local accessibility to schools so as to foster social inclusion, healthy child travel habits and a flourishing local school community.

Walking/cycling to school

The declining number of children walking or cycling to school in Britain is well attested. The decline is not only due to parental choice and longer distances to school (evidence suggests most parents still choose a school close by), it is also due to highly car-based lifestyles and the withdrawal of parental permission for children to be on the streets alone.

Lifestyle and health effects

A growing number of children are missing out on the regular exercise of getting to school. The patterns of physical activity established in childhood are key determinants of adult behaviour (Kuhl and Cooper 1992). This relates particularly to cycling: only a quarter of children now use bikes (Hillman et al. 1991); there is almost a 'lost generation' of cyclists. More sedentary habits are leading to worrying projections of future prevalence of obesity and heart disease (Roberts 1996, Recent review 2007).

Social effects

The children who do still walk to school see it not as a fall-back position but as having positive benefits: exercise, independence, meeting friends (Osbourne and Davis 1996). Parents walking with young children, meeting others on the way or at the school gates, create networks of mutual support. Cycling to school is consistently associated with higher levels of children's activity in other areas (EU youth heart study – ref MG). In addition the ability to walk/cycle to school reduces household travel costs: locally accessible schools are part of an equitable, inclusive society.

One study entitled 'Backseat Children' concluded that children driven to primary school are failing to develop road safety skills, a sense of independence or an understanding of their environment (Living Streets 2008).

ACCESSIBILITY POLICY

Accessibility to schools (preferably a choice of schools within easy reach) should be a significant factor determining school investment programmes and housing allocations/permission. Appropriate standards depend on local conditions in terms of density, settlement pattern and school provision policy. Standards need to be agreed by the education authority and the planning authority and written into spatial plans following consultation with parents and the wider community.

An overall strategy could involve:

- keeping schools as small as educationally/financially feasible
- using the accessibility standards to prioritise schools-investment decisions and help shape other development decisions
- gradually increasing residential densities
- ensuring a permeable neighbourhood pattern giving a choice of safe routes to school with the minimum deflection from the shortest possible route; and
- opening access to school sites from different directions.

Fortress school vs. community school

The reaction of some schools to perceived 'stranger danger' has been to take stringent security precautions. The school becomes an exclusive domain, with one controlled access. This forces some children into longer journeys than necessary, with concomitant reduction in walking. It also cuts the school off from the social and economic benefits of shared local use and the sense of the school being at the heart of the community. The integration of school and community makes good use of resources and can reduce vandalism, graffiti and anti-social behaviour in and around the school. More specifically, opening school playgrounds after school can increase the amount of children's play activity by comparison with locked playgrounds (Cooper 2009).

Remote playing fields or remote schools

Schools are sometimes shifted outside their main catchments in order to provide new classrooms and integral playing fields. The social and environmental costs of this decision – in terms of increased car reliance, pollution, congestion, lack of child exercise and loss of children's independence as well as poor community access – are significant. In situ redevelopment/reorganisation and dual school/community provision can offer viable alternatives.

Safely to school

This pilot project worked with nine schools in Suffolk to tackle the increasing problems associated with children's travel to and from school.

Objectives

Safety – reduce child casualties, increase pupils' road sense.

Environment – reduce school-related car journeys, promote walking, cycling and public transport, create a safer, more pleasant environment for everyone to enjoy.

Health and quality of life – encourage social inclusion, increase health and fitness, give a greater sense of personal safety to pupils and parents.

Lessons for sustainable neighbourhoods – Consultation is at the very root of the method. Surveys and the 'planning for real' technique elicited information about local needs.

Involvement – Children in each school made and painted a model of the local area. This worked well when the schools mustered an army of local volunteer helpers and tackled the construction over a marathon two days.

The children's reaction to the model was always very touching. The older children were fascinated and very eager to locate their own houses and their routes to school. Public consultation was well attended in almost all schools and attracted a wide range of people, young and old. The result was masses of comments that were easy to understand.

As a way of collecting a lot of local opinion the technique works excellently.

3.12

Figure 3.23

*Education
catchment
populations and
land needs*

Kind of school	Number of pupils	Implied catchment population	Typical land needs (range)
PRIMARY with shared classes	50–100	500–1,000	0.3–0.6 ha
PRIMARY 1-class entry	150–200	c.2,000	0.5–1 ha
PRIMARY 2-class entry	300–400	c.4,000	1–2 ha
SECONDARY 11–16- year olds, 4-class entry	500–600	c.8,000	4–8 ha
SECONDARY 11–18- year olds, 8-class entry	1,200–1,400	c.16,000	6–12 ha
COLLEGE 6th-form/technical		say 25,000	very varied

Proportion of children walking / cycling to school, by distance

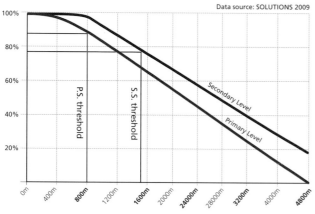

Data source: SOLUTIONS 2009

Figure 3.22

Accessibility thresholds for schools

Primary:
ideal = 800 m
tolerable = 1000 m

Secondary:
ideal = 1500 m
tolerable = 2000 m

At 800 metres 80–95% of children walk or cycle, depending on where they live.

At 1500 metres 65–80% of young people walk or cycle, depending on where they live.

Secondary school admissions

Admission criteria used where there is over-subscription

- *Children living in the catchment area of the school*

- *Children with medical or social needs that can only be met in the school of preference*

- *Children with brothers/sisters at the school*

- *Children with the nearest available safe walking route*

SOURCE: York City Council 2000

ACCESS TO PRIMARY SCHOOLS

Every urban neighbourhood, and every rural settlement, should have one or more primary schools. Ideally families should have a choice of accessible schools. At present the median length for suburban primary school trips is 1.3 kilometres (SOLUTIONS 2009). If areas were optimally designed, and primary schools evenly distributed, then at 60 ppha gross the closest schools could be within 600 metres. However, that is not practical in most situations because of the vaguaries of geography and site availability. Hence the target figure of 800 metres. At that distance the vast majority of children walk or cycle to school.

SECONDARY SCHOOLS

The significance of catchments

Despite the advent of parental choice, a large proportion of children go to close schools (Stead and Davis 1998). This is often encouraged by LEA admissions policy, favouring local catchment.

The downside of this policy is that in order to ensure the school of their choice parents may move to within the catchment area so their children will get priority. Popular, successful schools are thereby affecting the pattern of residential differentiation. The system of school place allocation may exacerbate social polarisation between neighbourhoods. The solution to this is not necessarily to abolish catchments (which has social, environmental and resource implications) but to consider density, housing policy and school size policies.

The size of schools

In a comprehensive system social polarisation is partly due to the sheer size of schools necessary to support an adequate sixth form. If schools were generally smaller then they could be located closer to where pupils live, and consequently shorten trip lengths, with more walking/cycling; and there would be greater choice of schools within a reasonable distance.

A 'sixth-form college' system (often associated with a technical college and thereby offering a very wide range of subjects and training) can enable the 11–16 schools to be more 'local', on the scale of the neighbourhood rather than the township, with more local choice.

Locational criteria

The suggested standards in Figure 3.16 are valid for areas with the potential for a reasonably even distribution of schools. Most students are willing to walk or cycle 1,500 m. New housing or schools should be located to facilitate this choice.

Public transport access: all secondary schools should be well located in relation to bus routes from their main hinterland areas. Clearly this is vital in dispersed settlement areas, but is also important generally to facilitate choice.

SIXTH FORM/TECHNICAL COLLEGE

The local college is appropriate to the scale of an urban district or market town, with a dependent population of 20,000–30,000. If colleges can be provided at this scale (rather than much bigger) then participation by less affluent/disadvantaged groups may be improved, and there is more opportunity for walking/cycling.

- Centrality in relation to public transport services is vital.

- An accessibility standard that could be achieved in most urban areas is 4 km (actual), which is a distance most cyclists are willing and able to cycle.

3.13 COMMUNITY HEALTH

Planning for public health involves much more than curative services. It is about a healthy human habitat and supportive social structures. Many sections of Chapters 2, 3, 4 and 5 are relevant. A healthy urban environment relies on the decisions of a wide range of bodies which do not have 'health' in the title. However, this section concentrates on what the health authority itself should do. Health authorities are major investors in the built environment. Their locational and design decisions impact on health just as do, say, education and transport authorities. Yet those locational and design decisions are often taken purely on the basis of operational and economic requirements with little regard to the

Exemplary York

Stead and Davis (1998) compared pupil travel behaviour for different types of school in a number of locations. In York they found both direct grant and city secondary schools served very local catchment areas, with average trip lengths of 1 km and very few over 2 km. There was no significant change between 1987 and 1997.

Number of people on the books

Solo doctor   = 2,000–3,000
Two-doctor surgery = 4,000–6,000
Four-doctor centre = 8,000–12,000

3.13

implications for health and well-being. Where this happens, health authorities are guilty of being anti-health.

LOCATING HEALTH CENTRES AND POLYCLINICS

Within a town or district of 20,000–30,000 people there should be a choice of surgeries, health centres and polyclinics offering together a wide range of services (e.g. midwife, district nurse, health visitor, family planning, drugs therapies, etc.) and giving accessible options to residents. The main responsibility for this rests with the Health Authority (Primary Care Trust), together with doctors, reinforced by policies within the spatial plan.

Criteria

- Is there a reasonably even spread of surgeries and health centres across the town/district to maximise the opportunity for pedestrian access by all sectors of the local community?
- Are all dwellings within 800 m (10 minutes' walk or more for the elderly/infirm/very young) of a health facility?
- Where local access is poor, are there plans to set up branch surgeries or to encourage more single practitioners?
- Are larger health centres and polyclinics (e.g. 4 doctors or more with a wide range of services) close to regular bus services giving good access to the whole township?

LOCATING OTHER HEALTH SERVICES

Accident and Emergency services

Emergency services are normally provided on a scale larger than an urban district or small town. But the danger of deciding scale of operation on the basis of increasingly specialised staff and equipment to cope with all eventualities is that the services become more and more distant from the clients. A fundamental principle should be that everyone can gain access to an A&E service without having to own a car. That implies each town having its own provision, and urban services being very carefully located. In some situations the health centres and polyclinics need to act as emergency services as well.

Dentists

People often choose to travel considerable distances to maintain contact with a dentist they trust. It is therefore important that dentists are located close to good bus routes. They should also be close to local shopping/service centres to facilitate multi-purpose trips.

Opticians

These are health providers but also increasingly retailers of comparison goods. In-centre location permits comparison shopping and facilitates multi-purpose trips.

Paramedics on cycles provision.

Natural health clinics

Similar criteria apply as for conventional health centres. Larger facilities should locate in or close to town centres or local high streets, permitting ease of access by bus, foot and bike. However, sole practitioners should be able to operate from home (subject to normal safeguards), to hold down costs and increase client choice.

Dispensing chemists

These should be in-centre, accessible by all modes of transport, and preferably close to health centres to maximise convenience.

HEALTHY NEIGHBOURHOODS

Broadening out from consideration of just health services, there are other types of services or activities where the potential health benefit is explicit – for example recreational, artistic, social and educational activities. There is also a benefit in bringing these together, so that they are more visible, can be linked sequentially, and be available to different family members at the same time.

Healthy Living Centres

Healthy Living Centres is the name of a UK Government funding initiative but also a concept dating back to an experiment in Peckham opened in 1935. Healthy living centres take a holistic view of health, recognising the varied social determinants. This approach recognises that strategies to improve health require a co-ordinated and imaginative approach including health, social and leisure agencies in partnership with local communities. The traditional GPs' practice is embedded within a facility that enables people to access easily the non-medical aspects of health. They are particularly relevant in communities suffering deprivation. The solution need not necessarily involve a single central provision building. Each Healthy Living Centre can propose a different mix of facilities and services responding to local circumstances.

Breaking out into the community

The principles of healthy living centres hold good for health provision in general. The concept can be used as an essential component of a healthy neighbourhood, pulling together some of the disparate elements of a healthy lifestyle and promoting mutual support. For example:

- Active community involvement and capacity building – around specific projects such as the provision of safe routes, access and support for local shops and affordable homes.

- Allotments, orchards and city farms: through the proved therapeutic and training benefits of horticulture and food production.

Healthy Living Centres

St Augustine's, Norfolk

This was the first Healthy Living Centre to open with funding from the New Opportunities Fund. The objective is to provide a one-stop shop for the wide-ranging health needs of people in King's Lynn. A large selection of facilities has been included:

- GP and primary healthcare
- childcare centre
- community café
- learning centre
- arts studio
- Citizen's Advice Bureau
- office space for community groups
- adventure playground
- garden for the disabled
- public transport, footpath and cycle links to surrounding area

Many different funding sources have been tapped into

- New Opportunities Fund
- Community Fund
- European Social Fund
- Department for Education and Employment
- Single Regeneration Budget
- Dow Chemicals – local sponsor

Figure 3.24
The original Peckham concept: by night, by day

A multitude of activities provided supporting a 'healthy heart' to the neighbourhood

SOURCE: Macfarlane 1950

135

- Schools, education and libraries: through after-school care, community education careers advice.
- Shared facilities, community halls: through social events, exercise classes, space for meetings.

Local recreational needs
outside the home

- *parent-supervised play*
- *playground activities*
- *informal play*
- *visiting the park*
- *picnicking/lunch hour*
- *organised sport*
- *casual sporting activity*
- *walking (including dog walking)*
- *cycling*
- *gardening in the allotment*
- *sitting and watching/reading*
- *sitting and talking.*

5.6 Green infrastructure

3.14 RECREATIONAL OPEN SPACE

BASIC PRINCIPLES

Local residents – particularly children, teenagers and elderly people – should have the realistic option of walking/cycling to an appropriate range of open-space facilities. They should be able to walk between such spaces on an attractive network of green parkways. As a general guide, open-space facilities should be available on the following basis

Within the home-place	toddler's playspace
Close to the home-place	allotments
	children's playground
	local greenspace/pocket park
Within the neighbourhood	kick-about area
	park, over 2 ha
Within the town	playing fields/tennis courts, etc.
	adventure playground
	'natural' greenspace over 20 ha

Note that green spaces, ranging from gardens to community forests, perform many functions within urban areas in relation to water, energy, food, pollution, biodiversity and cultural landscape as well as recreation. These overlapping functions are explored in later chapters. Here the emphasis is on recreation.

ACCESSIBILITY AND CHOICE

Leisure is one area of life where most individuals have relatively free choice. Spontaneity and enjoyment are of the essence. The key to local open-space provision is not simply a set of space standards but working from an awareness of local needs to ensure everyone has access to a range of attractive and well-managed recreational facilities.

The spatial plan can be used to establish which groups, and what neighbourhoods, are underprovided, and to set targets for existing neighbourhoods and requirements for any new development areas. In this context, land allocation standards and accessibility criteria are important. They can be used to help ensure equity and comprehensiveness, to point up priorities, and give a bottom line for negotiation with developers and service providers. Any standards of accessibility or land allocation have to be judged according to local preferences and the general character of the locality, and adjusted accordingly.

Kids play. Provide a choice of safe and exciting spaces or children will take what is there.

Accessibility thresholds

For both physiological and psychological reasons it is good for open space, especially greenspace, to be close to the home. This is particularly important for the young and old. More explanation is given in subsequent paragraphs, but in summary the desirable thresholds are:

- toddlers play area – 100 m
- playground and kickabout – 300 m
- local park/greenspce – 300 m
- access to the green network – 600 m
- playing fields 1000 m
- major natural greenspce 2000 m

Physical activity and mental well-being

Open spaces not only provide for specific recreational opportunities but also encourage healthy lifestyles, social contact and sustenance to the spirit. The evidence on physical activity (contributing to healthy lifestyles) varies from place to place but overall is strong. Time spent outdoors is a key determinant of a child's overall level of physical activity. The key factors are accessibility, quality and use (Croucher et al. 2007). Greenspace is most valuable as a trigger for physical activity if:

- it is close and well connected to living areas
- of sufficient size for informal games and walking/cycling without one imposing on the other
- is attractive and well-managed
- provides for a diverse range of activities to encourage good levels of use to maintain a sense of safety
- individual dedicated uses, such as sports fields, are interlinked with others.

The evidence on mental well-being is increasingly strong: there are often social benefits in terms of meeting up, playing, chatting, team-building, occasional major social events. There are also mental benefits. Nature, even in the form of grass swards, regimented trees and formal gardens, is important for well-being. Green space close to homes can lift the spirit and give health benefits. It appears particularly important for those poorer or less mobile groups who are more dependent on the local environment (de Vries et al. 2003; Greenspace Scotland 2008).

PLAYSPACE WITHIN EACH HOME-PLACE

The National Playing Field Association (1992) recommends a 'local area of play' (or LAP) for children up to five. This is a small area of open space for low-key games sited within one minute's walking time (or 100 m actual distance) of every home. As the picture suggests, this playspace may be part of the street scene but should be safeguarded from traffic, green in character, and overlooked by dwellings.

The Eight Qualities		Characteristics
1	Serene	Peace silence and calm. Sounds of wind, water, birds and insects.
2	Wild	Fascination with wild nature. Lichen and Moss grown on rocks, old paths.
3	Rich in species	Biodiverse, offering a variety of animals and plants.
4	Space	Offering a restful feeling of 'entering another world.' A coherent whole, like a beech forest.
5	The common	Green open place with vistas
6	The pleasure garden	Enclosed, safe and secluded. Where you can relax, be yourself and also play.
7	Festive	A meeting place for festivity and pleasure
8	Culture	Historical place offering fascination with the course of time

Figure 3.25
Basic experiential qualities that increase the attractiveness of the open spaces
After Grahn et al. (2005) based on a review of 86 studies cited in Benson and Roe (2007)

Local area of play – Some developers are incorporating the NPFA playspaces into their designs, without loss of housing space and at no greater cost, at the same time improving the estate's design quality and enhancing marketability.

5.16 Perimeter
block and
home-place

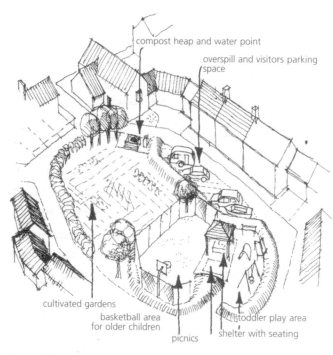

Figure 3.26
Communal garden with playspace

SOURCE: Barton et al. 1995

The principle of allotments very close to home has been adopted in many places, including Odense in Denmark, where allotments provide an attractive area around flats and offer an important outdoor social focus for residents. In Vancouver housing co-operatives have been surrounded by horticulture and gardens to great effect (Hopkins 2000).

4.14 Food growing

The need or appropriateness of such LAPs depends on the social mix and density of the area. Different policies for home-place playspace may be adopted. For example:

- **Medium-density areas: (50 dpha)**
Most back gardens are small and short excursions are necessary for toddlers/parents to gain exercise. The LAP model is ideal.

- **High-density areas: (100 dpha)**
Few households have private gardens and where there are families communal provision is vital. If the streets are too crowded/constricted for playspace then an alternative is shared playspace within housing blocks, in the communal garden/courtyard, managed by the residents' group.

- **Low-density areas: (25 dpha)**
There are fewer families within striking distance of any space provided, and large gardens provide ample play opportunities. There is therefore little justification for small-scale communal play spaces.

DISPERSED ALLOTMENTS

Access to allotments is a sustainability and health issue. Local organic food production in medium–high density areas has been greatly impeded in the UK by the convention of providing allotments (if at all) in large and poorly accessed fields. Anecdotal evidence suggests that this puts people off allotment growing and increases reliance on inorganic methods. It certainly results in more vehicle use.

Allotments should be close enough to homes to permit easy access by foot, carrying tools, organic wastes or produce. The guideline maximum distance suggested is 200 m, taken as a feasible wheelbarrow or bucket carrying distance. Clearly this standard could vary both with topography and local attitudes. One model of allotment provision is within the home-place in the form of community gardens, with potential for shared composting schemes and 'neighbourhood watch' over produce.

This implies a pattern of allotment provision radically different from at present. Spatial plans should require all new brownfield or greenfield housing developments over a certain net density to include dedicated community allotments and initiate appropriate management mechanisms. The corollary could be that there should be no net loss of allotment space within a township: sell-off of any under-used allotments could then proceed no faster than alternative more accessible provision was created.

NEIGHBOURHOOD PLAY AREAS AND GREENSPACE

Certain groups are particularly dependent on neighbourhood open-space provision – i.e. facilities within 400–600 m actual walking distance:

- parents with young children (often with pushchairs)
- young children playing, cycling, kicking around
- elderly people with limited mobility
- wheelchair users
- workers wanting a lunch break (or fag break).

The key to local provision is not the scale of specific land allocation but quality, access and safety. The needs may be met in a number of ways and often in the same or adjacent spaces. Any neighbourhood strategy is likely to involve some permutation of the following elements:

Play street

More children's play occurs on streets than in playgrounds. Access-only, semi-pedestrianised streets can provide well-supervised opportunities for informal play.

Playgrounds

Playgrounds for the 4–10-year-olds, with swings, seesaws, roundabouts, climbing frames and slides (not too tame!) should be within 5 minutes' walk or 400 m actual distance of every home (LEAPS: local equipped area of play). We recommend 300 m, as this would increase the incidence of casual, unsupervised youngster use, if the location is right.

Pocket parks

Small greens or quiet enclaves for sitting, talking, eating sandwiches and enjoying nature should be within a 300 m straight line, according to English Nature (1995). This equates with the 5-minute standard or 400 m actual.

Kickabout areas

Informal green spaces or hard surfaces open enough for ball games with a normal minimum size of 0.2 ha, and ideally adjacent to playgrounds.

Local wildplace

Children love mysterious, hidden places (though parents may not), which can be allowed to develop unkempt – copses, stream bottoms, old surface workings for example – where spontaneous creative play and games can evolve

The 400 m actual walking distance is based on research showing that most young children travel less than that to play. Safety of the route is equally important. Most young children are not allowed to cross main roads or for that matter go beyond

It isn't just the youngsters at play, Barcelona, Spain.

Incidental play and leisure in well designed pocket park, Freiburg, Germany.

Playing in the street, we accomodate our cars but not our children.

The 'six-acre' standard

The National Playing Field Association (NPFA) adopted the 6-acre (or 2.4-ha) standard of open space per 1,000 population in 1938. It has been used by local authorities ever since. It expressly includes space for sport, active recreation and children's play, but does not include decorative parks, allotments or 'landscaping'.

pitches, green and courts	1.6–1.8 ha
playgrounds	0.2–0.3 ha
informal play space	0.4–0.5 ha
total per 1,000 population	2.2–2.6 ha

This standard has not been independently validated and is not achievable in many inner urban areas. However, if written into local plans it can provide a good starting point for negotiation. As pointed out in the main text, quality, accessibility and safety are equally important criteria.

Parkland accessibility standards

While the linked parkland system should come close to every dwelling if possible, to encourage access and use, the facilities within it will necessarily be varied distances.

Parks – or non-sports greenspaces of at least 2 ha: target maximum actual walking distance from home 600–800 m depending on local conditions. 800 m is equivalent to 10 minutes' walking time or 3 minutes' cycling.

Playing fields – plus other appropriate facilities such as tennis courts, bowling green and hard pitch – target actual maximum distance 1–1.2 km, i.e. 15 minutes' walking or 5 minutes' cycling, subject to topography. Note potential for 'dual use' with schools/colleges.

Adventure playground – activities popular with local 8–14-year-olds, such as skateboarding, cycling, climbing and football need space of at least 0.4 ha: target maximum distance 1–1.2 km, or 15 minutes' walking, 5 minutes' cycling.

4.2 Integrated natural systems

5.6 Green infrastructure

clearly defined boundaries such as railway lines. The location of playspaces must therefore recognise these limits.

How *not* to plan local open space

'Prairie planning' of housing estates provides ample greenspace in the form of greens and wide verges. But the spaces have little recreational value and are expensive to maintain, creating open, often shapeless townscapes with little sense of place.

The other extreme is to hide the open space away, allocating land for play or for allotments in odd inaccessible corners of a development after the main layout has been worked out, without establishing who will look after it. This is called SLOAP – Space Left Over After Planning.

THE TOWN PARKLAND

At a broader scale specific recreational provision should be seen as part of an open-space system that percolates through the urban area, creating the opportunity for greenways (foot, bike, equestrian) and round walks. Where this linkage does not currently exist then 'virtual' linkage should be established, through new or improved connections, pedestrian/bike priority measures and tree/shrub planting as a signal of a possible route.

The town parkland helps to provide the landscape setting for the settlement. It should make use of the natural features of streams, lakes woods and hills, as well as ensuring it percolates through the town so that everywhere is within (ideally) 400 m of a part of it. The parks, greens, playgrounds, playing fields, allotments, small-holdings, local wild-places and locally distinctive habitats all find a place in the green parkland. The parkland network links out to major semi-natural access areas and to the countryside footpath system. The parkland also provides ecological services (in relation to water, air quality, energy, biodiversity) as part of the essential green infrastructure of the town.

planning for movement

3.15 NEIGHBOURHOOD MOVEMENT STRATEGY

STREETS ARE FOR PEOPLE

The key to a successful strategy is reclaiming streets for people: people walking, cycling, idling, playing, sitting, drinking, talking, even selling. Traffic has to be sufficiently tamed so as to pose little threat in terms of accidents, noise, fumes or space domination. This applies to all residential and shopping streets. Neighbourhood movement planning should open up choices for all groups – old and young, rich and poor – so that people have attractive options for how to get to friends, facilities and places.

5.5 Street networks

OBJECTIVES

Accessibility: easy access for all kinds of people to activities within and outside the locality, with a particular emphasis on non-car-users and less-mobile people.

Exercise: making it easy and attractive for people to gain healthy exercise by walking and cycling more – for both recreational and functional trips.

Safety: reducing the likelihood of road accidents and reducing the fear of assault and street crime.

Viability: a pattern of movement that maximises the chance of local business and social facilities being economically sustainable.

Community: creating streets and places where people can meet and thus foster local social networks, improving their quality of life and the sense of local community.

Environment: reducing transport-related levels of local air pollution and globally damaging greenhouse emissions.

Key to all these objectives is encouraging people from all sectors of society to walk. Research shows that people's propensity to walk is very significantly affected not only by distance but by how safe, convenient and pleasurable the experience of walking is. Safety is also a key factor in encouraging cycling, especially for children and older people. Public transport use is profoundly affected by distance to stops, reliability and the speed and comfort of service as well as frequency.

TAKING ACTION

In existing neighbourhoods, where outmoded traffic planning principles are dominant, change may well depend on effective community pressure. Local town councils, parish councils and transition town groups can lobby and motivate the powers that be, so that each incremental decision contributes to a coherent strategy. Achieving the objectives requires close co-operation between transport operators, policy-makers and local planners.

Township movement indicators

- *Percentages of people walking to key facilities (e.g. schools, supermarkets)*

- *Pedestrian casualties as a percentage of pedestrian activity*

- *Footfall in the township centre*

- *Number of Green Travel Plans adopted*

- *Number of 20 mph/home zones introduced.*

Transport should not cost lives!

According to the Department of Health 3,500 people are killed annually in road accidents, and 12,000–24,000 have their deaths 'brought forward' by exposure to traffic pollutants. That puts the occasional rail disasters into perspective.

CHECKLIST

Some groups with specific needs

- Parents with babies/toddlers (often in a buggy)

- Young children going to school/playground/friends

- Adolescents meeting together on neutral ground; going to school

- Young people shopping, pubbing, clubbing

- People going to work by bus or tram or bike

- Local workers at lunch times and before/after work

- Delivery vehicles to local shops/factories/offices

- Adult carers without access to a car, using local facilities

- Infirm/disabled people meeting/using facilities

- Elderly people with limited mobility, wanting local car access

- Dog walkers, runners and others wanting round walks off road

- Allotment holders with barrows/buckets of produce/compost

- Elderly/unemployed/leisured people strolling to the park or square.

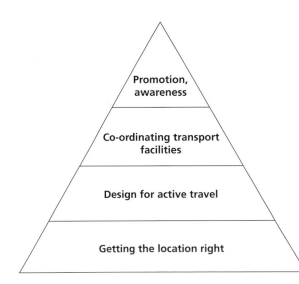

Figure 3.27
The travel planning pyramid

The latest guidance from the Department for Transport in Britain is a radical departure from the traditional traffic engineering approach. It reflects good practice in other Western European countries. The whole emphasis within residential areas is on the pedestrian friendly environment. Traffic is to be tamed, with junctions for example designed to slow traffic right down.

Neighbourhood travel plan

In areas with strong local communities, or where there is a significant new housing development, consider the feasibility of a residential travel plan. The initiative could be taken by a voluntary group (Transition Town, Residents Association, Neighbourhood Watch), or by the house builder (encouraged by the local authority) or by a town or parish council. Such a plan could include:

- A car share scheme (with willing participants, 25 households is sufficient)
- Support for community transport (this would require more households)
- Campaigning for better pedestrian and cycling provision

SOME BASIC PRINCIPLES

Equitable access

It is important to recognise the needs of different groups, not just the often dominant and ubiquitous car users, and then to plan a transport system that allows people to choose their own destinations, routes and modes with maximum freedom. This means opening up choice, and trying to ensure one person's choice does not become another person's constraint. The checklist of need groups having distinctive requirements can help orientate policy.

Designing for the most vulnerable groups (e.g. children, and those who are mobility-handicapped) will normally ensure choices are opened up for others as well. For example, easily graded ramps help elderly people and parents pushing buggies as well as wheelchair users.

Priority modes

The conventional approach in the late twentieth century was to plan the road layout first, providing for pedestrians, cyclists and particularly public transport as a secondary stage. This set of priorities can be reversed. Permeable, safe pedestrian and cycling routes and effective public transport routes should be the first considerations, with vehicle circulation second. Note, though, that this does not mean a rigid hierarchy of priority (as often portrayed) – it is a matter of designing for the various essential users in a compatible way. In basic terms:

- Pedestrians need direct frontage access to buildings and public spaces, with a dense, permeable network of safe, pleasant routes giving choice and opportunity
- Cyclists need the same direct access and freedom to roam, but with a network of identified longer distance routes
- Vehicles also need to be able to get close to all buildings – for emergencies, deliveries, recycling collections and disabled access – but do not necessarily need to park.
- Buses and trams need to have dedicated routes and their operational requirements fully understood to ensure efficiency
- Car traffic does not need the same high network density as pedestrians or cyclists, but does need on occasion to be able to percolate through to specific destinations
- Lorries and delivery vehicles are normally restricted to wider distributor roads, but also need direct access to shops and on occasion to homes

3.16 PLANNING FOR THE PEDESTRIAN

BASIC PRINCIPLES

Pedestrian activity is the lifeblood of the neighbourhood. Enabling free and easy pedestrian movement, with direct access to all buildings and public spaces, is therefore a very high priority. Every new development or transport investment should make a positive contribution to the pedestrian environment working to achieve the five 'Cs': connected, convenient, comfortable, convivial and conspicuous.

The benefits of walking

Walking is the most common form of movement, open to almost everybody. It constitutes most trips for people who do not own a car, especially children, young people and the elderly. Trips by public transport and car often involve a walking element. Like cycling, walking involves minimal resources but can be a healthy and pleasurable aesthetic and physical experience. Yet the pedestrian environment in many cities is increasingly hostile, and this is being exacerbated by the car-orientated nature of much modern development. In extreme cases the pedestrian option is being effectively excluded by inconvenience, danger, fumes and ugliness. The latest guidance from the UK government, however, rebalances the situation. The quality of the pedestrian environment is given priority over traffic flow (DfT 2007).

The health benefits of walking have been reinforced by recent research:

- Active travel to get to places is a key part of combating the trend towards obesity, especially important for lower socio-economic groups (Butland 2007)

Walking is healthy

For many people, walking is the best overall physical activity for maintaining and improving health and fitness, offering:

- *less risk of heart disease*
- *weight control*
- *less risk of high blood pressure*
- *less risk of diabetes*
- *less depression/anxiety*
- *less risk of cancer of the colon*
- *less risk of osteoporosis.*
- *no gym fees or expensive gear*
- *regular, everyday activity*

Walking for health Leicester

Promotes higher levels of awareness of the health and social benefits of walking and increases the participation in daily walking activity through increased opportunities, community action and improved environments.

Objectives include:

- *Developing environments and walking facilities – the focus of this is to make the links with future developmental priorities within transport and regeneration plans which seek to improve the environment in favour of pedestrians.*

- *Contributions to health improvement – reduction in coronary heart disease in Leicestershire.*

- *Providing better conditions for cyclists and pedestrians and thereby a reduction in accidents, in pollution from transport and hence in exacerbation of asthma.*

- *Regular walking for older people to strengthen their bones.*

Urban design solutions

Safer conditions for cyclists and pedestrians, wider footpaths, more seating and improved landscaping, slower-moving and reduced traffic, improved pedestrian street crossings, signposting walking routes.

3.16

Sketch View

Plan of the scene illustrated above

Figure 3.28
Clustering of facilities with natural surveillance

SOURCE: Barton et al. 1995

Roads can create tarmac deserts and an unfriendly environment for pedestrians unless properly integrated.

- Recreational activity - round walks, walks in the park, getting to open country – brings similar benefits
- Community networks are developed through informal street contacts while walking, helping to build a sense of a friendly, supportive neighbourhood
- These informal contacts can be important for mental well-being, reducing any feeling of isolation and anomie (Calve Blanco 2009)

Planning for pedestrian activity depends on there being places that people want to walk to. The land use and spatial aspects of this, together with guidance on urban design, are dealt with elsewhere in the book. Here we just rehearse the principles of sound pedestrian design.

CRITERIA FOR NETWORK DESIGN

The Institution of Highways and Transportation (2001) suggest there are five useful criteria for good pedestrian design, elaborated below.

Connected
- The network should be comprehensive, serving all significant desire lines.
- It should provide good permeability, i.e. a choice of routes filtering through an area allowing pedestrians to go which way they want.
- Easy, direct access to public transport facilities is vital.
- Green spaces should be linked into the network and allow for round walks, and where possible 'green routes' to major centres of activity.

Convenient
- Pedestrian routes should be as direct as possible in order to reduce distance to be walked and increase the pedestrian catchment of facilities.
- They should avoid steep hills, unnecessary barriers, steps or kerbs that might inhibit less agile people and those with pushchairs or wheelchairs.
- Where new routes are planned they should follow the contours, even if this does result in some route deflection. Alternative (direct) routes should also be provided for the energetic. Choice is important.
- Routes should be linked by safe and convenient crossings, with minimum diversion.

Comfortable
- Footways should be wide enough to allow easy passing and overtaking, without being pushed out into traffic – especially on heavily used roads where long vehicles on bends may be intimidating.

- Routes should be overlooked by nearby properties, giving a sense of surveillance and safety.
- The route should be well lit and feel safe, without dark corners or featureless, unconnected sections (e.g. blank factory walls) which can be intimidating.

Convivial

- Routes should be places where people can meet casually and talk in comfort, free from excessive noise or fumes.
- They should be designed for aesthetic enjoyment, giving pleasure by the variety of prospects, spaces and landscapes.

Conspicuous

- Main routes should be easy to 'read', distinctive, and clearly signposted. Landmark features (e.g. pubs, mature trees, public art) can help give a sense of place.

PROBLEMS FOR WALKERS

- The absence of seating en route. This affects the distance elderly people are willing to walk.
- Poorly designed subways – the fear of lurking danger.
- Lack of toilets in neighbourhood or town centres.
- Unkempt places with rubbish strewn around, e.g. dog dirt, graffiti.
- Intimidation by (possibly harmless) groups of young people/ adolescents and beggars.
- Shared surfaces with cyclists – specifically for those with hearing and visual impairments. See the next section on cycling.

SAFE ROUTES TO SCHOOL

The majority of children in England still walk to school (SOLUTIONS 2009) but the number is falling. The 'Safe Routes to School' programme involves local authorities working with individual school communities (teachers, parents, pupils) to raise awareness and improve the safety of pedestrian routes. It can lead to significant short-term shifts in pupil behaviour, but the decay factor is fast unless there are really significant improvements in the quality, directness and safety of the routes themselves. Some early schemes, trumpeted as successful at the time, subsequently showed a substantial increase in car reliance. A few good routes are unlikely to be sufficient because homes are widely dispersed. The moral is that a decentralised school-by-school approach, relying heavily on individual initiatives and external input being sustained, is no substitute for a city-wide integrated strategy with a comprehensive system of safe routes and high-profile political backing. The attitudes of a whole urban community have to be systematically changed. The approach of municipalities

3.12 Schools

CHECKLIST

Speed and time

Average walking speed = 3 mph, 5 kmph or 1.4 metres per second. Individual speeds vary widely in the 2–4 mph range

Walking time

Distance	400 m	Time	approx. 5 minutes
	800 m		approx. 10 minutes
	1 km		approx. 12 minutes
	1 mile		approx. 17 minutes

CHECKLIST

How far will people walk?

This varies hugely, depending on the person and the destination. Recent evidence for access to local facilities in English suburbs shows:
- *up to 600 m: 75+% of trips on foot*
- *600–1000 m: 50+% of trips on foot*
- *1000–2500 m: 25+% of trips on foot*
- *over 3,200 m (2 miles) less than 10% of trips on foot*

Actual distances walked varies with:
- *individual physical ability and fitness*
- *encumbrances, e.g. shopping, pushchair*
- *journey purpose and availability of options*
- *topography and weather conditions*
- *perceived pleasures and/or dangers of the route*
- *individual lifestyle choice.*

So while distance standards are useful they are only a starting point for local policy debate.

CHECKLIST

Standards for path design

Gradients
- *Normal maximum 5 per cent (1:20)*
- *Where necessary up to 8 per cent (1:12)*
- *For very short distances 12 per cent (1:8)*

Widths
- *Normal minimum 2 m*
- *Protected low-use routes 1.5 m*
- *Dual use with bikes 3 m.*

in Denmark and Japan, where car dependence for school trips has been cut to residual levels, demonstrates what is possible with commitment.

CRITERIA FOR NEW DEVELOPMENT PROJECTS

- **Location**: the location of new residential, commercial or social facilities should maximise the opportunity for people to walk.
- **Access**: every development, large or small, should have convenient and visible access for pedestrians – preferably directly off the street or square, not across extensive private car parks or grounds. Large developments should try to provide for direct pedestrian access from any approach road or path. This is particularly important for schools, supermarkets and other major trip generators.
- **Frontage**: new developments should face the surrounding routeways, presenting a friendly outlook to passers-by, inspiring confidence not fear or a sense of estrangement.
- **Connectivity**: they also provide an opportunity for reconnecting splintered parts of the urban environment, making new pedestrian links which can integrate the development and shorten trip lengths.

6.11 Choosing the right location

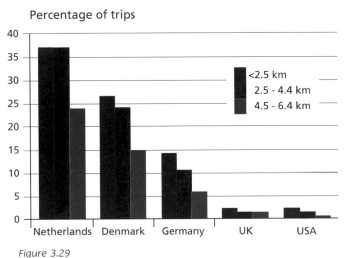

Figure 3.29
Cycling share of shorter trips

If the UK could increase cycling to the level of European neighbours, there would be a modest reduction in transport carbon emissions and a huge increase in active travel, combating obesity.

3.17   PLANNING FOR THE CYCLIST

BASIC PRINCIPLES

Ordinary streets throughout the neighbourhood should be managed for bicycle use, linking directly with surrounding areas. This requires that vehicle traffic be 'calmed', and levels of traffic modest. Where streets and junctions are heavily trafficked, continuous cycle lanes or segregated routes are important. There should in addition be a network of 'safe' routes, designed for children, which may be partly on-street and partly segregated, and serve local schools/playgrounds/shopping centres.

Characteristics of urban cycling

Cycling provides excellent exercise and improves accessibility. In some situations it offers the fastest as well as the least polluting method of travel. In the United Kingdom:

- The average cycling journey is 3 km, with normal use in the 1–5 km range.
- Beyond 5 km bicycle use falls off, with the normal maximum being 8 km.
- Average speed is about 15 mph (25 kph) on the flat, but less for the elderly, the very young, or bikes with trailers.
- Hills can deter trips. The normal maximum should be 5% (1:20), but 10% (1:10) is fine for able bodied cyclists over short distances, given modern gears.

A new approach to policing will be required for a network of cycling and pedestran shortcuts. Cycle-mounted police in Bristol.

The propensity to cycle is strongly affected by the safety and convenience of routes available. The cycling habit is best forged when young, so creating safe routes to schools, parks, local shops and around residential neighbourhoods is a priority. The challenge is to increase the amount of cycling while reducing accidents to cyclists. This is particularly difficult because cycling is a relatively anarchistic activity that is not easily regulated. Indeed, the freedom of cycling, the ability to go from anywhere to anywhere, is one of its attractions, with probable psychological benefits.

Promoting cycling

By European standards, levels of cycling in the UK are ridiculously low – the result of official neglect over several decades. According to the National Travel Survey (DfT 2006) only 15% of people cycle regularly – once a week or more. The percentage of total trips in some places is less than 2%.

Cycling promotion strategies need to involve carrots and sticks: better, safer cycling networks and disincentives to car use (e.g. parking restrictions). In the Sustainable Demonstration Town of Darlington there was, in addition, targeted personal and community travel planning. Those targeted increased their cycling by 79%, walking by 29% and public transport by 14%, while reducing car trips by 11% (DfT 2007). Modest shifts in the same direction were also evident in the wider population who were exposed to the general message but not the individualised travel marketing.

CRITERIA FOR CYCLE NETWORKS

Street access

General-purpose streets, which give direct access to homes and facilities, need to be bicycle-friendly and traffic calmed. One guide suggests that if cyclists share the common road-space, then a maximum traffic flow of 5,000 vehicles a day is desirable (Taylor and Sloman 2008). For more heavily trafficked streets there should be continuous cycle lanes or segregated cycleways. In existing settlements this is often not possible, and it is important to recognise that many cyclists will use the busy road if it is also the most direct, or gives access to relevant facilities. Segregated routes are fine, but are no substitute for a road network on which people can cycle safely.

Safety

Separate lanes or paths need to be provided if conflict with heavy or fast-moving traffic in unavoidable. Eighty per cent of accidents are at or near junctions where cars turn across the cyclist's path. Measures to give bicycles priority at junctions are therefore especially important. The provision of cycle space can be used to incidentally reduce traffic capacity.

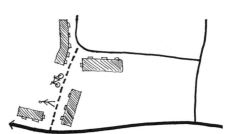

Figure 3.30
Pedestrian and cycling short cuts

Where the road layout is indirect a well-supervised and maintained pedestrian/cycling short cut is essential, giving an advantage over motorised traffic

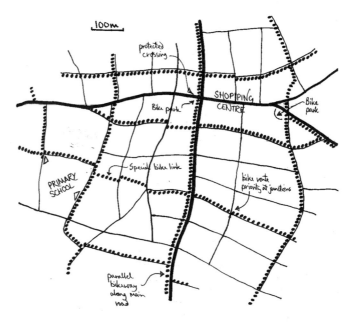

Figure 3.31
Safe bike routes forming a complete network across the town on a 2–400 m grid pattern

5.5 Street networks

147

Secure cycle parking in residential area, Rotterdam, the Netherlands.

Direct and safe route into the shops, Leicester, England.

The community provides cycles and maps for visitors without cars next to the railway station in Greena, Denmark.

Continuity

Main bicycle routes should be as continuous as possible, with few stops (momentum is important!). Fragmented stretches of bicycle path can actually increase overall dangers, and generally do not encourage cycle use. The designated routes (well signposted) should form a network that allows for a wide variety of origins and destinations. In some Dutch towns a 300 m cycling grid is provided. Investment can be focused where there are barriers to desired routes (e.g. a stream or main road).

Directness

Cyclists do not normally accept diversions that increase their journey length, time and effort significantly (for example, by more than 10 per cent). Segregated routes are sometimes impractical, except for young children under strict instruction, if they are clearly longer than the direct route along the road. In new development, priorities can be reversed, giving the most convenient route to cyclists and pedestrians, and making sure that it is obvious. This can help alter the psychology of modal choice.

Comfort

Special cycling routes need to be very carefully designed in detail, and subsequently maintained, to ensure easy gradients, a smooth surface, protection from the fumes from, and intimidation by, heavy goods vehicles or buses, and a visually attractive experience.

Bicycle parking

Secure end-of-journey parking in convenient locations is a factor affecting bicycle use – at railway stations, for example. Encouraging bike and ride effectively extends the catchment area of the station. Bike hire at stations and town centres creates further options for travellors.

CREATING THE SAFE NETWORK – THE HIERARCHY OF ROUTE OPTIONS

1   On-street provision shared with vehicles where traffic volumes are low, traffic is calmed, and junctions give bike priority.
2   Dedicated cycleways, with kerb- or contour-separation from pedestrians.
3   On-street provision of cycle lanes and junction protection, reallocating space from road vehicles where volumes are moderate or high.
4   Shared surfaces with pedestrians on segregated routes.
5   On-street provision shared with vehicles where volumes are medium/high but traffic is effectively calmed and hazards (e.g. cars pulling out) are managed.
6   On-street provision where traffic is travelling over 30 mph, lane widths mean cyclists are often threatened by vehicles

and turning movements may pose an unpredictable threat. No cyclist should be forced to endure these conditions – which apply frequently on British roads both in and out of town.

Cycle/pedestrian shared use

The sharing of a common surface can work when the route is well designed and cycle and/or pedestrian flows are modest. But pedestrians with impaired hearing or sight can easily be put off using such routes. Routes used by young families (with unpredictable movement and lack of spatial consciousness) are particularly inappropriate. This can occur on routes through a well-used park, for example. Reliance on shared use with pedestrians is therefore low down on the hierarchy of cycling provision – though still far preferable to sharing with heavy traffic.

Attractive pedestrian and cycle alley, but is there suficient natural surveillance? Delft, the Netherlands.

3.18 PUBLIC TRANSPORT OPERATION

BASIC PRINCIPLES

The pattern of bus services in a neighbourhood is too important to be left to the operators. The planners can significantly affect the viability of public transport and the route network in new areas by arranging roads, footpaths and land uses so that people are within threshold distance of services. At a wider scale, the quality of bus and train services is higher where the maximum number of people can reach their destination by the minimum number of routes. Urban linearity is therefore a key feature. The points where routes cross (nodes) then become the prime locations for local jobs and services and the focus for pedestrian and cycling routes.

5.2 Devising the spatial framework

Public transport accessibility needs to be considered not as an afterthought (left to the market) but as the starting-point for neighbourhood planning, with land uses then attached to the public transport network.

STARTING POINTS FOR NEIGHBOURHOOD PLANNING

- What is the current pattern of public transport provision and use?
- Which routes potentially offer direct connections to important destinations?
- How can the viability of existing/potential routes be reinforced?
- Can a strong mixed-use focus for public transport services be created?
- Can services be concentrated on to a few high-quality public transport corridors which still reach all homes/businesses?

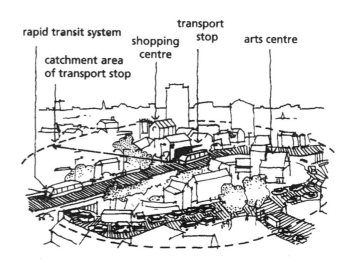

Figure 3.32
Public transport magnets

New retail, employment and leisure facilities in town/district centres can be clustered close around public transport nodes so as to benefit customers and underpin public transport viability

SOURCE: Barton et al. 1995

3.18

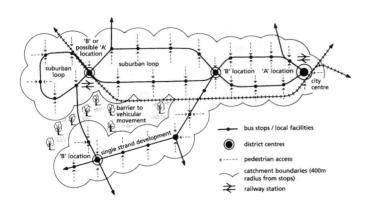

Figure 3.33
Principles of public transport planning

illustrating

- linear catchment zones
- magnets and nodes
- limited lateral movements
- fast and stopping services

SOURCE: Barton et al. 1995

Bus priority works!

Edinburgh's 'Greenways' cut journey times by 25 per cent and generated 250,000 extra bus trips in the first six months.

One Islington bus priority junction scheme saved over one and a half minutes for each bus passing through at peak times.

Rural bus services

The CLG considers that an 'adequate' service for rural settlements is an hourly service within 10 minutes' walk of homes.

SOURCE: Rural White Paper (DETR 2000b)

'A', 'B', 'C' and 'D' locations

Based loosely on Dutch planning principles, we can distinguish a three-fold hierarchy of centres which should be served by public transport. They can provide the basis for analysis of the existing and potential situation:

- 'A' locations are those with a range of facilities with a city-wide sub-regional attraction – major shopping centres, office headquarters, civic and cultural facilities, universities. These should be served by urban public transport services to all parts and inter-city rail

- 'B' locations are mixed use centres which provide for activities having a strong town or urban district attraction – superstores, district shopping centres, markets, libraries, technical colleges, swimming pools. These do not require inter-city services but should be a nodal point for local bus and tram services

- 'C' locations are those occupied by major local services but not necessarily part of a mixed use centre – secondary schools, outdoor leisure centres, industrial service estates. These should be well served by a main public transport route

- 'D' locations are those associated with low density facilities – wholesale estates, golf courses for example. These would benefit from public transport services but do not themselves justify them

KEY PLANNING PRINCIPLES FOR EFFICIENT BUS/ TRAM OPERATION

- Directness: provide direct routes between points of primary attraction – e.g. township centres (B locations on Figure 3.33).
- Speed/reliability: use bus-only lanes, junction priority and other measures to ensure that public transport vehicles are not unduly delayed by other traffic.
- Linearity: shape neighbourhoods so that journeys are naturally funnelled with little need for lateral trips, increasing linear demand and service quality.
- Density: grade densities so that the higher-density housing is close to stops, minimising the average walk distance.
- Clustering: locate along the route those activities that generate local trips, reinforcing visibility and potential for dual-purpose trips.
- Environment: ensure that the environment of the stops and main pedestrian access routes is pleasant and safe, avoiding physical or psychological barriers.
- Shelter: provide attractive and robust bus/tram shelters, with clear route information.
- Information: provide real time passenger information about services at key points.

ACCESS TO STOPS AND STATIONS

■   400 m standard for bus stops: all housing developments should be within easy walking distance of good public transport services that give access to the main centres of urban activity. A common standard for bus access across Europe is 400 m; and this is backed by time-honoured government guidance (DoE circular 82/73) and the Confederation of British Road Passenger Transport (Addenbrooke et al. 1981). Beyond that distance, the proportion of people willing to walk declines progressively and car dependence increases.

■   Restrictions on access: the 400 m criterion needs to be applied with care. It is the distance people generally are actually willing to walk; if routes are indirect, the straight-line distance may be much less. Access is also influenced by gradients (especially for older people) and psychological barriers such as subways or intimidation by road traffic.

■   Attractions for access: direct, safe and pleasant routes are important. Planting along the route can help refresh jaded travellers. Intervening opportunities – convenience store, pub, news stands etc. – can enliven the walk, provide the excuse to chat, as well as offer services.

■   800 m standard for metros: most people are prepared to walk 800 metres or more for high-quality metro or tram services: the critical factors are reliability, speed and frequency. Evidence suggests that properties within striking distance of a metro station are more attractive, and command a higher price, than those further away. At the same time the households living close not only use the metro much more but have lower car ownership (Taylor and Sloman 2009).

■   Parking and transfer at stations: ample cycle storage at tram or metro stations, connected into a good cycling route network, can hugely increase the carbon-neutral catchment of the service. At the same time the provision for cars should be limited in most situations. Instead of encouraging 'park and ride' the policy should be to ensure excellent transfer facilities to and from local bus services; ideally with a guarantee of meeting specific service times when frequencies are low, as on late evening or Sunday.

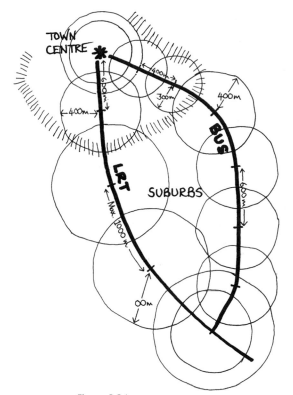

Figure 3.34
Stops and catchments

Optimum stop-spacing and catchment vary with service quality and origin/destination

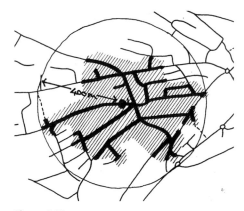

Figure 3.35
Bus stop catchments

The 400 m zone may be smaller than you think

Locating new development

5.12 Linear districts and towns

New housing and commercial developments must be located where they can be accessed, or are certain soon to be accessed, by good quality public transport. This applies as much to brownfield as to greenfield development, and is the 'bottom line' of sustainable development.

WHAT IS A 'GOOD' LOCAL SERVICE?

The main criteria are frequency, reliability, speed, cost and comfort.

Suggested standards for frequency are:

- Excellent: 5 minutes or higher. At this level of frequency travellers are able to change bus to bus with little time penalty.
- Good: 6–12 minutes. Travellers are able to wait for a bus on spec – casual use is possible.
- Adequate: 13–30 minutes. Dependable timetabling is essential but the wait is not long.
- Poor: 40–120 minutes. Journeys have to be carefully pre-planned, but can be programmed across the day.
- Dreadful: over 2 hours. A residual level of service. Awkward to use.

3.19   PLANNING FOR THE CAR

BASIC PRINCIPLES

The key to a healthy transport strategy is reducing reliance on private vehicular traffic. The capacity of the road system should not normally be increased, because it simply encourages extra trips by car and compounds problems of air pollution, carbon emissions and (sometimes) accidents. At the same time it undermines the inclination to walk, cycle or use the bus, and tends to compound social exclusion. Instead the general principle should be that road capacity is progressively reduced as a direct consequence of positive planning for pedestrians, cyclists and public transport. At the same time, traffic speeds (the prime factor in accidents) should be held low by design, and parking policy (or other forms of charging) used to deter unnecessary car trips.

ROAD NETWORKS

The main section dealing with street networks is 5.5. However, some basic points can be made here. Hierarchical road networks are compatible with sustainability because they can help keep heavy traffic out of residential areas, and well-managed main roads with limited access reduce accidents. However:

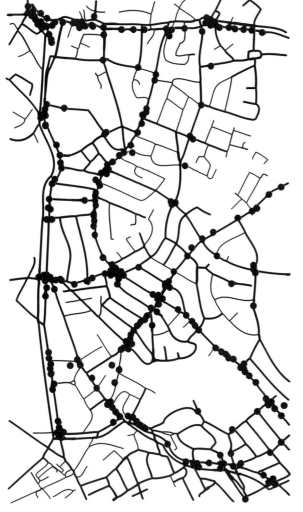

Figure 3.36
Road traffic incidents and casualties

Casualties and fatalities are not the only health impacts directly related to main roads; health impacts also arise from increased levels of air pollution and background noise.

Accidents between dates 01/01/1990 and 31/12/1998

SOURCE: Bristol City Council

- The secondary or distributor roads act as the natural concentrations of activity within or between neighbourhoods, and should be traffic-calmed and integrated into the townscape, with local facilities clustered on them (see Figure 3.37).

- The minor roads should not be a series of cul-de-sac but a street network giving vehicle permeability through the area. However, the vehicle through-network should not be every street. The minor streets can be access only for vehicles but provide throughways for cyclists and pedestrians. This is the principle of 'filtered permeability'.

- The bus routes normally follow the main distributors, which provide good connections between different parts of a town. It is therefore vital that the configuration of main distributors maximises the convenience and efficiency of bus services.

LOW CAR-USE ZONES

Vehicle access is essential for some users and for local economic vitality. It is not necessary right to exclude traffic (e.g. by pedestrianisation) unless the pedestrian flow is high in relation to street width. Nevertheless, local communities and planning authorities might consider defining existing and future home-places by different target levels of car use.

1   Car-free zones

- Developments where no cars are allowed except in an emergency, with controlled access for rubbish collection, and streets walking, play and community.
- Households pledged not to own a vehicle, relying on car rental, taxis or car pools with a limited supply of common vehicles.
- Highly accessible locations where local retail facilities are integrated/adjacent, walking/cycling is safe and pleasant, and public transport is excellent in all directions.

2   Car-limited zones

- Developments where car ownership is deterred – for example an ordinance or lease allowing one car only per household (as In Bermuda).
- Residents' parking limited to a maximum of one space per household, and this is grouped away from the access streets so that children's play takes precedence
- Accessible locations where alternative facilities (for walking, cycling, public transport) are good.
- Car pools, car clubs and car renting opportunities promoted.

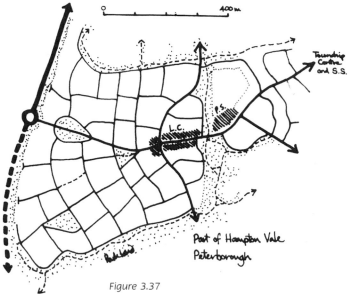

Figure 3.37
Hampton Vale masterplan

Hierarchical road networks are compatible with sustainability

The Hampton Vale masterplan illustrates:
- *A limited-access primary road.*
- *Secondary roads acting as the focus of local activity.*
- *Minor roads giving good permeability but discouraging short cuts/high speeds.*
- *A well-located linear neighbourhood centre.*
- *An open space network based around water management.*

Provide prominent space for car clubs.

Car tamed streets in new Freiburg developments; cycling and conversations dominate, but car space and access is available.

3   Car-tamed zones

- Areas where car ownership is unrestricted but vehicle speeds are moderated by design and by law.
- Car ownership decoupled from car use by gentle deterrence and excellent provision for walking, cycling and public transport.
- Design speed 5–10 mph in the home-place zones, and 20 mph in the wider residential area.
- Through traffic deterred and traffic volumes generally held low – this could include roads which function as local 'high streets'.
- Use road humps with discretion – they are awkward for buses and cause extra pollution as vehicles brake and accelerate.

SLOWING TRAFFIC, REDUCING CAPACITY

Road capacity for ordinary traffic may be reduced as a side effect of positive planning for other modes as well as traffic-calming techniques. The objective is not stop–start conditions, but steady, moderate, predictable, safe speeds.

- Widen pavements and reinforce pedestrian route continuity.
- Extend the pavement on corners to make bends tighter.
- Install bike lanes and bike priority on key routes/junctions.
- Insert tram-lines, bus-only lanes and priority junctions.
- Reduce sight lines at junctions (and warn motorists).
- Provide more on-street parking (and less off street).
- Enhance amenity: trees, tubs, seats.
- Install junction platforms, road cushions and rough surfaces (but make smooth routes for bikes).

PARKING THE CAR

In an era when we are concerned to make the environmental costs of our decisions visible, it is essential to charge the real costs of providing for the car. The car is a space hungry beast. The cost of providing it with a resting place should be specifically identified when possible. This is recognised when larger plots with drive space or garage for vehicles cost more to buy or rent. Shared parking space should be similarly charged, including the land value, the cost of construction and of maintenance in the calculation of price and/or rent. If the price of car storage is separately itemised it can affect the choices people make. Vauban in Freiburg has adopted this practice, with an initial capital charge and annual rent. It is of course very well served by the city tram system, excellent cycle ways and walkable facilities. Car ownership has fallen to 30%, and car use to a mere 10% of trips (based on Melia 2009).

■ In situ parking is desired for convenience, car safety and car washing/DIY. For some households (with an infirm or disabled member, for example) it is a practical necessity. Where density levels allow, integral parking can be provided for most households. However, consider first the needs of children to feel that they are free to colonise the street.

■ On-street parking has been designed out of layouts in the late twentieth century, but acts as a very flexible, visible car store with traffic-calming attributes. The prerequisites are modest traffic speeds and overlooked streets (informal car surveillance from the dwellings). On-street parking is particularly appropriate for visitor parking.

■ Parking courts can work well but only when the design is not too big/soulless, does not destroy the tranquility of back gardens, and when natural surveillance occurs from people passing or houses overlooking. Small courts serving the immediately adjacent properties should normally be the rule. Because they are hard surface they are attractive to children wanting to play ball games – which strengthens the need for some surveillance.

■ Grouped car parks away from the house can be a liability, but act as a natural deterrent to short-journey car use, and therefore may be favoured in 'car-low' developments. Normally the car park should be within 125 m of the home, with an absolute maximum of 250 m (De Knegt 1996). Distance from home needs to be compensated for by clear benefits, such as play streets, attractive planting, easy cycling, convivial spaces. Security at the car park is paramount – preferably achieved by having services grouped around it (for example, a repair shed, washing space, bike/car hire or small workshops/offices) and a clear allocation of monitoring/locking-up responsibilities.

Garages do not have to be eyesores, Poundbury, Dorchester.

On street parking is sometimes a good solution!

Parking courts made to work at New Hall, Harlow.

The city of Freiburg, in southwest Germany, boasts two new sustainable suburbs, constructed on brownfield sites. One is Reiselfeld – described briefly in Chapter 1. The other is Vauban, which, through often disarmingly simple means, provides a humane, inclusive safe environment that has become a place of pilgrimage for UK planners.

Vauban occupies 42 hectares of land, previously a French barracks, within 3–4 km of the city centre. It caters for 5,000 people and 600+ local jobs. There is a balance of social groups, with a significant proportion of families, despite the moderately high gross neighbourhood density of around 50 dph. The motto of the citizen's association 'Forum Vauban' is:
'Wir machen uns die welt widdi-wie sie uns gefällt' (we are re-making the world as we want it).

Community development

There have been three main bodies planning the development of Vauban: a dedicated committee of the city council, Project Group Vauban, including all the official agencies in co-operation, and Forum Vauban, which applied to co-ordinate the participation process and has done since 1995. The Forum, with the city council, has organised 40 workshops, excursions and festival events, helping to build social capital, and ensure effective participation of current and prospective residents in the planning process.

The plan and the aerial photograph reveal some key characteristics:

- *spine tram and access route*

- *direct connection to the rest of the city*

- *a very green environment*

- *open space penetrating the heart of the development*

- *opportunity for local food production*

- *solar-powered dwellings (bottom right of photo)*

- *the extent of 'car free' residences (orange on the map)*

- *multi-storey car park (shared by residents) over a supermarket, with solar roof*

The Freiburg planning department laid down strong but simple spatial principles:

- a grid of streets around the train spine route
- maximum of four storeys, in terraced style throughout
- green fingers linking to a linear park along the stream
- all streets traffic-calmed, many car-free.

In this context the land was divided into small plots, and preference given to private builders, households, social housing providers and housing co-operatives. Major house-builders were forbidden. The result is visually distinctive: much small-scale creativity and variation within a clear, standardised framework. There is evident commitment and care, both for private gardens and the public spaces. There is an exuberant community feeling.

Conviviality, convenience and free play

Local needs are met within easy walking (or cycling) distance:

- primary school and kindergarten
- thriving neighbourhood centre providing for social interaction
- local shopping centre and scattered shops along the spine route
- green spaces for recreation, inviting children to play
- traffic-free play streets, overlooked by the houses.

The child-friendly atmosphere reflects the design but also the freedom to roam the streets given by parents to quite young children.

High accessibility, no car

The tram service, extended in Vauban early in the development process, gives a frequent, reliable, fast service to the city centre and the city as a whole. The bike network encourages cycling for both longer and shorter trips. The streets provide a permeable, safe environment for walking. Those are the carrots. The stick is in relation to parking – which is not allowed except for unloading/frail elderly in the residential streets. Multi-storey car parking, at a price reflecting land and construction costs, is available on the fringes of the neighbourhood.

Car ownership is now about 50% of households. Over half of those without cars gave them up on moving to Vauban. Modal share is c. 30% walking, 35% cycling, 20% public transport and 15% car (one estimate puts car as low as 10%).

Vaubanallee: the main street, with shops, tram stop, green tram-lines to reduce noise and heat, and ubiquitous bikes.

Back street, pedestrians and cyclists only, with parallel SUDS system.

Photo: Steve Melia

Car-restricted street, safe for children to play in.

Design outline

The masterplan consists of a curvilinear street layout which ensures that most homes have a main orientation facing within 30° of south. The street pattern creates a through route to the main road running through Ketley, and allows for potential links to the existing housing on the western boundary of the site. Minor streets create informal perimeter blocks and homezones characterised by shared surfaces. A street design code was developed to delineate front boundary conditions, floorscape materials and treatment and building heights related to street widths. On street parking is an integral part of street design, as well as rear parking courts, which are designed as communal places.

An apartment building with offices at street level. Note the recycling storage to the right.

Homezone streetscene.

This is one of seven new communities being developed as part of the Millennium Communities Programme under the auspices of English Partnerships. At the time of writing, the Community is completing the first phase of approximately 103 homes out of the eventual 675 dwellings planned.

Location and context

The development is located on the edge of Ketley, a small but extensive, relatively low density settlement, predominantly early to mid 20th century in character. Ketley is one of a number of settlements based on mining and other small scale industries, which were amalgamated with the founding of Telford in the 1960s and 70s. It lies barely 3 km north of Telford town centre. Ketley has basic shops, an infants and junior school within 1 km of the site, and a community centre and bus stop within 100 metres.

The site is some 37 hectares, a classic brownfield area of mine workings vacated some years ago. Due to its disuse in the intervening years, wildlife habitats have developed which are now significant sources of biodiversity. Therefore remediation and conservation were major elements in the early stages of the project. The site is bordered by woodland to the north and east, with development edging its western and southern boundaries. It is elevated with extensive views to the north and west. The aims of Millennium Communities are to:

- minimise resource consumption
- protect and enhance local environmental capital
- maximise design quality
- improve construction quality and efficiency
- increase social inclusion and participation
- improve quality of life
- achieve long-term viability.

From these the brief for the developers and design team included:

- all households to be designed to meet internal specification of the Housing Corporation Scheme Development Standard requirement
- homes to be rated Eco Homes Excellent
- 50% reduction to embodied energy
- all materials to be Green Guide A rated
- 20% reduction in metered energy use
- 10% improvement in daylight and acoustics
- reduced construction waste to 23m3 per dwelling
- improvement upon national injury rates
- consideration of Sustainable Urban Drainage (SUDS), on-site renewables and local sourcing of materials.

Uses

A range of house types and tenures is provided in the scheme, from large semi-detached family houses to one bedroom apartments: 30% of the homes are classified as affordable. An element of home working is incorporated into the design of some houses. Some mixed uses are planned in the first phase, one of the house developers occupies a ground floor office in a block with apartments above. Other ground floor offices face the focal point square. The square is designed to accommodate the frontage of a junior school on its western side. This would be at the interface of the new and existing communities. Unfortunately at the time of writing, the education authority has decided not to proceed with the school. This is particularly disappointing as a school is often the 'glue' of successful community formation. However an encouraging symbol of the commitment to community cohesion is the completion of a large community play area on the western boundary of the site, which was designed with the involvement of the existing community.

Conclusions

The development of this Millennium Community coincided with the dramatic downturn in the housing market in the UK and the general recession. It remains to be seen whether subsequent phases will be completed, or will incorporate the undoubted high quality specification and design of the houses. The decision to abandon the school is a significant drawback, but looking at the overall number of houses planned for the site, it is doubtful whether there would be the critical mass of a new population to generate (a) the potential pupils for the school, or (b) additional facilities in Ketley.

There are many examples of good practice in the scheme, not least the creation of the frontage of the development as a continuation of the rather fragmented existing High Street, including its proximity to existing bus stops and facilities. A ramped walkway (although quite steep) directly links this phase with the bus stop. The streetmaking and block design, and the quality and specification of the built environment is high and will no doubt be softened by the landscape when it matures. As usual the quality of the public realm will only be assured by a continuing commitment to a maintenance regime.

A rear court parking and communal area.

The play area at the interface with the existing settlement in the background. The play area was designed with the participation of the local community.

The interface of the new 'village' apartments on the left with the existing main road to the right. A bus stop is situated just beyond the pedestrian crossing. The former school now community facility is seen in the background.

159

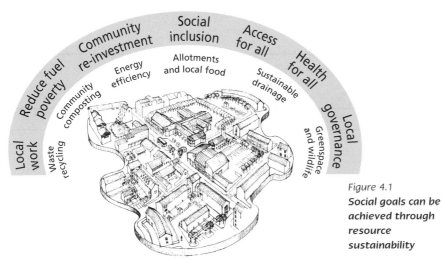

working with natural systems | chapter 4

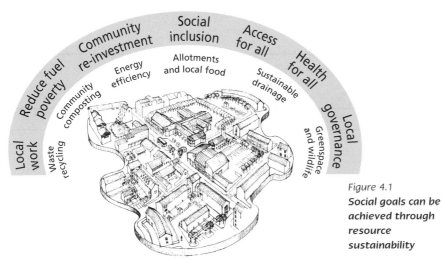

overview

4.1 THE LOCAL GLOBAL SYSTEM

This chapter focuses on wise use of natural and man-made resources through addressing the neighbourhood as a system. More correctly it is a key sub-system and building block of human habitats , influencing and being influenced by systems at smaller scales (e.g. households) and at larger scales (towns, districts and cities). The chapter deals with five basic resources in detail whilst acknowledging that others such as air, soils and land have not been covered.

In order to 'get things right', we need to plan this scale very carefully. Projects at the neighbourhood scale – whether incremental changes, renovation, major regeneration or new build – give us tremendous opportunity. At this scale we can reap rewards of synergy that are not available when working with individual buildings. This scale also allows plenty of opportunity for ownership, participative planning and co-management.

The basic environmental ideas outined have been around for a long time, but they are still rarely implemented in a comprehensive manner in neighbourhood planning. This chapter demonstrates how health, local quality of life and social goals can all be underpinned through mindful planning of the local resource system.

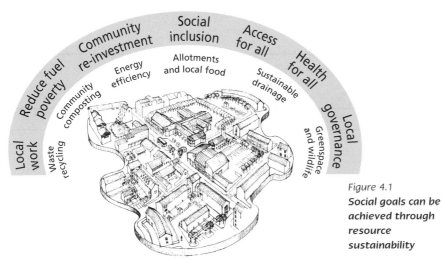

Figure 4.1
Social goals can be achieved through resource sustainability

4.1

'Resource planning at the neighbourhood scale can give rise to benefits for developers and communities that go far beyond what can be achieved for an individual building or small site.'

SOURCE: (Planning 1999)

Figure 4.2
A web of resource management

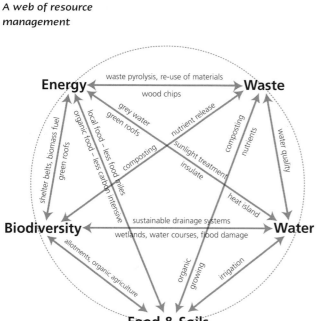

'Land should be regarded as a scarce finite resource. Development projects should be as compact as possible and should enhance the environment, not just limit damage, by respecting biodiversity, harnessing natural resources and reducing the call on non-renewable resources.'

(DETR 1999i: p. 71)

THE RESOURCE SYSTEM

Systemic working

A fundamental systemic plan of resource flows underpins all the leading examples of low impact, liveable neighbourhoods. Early thinking should focus on the basic pattern of the resource plan, the details can follow later. The physical form of the locality, the resources available and the resources needed must be planned as a single system at the outset. There can be no repeatable template – the proposed resource system needs to respond to the local situation.

Systemic working for human settlements has been codified into several named approaches such as natural step, permaculture, 'cradle to cradle' or the tenets and approach of the transition movement. These approaches are all useful ways to communicate systemic work.

A resource system plan for a neighbourhood needs to show the following elements:

- All flows into and out of the system – water, electricity, heat, materials.

- All main system functional components – housing, allotments, water bodies, woodland, surrounding uses.

A resource system plan for a neighbourhood needs to embody the following goals:

- A high degree of internal (re-)cycling and re-use of flows.

- Built-in flexibility and redundancy.

Spatial integration

- The neighbourhood systems need to integrate with resource flows at larger spatial scales.

- The neighbourhood system needs to support connection to the systems at smaller spatial scales, the local living zone, the street, the building.

APPROACHES FOR NATURAL SYSTEMS AT THE NEIGHBOURHOOD SCALE

■ Social, health and economic outcomes

When dealing with neighbourhood resource issues it is important to break out of a purely environmentally focused vision. Social, health and economic objectives should also be pursued. Interventions should seek to improve social capital and inclusion, these can have important mental health outcomes. The aim is to support a range of options for the adoption and maintainance of healthier lifestyles.

Economic objectives need to be carefully chosen so as to support the higher level social and health outcomes, all to often not enough effort is put into developing the financial models which support these outcomes and economics is left to be in conflict with the other goals of sustainability. For example, if the 'payback' cost of installing effective carbon neutral technologies is too high for individuals to bear, then a more suitable financial model or approach must be developed. Innovative technologies often demand innovative delivery mechanisms. These often result in long-term savings and can often create local jobs – financial efficiency and environmental efficiency aligned!

■ Integrated resource planning

Integrated resource planning is needed. Good neighbourhood resource development builds collaboration between social providers and private utilities. This may result in increased initial design and implementation costs but there will be year-on-year benefits providing social, environmental and financial payback in the medium and long term.

■ 'Soft infrastructure'

This means people's behaviour, motivation, knowledge and support. As individuals we often don't choose to live in a resource-efficient way. Research has shown that merely redesigning neighbourhoods or installing the latest technology will not necessarily provide the results envisaged. Measures that acknowledge the role that soft infrastructure has in changing behaviour need to be built into neighbourhood development initiatives.

4.2 IMPLEMENTING AN INTEGRATED STRATEGY

The principle of an integrated resource strategy applies at several different levels: general policy, township spatial framework, development area brief, detailed design, and ongoing management. The whole sequence is vital if sustainable resource use is to be achieved on anything more than an occasional or trial basis.

For a new urban extension an integrated approach from the outset is feasible. But most of the development we will be living with for the next 150 years or more has already happened, we must recognise the difficulties of an integrated approach but also rise to the tremendous opportunity. For existing localities the agenda for change happens in a thousand independent incremental upgrades to infrastructure and a hundred thousand planning applications. We must send the right signals in high level planning strategies (both locally and nationally), in government fiscal policies, in new remits for agencies, in support for community initiatives and in setting up the right ownership and business vehicles.

LOCAL RESOURCE PARTNERSHIPS

Different resources are managed by a wide range of organisations, each with their own remit. Common goals, and a collaborative

4.a Hammarby sjostad

1.12 Neighbourhood design principles

2.3 Collaborative communities

Increasing local autonomy

We do not advocate a blanket goal of resource autonomy for all neighbourhoods. However, in the driver for improved local quality of life and healthier lives, together with reductions in global environmental impacts, greatly increasing local autonomy will be beneficial for most neighbourhoods. The exact balance of autonomy and dependence needs to determined with sensitivity and understanding of each locality, its demographics and its context. Some benefits from increasing local autonomy:

Energy
Reducing energy costs
Tackling fuel poverty
Safeguarding future fuel flexibility
Reducing global warming emissions

Water
Reducing flood risk
Improving attractiveness
Enhancing wildlife
Adding amenity
Reducing scarcity

Food
Easier choice for a healthy lifestyle
Fostering social inclusion
Supporting local vitality – growers and shops
Improving access to food (resisting food deserts)
Reducing food transport and traffic

Waste
Providing training and local employment
Opportunities for fostering social capital
Reducing waste transport and traffic
Meeting waste recycling targets

Biodiversity
Creating a better-quality environment
Improving wildlife amenity
Meeting biodiversity targets
Buffering climate change

Local resource partners

- *Local planning and environment department*
- *Waste collection and disposal units*
- *Housing, parks and education departments*
- *Health authorities*
- *Energy supply industries*
- *Water companies*
- *Developers' representatives (such as builders trade federations)*
- *Wildlife interests (national agencies and non-government organisations)*
- *Environmental and recycling interests (national agencies and non-government organisations)*
- *Countryside agencies and regional development agencies*

Utilities in a proactive development role

Hammarby Sjöstad, Sweden

An example of a proactive partnership where the utilities are leading the development concept for Hammarby Sjöstad – a new district 'where technology meets ecology'. The partnership is between
- *The waste management company – Skefab;*
- *The drinking water supplier – Stockholm Vatten AB;*
- *The energy company – Stockholm Energi AB.*

These utilities have jointly formulated a set of proposals for the energy supply, water, sewage and waste management for a city extension to the south of Stockholm.

The new district will be resource efficient and environmentally planned. It will exploit recycling technology and is aiming to achieve high levels of resource recovery.

The objectives are to close 'eco-cycles' at as local a level as possible and to minimise import of resources.

Further details can be found in Case Study 4.a at the end of this chapter. www.hammarbysjostad.stockholm.se

1.13 Neighbourhood design principles

approach, must be agreed under the auspices of an existing local process depending on the situation. Some countries have a community strategy, which emanates from the local authority as a whole. In the UK, unfortunately the Local Strategic Partnerships that produce these strategies may well not include some of the key actors. While health authorities and biodiversity groups will be members, energy providers and water companies may not. In many situations the local statutory development planning process will offer a way forward.

Whatever the local details are in terms of planning processes and at whatever scale of development is being envisaged, we suggest that a Local Resource Partnership is created, under the auspices of the appropriate statutory process. The Resource Partnership, possibly as a sub-committee, would aim to agree a co-ordinated programme promoting sustainable resource use. It would try to ensure that optimistic aspirations and policies incorporated in development documents would be reinforced by the agencies involved in delivering and managing resources. The Partnership would provide the context within which spatial frameworks and specific development projects would lead to an integrated resource plan.

APPLYING THE SIX NEIGHBOURHOOD DESIGN PRINCIPLES

New build, regeneration or renovation projects all need to have a clear strategy for dealing with resource issues. This strategy will be set within the wider policy context, influenced by relevant planning policy and the resource utilities and regulators. To determine the level of detail and scope, address the six principles of neighbourhood planning.

- **Stakeholder involvement**
  Planning more efficient resource use can be a galvanising issue for encouraging participation. Not only can people forge a better environment for themselves, but there can also be financial rewards. Additionally, raising the level of local control is *per se* good for health!

- **Increasing local autonomy**
  Dealing with resources in a holistic way will help to increase local autonomy; reduce the 'ecological footprint' of the neighbourhood and close resource loops. People's local, regional and global environment will benefit (see side column).

- **Connectivity**
  Connectivity between resource issues and social provision is the key to winning support, securing funding and long-term success. Good examples are allotments and community gardens. These can produce local food for a community centre, they can be part of a training and employment project and also linked to the composting and recycling process.

- *Diversity*
  Diversity results in a richer and more robust neighbourhood. Optimum use can be made of variable local conditions, of local opportunities. Locally distinctive solutions can arise.

- *Response to place*
  For each resource there are a range of options to pursue. The appropriate choices will be determined by local conditions, such as soil types, climate, available energy sources, aspect, infrastructure. If an adequate survey is undertaken, local solutions will arise.

- *Adaptability: the life-time neighbourhood*
  Adaptability underlies the resource approach developed in this chapter. Future flexibility of options is built in (in choice of fuel, for example).

TOWNSHIP SCALE SPATIAL FRAMEWORK

The town or district spatial framework can tie general policies to physical reality, and provide a context for the pursuit of specific projects. To have any authority the framework needs to be adopted by the local planning authority as local guidance, and also be backed by the 'local resources partners'. The 'community checklist' in Chapter 6 offers a quick set of relevant resource criteria. The framework can also point the way towards integrated solutions that give maximum return on land and financial investment. Given a willing investment company, specific development projects (large or small) offer a tremendous opportunity to achieve sustainable resources use.

The 'development checklist' in Chapter 6 sets out the key issues in terms of location, appraisal and design, and can be cross-referenced to material presented in this chapter. The local planning authority can, up to a point, encourage a responsible attitude from the investors by requirements in a development brief, masterplan or design guide. The limits are set by the degree to which progressive natural and human system win-wins are backed by the statutory local planning documents.

Examples of integration at the town or district scale.

6.8 Green infrastructure

- *Safeguard a green/open space network that preserves water courses and floodland, provides for a town farm, enhances wildlife potential, maximises tree cover, safeguards renewable potential, manages climates and pollution as well as providing for recreation; establish collaboration agreements on investment programmes and management regimes.*

4.17 Waste parks

- *Plan a town/district waste and recycling park, with a community composting scheme and perhaps a combined heat and power (CHP) plant using waste materials and coppice from an adjacent wildlife resource and parkland.*

2.9 Agreeing a programme

- *Shape the town/district in terms of density, landscape, layout and aspect, mixed use and linearity so as to enhance the long-term viability of community heating and solar power as well as public transport.*

5.00 Urban design

- *Promote criteria-based policies to foster specific resource strategies – for example, the local availability of allotments, the creation of wind breaks, the local disposal of waste water, recycling provision in home and wildlife 'threads' through development (see 3.10: criteria-based planning).*

165

THREE SYSTEMIC MODELS

The Natural Step

The Natural Step is a framework for sustainable development. Initially developed in Sweden during the early 1990s, it has been refined through application internationally.

The Natural Step framework's definition of sustainability includes four 'system conditions' that lead to a sustainable society. These conditions must be met in order to have a sustainable society;

In a sustainable society, nature is not subject to systematically increasing:

■ *concentrations of substances extracted from the Earth's crust;*

■ *concentrations of substances produced by society;*

■ *degradation by physical means and in that society;*

■ *people are not subject to conditions that systematically undermine their capacity to meet their needs.*

Underpinned by a science-based framework, it assist individuals and organisations in understanding sustainability and creating sound responses. In application the framework leads to a planning methodology for assessment, visioning, action and monitoring.

FFI: www.naturalstep.org

Cradle to Cradle

In a single innovative leap, the life cycle costing brigade and the recycling camps, have been challenged by ideas coming from Michael Braungart and William McDonough of EPEA (Environmental Protection Encouragement Agency). Cradle to Cradle, taking its inspiration from nature, allows no place for the concept of waste. In nature; waste = food. Although developed primarily for commercial product design, some tenets of the approach are useful at the neighbourhood scale.

Maximise ECO-EFFECTIVENESS: *the concept of eco-effectiveness presents a positive agenda based on maximising the ability of industry to support the natural and human world.*

Build-in ECO-INTELLIGENCE: *The intelligence of natural systems (such as nutrient cycling, interdependence, celebration of diversity, solar power use, regeneration, etc.).*

Reduce DOWNCYCLING: *Recycling a material in such a way that much of its inherent value is lost (e.g. recycling plastic into park benches).*

Increase UPCYCLING: *Recycling material in such a way that it maintains and/or accrues value over time (the opposite of downcycling).*

Design PRODUCTS OF CONSUMPTION: *Designed for safe complete return to the environment where they become nutrients for living systems.*

Support PRODUCTS OF SERVICE: *The manufacturer maintains ownership of the material for continual reuse while the customer receives the product's service without assuming its material liability.*

Control UNMARKETABLES: *Products which cannot be consumed in either an organic or an industrial metabolism. In the long-term, these products should not be manufactured. As existing unmarketables are discarded, they should be stored until a safe recycling process is developed.*

(McDonough and Baungart 2002)

FFI www.epea.com

Permaculture

Permaculture seeks to define some tenets for living in tune with surrounding natural systems. Many practitioners internationally have contributed to the development of the approach, most notably the creators, Bill Mollinson and David Holmgren, who developed the basics in Australia in the 1970s. The following permaculture principles are particularly relevant to urban neighbourhood development.

Design from patterns to details - By stepping back, we can observe patterns in nature and society. These should form the backbone of our designs, with the details filled in as we go.

Integrate rather than segregate - By focusing on relationships between things they can work together to support each other.

Produce no waste - By valuing and making use of all the resources that are available, nothing goes to waste.

Use and value diversity - Diversity reduces vulnerability to a variety of threats and takes advantage of the unique nature of the locality.

Use and value renewable resources and services - Make the best use of nature's abundance to reduce consumptive behaviour and dependence on non-renewable resources.

Catch and store energy - By developing systems that collect resources when they are abundant, we can use them in times of need.

Use edges and value the marginal - The interface between things are often the most valuable, diverse and productive elements in a system.

Use small and slow solutions - Small and slow systems are easier to maintain and more eco-efficient than big ones and/or fast ones.

FFI: www.permacultureinternational.org

energy

4.3 ENERGY SYSTEM BASICS

In this chapter, energy as it is used in homes and workplaces in the neighbourhood is the focus. Reducing energy for personal transport is covered under movement in Chapter 4. Energy is also embodied in products and materials, elements of this agenda are touched on in material on food and sustainable construction.

Key tenets

■ *Attention to the soft infrastructure*

Local involvement and control – support change through making energy efficient behaviours easier; use feedback through visible metering; use energy service companies (ESCOs) for local involvement and investment in alternative energy sources. Ensure residents understand how to live in comfort efficiently.

■ *Reduction in needs*

Efficient site layout and design – use passive solar capture and storage; pay attention to orientation, overshadowing, shelter belts and microclimate modification; design buildings with high levels of insulation and thermal mass as appropriate.
Efficient technologies – provide neighbourhood heat infrastructure (community heating), ensure efficient generation using combined heat and power, provide future flexibility in choice of fuels (via community heating), install efficient appliances.

■ *Renewable and decentralised energy systems*

Harnessing low-impact energy – use solar water heating, photovoltaic cells, wind turbines, energy from waste, energy from biomass, heat recovery, heat pumps, water turbines, geothermal, waste heat from industry.
A mix of local and distant sources – mix local microgeneration of energy (with heat where viable) with bought-in or co-owned distant renewable sources.

Reasons

The extent and nature of our current energy use, with its rapid depletion of fossil fuels, contributes to climate change. Yet, we still have winter deaths and ill-health linked to fuel poverty. Cold living conditions increase the risk of cardiovascular illnesses; damp homes are associated with a range of respiratory and allergic conditions. Not only are we wasteful in our use of energy but we don't even bother to make use of locally available sources of renewable energy in our neighbourhoods.

Social capital can be strengthened by involving people more closely as the consumers of energy, in new-build or regeneration schemes. This involvement is essential since lifestyle and behaviour have a critical impact on energy use. Fuel poverty can be tackled at the same time as a long-term strategy that helps to build-in future flexibility and reduce carbon emmisions.

- *European Common Indicator 2*
  Local contribution to global climate change

- *UK headline indicator*
  Emissions of greenhouse gasses

- *UK core set of indicators*
  Electricity from renewable sources

- *Neighbourhood indicator*
  Heat loss from buildings
  Household gas and electricity use

Energy efficiency for health:

Cost savings through *ending* fuel poverty!

The feasibility of a national 15-year energy efficiency programme for all poorly performing UK housing was assessed. The total costs are outweighed by the savings once the social benefits are taken into account. In particular, there are lasting health benefits.

Total programme costs	£12,612 million
Savings	
To the NHS	£5,234 million
From fuel costs	£5,630 million
From jobs created	£1,405 million
Others	£2,736 million
Total savings	£15,003 million

Goodacre, Sharples and Smith, 2000

Energy is central to all three strands of sustainable development:

- *Environmental – through climate change, pollution and ecological impacts*

- *Social – through contributing to quality of life and maintaining good health, and the eradication of fuel poverty*

- *Economic – through (literally) fuelling the economy and providing jobs*

LGA and LGMB 1998

Mitigating heat island effects

Heat islands occur in urban and suburban areas and are significantly warmer than their surroundings. The main causes are highly absorptive construction materials and a lack of effective landscaping. Heat island problems in large conurbations can reduce air quality and affect human health. They can also lead to increasing energy demand in the Summer for cooling.

Temperatures of dark dry surfaces in direct sun can reach 88°C, while a vegetated surface with moist soil might only reach 18°C under the same conditions.

Heat island health problems include:

- heat related health problems; heat exhaustion and heat stroke

- air quality related health problems; lung function, asthma and allergies

- sunlight-related health problems; skin cancers and eye disease

(Gartland 2008)

Fuel poverty defined

Fuel poverty housholds needing to spend 10% of income on fuel (2.5 million homes in the UK; approximately 8 per cent of the population).

Severe fuel poverty: households needing to spend 20% of income on fuel (1.5 million homes in the UK; approximately 5 per cent of the population).

Extreme fuel poverty: needing to spend 30% of income on fuel (1 million homes in the UK; approximately 3 per cent of the population).

Energy services

'Base energy policy and all decisions on the principle of providing the services needed with less use of damaging forms of energy.'

(LGA and LGMB 1998)

1.4 climate stability

TRENDS, DRIVERS AND CONTEXTS

Global warming

The Royal Commission on Environmental Pollution's report, Energy: the changing climate (RCEP 2000), called on government to reduce CO_2 emissions by at least 60 per cent over the next 50 years. Other reports and think tanks suggest more stringent cuts. All governments are using a number of mechanisms such as building regulations, planning policy and tax controls to achieve these cuts.

Mitigating the effects of climate change should also be of concern. With hotter dryer Summers (southern England could have the summer conditions of southern France by 2080) thermal safety and also comfort in the public realm needs to be considered.

Provision of shade, vegetation and specific materials and surface design to combat the heat island effect needs to be considered in heavily built-up areas.

Fuel poverty and energy costs

A household is in fuel poverty if, in order to maintain a satisfactory heating regime and cover other normal fuel costs, it would be required to spend more than 10% of its income on all household fuel use. Combating fuel poverty is a key government objective. The approach advocated in this guide will help to make buildings cheaper and easier to heat.

Zero-carbon and carbon-negative development

Zero-carbon means fossil fuels are not burned, or the emissions arising from such use are prevented from entering the atmosphere. Carbon-negative means that carbon is taken out of the atmosphere, such as by increasing the amount of woody plant material or by burning biomass with carbon sequestration. Climate change demands rapid and radical action. To support this the visionary goals of zero-carbon or carbon-negative development should be adopted. It is widely recognised that there are now no technical barriers to the construction of zero-carbon buildings, so lets now aim higher – for carbon absorbing neighbourhoods.

The zero-carbon neighbourhood, which also needs to support zero carbon lifestyles, needs careful attention. This guide provides an essential tool for those wishing to make this step.

Why use energy anyway?

People and businesses do not primarily need energy supply: people need the services energy gives them (warmth, light, cooling, transport, heat for cooking, machines to do tasks, etc.). We need to make a conceptual shift away from the 'provision of energy' to the 'provision of energy services', a re-focus on the actual need. The delivery of some 'energy services' may not require the use of any energy at all!

4.4 NEIGHBOURHOOD ENERGY PLANNING

An energy plan will develop a 'best fit' between the energy demand of a neighbourhood and the energy resources of its locality. Every neighbourhood is unique: even within a neighbourhood certain measures will be best suited to specific sub-areas, certain types of house or forms of tenure.

What opportunities exist to develop such a plan?

Major regeneration schemes as well as new build represent ideal opportunities for the comprehensive and strategic review needed for energy planning. In areas where change is incremental, processes such as Agenda 21, local planning partnerships and refurbishment schemes present possibilities for energy planning.

Who should prepare the plan?

The lead should be taken by a partnership involving the main development agent, local authority and an energy provider or Energy Service Company (ESCO – see below). A local strategic partnership, where one exists, should take the lead. It will be especially important to include residents/workers (regeneration and renovation) or make provision for their inclusion plan later (new build). Occupier behaviour is a very significant factor in energy use.

PARTNERS, PARTICIPANTS AND CONSULTEES

Local Authorities

Buildings and their localities are major determinants of energy intensity and supply options. Local authorities, through years of urban policy have significantly affected most facets of energy demand and supply. Physical planning specifically affects at least 70 per cent of use (Barton 1989). Local authorities need to acknowledge this critical impact and seek to increase the energy-autonomy and use of renewables in each settlement and every neighbourhood.

Developers

Developers can anticipate future regulations. A forward-looking response is to research and promote schemes that are innately energy efficient, both at the building and neighbourhood scale. An energy plan can offer a scheme planning and market advantages.

The Carbon Trust

The Carbon Trust was set up by the UK Government to accelerate the move to a low carbon economy. It works with organisations to reduce carbon emissions. It can provide advice and access to other forms of support. FFI: www.carbontrust.co.uk

Community Action for Energy

Tenant and residents groups and a community association save energy and improve health at Beacon Energy Action.

The initiative is a good example of the benefit of forging links between health and energy. The project is situated in a Health Action Zone and part of Beacon Community Regeneration Partnership, Cornwall, an area characterised by poor housing, low incomes and high rates of respiratory disease.

The project was designed to improve the energy efficiency of housing, regardless of tenure, in an area. Improvements in health, reduction in fuel poverty and involving and empowering local people were all goals. As part of the project local people were be trained as 'Energy Wardens' to extend the momentum beyond the 3-year project.

This project was part of Community Action for Energy. A range of help and support for making community buildings more energy efficient, bringing renewable energy to communities and helping local people save money on their fuel bills.

FFI: www.energysavingtrust.org.uk/cafe

Solar capture on the roofs in Vauban, Germany.

4.4

Urban Splash are housing developers known for innovation in urban architecture, this development in Altrincham is a good example the role of an Energy Service Company in an refurbishment project. A former Budenberg office building has been convered into 290 apartments.

*Budenburg Haus works on a 'private wire' system – it has its own internal electricity grid and heat network. Much of the energy needed is generated on-site, through combined heat-and-power (CHP). Extra electricity is imported wholesale from the grid when needed. Both sorts of power are sold on to the individual apartments. As the energy centre knows how much heat, water and electricity each flat is using, it can build up information about when power is most needed. At times of low demand, during the middle of the day when people are at work and at night, excess heat is stored as hot water in a tank under the car park ramp. Residents are charged for units of heating and hot water and not the energy per se. So it is in the interests of the energy services company, EcoCentroGen, to generate as efficiently as possible. Like all domestic customers, residents are free to switch to another energy supplier – but as EcoCentroGen promises to match competitors' prices, people have little incentive to go elsewhere.
The building's green features are used by Urban Spalsh as a selling point.*

Critics of the scheme have pointed out that in this case there are no onsite renewables and the energy centre is not equiped to sell excess power back to the grid. However this is one of a new generation of residential schemes to use a CPH system, claims are that it has reduced CO_2 consumption by 82%.

Utilities and ESCOs

Energy utilities can be a key stakeholder in larger schemes. Involving them early on will help match essential infrastructure suitable for low impact solutions. In addition to the national and international 'brands', smaller energy providers are emerging in response to local energy agendas, in the UK these are called Energy Service Companies (ESCOs).

Energy Service Companies are legal partnerships (public/private) formed to provide energy services. These are good vehicles for sustainable energy as their energy service provision can be tailored to local requirements.

Residents

Attitudes, understanding and behaviour are at the heart of low energy living. Profligate lifestyles will undo even the most energy efficient housing. Residents, resident groups and social landlords must be on-board and be given the information they need to support a less energy intensive homelife.

Houses which actually generate net electric power in Vauban, Germany. The energy company pays the occupiers for electricity.

2.2 the seven stage process

NEIGHBOURHOOD ENERGY PLAN

Phase 1 – Take the initiative and define a vision

A neighbourhood energy plan needs to be in the interests of the whole community and democratically accountable. The local authority must therefore be centrally involved. It may be in partnership with a major energy provider or providers, and liaise with companies/agencies/farmers with waste surplusses after re-use and recycling. Residents and businesses may be antagonistic if they percieve their territory is being imposed on from outside – for example constructing wind turbines. It is vital from the outset to share ownership with the community.

Engage partners and potential users in a briefing and future visioning workshop. Define the scope, objectives and agree a broad approach.

Phase 2 – Understand the locality and learn lessons

Assemble basic local information. Conduct a demand and user survey, a site and energy source analysis, and an institutional, management and stakeholder audit. Review the surrounding context such as large heat producers or users – industry, swimming pools, hospitals, schools, shopping malls. Research good and best practice.

The stakeholder group should respond to this information by developing a stategy, the group may need to be extended following this stage. Factor in longer-term strategic issues for the area and ensure that social and health outcomes are included in the energy planning.

Phase 3 – Develop ideas and options

Generate basic proposals and options with key actors. Carry out scoping for viability of Community Heating/Combined Heat and Power (see CHP Checklist 5.6). Create a 'long list' of possible measures to be employed:

■ **Spatial and built measures**
Built form: low energy design, layout, orientation and landscape.
Community distribution: local energy and heat distribution.
Local sourcing: microgeneration and locally controlled energy generation.
Buildings: insulation, double glazing, passive solar, active solar, thermal mass.

■ **Non-spatial measures**
Soft infrastructure: user control and usage feedback, low-energy clubs, energy wardens.
Kit: heat-recovery equipment, and low-energy appliances and light bulbs.
Green electricity: buying energy from suppliers who will provide energy from renewable sources.

Review proposals and options at a second briefing workshop with stakeholders. Include assumptions for user advice/training and support during and after implementation.

Phase 4 – Agree a programme and take action

Integrate the revised energy plan within the main spatial framework for the neighbourhood. Technical consultants will be needed to complete a detailed scheme. It is very easy to lose the required investment in 'soft infrastructure', ensure that users will be supported during and after hand-over.

> **CHECKLIST**
>
> **Universal Energy Sequential Test**
>
> *For use in new build, regeneration, refurbishment and appliance replacement.*
>
> **The energy hierarchy**
> 1 *reduce the need for energy*
> 2 *use energy more efficiently*
> 3 *use renewable energy*
> 4 *any continuing use of fossil fuels to be clean and efficient for heating and co-generation (CHP)*

2.9 Agreeing a co-ordinated programme

4.6 Community heating checklist

2.10 Taking action

Sources of advice and access to funding
Energy Efficiency - www.est.org.uk
Renewables - www.etsu.com
Combined Heat and Power - www.chpa.org.uk

Information about best practice in energy-efficiency and fuel-poverty strategies is available from the Centre for Sustainable Energy - www.cse.org.uk

4.5

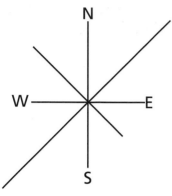

Figure 4.3
Wind rose 1

Understand local wind by plotting a wind rose for summer and winter

Wind chill greater than 900 w/m²

Per cent for all wind directions

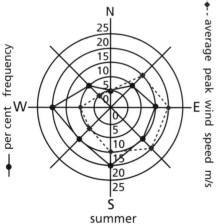

Figure 4.4
Wind rose 2

Plot wind chill percentages for eight compass points

summer

Figure 4.5
The feasibility of passive solar varies with latitude

A successful neighbourhood energy strategy begins with site planning.

The savings in lifetime fuel costs will be greater than the extra capital cost spent in reducing energy requirements. The synergistic appraoch avocated here also assumes that social and health benefits will also be sought as part of a holistic approach to energy planning.

The first aim should be to reduce wind speeds across the neighbourhood and to optimise solar access to all buildings through considered design of the layout and landscape. A step-by-step method to achieve this is described below.

STEP 1   NEIGHBOURHOOD CLIMATE

A careful assessment of the local climatic conditions combined with layout strategies to optimise the microclimate can reduce energy costs by 10 per cent (DETR 1997a).

Every neighbourhood will have its own local climatic conditions. For an efficient energy layout, the designer will need the following information:

■ *wind* – direction, strength and seasonal variations

■ *sun incident angles* – determined by latitude

■ *slope* – will influence solar access through lengthening shadows

■ *landform and landscape* – dips, escarpments, frost pockets, sheltering ridges, shelter belts

Latitude/ typical location		All year	10 months 21 Jan–21 Nov	9 months 6 Feb–6 Nov
60°N	Lerwick	66 m	40 m	25 m
58°N	Ullapool	46 m	31 m	21 m
56°N	Edinburgh	32 m	25 m	17 m
55°N	Belfast	31 m	23 m	16 m
54°N	York	28 m	21 m	15 m
52°N	Milton Keynes	23 m	17 m	< 15 m
50°N	Penzance	19 m	15 m	< 15 m

Spacing between houses for a minimum of 3 hours' solar access per day. Assumes solar access to ground floor windows on a flat site of two-storey houses with 30° pitched roofs (*DETR 1997A*).

STEP 2 SLOPE AND ASPECT

For solar access, the building density, house design type and orientation should be informed by the degree and aspect of slope. The balance between lower densities, enabling solar access for heat gain, and higher densities, supporting other aspects of sustainability, needs careful consideration. Passive solar gain is maximised when buildings are about 20 m apart, but this could conflict with the current density requirements. To prepare an optimal density plan the slope factors must be taken together with planned facility nodes and access requirements.

Slopes within 45° (or better 30°) of south will be especially valuable for siting houses designed for solar gain. Here, higher densities will be possible without losing solar access. Buildings on slopes with a northerly aspect may need to be more widely spaced to avoid overshadowing – or use higher densities here and alternative energy service provision since passive solar is less viable.

Figure 4.6
Shelter belt on a ridge

Use landform to increase the windshadow

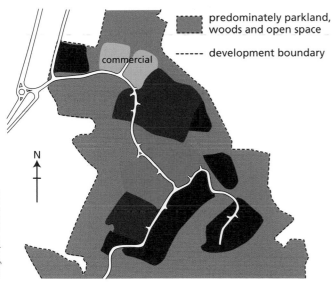

predominately parkland, woods and open space

------ development boundary

commercial

N

Image: After Tibbalds TM2

■ passive solar area
minimum of 70% of dwellings orientated within 25⁰ of south

■ mid density area
at least 60% of dwellings orientated within 25⁰ of south

■ urban development
maximise the number of dwellings orientated within 25⁰ of south

Figure 4.7
Zone the site for different objectives according to slope, aspect, access etc

SOURCE: Based on Tibbalds TM2

5.4 Graded densities

STEP 3 SHELTER BELTS

An ideal way to reduce wind speed at the neighbourhood scale is by the use of shelter belts. These should be designed to give other health benefits by providing amenity and wildlife (be careful to mainly use native species and avoid the quick-fix trap of leylandii).

Figure 4.8
Typical shelter belt composition

Use a variety of trees and shrubs to increase density

Design criteria for layout of neighbourhood shelter belts

- Place the belt perpendicular to, or within 45° of, the incidence of the prevailing wind.

- The area behind the belt protected from the wind is determined by the height and degree of porosity to wind.

- A 50 per cent porosity belt should be 15 m wide (10 m minimum), with a minimum length of 20 m.

- At 50 per cent porosity wind protection is effective for a height of up to half the height of the shelter belt. Figure 4.9 gives distances and heights of protection for two different values of porosity.

- To ensure good solar access do not position a building to the north closer to a shelter belt than 3 to 4 times the shelter belt's height.

Design details for achieving an effective 50 per cent belt

Porosity is determined by species composition and width – aim for 50 per cent porosity. Denser shelter belts provide more wind speed reduction but for a shorter distance.

- Use a mixture of climax and sub-climax deciduous and evergreen trees for the core. If deciduous trees are used for the main height, the solar 'stand-off' zone can be at the narrower end of the scale.

- An irregular top profile, clumps of taller trees, will further break up the air stream.

- The windward face should be fairly abrupt in the vertical plane but gently irregular in plan.

- Both faces should be well clothed with smaller trees and woodland edge/hedgerow shrubs lower down.

Figure 4.9

Calculating wind shadow characteristics for shelter belts

For two-storey buildings Protection:	Shelter belt height	'Stand-off' distance for solar access (MEASURED WITHIN 30° TO THE NORTH OF THE BELT)	zone experiencing up to 50% reduction in wind speeds	
			medium belt: 50% porosity	dense belt: 20% porosity
up to the eaves (5 m)	10 m	30–40 m	10–80 m	0–65 m
up to the ridge (7.5 m)	15 m	45–60 m	15–120 m	0–100 m
well above the ridge (10 m)	20 m	60–80 m	20–160 m	0–130 m
maximum protection afforded			65% reduction	75% reduction

Figure 4.10

Effects of a shelter belt on windspeed

Typical percentage wind reduction for a shelter belt, height = h

wind direction

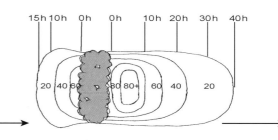

Figure 4.11

Shelter belt characteristics for some common tree species

SOURCE: PSA 1988a, 1988b

Shelter belts can encourage wildlife and provide amenity for greenways.

4.19 Increasing wildlife planning

5.6 Green infrastructure

Name	Porosity		max ht (m)	Full leaf
	SUMMER	WINTER		
Acer platanoides: Norway maple	1	5	15–25	mid April–mid Nov
Aesculus hippocast: Horse chestnut	2	5	20–30	early May–early Nov
Betula pendula: European birch	3	6	15–25	early May–early Nov
Fagus sylvatica: Common beech	1	6	18–30	late May–late Nov
Fraxinus species: Ash	2	5	15–25	early May–early Nov
Platanus acerifolia: London plane	1	4	30–35	late May–late Nov
Populus tremuloides: Aspen	3	6	12–15	mid April–mid Nov
Quercus robur: English oak	2	6	20–30	early May–early Nov
Taxus baccata: English yew	0–1	0–1	12–15	evergreen
Tilia cordata: Small-leaved lime	1	4	15–25	late May–late Nov

Porosity: 0 = low (stops wind more); 6 = high (lets wind through more)

STEP 4 ORIENTATION PLUS PLACEMAKING

To optimise passive solar gain, housing front/back walls should be orientated to face within 30 degrees of south/north up to 45 degrees is still worth it on south facing slopes and this can narrow to 20-25 degrees on north facing slopes. These requirements must be fulfilled by a layout which also gives rise to an interesting and varied neighbourhood character and makes a successful place.

Image: © Tibbalds TM2

Figure 4.12
Housing layout for solar access can provide good urban form

Figure 4.13
Housing layout for solar access can respond to context

SOURCE: R. Guise

A. A layout which has the sole aim of achieving south facing elevations to maximise solar gain. This approach can, however, result in a poor street frontage and monotonous spaces between buildings.

B. A layout which achieves south or south west orientations for almost all units and (a) responds more sympathetically to the street scene, (b) creates more appropriate spaces between buildings.

Source: Building Futures at www.hertslink.org

Passive solar design can fit into the volume builder's portfolio

Standard house type but with nearly twice as much glazing on the south elevation. Design study by Barratt (Southern Counties), James and Keearns Architects.

SOURCE: DETR and DTI 1999

Front: North elevation; 7.15 m² glazing

Back: South elevation;13.2 m² glazing

Financial and technical support for CHP

Grants can be available for the development of plans for CHP schemes, and in some cases to support the capital cost of a scheme.

The Energy Saving Trust supports community heating schemes as part of its energy services programme. www.est.org.uk

The Combined Heat and Power Association exists to operate a programme of support, advice and consultancy for CHP and mCHP development. www.chpa.co.uk

STEP 5 BUILDING FORM

Unless buildings are superinsulated less external wall for a given internal volume means less heat loss. With an internal living space of some 500 m³, a detached house will have an external wall area of 200 m². A semi-detached house with the same internal dimensions will have an external wall area of around 150 m², and in a terraced house the external wall area will be reduced to about 100 m². With inadequate insulation this will halve the heat losses through the walls. Reducing exposure to the external environment, for instance by setting elements of the building into the ground, should also be examined. In designs with very high levels of insulation, there will be no difference in heat loss through the walls; however the environmental impact argument then revolves around energy embodied in the insulating materials and wall thickness. The walk-up terrace form having a reduced embodied energy. The use of four storey walk-up flats as a building form takes the reduction in enegy (embodied or in heat loss) to the next level.

Maximise solar gains and minimise losses by providing 60–75 per cent of the glazing on the south elevation. This approach, often found in vernacular cottages, can provide some very desirable homes. The impact of this approach on standard estate house types and internal layout of rooms needs consideration. These aspects of building design are outside the scope of this guide, but typical layouts and further details can be found in Chapter 5. Thermal buffering (the use of an atrium or conservatory) and high levels of insulation should also be explored.

Wind friction

4.21 Urban trees

Plan for additional dispersed tree planting (in addition to shelter belts) across the neighbourhood to reduce wind speeds through increasing wind friction. Tree location and groupings can be chosen that enhance character and sense of place.

4.6 SOURCING AND DISTRIBUTING ENERGY

The deregulated market provides the context for using a variety of energy sources. A diversity of local and small scale supply will help meet all six principles of neighbourhood design in a way that large remote powerstations and the current national distribution grid never can.

Using a 'private wire' system and a meter to the national grid, locally generated energy can be combined with energy bought in from the grid (this can also be renewably sourced). Excess energy generated locally can be sold back through the national grid. The details of buying and selling electricity are governed by electricity trading arrangements. This is a complex area and up-to-date advice will be required. Social landlords can also sell locally generated electricity to their tenants.

SOURCING ENERGY

Collective purchase

Collective purchase agreements can allow neighbourhoods to influence and support renewable energy generation. These are group contracts whereby a bulk purchase of electricity is agreed with a nominated supplier.

Small-scale wind turbines and community windfarms

Appropriate wind initiatives in an urban situation are either small wind generators or community/cooperative windfarms. Usually roof mounted, a number of highly efficient systems are on the market. These provide an alternative to the larger scale rural or offshore windfarms. There is good compatibility with local demand since it tends to be more windy in the seasons that require more lighting and space heating. The city farm, a large allotment site, a parks depot or local refuse tip: are all locations that could both use and accommodate small-scale wind turbines (2.5kW to 6kW). For urban residential settings, there are also a range of micro-tubines (1kW to 2.5Kw) both horizontal and vertical axis technologies, that are almost silent, with very low operational wind speeds. Normal planning regulations – regarding noise, visual intrusion and safety – would apply. In general, wind turbines on domestic buildings can be uneconomic and frought with structural and vibration issues.

Essential conditions:

- *Area wind speed* – area with a local annual average windspeed of 6 m/s or more at the height of the proposed installation. Check on meterological website or for the UK visit the Department for Business Enterprise and Regulation Reform windspeed database.

- *Micro wind speed and quality* – no significant nearby obstacles such as buildings, trees or hills that are likely to reduce the windspeed or increase turbulence.

The added value of pursuing wind at the neighbourhood scale, rather than building by building, lies in the potential for collective investment, in larger scale turbines. Ideally these would be situated in an appropriate nearby situation in open land and on higher ground. Suitable investment management vehicles would be a social landlord, a local management group set-up by inspired developer or set up by other local organisations; maybe growing out of the transition movement or other concerned interests.

The first community-led windfarm in the UK

Awel Aman Tawe, Upper Swansea Valley

This will be the first community-led and fully community-owned windfarm in the UK. Awel Aman Tawe is a community-led project to develop a small windfarm as a major community asset providing sustainable funding for local regeneration and a source of renewable energy to UK customers. In addition, it will disseminate valuable lessons to the renewable energy industry regarding the processes of gaining community support.

The objective is to establish a small community-owned and managed windfarm which will generate sustainable funding to:
- *assist in the regeneration of the Upper Amman/Swansea Valley areas; and*
- *support the implementation of Local Agenda 21 (LA21) objectives.*

A comprehensive participatory assessment and collaborative planning process aims to explore the issues pertinent to communities, and generate a series of lessons as to how to replicate the process of community leadership in this sector.

Cost: £3 million

Projected income of windfarm: £192,000– £383,000 per annum

For further information, contact www.awelamantawe.co.uk

Photo: Tom Albery

Small scale wind turbines on urban industrial park, Thatcham, Berkshire.

Rotterdam

Mass heat generation: Road decks, Rotterdam

Innovative heat generation systems have been installed on a motorway flyover in Rotterdam, by a Dutch building company called Ooms, and also in Scotland, by Invisible Heating Systems. The Scottish example generates 108 megawatts a year from a 400-square-meter parking lot, which heats a 1,500-square-meter office building and adjacent workshops. Such systems take advantage of the high absorption capacity of asphalt.

In Rotterdam the system extracts about 270 kilowatts per square meter a year, about half that of a solar panel on a roof. But the designers say that the cost is about a twelfth that of a solar panel and there is a much larger area of tarmac available. Claims have been made that for every kilowatt of electricity the system needs to pump water around the pipes, it generates 25 kilowatts of heat.

Solar panels retrofitted to this housing block in Freiburg, funded by the construction and sale of an additional penthouse floor of accommodation.

Solar electricity

Photovoltaics compliment wind energy as they are more efficient in summer with more sunlight available. This renewable technology is highly compatible with the urban realm as it can easily be integrated into the built form as roofing material, shading, and cladding. The technology is also one of the easiest to retrofit and should be given close consideration in all refurbishment projects and renwal programmes.

In Germany, large numbers of solar voltaic systems are being installed by individuals and house builders supported by central government policy. This has ensured financial security for pay-back of the installation investment through guaranteeing a good price for domestically generated excess electricity. Basically the Government, through subsidy, has supported an attractive selling price (or 'feed-in tarrif', as it is known) for householder produced electricity.

Solar hot water – building scale

It is more productive to heat water directly with dedicated solar thermal equipment than it is to use photo voltaics for electrical heating of water. Thermal collectors can be used to provide hot water for space heating or for washing requirements.

Solar heat collectors – large scale

Systems involving the use of large areas of tarmac as heat collectors are being investigated and trialled – see side box. For economic efficiency these systems should be installed during road maintenance or when new roads, car parks, or airport runways are constructed, rather than attempting retrofitting.

The system involves the hot asphalt transferring heat to water via a series of embedded water pipes. The hot water is then pumped into an underground aquifer where heat exchangers extract the energy from the circulating water before it returns to the surface. The aquifer acts as a heat store, which in winter can be tapped by pumping water through the aquifer, up to the surface, and into buildings. Through keeping a road frost free maintenance costs and accident costs are reduced. The installed system can also be used to circulate cool water in Summer using a second aquifer, as cool store, this can be used to keep buildings (and road surfaces) cool.

Heat pumps: ground, air or water source

Heat pumps work on the same principle as a refrigerator, only in reverse. The technology transfers heat from one location to another. In a heat pump, 'low grade' dissapated energy is extracted from ground, air or water and is released as usable heat within buildings. The heat being collected is from the sun's warmth, a small amount of electricity is needed to run the techology. If this is also from a renewable source the techology is carbon neutral. In a typical urban area available heat collecting areas are gardens and lawns, road surfaces and hard standing.

Small-scale water turbines

In some areas small water turbines may provide a useful local power source. In the smallest hydroelectric schemes, the head of water can be a few metres. Hydroelectric systems can be connected to the main electricity grid, or can be part of a stand-alone power system. Any electricity generated in excess of consumption on site can be 'sold' to electricity companies.

The simplest schemes are known as 'run-of-river', they utilise the natural flow of a river, continuity of flow can be enhanced by a weir. 'Storage' schemes would also be viable for a neighbourhood scale development, where a dam impounds water, giving more continuity and control of supply. Both storage and run-of-river schemes can be diversion schemes where water is channelled from a river, lake or dammed reservoir to a remote powerhouse containing the turbine and generator. A canal or low-pressure tunnel transports the water to this facility and then back to the river or to another watercourse.

Biomass

Fast-growing species such as willow can be grown as a crop to feed into a boiler/CHP generator. In a neighbourhood context, such biomass production fields can be designed to fulfil additional functions. With controlled access and zoning, amenity uses, buffering from noise/roads and foul waste treatment can be accommodated. Foul waste can actually increase the growth rate of some of the biomass species. As a local resource, some parts of the country have surplus wood available from tree maintenance and sustainable woodland management.

Waste

Although deriving energy from large-scale district incinerators is sometimes seen as an environmentally dirty source, on a neighbourhood scale there may be specific wastes which can be cleanly burnt for heat or power (tree surgery arisings, for example). These are termed carbon neutral as the carbon emmited has been captured in recently and is not fossil.

Eighty local investers clubbed together to fund this large solar photovoltaic installation. The location is inspirational, and uses a south facing road verge.

4.6

'Only around 40 per cent of primary energy input (coal or gas) used in power stations is converted into usable electricity, the rest is wasted heat. A further nine per cent is lost as the power moves through the transmission and distribution system. Then a further third is lost in our homes and offices because they are poorly insulated, not designed with energy in mind, and inhabited by people who do not see themselves as players in the energy game.'

Quote from Grid 2.0: The next generation (Willis 2006, p. 6).

CHECKLIST for a community heat distribution scheme

Basic scoping. Listed below are some indicators for a successful community heating/combined heat and power (CH/CHP) scheme (note these are not requirements for every scheme, but where four or more are present success is more likely).

- A project champion

- A core institutional user present or nearby

- A social landlord or management company

- 300 dwellings or more

- A medium- to high-density built form

- An existing CH scheme in the locality

Other factors for success. These secondary factors will also assist if present:

- An opportunity for cooling requirements

- A source of waste heat

A preliminary discussion with people involved in the field can help. A first point of contact is the Energy Services Association, who may be able to put you in touch with someone involved in a similar scheme.

Feasibility study and layout. The addition of a CH/CHP scheme is not a key determinant of the spatial framework of a neighbourhood. Following basic scoping, a full feasibility study will be needed to determine what configuration the system should have and how it could be financed. Grants may be obtainable for this. Where possible, plan to route heat pipes through 'soft' landscape and avoid major roads.

Geothermal

Based on hot rocks and hot aquifers. Over the longer term this energy source becomes locally depleted. However, due to hot aquifers at a depth of some 1.5–2.0 km in several areas of the UK, it is a useful energy in the medium term and can be a viable energy source to help kick-start a heating distribution network. In Southampton, UK, a local geothermal source has been successfully linked into an extensive community heating network.

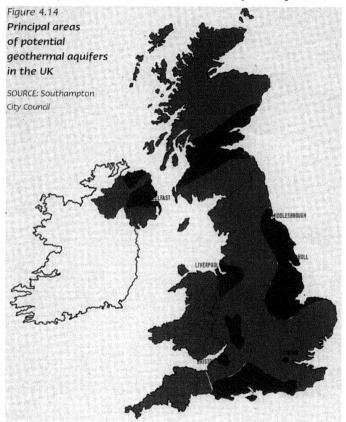

Figure 4.14
Principal areas of potential geothermal aquifers in the UK

SOURCE: Southampton City Council

Combined heat and power: Conventional (CHP) and micro/mini (mCHP) systems

These are highly efficient energy-production systems. They supply both electricity and heat. In conventional CHP the heat is distributed by community heating schemes. In mCHP the unit is integrated into the buildings heating system, being little larger than a domestic condensing boiler. Unlike conventional CHP with mCHP heat is the main output and electricity is the by-product often not needed in the building at the times generated. Viability depends on the details of feed-in tariffs. Both types of plant can also be used to provide cooling if required. The installation of a CHP plant is the ideal catalyst for the laying of community heating distribution: see 'Distributing energy' below. Some plants can use a mixture of fuel sources, including waste, to generate power.

This type of energy source is ideal for new housing at all scales and an especially good solution for social landlords or where an element of co-housing or a management vehicle is envisaged. CHP is especially compatible with 'mixed use' urban design since it is more viable with a broad range of heat consumers. Use new major investment in swimming pools, hospitals or town centres as a trigger.

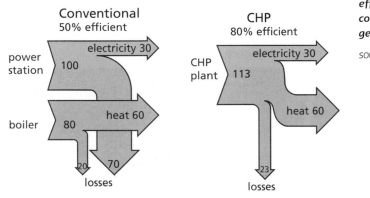

Figure 4.15
CHP is more efficient than conventional generation

SOURCE: DETR 1999H

'Buildings account for almost half the UK's energy consumption ... Combined Heat and Power schemes use waste heat and can increase fuel efficiency to 70–90 per cent (compared with 30–50 per cent with conventional electricity generation).'

SOURCE: Space For Growth, English Partnerships

DISTRIBUTING ENERGY

Community heating is the distribution of heat to users using an infrastructure of heating mains pipes. The heat can be fully controllable by the end users. End uses can be water heating, space heating or conversely, cooling (via absorption chillers).

Significant savings in fuel bills can be achieved by community heating, usually in the order of 10 per cent below the cheapest other option. It has often been called district heating, though the first-generation district heating systems had less user control and gave the technology a poor reputation. An advantage is that the basic infrastructure (heat mains and a heat exchanger for each user) needs less maintenance and has a longer working life than the conventional best practice of providing every user with a high-tech (condensing) boiler.

Community heating systems provide future flexibility and can distribute heat from any variety of energy sources – biomass, heatpumps, domestic waste, gas, 'waste' heat from industry. This flexibility gives opportunities for connection of renewables even when continuity of supply may not be assured. For the end user, a simple heat exchanger replaces the traditional boiler. The heat is controllable and can be metered.

Community heating schemes usually include a combined heat and power plant, though even in their absence there are economic and environmental benefits for community heating through bulk purchase of fuel, load diversification and future fuel flexibility. Laying heating pipes can be disruptive and expensive, therefore it makes sense to do this as part of area-wide infrastructure development prior to building or major refurbishment. For viability,

4.6

Heat and power plants are particularly compatible with mixed-use neighbourhoods for two reasons:

1 The wider spread of heat demand throughout the daily, weekly and seasonal time cycles creates a more even demand profile.

2 The closer proximity of users and plant reduces the amount of expensive heat-pipe infrastructure required.

The urban design planning implications are further developed in Section 5.3 – a mix of uses

consumers will have to be committed to buying their energy from the scheme, this requirement needs addressing as part of the soft infrastructure package. Community Heating and Combined Heat and Power plants are particularly compatible with mixed-use neighbourhoods for two reasons:

1 The wider spread of heat demand throughout the daily, weekly and seasonal time cycles creates a more even demand profile.

2 The closer proximity of users and plant reduces the amount of expensive heat-pipe infrastructure required.

The urban design planning implications are further developed in Section 6.7 – Space and energy sharing.

Figure 4.16
Southampton community heating

The network delivering heating and cooling to buildings in the city centre, Southampton. Heat is provided from a geothermal generator and a CHP generator that also provides electric power

SOURCE: Southampton City Council

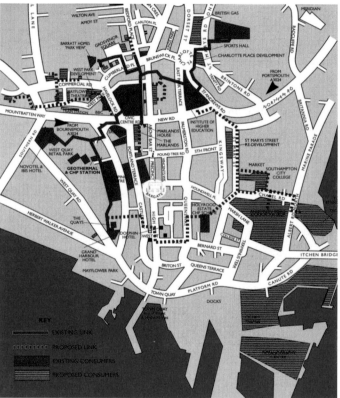

Figure 4.17
Community heating idealised layout – mixed uses make infrastructure more economic

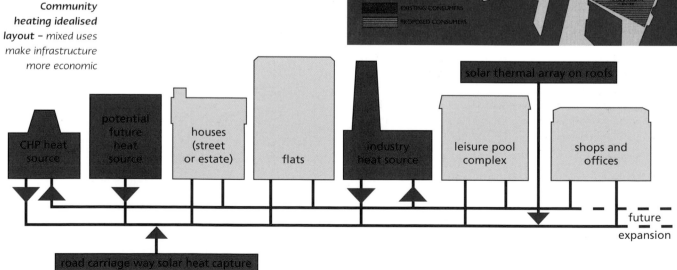

water

4.7 WATER CYCLE BASICS

Sustainable water practice has implications for the public realm and layout of a neighbourhood. In order to ensure the best public health and sustainability outcomes, an integrated approach needs to be developed from the outset.

There are potential synergies with objectives for wildlife, movement, food, qualty of life and reducing carbon emmisions. There is also great potential for creating special landscapes and attractive places.

Key tenets

The tenets below can be applied to new build, renovation and regeneration. They can make neighbourhoods more desirable with improved market value, hand in hand with environmental benefits.

■ *Value the asset*

Reduce reliance on distant sources – survey and use local sources such as rain, streams, wells and springs.
Reduce use – match use to water quality – use rain water and grey water where possible; collect and re-use water within the neighbourhood.
Celebrate urban watercourses and ponds – provide access to streams, use ponds for amenity settings and wildlife.

■ *Control downstream impact*

Reduce flood risk – use sustainable urban drainage systems to even out the flows and improve the quality.
Recharge aquifers – use porous surfacing and soakaways where possible.
Subsidiarity principle – manage quality and quantity issues as close as possible to their source.

Reasons

We traditionally build our neighbourhoods in a way that contributes, almost negligently, to the persistent waste of this resource. We design houses to flush drinking quality water down toilets and, in the past, to pour useful rain water falling on our rooftops straight into sewers. Streams that could be valuable for wildlife and contribute to our quality of life lie in underground pipes or suffer from habitat destruction through chronic low flows.

In the UK recently, we seem either to have an abundance of water and flooding or a drought. Strategic water planning is catchment based. Each neighbourhood has a part to play in water management – reducing downstream flood risk, reducing scarcity, improving quality. When properly planned for in a neighbourhood, the water resource can benefit amenity and wildlife, whilst evening out glut and scarcity.

- **UK Core set of indicators**
  Household water use and peak demand
  Water demand and availability

- **UK Headline indicator**
  Rivers of good or fair quality

- **Neighbourhood QOL indicators**
  Metered domestic water use
  Watercourse or waterbody quality

Smart growth
Creating quality developments
the role that water can play

- *Reduced risk of flooding and consequential liabilities*

- *Improved quality of landscape setting and amenity through use of wetland habitats*

- *Opportunity for reduced water and sewerage charges*

- *Increase in wildlife range and quality*

- *More water available for gardens/ allotments during drought*

4.8

Including water strategy in planning documents

Supplementary planning guidance produced by Reigate and Banstead Borough Council, the Horley Design Guide, relates to the expected provision of some 2,600 dwellings after 2001. Water resources, both surface water and water consumption, are dealt with comprehensively.

An open space, the 'Riverside Green Chain', is proposed as a location for attractive new features that are functional parts of the source control regime, such as shallow watercourses, ponds and reed beds. This will have biodiversity and amenity benefits.

Other measures detailed include rain water storage of 225 l per curtilage, downpipe discharge to grass swales, and wet and dry ponds and minimising mains water consumption.

Maintenance of the drainage features has also been included.

*Environmental Policy Services
Reigate and Banstead Borough Council
www.reigate-banstead.gov.uk*

4.8   NEIGHBOURHOOD WATER PLANNING

At a local level the water planning for a neighbourhood, town or district needs good fit with the larger functional component in which is sits – the catchment. In all areas some form of water planning process will already be in operation.

PARTNERS, PARTICIPANTS AND CONSULTEES

National or Regional Water Agencies

These bodies have the responsibility for many aspects of the water environment, including issuing consents to abstract water or discharge water, environmental protection, water resource management and flood risk management. These bodies manage water planning processes, including water quality/flooding and water demand management.

Water companies

In the UK, the Environment Act 1995 placed a duty on water companies to promote the efficient use of water by their customers. Water companies local to a neighbourhood have been major players in sustainable neighbourhood development schemes on the continent. Water companies can reduce charges for customers who implement water-efficiency measures.

Professional institutions for water management

In the UK, the professional body is the Chartered Institution of Water and Environmental Management, it can provide a range of expert advice and assistance in developing a strategic approach to local water resources (www.ciwem.org.uk).

Environmental health officers

Local environmental health officers should be kept informed and involved in schemes dealing with issues such as local bore holes or grey water recycling. The local authority environmental health section can also be a good source of advice and regulatory information.

Consumers

Residents will need to be involved and to understand a local water regime that may be different from conventional approaches. New skills must be learnt; a certain degree of monitoring or even management may be required. In domestic situations, for example, there may be some water that is non-potable. Inappropriate disposal of chemicals into one part of the system could lead to adverse consequences: for example, a noxious chemical disposed of in a paving gully may end up being watered on plants. In-house grey water treatment units require periodic checking and top-up of decontamination chemicals.

NEIGHBOURHOOD WATER CYCLE PLAN

Phase 1 – Take the initiative and define a shared vision

A full understanding of local water resources and the water cycle is needed as a precursor to developing low-impact solutions. Take up this remit early on and feed it into the spatial planning process.

- The development does not exist in isolation. It is influenced by discharges 'upstream' and it will in turn influence areas 'downstream'.

- A partnership will be needed between local authorities, water companies and the relevant public water agency. Residents and businesses will also need to be brought on board as a more clear strategy emerges.

Phase 2 – Understand the locality and learn lessons

Widen the horizon from just thinking about mains supply of drinking water and off-site disposal of waste water – to a review of all water sources, water movement and possible options for use/re-use, drainage and aquifer recharge. Exchange information with other neighbourhoods and regions who are further ahead and learn from their experiences.

- Conduct a basic review of water resources in the neighbourhood, including 'hidden' water such as rainwater, culverts and storm water entering from adjoining areas.

- Differentiate between the different qualities of water found both in use, after use, and in the landscape.

Phase 3 – Develop ideas

A comprehensive water management strategy will be needed with calculations of estimated flow. Create and discuss a long list of measures including:

- **Spatial and built measures**
Large scale lansdscape features: water bodies for storage, control and treatment, permeable surfaces and swales,
Local sourcing: water harvesting, rain water collection,
Buildings: living machines, green roofs

- **Non-spatial measures**
Soft infrastructure: user buy-in, visible water metering
Kit: grey and rainwater systems, dry closets, low use applicances

Phase 4 – Agree a programme and take action

The developing water plan needs to be continually adapted for best fit with the other emerging resource system plans, health and well-being objectives, and the developing spatial framework.

2.2 The seven stage process

2.7 Understanding the locality

2.10 Taking action

CHECKLIST

Recognising water		Options for use or discharge
Type	Source	
Blue	Running or standing water	Use to enhance amenity and wildlife on site
White	Mains water	Drinking, body washing, cooking
Grey	Baths, showers, washing machines	Treat then use for washing cars, watering gardens, flushing WCs. Dispose to reed bed or other local biological treatment and nutrient capture
Green	Captured roof rain water	Washing cars, watering gardens, flushing WCs
Black	Flushing WCs, kitchen sinks	Dispose to mains sewer, cess-pit or local biological treatment for nutrient re-cycling

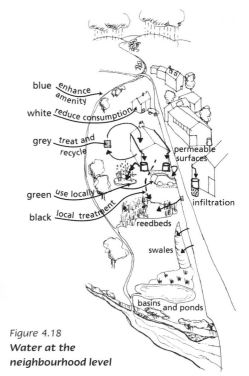

Figure 4.18
Water at the neighbourhood level

4.9

Ekostaden, Malmö, Sweden

A partnership between the housing association and neighbouring industrial estate landlord (the municipal authority) is developing an innovative programme to solve problems and enhance the quality of local life. The 1 ha of flat roof on the industrial site is being retrofitted with a shallow cover of plants. This has resulted in a 60 per cent attenuation of water run-off, better insulation and longer life for the roof covering.

Downpipes in the housing area are being fed into a system of newly created open channels alongside pavement and reed beds. The aim is to relieve pressure on the combined sewer system and reduce flood risk. This is being achieved and with positive spin-offs for local amenity, biodiversity and water quality.

Residents and the local authority are supporting the project, which is leading to improvements in quality of life.

SUDs component making a strong contribution to the urban scene

SOURCE: John Dolecek

WATER NEUTRALITY

Water neutrality has two aspects. In supply, it is achieved when the contruction of a new development results in no overall increase in total water demand. Water neutrality in discharge is achieved when run-off from a new development mimics the situation of a vegated undeveloped site in quantity and quality.

Neutrality in discharge should be the ambition for all new developments and is acheivable. Neutrality in supply is a worthwhile ambition but very challenging. It could be met by 'off-setting' some of the extra water demand through water saving measures in surrounding buildings financed by the development.

4.9   LOCAL SUPPLY AND TREATMENT

WORKING WITH SURFACE WATER

■   *Restore watercourses and replenish ground water*

In dense urban areas water courses can run in an open channel alongside verges, walkways and roadways. Where there is more room a natural channel can be re-formed though parkland or other green space. De-culverting and restoration is closely linked to flood risk control and re-construction of natural watercourse features. The Institute of Civil Engineers considers that all urban watercourses, no matter how small, should be considered for restoration back to nature.

Recharge local aquifers where possible through use of soakaways, permeable surfaces and wetland features.

■   *Celebrate urban watercourses and ponds*

Well-designed water 'features' can enhance the quality, amenity and values in a neighbourhood. Both ponds, lakes and moving water-courses can safely be incorporated into even the most urban of schemes. Where possible, facilitate access to water but have regard to safety. There may also be access requirements for maintenance.

Risks associated with open water features are often raised by the community. The myth of the danger is far greater than any actual risk. Once this has been dealt with by exploring the statistics with concerned stakeholders, the actual risk can be minimised by good design and community education.

REDUCING DEMAND

In addition to rainwater harvesting and recycling, in new build or comprehensive refit/regeneration the developer has an opportunity to reduce neighbourhood water demand through the installation of water-efficient devices and appliances. A range of products are available – showers, water-saving baths, low flush toilets (and retrofitting water-saving 'hippos'), spray taps, more efficient dishwashers and washing machines.

In some locations significant reductions in quantity can be possible by using a dry composting toilet system. For initial public acceptance, these can be introduced on allotments, community orchards and city farms.

HARVESTING RAINWATER

Rainwater can be collected from roofs. There are methods for disposing of the initial run-off or first flush, which contains most contaminants. At its simplest, roof rainwater can be collected for an individual house by a rainwater butt: this is then used to water the garden. However, if integrated at a larger design scale (street, home-patch or even neighbourhood), rainwater can be fed into a communal treatment and distribution system – broadening the choice of end-uses.

Rainwater collected as run-off from paved surfaces will tend to be more contaminated than that from roofs. In some situations, though, this can be infiltrated directly into the ground or fed in to surface water systems such as reed beds or ponds.

GREY-WATER RE-USE

While water recycling is a sustainable approach and can be cost-effective in the long term, the installation of grey-water systems can be initially expensive. There are public health concerns that can make it difficult to implement water recycling projects. These are not insurmountable and their remedy lies in regular system maintenance.

There are two main approaches for grey-water recycling, with differing impact on neighbourhood design and layout. Decentralised grey-water systems and shared biological treatment, these are outlined below.

Decentralised grey-water re-use

There are several proprietary domestic systems available. Basically these work by collecting, filtering, treating and storing used water on an individual house by house basis. The equipment will require periodic maintenance and a pump is used to pump the water back-up for re-use.

Shared biological treatment

The neighbourhood design scale presents the opportunity for shared grey-water treatment systems.

Living machines: A living machine is a specially designed glazed facility which uses a combination of sunlight and vegetative processes to treat the communal grey water. The facility can also provide a communal indoor gardening amenity (see side box).

Communal grey-water use

Shettleston Housing Association, Glasgow

This scheme comprised sixteen units of new-build terrace and flat development.

Low resource impact was designed for in both construction and management.

The homes are partially heated using geothermal energy from a disused mine below the site. After the heat is extracted from water pumped up from the mine, this water is then fed into a grey-water system serving all the WC cisterns in the housing.

Grey water integrated with renovation

Kolding, Denmark

The Municipality of Kolding is in the process of carrying out an urban ecology pilot project sponsored by the Danish Housing Board. This project covers ecologically orientated urban renewal in a block of flats with 129 existing flats and plans for 14 new flats. These houses lack a number of things as regards modern installations, insulation and maintenance.

Housing improvements in the individual properties are in progress. The owners have had the opportunity of receiving support for energy and water saving schemes, such as extra insulation, active and passive solar heating, water-saving toilet closets and fittings and recycling of rainwater for flushing the toilet.

Sections of the former private backyards have been fitted out as a common area with space for community purposes such as composting household waste. In the centre of this common area, a large glass pyramid, in which there is a biological purifying plant for waste water, has been built. The cleaned waste water is led outside the pyramid to permeate the soil in the area.

Water Safety

Accident-preventative approach

Care needs to be taken in the design of features with standing surface water to minimise risk of accidental drowning.

The Royal Society for Prevention of Accidents runs a consultancy and advice service. They have uncovered four links in the chain to drowning. A preventive strategy must be designed to break these links.

1 Ignorance, disregard or misjudgement of danger

2 Unrestricted access to hazards

3 Absence of adequate supervision

4 Inability to save oneself or to be rescued

Water bodies should be designed from the outset both to minimise the hazard (though gently shelving margins) and to reduce access to deep water (through location of paths and the use of vegetation).

Water balancing system as part of the local play amenities in Reisfeld. The culture seems more concerned with health and has concerned with 'health and safety.' Notice the design provides for good overlooking and no fences.

Reed beds: Where space permits, a system of reed beds can be used to treat grey water. In some instances this can be designed to accept 'black water' in a fenced-off section. This is only acceptable in certain areas where there is no risk of groundwater or run-off contamination and where traditional sewer systems are unavailable. There are of course important maintenance issues though the reed-bed system can also be managed for biodiversity.

Approach	Description	Pros and cons
Individual house systems	Grey water collected by waste pipe from appropriate sources. In-house collection, treatment header tank for use in WCs	**Pro**: No influence on neighbourhood spatial design **Con**: Increase in household plumbing maintenance
Shared systems living machines	Grey water collected by waste pipe from appropriate sources to central treatment facility Distribution back to houses by secondary 'recycled water' rising main Bespoke design at the terrace, living zone or sub-neighbourhood scale	**Pros** Treatment plant can be integrated with amenity uses Centralised maintenance. Treatment possible to higher quality therefore more uses for the water produced **Cons** Land required for treatment. Community or residents' management company required

Nutrient recapture

Conventional sewage systems adopt a mix first and separate later approach to waste and water. Faeces is mixed with the liquid of urine and (usually drinking quality) fresh water to be carried to treatment works to then separate out dry matter and liquid. There are important system issues to deal with here both in terms of water and nutrient cycles. These are only beginning to be addressed within the urban sustainability debate. Further coverage can be found in the material section under local resource recovery.

4.17 Local resource recovery

4.10 FLOODING, DRAINAGE AND RUN-OFF

SURFACE CONTROL

The basic philosophy is for a developed area to mimic a natural area in terms of quantity and quality of run-off. This is the concept behind sustainable drainage systems. These use a multitude of techniques to control quality and quality of run-off as close to the source as possible. The method, set out fully in any good design manuals for sustainable urban drainage systems, entails reviewing and modelling a number of options to find the best solution.

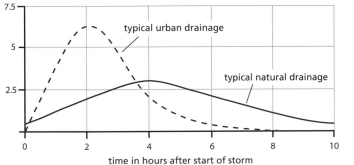

Figure 4.19
Comparison between natural drainage and a developed area with no storm water retention

SOURCE: After Hough 1995

SUSTAINABLE DRAINAGE SYSTEMS

Key objectives

- Attempt to control water discharge as soon as possible after precipitation (source control).

- Slow down the speed of discharge off-site (control of quantity).

- Use passive techniques to filter and settle suspended matter (control of quality).

- Fully integrate design of the sustainable drainage sytem with the emerging layout plan to add value to the development footprint, landscape character, amenity, movement routes and wildlife.

Additional measures may need to be taken if releasing SUDs water into sensitive environments, such as:

- bathing areas or public parks/formal areas

- designated freshwater or shellfish fisheries.

- sites with statutory protection

SUDs maintenance

The basic framework is for the local authority to adopt all above-ground works and for the water company (or authority in Scotland) to adopt below-ground structures. The developer should be prepared to have the SUDs managed as a private system, handing it over to a grounds management company specialising in this area. It is vital to ensure that the necessary high quality of landscape management and presentation is maintained once an area has been adopted by a local authority.

Swale park storage

North Hamilton, Leicester

The sutainable urban drainage systems or SUDs concept is very flexible and can be incorporated into a development scheme in various ways.

The urban design framework at North Hamilton uses a system of swales set in 'swale parks' as drainage channels and on-site flood storage. This provided a more attractive and cheaper alternative to the traditional solution, which would have meant a large retention pond at the bottom

A swale park serving adjacent housing areas

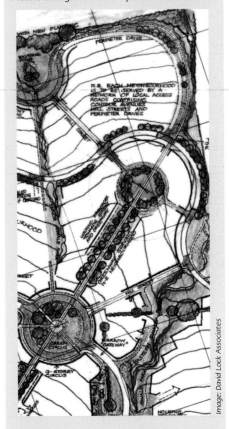

Image: David Lock Associates

of the site.
A small swale park is shown in the illustration; a larger central swale park includes more open water and a greenway connecting the housing to the main high street.

The urban framework for North Hamilton was developed by David Lock Associates: www.davidlock.com

4.10

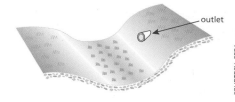

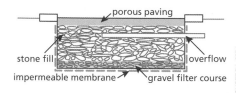

COURTESY: SEPA

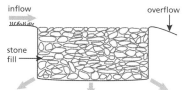

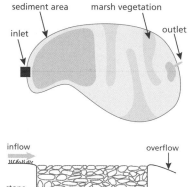

COURTESY: SEPA

Figure 4.20
SuDS information

Comprehensive design manuals for sustainable urban drainage systems are available from the Construction Industry Research and

Filter strips and swales

Vegetated surface features that drain water evenly from impermeable areas. Swales are long, shallow channels. Filter strips are gently sloping areas of ground. They can be designed into public open space or road verges. Native grassland species can be introduced for wildlife and visual amenity.

Infiltration devices

Infiltration devices drain water directly into the ground. A common examples is a soakaways, but they can also be in the form of trenches, swales and basins.

These areas can be used as playing fields and public open space. They can also be planted with trees and shrubs for biodiversity.

Basins and ponds

Basins are usually dry, such as detention basins and flood plains. Ponds are designed to remain wet (for example, balancing ponds, wetlands, lagoons).

Basins can be used for sport and passive recreation. Ponds can provide public and wildlife amenity.

Filter drains and permeable surfaces

Filter drains are linear devices with a volume of permeable material below ground to store surface water.

Permeable surfaces are area-wide such as grass, gravel block paving or other permeable paving. Permeable surfaces can be designed to be trafficked and used as car parks and non-adopted access roads.

GREEN ROOFS

4.3 Greenroofs and heat islands

4.11 Greenroofs and food

4.20 Green roofs and biodiversity

Green roofs can be considered a sustainable drainage technique in that they control the speed of rainwater discharge following precipitation. They do this without the obvious land take necessary that can make some sustainable drainage elements less compatible with higher density development. Green roofs can be broadly considered as being one of two types:

Intensive – high mainenance, gardens with bedding, shrubberies and/or lawns.

Extensive – low mainentance, clothed in sedum. mosses or low fertility grass species.

Extensive green roofs, in particular, offer the following environmental health benefits, they can:

- contribute to a reduction in the heat island effect
- act as a sponge store for water thus reducing the severity of peak run-off flows and evening out rain water discharge
- have excellent Summer heat and Winter cold insulation properties
- absorb air pollutants, dust and carbon dioxide
- provide opportunities for contact with nature
- provide opportunities for meeting local biodiversity targets and supporting wildlife.

In terms of development economics, they have potential to:
- reduce water costs
- extend roof life
- have excellent noise reduction/acoustic properties
- reduce heating and cooling costs
- increase development values.

A typical green roof can hold 55 per cent of its volume in water, this can be as much as 110 litres per square metre (Brighton & Hove Council 1998).

Green roofs can be retrofitted to existing buildings or designed in to new ones. They can be, and have been, installed on buildings of virtually any function, residential houses and flats, industrial, office, retail and leisure. The cost is comparable to other roof coverings and structural load needs consideration.

BUILDING IN THE FLOOD PLAIN

Living with water

With climate change comes the increased periodicity and intensity of flooding, this can take many forms, inland flash floods, river overspill and flooding from the sea. The combination of development pressures, increasing densities and greater areas of open surface water storage will inevitably result in temptations to build on potential flood risk areas in some pretty accessible (and even town centre) locations. Building in close proximity to water can provide amenity benefits and some valuable real estate. In the Netherlands, careful control of water levels, in a pumped landscape, with large areas of open water and surface water storage has given rise to some award winning housing in highly sustainable neighbourhood developments. The approach we advocate throughout this guide, is not to stick to a hard rule (e.g. never build in a flood plain) but to view the system as a whole and determine a neighbourhood development solution which is sustainable and benefits health - that way lies innovation.

Retrofit of green roofs on these industrial units put a stop to annual flooding of school grounds nearby in Ekostaden, Malmö, Sweden

Photo: John Dolecek

Green roof retofited as part of adding another floor to this office block in Freiburg, Germany

Water housing in the self-development zone at Nesselande, Rotterdam.

FFI:

Sustainable Water Management: Eco-towns water cycle worksheet. From the Town and Country Planning Association www.tcpa.org

The LifE handbook - Long-term initiatives for flood-risk environments. From the Building Research Establishment www.brebookshop.com

4.11

food

> - **Core indicators**
>
>   *Organic farming; land use area and economic value*
>
>   *Food transportation; by urban roads, by air, by heavy goods vehicle*
>
> - **Neighbourhood quality of life indicator**
>
>   *Percentage of population who have five or more portions of fruit or vegetables a day*
>
>   *Percentage of population with access to a food shop selling fresh fruit and vegetables*
>
>   *Percentage of population within ten minutes' barrow journey of an allotment*

Food for health

Food has been recognised by WHO as a social determinant of health. The pattern and nature of food supply at the neighbourhood level can adversely affect health and the global environment.

'A good diet is an important way of protecting health. Unhealthy diets are linked to cancer, heart disease and stroke.'

Our Healthier Nation; a Contract for Health (DoH 1998: Chapter 2).

'Poor diet is responsible for nearly a third of life years lost in disability and death.'

World Health Report 2002: Reducing Risks, Promoting Healthy Life (WHO 2002).

Food and sustainable development

Access to locally grown, healthy and safe food is emerging as an important consideration in urban sustainable development.

4.11 FOOD BASICS: STAPLE ISSUES

Food is a cross-cutting issue. Focusing on food in neighbourhood planning allows deep access into health and sustainability agendas. There is a history of ignoring food in urban spatial planning, let the market sort it out! We suggest a different approach, the potential beneficiaries (or losers) include obesity, climate stability, social capital and employment.

Key tenets

■ *Increase access for local people to food*

Improve access by providing adaptable space for local shops and small-scale supermarkets and supporting those already present.

Plan safe and pleasant pedestrian and cycling routes linking retail and residential areas.

Plan for well distributed superstores in each town/district.

■ *Maximise opportunity for local food production*

Support productive urban soils – Maintain or provide allotment land, provide sites for locally managed organic orchards, provide back gardens/roof gardens of a size to enable food production, plan for community growing projects.

Support hinterland agriculture – Improve access to markets through farmers' markets and local produce labelling. Promote health through community supported agriculture.

■ *Increase community links to food*

Use food projects as a focus for health, inclusion, training and employment; at the town/district scale, plan for city farms.

Link allotments to communities physically and through school and health projects.

Reasons

The concept 'food miles' refers to the distance food has to travel from where it is grown to where it is purchased and then on to where it is consumed. Food transportation by road has been the fastest growing transport sector in the UK and a major contributor to air pollution and carbon emissions. Food is often abundant in retail parks served well by cars and articulated lorries, but the term 'food deserts' has been coined to describe neighbourhoods where access to fresh food in small local shops is scarce. Recent research (Guy 2008) indicates that this may not be having the impact on diet once feared due to a decrease in daily 'basket' shopping and an increase in weekly supermarket food shopping.

Modern industrial farming has had a devastating impact on biodiversity and soil fertility. Encouraging local organic growing reduced food emissions from the energy intensive nitrogen fertilisers and from having to transport green watse out of the settlement.

CONTEXTS AND TRENDS

We have created a vast international system of food production, procurement, processing, packaging and preservation. We have ensured that people can eat in urban settlements dislocated completely from any food growing and increasingly even from cooking. Although not 'hard wired' like the energy or water systems, to ensure that the food urban system does not work against health and sustainability, it needs re-planning and nurture at a local level.

Food access

The term 'food access' takes into consideration the complexity of factors that affect a person's ability to obtain sufficient, adequate food for enough money to buy food, being physically able to walk, or drive to shops which can provide this, and understanding how to prepare and use healthy foods.

Food and health

The WHO estimates that by eating five portions of fruit and vegetables a day deaths from diseases such as coronary heart disease could be reduced by up to 20 per cent. The shift towards processed food and away from fresh produce, combined with a decline in cooking skills and nutritional advice have contributed to increased ill health, including coronary heart disease. A study of health issues in planning for London (GLA 2007) stated that improvement of residents' collective diets could deliver significant benefits including reduced incidence of cancer, coronary heart disease and type-2 diabetes.

Inclusive communities and health inequalities

Research suggests that the poorest in society are paying more but getting less for their money. They are being disadvantaged by their poverty three times over:

*   the shops which are most accessible to low-income consumers provide less variety and choice;

*   prices are higher; and

*   the quality is often lower.

The research found that the cost of choosing a healthy option to be a staggering 88 per cent more in a local shop than at a town-centre supermarket. Estimates put at 4 million the people in the UK who cannot afford a healthy diet (NCC 2004).

In start contrast, urban food production provides an excellent means of involving groups who often face discrimination, or marginalisation, in a social and productive activity. It can provide an opportunity for expression of cultural or ethnic identity through the varieties and cultivars selected and the growing methods (Garnett 1996). There are also numerous examples

Haringey Good Food Directory

To support health through access to good food a directory has been produced. This lists some of the food resources that exist locally in Haringey, North London

Food growing

Being involved in a rewarding activity, being in the open air and being in contact with nature can lower stress levels

London food studies

Inequalites

Wealth: *The highest income households in London consume 2.5 times more fruit and vegetables than the lowest income households.*

Ethnic communities: *the high fruit and vegetable consumption of some ethnic groups in London (e.g. Chinese men and women) hides the very poor diet of other groups, such as the Bangladeshi and Irish communities.*

Healthy ageing: *The elderly in London are particularly vulnerable to under-nutrition, with 40 per cent of admittances to hospital aged 65 years or older being qualified as undernourished, while 12 per cent of those living in the community and 20 per cent in care homes are at risk of under-nutrition*

Information from www.lda.gov.uk

Food can express culture and diversity with local varieties and tastes, recipies and cooking, the colour of the local market.

4.11

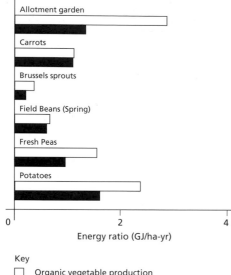

Figure 4.21

Comparison of energy inputs and useable energy outputs in organic and non-organic UK vegetable production

The energy ratio is the edible energy in a food stuff divided by the energy input necessary to produce the food. The energy inputs represented by the fertilisers, all field working, spraying and storage are taken into account. Output is in terms of edible energy and protein in the foodstuff (Leach 1975; Viljoen 2005).

	Fuel costs	
Farm	Overall proportions	accounted for by transport or fertiliser
Mill	19%	11.6% fertilizer
Bakery	13%	1.4% transport
Bakery	47%	5.0% transport
Retail	21%	12.2% transport
Total	**100%**	**30.2% of total fuel costs**

Figure 4.22

Fuel costs of a standard white loaf

30% of the fuel cost is due to fertilisers or transport; local organic food minimises these fuel components.
(After Chapman 1975, in Viljoen 2005, p.23).

of food growing projects associated with gaining nationally recognised horticultural and vocational qualifications, often for those who have faced past disadvantage (Howe and Wheeler 1999).

A study revealed that the highest income households in London consume 2.5 times more fruit and vegetables than the lowest income households. When examining variations in ethnic groups, diversity needs to be acknowledged and not aggregated. The study found that the high fruit and vegetable consumption of some ethnic groups in London (e.g. Chinese men and women) hid the very poor diet of other groups, such as the Bangladeshi and Irish communities (LDA 2006).

In terms of healthy aging, the London study reported that the elderly in London were particularly vulnerable to under-nutrition, with 40 per cent of admittances to hospital aged 65 years or older being qualified as undernourished, while 12 per cent of those living in the community and 20 per cent in care homes are at risk of under-nutrition.

Social and therapeutic horticulture

The use of horticulture and gardening to promote health, well-being and social inclusion, particularly working with vulnerable people has been called social and therapeutic horticulture. Research indicates the validity of range of benefits to different groups:

■   Vocational horticulture may be a tool to improve social bonding of juvenile offenders, evoking changes in attitudes about personal success and individual perceptions of personal job preparedness.

■   The nature of horticultural activities lend themselves easily to communicative disabled individuals, gardening is a good gentle but active and social workout for the elderly.

■   Horticultural activity has been shown to be particularly effective for those with mental health difficulties.

The beneficial effects stem both from active and passive engagement with nature. Both cognitive (reasoned) and evolutionary (inherited) components are present in the restorative effects (Aldrige and Sempik 2002).

Food carbon and nutrient cycles

■   Special fare: Growing and eating more local food brings back seasonality. It enables the carbon intensive – the world-wide – the out of season – the exotic flavours and colours – to appear more special again and not just part of an everyday diet.

The combination of the loss of connection between urban areas and their hinterland; decreasing rural population and non-organic food production is having a profound impact on nutrient cycles and food carbon emissions

An important cycle of nutrients links the elements which sustain both human populations and maintain food plant and animal growth – the nutrients carried in foodstuffs travelling back to the land through waste and sewage processes. 'Modern' neighbourhood design and city development breaks this cycle and has created instead an unsustainable linear flow, whereby we continually apply artificial fertilisers to the land, import food to urban areas and disperse and dispose of valuable nutrients in sewage and waste in landfill, incineration, rivers and the ocean. Not only does the current situation lead to nutrient waste but it is also carbon intensive both in transport of food and in fertiliser production and transport.

For sustainable neighbourhoods there are two important factors that address both nutrient cycles and carbon emissions in food; keeping food more local and using organic production methods (see Figures 4.20 and 4.21). Both of these can also be supported by
re-connecting urban areas to food growing and to their hinterlands.

Food transport

In terms of an individual's carbon footprint the continual increase in the distance food travels, often by air and road, is significant. Sometimes refered to as 'food miles'; food production, processing and distribution is leading to increasing quantities of food being transported over increasing distances.

Synergy: Green roofs, food and climate change

Some cities are realising that food growing on rooftops can reduce the heat island effects, whilst also providing employment. In Tokyo, a number of building owners in the capital have introduced roof-top gardening as a way to prevent overheating whist also harvesting sweet potatoes, which grow well in the roof-top environment of harsh sun and strong wind. The plants are particularly good for roof-tops because their wide leaves can cover the whole surface and are efficient at transpiration, evaporating water, which has a cooling effect.

Institutional roof garden food project, Moscow

The temperature of a roof area not covered by potato leaves was as much as 27 degrees Celsius hotter than an area covered by the leaves, according to a survey on one site.

4.12

Salop Drive market garden

In 1996, a Sandwell Regeneration Partnership feasibility study looked at establishing a community agriculture programme. This led to the investigation of parcels of derelict and underused land in the borough. Salop Drive, an overgrown allotment site, was found in 2000, and plans to establish a market garden began to take shape. Figures on ill health and death from preventable lifestyle-related illnesses are high in Sandwell compared with other similar areas. In 2000 a 'Charter for Healthy Sandwell' suggested community gardens for productive physical activity, mental reflection, building social links and growing healthy food.

Over a number of years, local residents and disabled people reclaimed Salop Drive's three-acre site, and now have mainstream funding from Sandwell Primary Care Trust.

The site includes a glasshouse, polytunnels, community gardens, wildlife area, outdoor beds and mini-allotments, all designed to be accessible for the disabled. There are demonstrations of composting, recycling, and sustainable growing methods to local schools and a work experience programme. The market garden delivers up to 80 bags of produce to local households every week, a saving of 6,400 to 9,600 food miles per year.

With the Salop Drive experience as a hub, Sandwell has now pioneered a local 'Community Agricultural Strategy' for 2008–2012 called 'Growing Health Communities' this sets out the practical vision for an extended programme of community agriculture across the borough.

Photo: Ideal for All.

PARTNERS, PARTICIPANTS AND CONSULTEES

For sucess form a wide partnership – typically involving local health groups, city farms/allotment associations, training and employment agencies. The principle for food in neighbourhoods is to make 'local food links'; growing, buying, cooking and enjoying.

Health Authorities

Health Authorities recognise that getting involved with the food aganda provides opportunites for positive impacts on physical and mental health through nutrition and exercise and through social contacts. Gardening and horticulture activities also assist mental health by relieving stress.

Local Authorities

Food is at the heart of our well-being and is a potent Local Agenda 21 topic. Food initiatives have demonstrated: improved physical and mental health; opportunities for greater social cohesion; and potential for employment and training.

Local shops and other food related initiatives

In addition to local shops food projects can be included in wider initiatives such as: Healthy Living Centres, cooperative buying schemes, Fairtrade (health for overseas food workers) and promotion of local countryside products, such as forestry, fibres, biomass.

Soil Association

The Soil Association exists to support sustainable agriculture. It can offer support to food initiatives including local regeneration organisations. It also offers training seminars and workshops on a number of local food issues. The Association publishes a comprehensive outline of local food issues. FFI: www.soilassociation.org

Sustain

Sustain is an alliance for better food and farming. Sustain advocates food policies and practices that enhance health and enrich culture. They provide a Food Indicators Toolkit and support a food access network: www.sustainweb.org.

Other organisations

Common Ground – supports community orchards, community gardens and apple day. FFI: www.commonground.org.uk
National Association of Farmers' Markets – disseminates information about farmers' markets: www.farmersmarkets.net
Federation of City Farms and Community Gardens – offers support and advice: www.farmgarden.org.uk. See 4.14 for more details.
Local Government Association (LGA) – has policies and publications, including support for allotments: www.lga.gov.uk
Rural Shops Alliance – support for independent village shops: www.rural-shops-alliance.co.uk

LOCAL FOOD PLAN

Phase 1 – Take the initiative and define a shared vision

Food projects come in many shapes and sizes. Draw up a list of key stakeholders according to the local circumstances. Prepare the ground and run a briefing, scoping and future vision exercise.

2.2 the seven stage process

Phase 2 – Understand the localities and learn lessons

Depending on resources conduct a basic audit, or food mapping, of the current situation. Find out how others have run projects in the past.

- **Food mapping:** Basic spatial audit of food sources and food quality.

- **Food radar:** Walking distance to food sources mapped, population coverage and gaps in provision noted.

- **Food access:** Cross referencing physical accessibility data with known statistics of population deprivation, health and other demographics of vulnerability.

Phases 3 & 4 – Develop ideas, agree a programme and take action

- **Spatial and built measures**
  Farmers' markets and Women's Institute markets
  Growing at home, on allotments, at school
  City farms and community gardens and community orchards
- **Non-spatial measures**
  Subscription farming and box schemes
  Community-owned farms and other investment for local food production
  Food co-ops and community buying groups
  Local food directories

Food, the polluter?

Comparison of annual CO_2 emissions for an average four-person household:

- *Running a house – 4.2 tonnes heating, cooking, lighting, etc.*
- *Running a car – 4.4 tonnes 20,000 km average fuel consumption*
- *Food consumed – 8.0 tonnes growing, processing, packing, transport and cooking*

SOURCE: BRESCU GIR 53, 1998

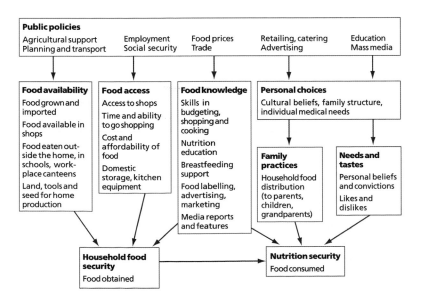

Figure 4.23

Influences on food choices

World Health Organization (2002) Food and Health in Europe. WHO: Copenhagen

4.13

Policy in relation to food access

The Acheson Inquiry 28 into health inequalities noted that food access and 'food deserts' were best approached through a planning and policy framework, as opposed to one based on self-help and education.

Acheson D. (1998) Independent Inquiry into Inequalities in Health Report. The Stationery Office: London.

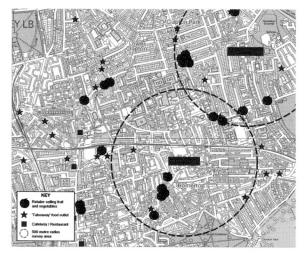

Figure 4.24
Mapping of Daubeney and Berger School areas showing shops selling fruit and Vegetables. Bowyer et al. 2009

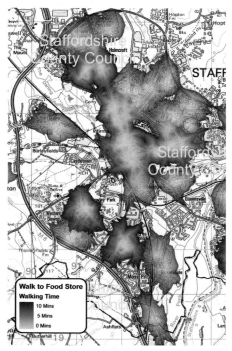

Figure 4.25
Isochrones showing a ten-minute walk to a shop

Putting Food access on the radar. O'Neill (2005) M. London: National Consumer Council

There are a number of tools available to analyse what is happening with food access at the local level.

In England, the Department for Transport and the Department of Health have issued guidance on accessibility planning which sets out the main objectives for improving access to key services, including food shopping, and encourages those involved with delivering health improvements to work with local transport authorities on producing accessibility strategies for their area. (D H 2004).

THE FOOD BASKET

For comparative work a basic food basket needs to be established. Through a mixture of survey, focus groups and literature review of previous studies, a list of basic food shop items representing the total weekly family food shopping can be established. In practice several food baskets may need to be established, with common basic items complimented by others to allow for diversity in diet of different local demographic groups. The baskets should contain what would be called a healthy and balanced diet. In the UK, data from the Food Standards Agency and NHS recommendations daily intake provide a basic steer. A basket should contain food from the five basic groups, in healthy combination and that is affordable and acceptable to the local population.

A person will be provided with a wide range of necessary nutrients from a variety of foods – 'fruit and vegetables' (5–9 portions per day), 'bread, cereals and potatoes' (5–14 portions per day), 'meat, fish and alternatives' (2–3 portions per day), 'milk and dairy foods' (2–3 portions per day). The fifth group, 'foods containing fat and/ or sugar', contains items that are not essential but add variety and palatability to meals and should form the smallest part of the diet (Bowyer et al. 2000)

FOOD MAPS

Understanding the relationship between food shops and the population can yield essential data. At a basic level this can be plotting on a map the location of food shops together with physical accessibility information. Using a pedshed approach, described in Chapter 4, population within critical 5 minute (cornershop) or 10 minute (local centre) walk times can be plotted. Don't just look at healthy food access but also plot unhealthy food access, such as the density and ease of access to fast food in areas around schools.

Geographic information systems can take this form of analysis to new levels through cross-referencing food location with demographic data such as levels of deprivation, lack of car ownership and age. Also actual residential population levels can be plotted to give percentage accessibility and accessibility dead spots.

LOCAL SHOPS

There is a strong case for supporting local shops which give easy access to food, and often supply fresh local produce. In rural villages there are several examples of shop support schemes coming to the aid of the threatened local shop. These could provide models for urban areas.

Co-operation between local producers, LETS groups, allotment associations and retailers, maybe supported by initial funding from the health authority or community/regeneration funds, could help the local store to become again a valued community asset.

FARMERS' MARKETS

Farmers' markets sell locally produced goods to local people. The concept is obviously not a new one. Farmers have bartered and sold goods as far back in history as agriculture itself.

- Plan for or identify public open space in a local commercial centre that can serve as a market space.

It is generally accepted by most farmers' markets that stall holders must have grown, bred, caught, pickled, brewed or baked the goods themselves. The main emphasis is to help local producers and processors to sell their goods direct to the public, near their source of origin, creating benefits to them and the local community. Farmers' markets benefit farmers, consumers, the environment, and the local economy

- They help bring life into towns and cities, aiding regeneration.

- They encourage social interaction particularly between rural and urban communities.

- They help to improve diet and nutrition by providing access to fresh food.

- They provide direct contact and feedback between customers and producers.

- They provide a secure and regular market outlet for producers, especially valuable for small-scale producers, new producers and producers in organic conversion. This stimulates the economic development by increasing employment and encouraging consumers to support local businesses.

- They cut out the middle man, allowing increased financial returns through direct selling and improved cash flow.

- They help reduce food miles and packaging.

- They raise awareness about where food comes from and how it is produced.

The National Association of Farmers' Markets: www.farmersmarkets.net

3.10 local shops and services

● Food retailers in and around the three survey areas

○ Survey areas - 500 metre radius around the specified locations

Figure 4.26

Shopping for Food: Accessing healthy affordable food in three areas of Hackney.

A survey availability of key food items for a healthy food basket, costs and services offered in 37 shops was carried out. This data was later used to develop maps of access and shopping patterns.

SOURCE: Bowyer et al. 2009

Long established farmers' market in Los Angeles, USA

4.14

URBAN SOILS

With food growing in urban areas so important for health and social inclusion, the protection of urban soils is an important issue. In the UK, soil quality as an urban resource has been largely neglected by urban policy for many decades.

Soil is an all too often ignored valuable urban resource. It is a fundamental link between the abiotic world of water, rocks, chemistry and air and the biotic world of living plants, animals and microbes. Soils are a store of great biodiversity value and in turn support above ground biodiversity. Soils are continually lost in urban development, not only at the time of initial development but continually – witness the skips full of soil arising from garden makeovers, front garden paving and house extensions. In addition to loss per se, the sealing of urban soils by urban development can increase run-off by up to 50 per cent. Sustainable soil management in the built environment is now on the agenda.

> Where urban growth is to occur on good-quality agricultural land or in areas with fertile soils, such as alluvial soils and sites of former horticultural industry;
>
> - In planning – inlude soils as a community asset. Housing should have twice the standard quantity of allotments, plan for a city farm and community orchards.
>
> - In construction – ensure topsoil in areas under proposed building foot print is stripped and re-used elsewhere.
>
> In all urban areas:
>
> - Safeguard soils from contamination and compaction during construction.
>
> - Provide a 'disposal to re-use' route for householders or refuse companies with surplus soils.
>
> - Discourage sealing of surfaces where unnecessary, such as front gardens, use permeable surfaces wherever possible.

Although it is possible to create artificial growing media and to reclaim contaminated land in some instances, soil iteslf needs to be treated as a fundamental and irreplaceable finite natural resource.

The Blue Finger – Bristol, UK

As with many conurbations all over Europe, fingers of countryside have been deliberately left undeveloped to provide the 'lungs' of the settlement, good access to counrtyside and routes for biodiveristy. Although these often harbour good quality soils; being so well connected, these areas are always at risk of development. In Bristol, such a finger, with soils that have even supported a market garden industry in the past, is at risk from housing expansion pressures.

Image: Richard Spalding

Soil quality map

Blue denotes good quality agricultural land, dark blue denotes best quality.

Threats to urban soils come from:

- *The sealing of surface areas; leading to increased run-off and loss of biodiversity*

- *Continual loss of good-quality soils in residential areas as waste; for examaple through 'garden improvements', soil is just thown away in mixed skips*

- *Construction of homes and offices on good-quality agricultural land*

- *Contamination of soils during the contruction process*

ALLOTMENTS AND ORCHARDS

Allotments seem to send mixed messages: on the one hand, some view them as relics from 'the war', as half-derelict eyesores. On the other, rumours abound of 5-year waiting lists for those wanting to rent an allotment. Many organisations now see allotment renaissance as representing an important tool for delivering sustainability to neighbourhoods.

There are tangible benefits for planners, developers and communities in developing allotments; increasing their accessibility in regeneration and new-build schemes.

Allotments connect to social and health themes such as

- recreational activity, keeping fit
- health initiatives (healthy living centres, for example)
- urban renewal and green space provision
- community education and life-long learning.

Allotment initiatives are especially useful in increasing public participation: and helping to combat social exclusion. Allotments are accessible to all social groups, and are widely used to grow food by the elderly and other people on low incomes.

In particular for local councils, promotion of policy delivery through allotments is in keeping with Best Value and provides an integrated route to service delivery. As such allotments can have a seminal focus in Community Strategies for the promotion of well-being. Planners and designers considering the neighbourhood spatial framework should embed new or existing allotments into the layout looking for synergy with other spatial uses. Allotment provision is particularly compatible with:

- sustainable urban drainage
- local pedestrian access
- community recycling and composting
- wildlife and biodiversity
- shelter belts
- community orchards, see below.

COMMUNITY ORCHARDS

Community orchards can be successful in urban and rural areas. They provide many opportunities for strengthening community links through sharing knowledge, skills and activities. They can enhance the environment of housing estates, industrial estates, hospitals and schools whilst also increasing biodiversity. Community orchards can provide endless opportunities for fun events including tree dressing, blossom parties, apple-day fairs (National Apple Day is in the autumn) and apple bobbing. Land requirements are upwards from 0.1 ha for about ten trees.

Allotments to orchards

Blondin Orchard, London

Following a decline in allotment use, when consulted, the local community were keen on planting an orchard on the allotment site.

Local people helped to plant 46 old and local varieties of apples on a 0.5 ha site. A 50-strong Friends Group co-ordinate regular maintenance activities.

Project objectives:
- *good fruit production*
- *community involvement*
- *enhancment of wildlife value*
- *use of redundant land.*

Project partners include: London Borough of Ealing – Parks and Countryside; London Ecology Unit; Common Ground; Friends of Blondin Nature Area

Common Ground provide information through a series of orchard advice notes, including sources of grant funding. www.commonground. org.uk

---

4.10 Flooding

3.8 Accessibility

4.17 Recovery

4.20 Biodiversity

4.5 Energy

Local Agenda 21: Estate allotment and leisure gardening

QED Allotments Group, Dartford, London

This group promotes the sustainable development of allotment gardening. The group concentrates on ten action areas including:
- *Waste disposal and recycling*
- *Helping to meet local needs locally: for food, water, shelter and fuel*
- *People's health*
- *Access to facilities, services, goods and other people*
- *Participation in decision-making*
- *Valuing and protecting local features*
- *Satisfying employment.*

Early successes have proved this an effective method of tackling problems common to many inner-city areas.

Allotments: an accessible shared resource and a meeting place for communities.

Allotment mindmap

Emma Southward

Figure 4.27
The integrated allotment site

Allotment sites can underpin local access to food and open space whilst performing valuable water and biodiversity services

CITY FARMS

City farms have an important role to play in urban sustainability and there is growing government recognition of their value to local communities. As a major local resource they should probably be planned for at the district/town scale: every district/town should have one. Benefits are manifold:

■ improvements to physical and mental health through being active, social interaction, contact with nature;

■ production of fresh food and contact with food and food processes

■ provision of productive, creative, safe, high-quality open space

■ opportunities for people to learn new skills and abilities, either informally or on formal accredited training courses

■ additions to the economic wealth of the area

■ provision of facilities that can bring people of different abilities, ages, and cultures together socially, and aid community development

■ fostering community pride and independence through involving local people on management groups

Community city farm at St. Werbergs, Bristol.

The Federation of City Farms and Community Gardens (FCFCG) *is the UK organisation representing groups involved in community-led development of open space through locally managed farming and gardening.*

Advice and support - www.farmgarden.org.uk

Figure 4.28
Some farm sizes and facilities offered

Approximate farm size	Typical facilities	Example
0.5 ha	Small herb gardens and pond areas; 22 private allotments; spinning room; dyeing area; visitors' room. Animals: poultry, cow, donkey, duck, horse, goat, pig, rabbit, sheep	Vauxhall City Farm, London
1 ha	Community garden, polytunnel, large adventure playground, craft and art rooms and workshop, café. Animals: poultry, goats, pig, rabbit, sheep	New Ark Adventure Playground and City Farm, Peterborough
2 ha	Kids and pensioners allotments, classrooms; run a riding programme and NVQs in horse care and animal care. Animals: poultry, cows, ducks, horses, goat, pigs, rabbit, sheep	Kentish Town City Farm, London
3–4 ha	Interpretation centre/classroom, café. Gardens including wildlife pond. Animals: poultry, cows, ducks, donkey, goat, pigs, rabbit, sheep	City Farm Byker, Newcastle
over 5 ha	Café, dairy, classroom, polytunnels. Animals: poultry, cows, donkey, geese, goats, pigs, pony, rabbit, sheep	Rice Lane City Farm, Liverpool (10 ha)

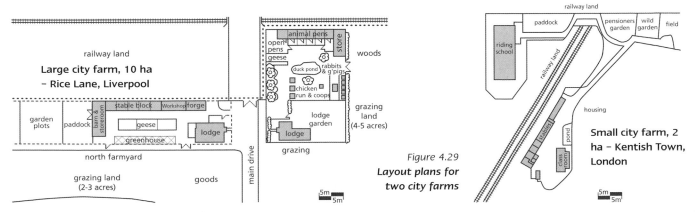

Figure 4.29
Layout plans for two city farms

- *EU indicators*

  Waste landfilled

  Waste incinerated

  Hazardous waste generated

  Municipal waste generated

  Industrial waste generated

  Waste recycled/material recovered

- **Neighbourhood indicators**

  Total household and business waste

  Percentage of household and business waste recycled

  Percentage of household and business waste composted

Figure 4.30
Material flows; linear and complex

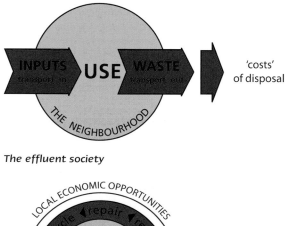

The effluent society

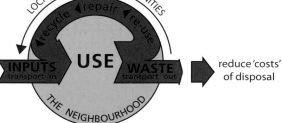

The sustainable society

materials

4.15 WASTE NOT

Materials brought into the neighbourhood becomes 'waste' through being placed in the waste stream by the actions of those no longer requiring its use. Much of the material in the waste stream can still perform important functions in the neighbourhood, and if not in the wider economy. Therefore, when planning and designing neighbourhoods for sustainability, approach waste as a resource – a flow of useful local materials.

KEY TENETS

- *Close resource loops*

Repair, recover, re-use. Use local waste stream as a materials bank providing new life to discarded items supporting innovation, creativity and jobs. Examples include furniture recycling stores and community compost sites.

Separate waste stream materials. Separation of materials at source in the waste stream makes re-use through recovery more viable and recycling more economic.

- *Create local solutions*

Localise the waste facilities where possible. There is a balance to be struck between closing the resource loops locally or passing sorted waste streams on to a larger spatial scale. The more local; the less transport is required.

- *Involve people*

Make recycling the easy option. Recycling should be the final option after reducing waste and re-use have been explored. A change in habit comes when people have to tackle these issues in their homes and businesses.

Involve people in the community. Effective schemes make use of not-for-profit groups and community development: for example, locally managed community recycling and compost sites.

Reasons

The creation of 'waste' demonstates failiure. Homes and businesses usually just dispose of all unwanted items to 'refuse' – this 'waste' gets dumped in landfill or incinerated. Perversely, this 'waste' contains resources that we need and that we actually mine, manufacture and purchase in great quantities: for example nutrients to feed soils, all sorts of containers and packaging, metals, paper, clothing, furniture and appliances. Neighbourhoods need to go beyond just recycling. Local materials recovery generates opportunities for business innovation, training and jobs.

Identifying and separating useful material in the waste stream not only releases its value for re-use but also reduces the transport required for import of new products/materials and export of waste, saves resources and reduces pollution.

4.16 LOCAL MATERIALS MANAGEMENT

At the local scale there is an important role to be played by the community not-for-profit sector in providing services and raising awareness.

Sustainable construction

The material in this chapter deals with the neighbourhood in use – however, waste must also be minimised during the construction phase. Sustainable construction includes re-use of buildings, re-use of materials and construction waste and local sourcing of construction materials. Best practice in this respect can deliver better profitability and competitive advantage for developers, as outlined in the UK strategy *Building a better quality of life: A strategy for sustainable construction* (DETR 2000i).

PARTNERS, PARTICIPANTS AND CONSULTEES

Community waste sector

A strong community waste sector has a vital part to play in the delivery and promotion of sustainable resource management. The sector comprises local community groups, charities, community-based waste management companies and other social enterprises and provides both permanent and voluntary employment to a wide range of people. In many countries, individual organisations work at neighbourhood levels delivering a wide variety of services to communities through reduction, re-use, recycling and composting projects. Together this sector can benefit local communities across the whole 'Triple Bottom Line':

- income and profits are retained and invested in the local economy

- social benefits include work and training opportunities, affordable goods and services and infrastructure improvements for people in local communities

- environmentally, schemes reduce CO_2 emissions and the amount of local pollution caused by long-distance waste management activities.

Other voluntary groups

Voluntary groups outside the community waste sector can also have specific roles with regard to local materials re-use. These include allotment associations (green waste to compost), religious groups and those owning premises (used clothes swaps and sales) and school support groups and those owning outdoor open space (markets and car boot sales). Re-use can be increased though providing small premises and other support to special interest groups who can specialise in repair, upgrade and component re-use for items such as bicycles, computers, furniture, and domestic appliances.

Sustainable construction in the UK

The Royal Institute of British Architects (RIBA) has stated that architecture is responsible for about 45% of the carbon dioxide emissions in the UK and that architects are a large part of the problem. In response the RIBA has a sustainability and climate change programme and has developed a number of design toolkits for reducing the impact of buildings on climate change. These toolkits and further information can be found on the RIBA website www. architecture.com.

The Board of Trade and Industry, in the UK called the Department of Business, Enterprise and Regulatory Reform, is co-ordinating an ongoing national sustainable construction initiative. Called the Strategy for Sustainable Construction, it is a joint industry and Government initiative intended to promote leadership and behavioural change, as well as delivering benefits to both the construction industry and the wider economy. For further information see www.berr.gov.uk

Sustainable construction and construction material re-use

Starting points for further information

Sustainable construction information at the Building Research Establishment: www.bre. co.uk and the Construction Industry Research and Information Centre: www.ciria.org.uk

Materials information exchanges matching waste supplies with potential users: www. salvomie.com and www.smartwaste.co.uk

Green specification information and sources for green specification for construction: www. greenguide.org.uk

4.17 Local resources recovery and waste parks

Best Value indicators for waste

- *Of the total tonnage of household waste arisings*
  - *percentage recycled*
  - *percentage composted*
  - *percentage used to recover heat, power and other energy sources*
  - *percentage landfilled.*

- *Weight of household waste, per head.*

- *Cost of waste collection per household.*

- *Cost of municipal disposal, per tonne.*

- *Number of collections missed, per 100,000 collections of household waste.*

- *Percentage of people expressing satisfaction with*

  - *recycling facilities*
  - *civic amenity sites.*

- *Percentage of population served by a kerbside collection of recyclable waste, or within 1 km of a recycling centre.*

SOURCE: DETR 2000

2.2 The seven stage process

CHECKLIST

Waste: the ranking of priorities

1 Reduce: the amount of material that is being brought in that is not required

2 Repair: mend and make good

3 Re-use: the item or product where possible

4 Recover: elements for re-use, strip out the value

5 Recycle: the components or materials where re-use is not possible.

Design waste management processes to provide benefits

• Economic – through employment, repair and re-use of resources

• Health – through involvement, less transport, less incineration/landfill

• Environmental – reduction in material use, reduction in impacts.

Local Authorities

Waste management is a key service provided by local authorities and a number of targets have been set for waste management services. It is not only environmental and technical services who can influence the ease of meeting these targets. Planners and designers involved in neighbourhood schemes can also make a significant impact.

LOCAL MATERIALS PLANNING

Phase 1 – Take the initiative and define the vision

There should be wide interest in setting-up a local materials recovery plan; stakeholders interested in local jobs and environmental issues can make a common alliance. Include voluntary interest groups.

Phase 2 – Understand the locality and agree a strategy

Policy and legislative guidelines are increasingly demanding the creation of a neighbourhood with effective re-use and recycling regimes.

- Recognise the small but crucial space and design requirements needed in new build or regeneration of neighbourhoods for minimising waste.

- Consult with experience in the community not-for-profit sector and with the relevant council departments.

- Aim to provide facilities that embed re-use and recycling in the daily life of residents and businesses in the locality.

To determine how far waste and arisings should be transported use the proximity principle – close resource loops as close to the source as possible (see Figure 4.31).

Phase 3 – Develop ideas and options

- **Spatial and built measures**
  Community compost facilities on allotment sites, waste parks, urban mines
  Buildings: Pyrolysis plants and heat mains; low rent places for start-up repair workshops
- **Non-spatial measures**
  Soft infrastructure: Kerbside collections
  Kit: public realm separation on streets, in parks and on public transport; household recycling and compost bins.

Phase 4 – Agree a programme and take action

Maintenance and management are vital for long-term viability and ecological efficiency. Success is dependent on a continual flow of materials through the system; networking with other neighbourhoods and districts involved in materials recovery will be important.

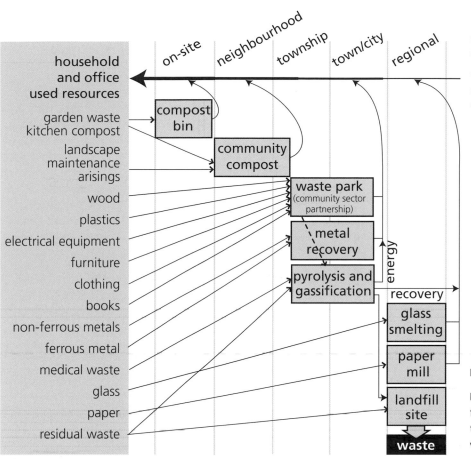

Figure 4.31
Proximity principle

*Close the resource
loop as close to the
source as possible*

EU Landfill Directive

Mandatory targets for reduction in landfill
for the next 20 years. It sets reducing
targets for the amount of biodegradable
waste going to landfill.

*The tip of the iceberg. Emptying a below ground public realm recyling and waste storage facility.
Small bin above ground; large below ground storage capacity, Tignes, France.*

Further information on local materials use

Community Composting Network
www.communitycompost.org

Community Recycling Network
www.crn.org.uk

Furniture Re-use Network
www.frn.org.uk

4.17

East London Community Recycling Partnership

Many flats on housing estates were built with a waste system consisting of communal chutes at the end of each landing area, leading down to large shared bins in the basement of each building. Meant to be efficient and convenient, in practice it was unreliable, smelly, very difficult to clean and a health hazard. The accumulated waste in the chutes and bins attracted infestations of rats, flies and other pests.

The East London Community Recycling Partnership have solved these problems with a community composting schemes on 10 estates in Hackney and several others in neighbouring boroughs. Their system is a success since the residents find it easy to use and understand and it causes less problems than the existing system. The prospect of keeping old food waste in an apartment cannot have seemed attractive, however, the new system gets around this problem by using a fermentation system to arrest the inevitable putrefaction. The residents are supplied with a 10 litre bin with a sealable lid, corn-starch biodegradable liners and a small bag of 'Bokashi' (bran inoculated by a strain of yeast). The sealable lid not only prevents flies and maggots entering the food waste, it also provides a good growing environment for the fermentation organism.

Participation rates, the number of people signing up for the scheme and receiving a kit and instructions, are as high as 85% in Seaton Point high-rise block, the lowest rate of uptake is still an impressive 55%. The high rates can be attributed to the work put into knocking on doors, meeting residents and explaining what the project was about i.e. basic but intensive interaction with the community. Involvement of the Tenants' Associations is a critical factor, residents need to have ownership or the scheme will fail.

Household collections are weekly. Every 100 tons of food creates 20 tons of compost, therefore 80 tons of food disappears.

4.17 LOCAL RESOURCE RECOVERY

SEPARATION AND STORAGE AT THE HOME

In many areas there is a kerbside waste collection of separated materials direct from households. These schemes should be extended to more areas in the future to meet national mandatory recycling targets. The motivation and even the ability to participate will be influenced by the provision of in-house storage for separated waste. Developers can assist through provision of storage under the sink unit for immediate storage of recyclables prior to them being taken outside the house. A number of proprietary systems are available. Designers should give thought to providing for four types of waste: organic matter, dry recyclables (glass, tins, cans, textiles and shoes), used paper and residual waste.

Separating waste in the house necessitates more than a single 'rubbish' bin outside the house. Ideally, waste streams are kept separate. Reusable and recyclable materials suitable for kerbside collection are placed separately with residual waste being put in a rubbish bin. Where wheelie bins are provided, the size can be an important factor in determining quantities sent to residual waste stream. All new housing should have a garden compost bin provided.

SEPARATION AND STORAGE IN THE PUBLIC REALM

Mini-recycling centres

In estates or blocks of flats where there are already communal rubbish collection facilities these can be expanded to become mini-recycling centres. An effective way is to provide, in addition to the communal rubbish receptacles, storage room for separated wastes. To ensure that these are actually used there needs to be investment in the 'soft infrastructure'.

Benefits

- Can encourage high participation rates if suitable banks, bins, etc. can be located close to people's homes.

- Are cheaper than separate collection from households.

Disadvantages

- Badly sited banks can lead to an increase in traffic movements and may deny some people the opportunity to participate.

- Care has to be taken to ensure people put the right material in the right bin as contamination can damage the value of the collected materials.

Street-scale facilities

Even in areas with a standard street layout, there is also the possibility of including a recycling facility for a group of streets, at living zone scale. In some countries, a small covered and gated local enclosure is used as a local storage and collection point for large items such as fridges, batteries, furniture, other white and brown domestic goods for collection and repair/re-use.

Local recycling point in Hiriazumi, Japan

Car batteries, sump oil, fridges, electrical goods, plastics, different types of canisters, etc.

Collections are twice a week.

A wide range of household items can be placed in the facility, which are graphically illustrated on the notice.

COMMUNITY COMPOSTING

Kitchen and garden waste make up 30–50 per cent of household waste. It is valuable organic material, and none need go to landfill.

In terms of climate change, landfills released 25% of the UK's methane emissions in 2003, representing 2% of total UK greenhouse gas emissions. The anaerobic decomposition of organic material in landfill sites is the primary source of methane in the atmosphere. Methane has 20 times the global warming potential of CO_2.

In order to meet EU Landfill Directive Targets the UK needs to separate and collect household biodegradable waste (known as putrescible waste) for composting. At one end of the scale there are centralised composting sites. These are large commercial operations needing waste licences and industrial or farming locations.

At the other end of the scale, in addition to home composting, is the growing network of community sites. Sites not storing over 1,000 m² (500 tonnes) at any time can apply for exemption from waste licensing regulations. Sites at this scale can be integrated into neighbourhood planning, providing local employment and community participation, in addition to recycling. Experience shows that there is scope to widen the social benefits through training schemes or, for example, working with adults with learning difficulties. In terms of physical planning, links can be made with allotments and city farms.

Composting

It is estimated that only 7 per cent of houses with gardens have a compost bin.

Local effort supported by County Council

Devon Community Composting Network

A network of some 25 local compost initiatives. The network itself is funded by the Devon Authorities' waste reduction and recycling committee. It provides a forum for advice and shared problem-solving, greatly assisting local organisers in setting up their own projects.

Projects are funded by landfill credits, sales of compost, charges for collection, grant funding and volunteer hours used as matched funding. Many sites are small but even with only a site measuring 6 m by 8 m, 50 tonnes can be processed per year. With landfill credits, sales and collection charges, this creates an annual income.

4.14 Food growing

'The Government looks to community groups to

- *be fully involved in Local Authority efforts to build partnerships for more sustainable waste management*

- *draw on the guidance on Best Value recently published by NCVO in developing partnerships with Local Authorities.*

- *continue their valuable work in motivating public involvement and increasing participation in recycling and composting schemes.*

- *take advantage of funding from the landfill tax credits scheme where possible'.*

SOURCE: Waste Strategy 2000, Section 4.32 (DETR 2000k)

Figure 4.30
Idealised layout for community compost facility serving 200 households

Note progressive reduction in size of boxes as the compost matures and shrinks in volume

Indications are that community composting schemes can be a good generator of local partnerships. Councils can pay groups recycling credits for every tonne diverted from landfill, though not all councils take up this opportunity to promote community recycling. Income can also be generated by charging for special collections/garden clearance, selling compost, education visits.

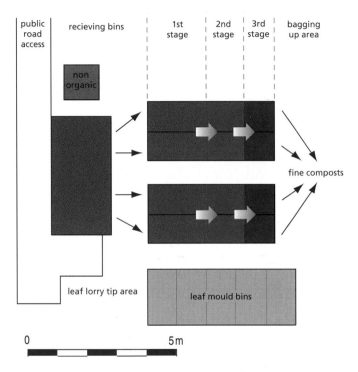

Substantial community compost site at Thornbury, South Gloucestershire (approx. 400 m²).

Communal compost rotating bin in shared courtyard garden, part of social housing eco-renovation, Vestebro, Copenhagen.

Example	Site Size	Details
Chagford Old Site, Devon	50 m²	60 tonnes compost processed pa. Comprises 6 bins, each 1.2 m x 1.2 m. Collection, and bring system, of local households' garden waste; village 1,400 pop.
Healy City Farm Site, Sheffield	50 m²	50 tonnes compost processed pa. Collection of kitchen waste from 200 households; city farm waste; hop waste from local brewery; commercial grass cuttings
Uffculme Project, Devon	900 m²	250 tonnes compost processed pa. Bring system for village of 2,000 pop. Some use by hinterland of 10,000 pop. Charged for collection for disabled and elderly

Figure 4.31
Sample land requirements for community compost schemes

WASTE PARKS

Local authorities provide civic amenity sites where people can bring their household waste. This consists generally of bulkier items such as furniture, DIY waste, kitchen equipment and garden waste, as well as recyclable waste.

Built at the township or whole-city scale, a waste park is like a civic amenity site but the aim is to reclaim, repair, renew and return for re-use. At its best the site will have permanent core staff and involve a partnership of organisations involved in salvage and manufacture, running workshops, craft production, training and business development. Partnerships with local business and the community sector can provide both sources of material and routes for end use.

receipt of waste → materials recovery and sorting → aggregates / textiles / paper / electronics / timber / tyres / packaging → on-site conditioning repair and processing → raw materials to manufacturers / repaired and reconditioned items / products made from salvage / products made by processing on site

Figure 4.32
The waste park concept

ENERGY FROM WASTE

A well-designed new generation incinerator, a pyrolysis and gasification plant, can accept a very wide range of fuel types: household, commercial and industrial waste, clinical waste, shredded used tyres and biomass. These facilities offer a clean burn waste facility. The process can produce energy and heat (CHP). The maintenance of high temperatures is claimed to ensure that dioxins are not generated and the lack of air during the burn (in a process more akin to charcoal making than a bonfire) means a very reduced emissions quantity compared to incineration.

Unlike conventional incinerators the plant is modular; the smaller-scale units would fit on a standard town industrial estate and could be incorporated as part of a waste park. Since they burn clean and emit only very low levels of noise, they can be located nearer to centres of population, users for the heat output.

URBAN WOOD AND WOODLAND CYCLES

Urban wood and tree management needs facilities to support conversion from a largely linear process to the cyclical and systemic processes necessary for sustainability and health, whilst also dramatically increasing tree cover, in line with responses to global warming and urban health. A facility can bring together;

■ volunteers, skilled professionals and training opportunities;

■ collection points for waste wood and tree surgery arisings with processing opportunities for woodchip biomass, wood storage, curing and re-use as sawn wood, charcoal production

Converting linear flow to a (re)cycle

Sustainable Growth Park, Urban Mines

A proposed industrial park dedicated to reprocessing materials from the local waste stream to supply on-site manufacturers with quality secondary raw materials.

The concept is designed as an engine for economic development, urban renewal and job creation within an environmentally sustainable and financially self-supporting framework.

Principal features:

* *State of the art 'Materials Recycling Facility' to separate materials by a combination of manual and mechanical methods.*

* *Reprocessing plant to refine the various materials to a tightly controlled quality assured specification.*

* *Units for small and medium enterprises to use the raw secondary material produced on site.*

* *Areas for aggregate treatment, composting of organic wastes and a re-use centre for refurbishment of discarded manufactured products.*

For further information, see: www.urbanmines.org.uk

A different scale!

Compact Power's trial pyrolysis and gasification plant next to a redundant incinerator at Avonmouth. The plant can generate local heat and power. For further information see: www. compactpower.co.uk

SOURCE: compact power

Incinerator   Pyrolysis plant

4.17

Flemish network of re-use centres

Re-use centres have been set up to tackle waste, employment and environmental issues together. Waste is collected, sorted, repaired and re-sold.

The environmental objective is to encourage re-use and extended life of secondhand household goods. Employment is provided for low-skilled long-term unemployed people. The socio-economic objective is to provide cheap but decent products for people with lower incomes.

The network has 40 sites and now covers 6 million inhabitants, who produce 16,000 tonnes of waste a year: 10 per cent of this now is dealt with by the re-use centres.

The regional government provides start-up investment, and local authorities get grants for working with the centres.

- local people with demonstrations and involvement in local tree, resource and biodiversity support;

- good practice in urban tree management and buy-in from residents for greater urban tree cover.

Bioregional have set up such a facility, called an 'urban tree station', together with the London Borough of Croydon. They estimate that it is diverting 10,000 tonnes of wood a year from landfill (FFI see www.bioregional.com).

NUTRIENTS FROM SEWAGE

Vast quantities of nutrients are transported into all settlements in our food. These potentailly valuable nutrients, having found their way into the sewage system, often end up dispearsed into rivers and the sea.

Re-use of sewage nutrients

Bulk treatment and processing: The solids settling out in the sewage treatment process are referred to as sewage sludge. These can be heat treated into virtually pathogen free combined soil conditioners and natural slow release fertilisers, rich in minerals and nutrients. As well as providing an agricultural product some sewage utilities are experimenting with developing granular products for domestic scale use in urban areas.

Urine separation and 'night soil' at the domestic scale: Urine has a high nitrogen content and a number of simple treatments can enable safe and sanitary storage and handling for use as a liquid fertiliser. Composting toilets of various kinds can enable faecal solids to be broken down, although legislation prevents the use of untreated product on the land. In many countries and in areas of low population there are traditional and vernacular facilities and processes enabling domestic re-use. Technologies for modern high density safe urban treatment and re-use are still in their infancy. A few allotment sites and city farms in the UK are now installing composting toilets and urine collection facilities.

In Adelaide, Australia, construction is underway on a major pipeline to send wastewater from the main sewage treatment plant to water Adelaide's parklands for irrigation and vegetable and fruit growing. The pipeline will eventually circle Adelaide and save the City Council from using drinking water to water the parklands, saving an expected five billion litres of fresh water a year.

biodiversity

4.18 WILDLIFE: A HEALTH ISSUE?

'Nature' finds it tough in many of our urban spaces. All too often, municipal green space maintenance ethics demand barren and costly short grass, chemically scorched earth shrubberies and weed-controlled hard surfaces. Sometimes it is only private gardens and derelict sites that give succour to nature.

We can benefit the planet and ourselves by considering biodiversity issues in each development scheme. There is room for more greening in towns and cities whatever the density – from the verdant and lush of the 'garden suburb' to green roofs, street trees, wall climbers and pocket community gardens – bringing nature and the seasons even into crowded urban centres.

Key tenets

■ *Develop the partnerships*

Health interests – Involve local health interests in supporting health through contact with nature

Wildlife connections – make links with local wildlife interests, local authority parks and landscape officers to meet local Biodiversity Action Plan targets

■ *Build wildlife capacity – enhancement*

Enhance the developer's investment by providing landscapes thriving as healthy habitats for local flora and fauna.

Provide habitat enhancement, and habitat re-creation whenever there is a significant development or renewal project

■ *Improve links*

Wildlife to wildlife – connectivity is the maxim, connect local wildlife areas to each other and to the countryside.

Wildlife to people – provide local people with the maximum of contact with nature and access through nearby nature, developing walking and cycling in nature, using the outdoor as health gym and through involvement in management.

Reasons

People enjoy nature: positive effects on health and well-being have been demonstrated. But this positive interaction is less and less available: in towns and on farmland, species are in decline. The song thrush, a good indicator species, once a common sound in towns, has shown a 59 per cent decline over 20 years. Even if only looking at our own needs, supporting urban biodiversity makes social and economic sense:

■ people prefer living in neighbourhoods where nature can thrive (DoE 1994)

■ people live healthier lives when they have contact with the natural world (Rohde and Kendle 1994).

- **EA key indicator**
  Achievement of Biodiversity Action Plan targets

- **UK headline indicator**
  Population of wild birds in the UK

- **Neighbourhood indicator**
  Percentage of residents who see birds nesting
  Percentage of residents who are satisfied with the quality and amount of green space

So with the healing professions, the primary concern must be to maintain the integral well-being of the planet. Not even with all our medical sciences and technologies can we establish well human beings on a sick planet.

SOURCE: Thomas Berry 1991

Nature adds to local diversity by colour shape, sound and season.

Towards an urban renaissance

'We also need to promote the idea of the **ecologically sensitive city** in which humans recognise that they cohabit with nature. Trees, woodland and other open space are all important in fostering biodiversity, in enhancing human health and well-being, and in reducing noise and pollution. We can use some of our previously developed land to create new areas of urban green space.'

SOURCE: (DETR 1999i)

4.18

Human well-being and urban wildlife

Contact with nature may be one of the conditions that protects individuals from a breakdown in health and supports resistance to disease. Benefits of contact with nature include:

- *restorative effects – reducing fatigue, 'recharging'*

- *cognitive effects – enhanced self-esteem, sense of peace*

- *behavioural effects – encourages play, exploration, adventure*

SOURCE: Rohde and Kendle 1994

'The quality of our natural environment demands that the development decisions respect the direct relationship between man and nature.' (DETR 1999i: 29)

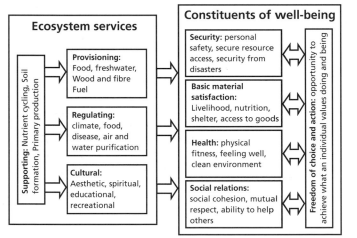

Figure 4.33
Ecosystem services support our well-being.
After Millennium Ecosystem Assessment, 2005

The Millennium Ecosystem Report (2005) provided a detailed assessment of the state of the world's ecosystems. It also reviewed the way in which the services that these ecosystems give, which they termed 'supporting', 'provisioning', 'regulating', and 'cultural', provide humanity with a platform for well-being. Worryingly, the assessment found that the ability of ecosystems to provide these services is rapidly declining due to the impact of what we should defined as unsustainable development.

CONTEXTS AND DRIVERS

Nature and health

Humankind evolved within landscapes of great biodiversity and now increasingly creates and inhabits an environment of biodeficiency. Evidence of the effects on health and self-fulfilment of what has been an incremental change for hundreds of years is difficult to interpret. There are, of course, theories of biophilia (Wilson 1986), placing contact with nature at the centre of human identity and well-being. Several recent empirical studies seem to support such theories and point to a strong relationship between contact with nature and human health. These studies indicate that: (See side column)

For further information see Health, place and nature - How outdoor environments influence health and well-being: a knowledge base (SDC 2008).

The Royal Commission on Environmental Pollution state, 'From our evaluation of the evidence, we are strongly persuaded that access to good quality greenspace provides an effective, population-wide strategy for the promotion of good health, wellbeing and quality of life. We are convinced that the evidence is sufficiently strong to warrant amending planning guidance to recognise the health benefits of greenspace and to build greenspace into new and existing developments' (RCEP 2007).

Biodiversity and habitat re-creation

The climate change 'press' seems to have temporarily eclipsed an equally dire prognosis for the world's ecosystems. Both of course are symptoms of a single underlying problem, the unsustainbility of current global economic systems and politico-cultural mores. The Millennium Ecosystem Assessment (MEA 2005) provides stark evidence of dramatic changes in the biosphere. Species extinctions are at their highest rate since the last great period of extinction 65 million years ago and further increases are predicted. The term 'biodiversity' actually refers to an aggregate measure of diversity in the gene pool, of species and of habitats. The broad direction of evolution since life first emerged has been to add diversity. With diversity came stability, adaptability and the flourishing of a range of ecosystems clothing the earth, which eventually created the conditions for the emergence and maintenance of the human race. Damage to biodiversity puts all this at risk.

The Millennium Ecosystem Assessment divides the part that biodiversity has in supporting human well-being into four 'roles:'

- supporting roles include the underpinning of ecosystems through structural, compositional, and functional diversity;

- regulatory roles through the influence of biodiversity on the production, stability, and resilience of ecosystems;

- cultural roles from the nonmaterial benefits people derive from the aesthetic, spiritual, and recreational elements of biodiversity;

- provisioning roles from the direct and indirect supply of food, fresh water, fibre, and so on.

All these roles are strongly interrelated. The assessment estimates that current extinction rates are around 100 times greater than rates found in the fossil record. Other estimates, some of which refer to extinctions hundreds of years into the future, estimate extinction rates 1000 to 10,000 times higher than previous rates (MEA 2005).

Ecological intensification in the urban realm

Creating and maintaining rich urban biodiversity is a strategic issue. The term 'ecological intensification' captures well the required policy approach. This is not, as may first appear, incompatible with achieving higher densities to support the viability of local services and facilities. Indeed a more biodiverse public realm can play its part in socially focused outcomes such as health, well-being and quality of life even where space is at a premium. The other key outcomes covered in the sections on food, waste, energy and water are not only compatible with implementing strong biodiversity policies, but benefit from a high degree of mutual synergy.

An example of this approach can be found in work undertaken in Basel, Switzerland, on the role of green roofs in meeting biodiversity objectives. Rare species often colonise urban brownfield land. Development causes a loss of this type of habitat. Following research and piloting, it was found that a regime of various substrate depths, supported the provision of low nutrient well drained extensive green roof (termed the brown roof) mimicking the valuable neglected brownfield sites being lost through urban intensification. In accordance with national biodiversity obligations, the canton of Basel mandates the design and use of substrates for extensive green roofs as part of its current biodiversity strategy (Brenneisen 2006).

Health benefits of nature: the evidence

- *People with access to nearby nature are generally healthier than those without (de Vries et al. 2003, Pretty et al. 2007).*

- *The percentage of greenspace in a person's residential area is positively associated with their perceived general health, a relationship that is strongest for lower socioeconomic groups (Mitchell and Popham 2008, Maas et al. 2006).*

- *Populations in urban areas with greenspace and gardens have fewer mental health problems (Pretty et al. 2007). Contact with nature specifically impacts positively on blood pressure, cholesterol, outlook on life and stress reduction (Maller et al. 2005).*

- *A 10 per cent increase in greenspace in the living environment can lead to a decrease in health complaints equivalent to a reduction in age of five years (de Vries et al. 2003).*

- *The human response to nature includes feelings of pleasure and interest and a reduction in anger and anxiety (Rohde and Kendle 1994). Residents living in areas with more trees and grass see their problems as more soluble and less severe (Kuo 2001).*

- *Natural spaces have a restorative effect, helping people recover more quickly from attention demanding tasks (Hartig et al.1991, Hartig et al. 2003) and play a role in recovery from stress and can benefit concentration and mood (HCN and DAC, 2004).*

- *Contact with nature can enhance child development, by encouraging recovery from stressful experiences and providing opportunities for exploration (HCN and DAC 2004). Street trees were found to be associated with a lower prevalence of early childhood asthma (Lovasi et al. 2008).*

- *In adults contact with nature provides opportunities for personal development and well-being, stimulating feelings of relaxation, autonomy and competence. (HCN and DAC 2004).*

4.19

Health benefits of greenspace
An overview

Hundreds of independent studies whose conclusions bear on the relationship between urban greenspace and inidivdual and population health have been carried out. Each study may have used different socio-cultural groups and different parameters of greenspace and health. However, reviews of these studies provide the following broad conclusions:

General health and well-being
Regardless of socio-economic status there is evidence of a positive relationship between greenspace and general health.

The quality and quanitity of greenspace is important, poor quality greenspace may have a negative health effect.

Physical environmental health
Large trees and shrubs can protect people from detrimental environmental expoure to flooding, air pollutin, noise and urban temprature extremes.

Saluatory health and well-being
Experiencing greenspace has a positive impact on levels of stress. Effects can occur relatively immediately after expossure to greenspace. Stress reduction can occur through elements such as sensory stimulation, aesthetic expereinces and promotion of outdoor activity and excercise.

The degree to which biodiversity, per se, plays a role is unclear, although some evidence points to the importance of visual and spatial diversity in landscape having an important role in human restoration and recuperation.

Promotion of physical activity
The following factors were found to be involved in realtion to activity and use of greenspace:
- *distance to home*
- *ease of access*
- *attractiveness of the resource (boidiversity and cleanliness)*
- *connectivity to other uses (e.g. shops, jobs)*
- *range of amenity supported (e.g. play areas, quiet areas, picnic facilities)*

SOURCE: Greenspace Scotland 2008

Local wildlife trust offices can be found via www.wildlifetrusts.org.uk

In the neighbourhood setting, biodiversity objectives should be pursued in tandem with social and economic objectives. Financial support can be strengthened through forming partnerships with urban regeneration, employment, training and health initiatives.

National planning policy will set out the framework for designation and protection of national and local sites. However, in a typical neighbourhood, the basic or 'background' level of biodiversity will not usually attract protection through these measures. This section sets out an approach to be followed in non-designated areas under development or renewal.

Policy support for biodiversity in residential or mixed neighbourhoods can be drawn from Biodiversity Action Plans, some of which are starting to address typical urban land and can and should be refered to in any local planning guidance.

PARTNERS, PARTICIPANTS AND CONSULTEES

The developer

People prefer living and working in areas with good access to greenspace. The connection between development value and such access is proven. The developer will be interested in quality design to minimise any disbenefits. Poorly planned landscape can give rise to crime and fear of crime.

Householders

People enjoy nature. Householders need to be fully on board and aware of what they can do to encourage nature. Options for a 'wildlife garden', for bird tables and bird nests, bat boxes can be made in new build and regeneration. Householders can adopt a new street tree, greatly increasing survival chances through watering and checking regularly. Calls need to be made for 'planting not parking' to help stem the tide of front garden car parks.

The local authority

Local authorities balance their statutory duties to protect the natural environment with many other responsibilities. The local plan and local Biodiversity Action Plan are essential tools in setting the policy scene for the role of the neighbourhood in nature conservation.

Local wildlife interests

A local wildlife group or trust will be a valuable first point of contact for information about wildlife in the neighbourhood and is often the lead partner in preparing local Biodiversity Action Plans. In the UK, the Urban Wildlife Partnership is a national charity devoted to promoting the well-being of wildlife and the places it lives in towns and cities.

THE BIODIVERSITY PLAN

Using the analogy of a body; the town-scale wildlife network of corridors, reservoirs, stepping stones and links provides the major arteries and organs of the urban wildlife habitat system. Although comprehensive, most urban territory will inevitablly fall outside all the identified areas in this town-scale approach. The body still needs the detail of tissues, sinews and capillaries to be viable. These details can be provided by attending to biodiversity at the neighbourhood scale. The biodiversity goal at the neighbourhood scale is to increase wildlife capacity across the whole spatial territory. The policy and tools needed for this are set out below as four mutually reinforcing activities.

Phase 1 – Take the initiative and create a shared vision

A coalition for biodiversity is often intitiated when a valued local habitat is under threat. Even in the absense of such a threat, the response to a major proposal should be to undertake a neighbourhood habitat appraisal; use this process to draw in partners and interested parties.

Undertaking a neighbourhood appraisal would also be a way of examining the environmental function of the site in context and also in terms of human well-being (see Section 3.8).

Phase 2 – Understand the locality and learn lessons

- What species are locally important?

- What does the relevant Local Biodiversity Area Plan say?

- Is there an urban tree strategy?

- What has worked well in other neighbourhoods?

Phase 3 – Develop ideas and agree a programme

These four spheres of action need consideration. Details of activity in each of these spheres can be found on the following pages.

- Wildlife promotion at the town scale: see 4.20

- Neighbourhood biodiversity enhancement: see 4.20

- Protection and enhancement of biodiversity in the development project: see 4.22

- The pivotal role of urban trees in biodiversity and health: see 4.21

Phase 4 – Refine solutions and take action

The four agendas for action above are mutually supportive and as an integrated package provide, not only a valueable safety net for urban biodiversity, but also the ground plan for a radical enhancment for health and well-being.

2.2 the seven stage process

Nature conservation as urban regeneration

Neighbourhood Nature Programme Walsall, West Midlands

This is a nature conservation project that strengthens local communities whilst also improving local environments and biodiversity.

The project ran from 1993 to 1998 as part of an urban regeneration programme.

The project officer was guided by the local community and representatives of partner organisations. The project was promoted through a travelling exhibition, it included:

- *new woodland planting*

- *community-led activities/events*

- *free trees for private gardens*

- *wildlife monitoring by young people; and*

- *improving school grounds.*

Further information can be found in Best Practice in Urban Forestry achive, available from the Wildlife Trust for Birmingham and the Black Country.
www.wild-net.org/wildbbc

Figure 4.34
The costs of three basic landscape approaches to open space.
Biodiverse landscape can cost a lot less.
SOURCE: Benson and Roe 2007

Type of approach	Mean costs £ per ha relative to native maintenance		
	Capital	Establishment (0-5 yrs)	Maintenance (5-10 yrs)
Native Derelict areas that have been colonised adequately to allow minimal reclamation thus retaining the colonised vegetation	7.0	2.7	1
Naturalistic Derelict areas that have been treated so that they simulate natural habitats	56.5	16.5	5.6
Amenity Derelict areas that have had traditional reclamation to grassland with or without trees and shrubs	32.3	11.7	8.6

4.20

Section 37 of the UK Habitats Regulations 1994 includes policies 'encouraging the management of features of the landscape which are of major importance for wild flora and fauna' including links, corridors and stepping stones that 'are essential for the migration, dispersal and genetic exchange of wild species.'

4.20   BIODIVERSITY FRAMEWORK

Creating and maintaining rich urban biodiversity is a strategic issue. The term 'ecological intensification' captures well the required policy approach. This is not, as may first appear, incompatible with achieving higher densities to support better services. Indeed a more biodiverse public realm can play its part in socially focused outcomes such as health, well-being and quality of life even where space is at a premium. Many key outcomes covered in the sections on food, waste, energy and water are not only compatible with implementing strong biodiversity policies, but benefit from a high degree of mutual synergy.

WILDLIFE AT THE TOWN SCALE – THE WILDLIFE NETWORK

Most local authorities have a wildlife plan or local Biodiversity Action Plan. This should set out the strategic framework for town-wide nature conservation and wildlife support. Current best practice for wildlife strategies is to adopt a wildlife network approach. This involves the identification of a number of key resource types that are then mapped for the entire conurbation. Some of these resources will be sites that have statutory national or local designation. A neighbourhood project should be seen in the context of the settlement wide network and seek to strengthen it.

KEY

The wildlife network at the town scale includes

green wedges and country-side links *– tracts of countryside extending into the town. The largest scale features, often associated with river floodplains or escarpment that have escaped built development*

wildlife corridors *– linear tracts of habitat, sometimes connected with the surrounding countryside. Often land bordering transport corridors (especially river, canal and rail)*

wildlife reservoirs *– large areas of urban green space and/or those with large biodiversity capacity. Some may have national or local designations*

stepping stones *– small areas of urban green space and/or large areas of low biodiversity capacity*

wildlife links *– shorter or weaker tracts of habitat linking the other features. For example hedgerows/lines of trees*

Figure 4.35
The townscape approach

NEIGHBOURHOOD BIODIVERSITY

At this scale, involving local people is paramount. Effective contact can be through local schools, wildlife networks, and other interest groups.

Measure 1 Increase 'background' wildlife capacity

Aim for a very high level of biodiversity at the neighbourhood scale. This is not to say that the entire built environment must be cloaked in green, but to recognise that every development, whether renovation, enhancement or new build, has a part to play in replacing the local biodiversity that has been lost in many industrialised nations, especialy in the last 25 years. With regards to bird populations it would be true to say that literally global problems can be addressed with small-scale local solutions. For example, modern house designs rarely offer opportunities for swifts and house martins. These can be given an opportunity by mounting nestboxes under eaves or on gable ends.

This capacity approach needs to encompass streets, commercial nodes, business parks, education facilities, health centres, transport corridors and public open space.

Tools
- Plan for 10 large, native trees per ha in high-density areas, increasing to 25 in medium-density areas and 50 in low-density areas.
- Optimise all other resource interventions for wildlife
  Energy – shelter belts, biomass coppice
  Water – treatment and attenuation wetlands
  Food – allotment windbreaks
  Waste – community composts, ground mulches
- Restore old hedgerows or plant new ones (even in urban areas).
- Provide green roofs and wall climbers.
- Provide bat boxes and bird boxes, garden ponds.

Measure 2 Create threads

Use a spatial design to provide a wildlife network on a finer scale than the corridors of the town scale. This should comprise a fine and near continuous network of hedges, shrubs and trees.

Tools
- Locate, protect and enhance existing features (for example remnant countryside hedgerows).
- Consider providing hedgerows instead of fences as back garden boundaries.
- Use linear features to provide opportunities for threads. For example along boundaries or movement corridors.

Measure 3 Provide local wildlife nodes

Design or improve the wildlife quality of local nodes in the urban fabric. Also remember that, in wildlife terms, two plus two equals

4.21 Urban trees

4.10 Flooding, drainage and run-off

5.6 Green infrastructure

Biodiversity

'biodiversity is ultimately lost or conserved at a local level'

'Local Biodiversity Action Plans should reflect the views, values and individual character of their area as well as the national priorities'

SOURCE: (UK Biodiversity Steering Group 1995)

Target species

Start by identifying locally important species from the Local Biodiversity Action Plan. In general, the following species can all be assisted in gardens and allotments. They have all also been cited as of particular concern nationally by the UK Biodiversity Steering Group Report (1995)

- *Birds: blackbird, blue tit, house sparrow, robin, song thrush, house martin, swallow, swift*
- *Several species of bat*
- *Other animals: badger, hedgehog, great crested newt.*

As wildlife capacity increases, small-scale measures are more likely to succeed.

4.20

Birmingham and the Black Country Biodiversity Action Plan (BAP)

This is a good example of how to include urban biodiversity in a local BAP.

Garden ponds, urban wasteland and allotments are the subject of habitat action plans in this BAP. The plan was prepared as a process involving a wide number of local stakeholders. The action plan recognises buildings and structures such as bridges and tunnels as valuable habitat. Species identi-fied for protection and enhancement in the urban area are the song thrush, bats, black redstart and skylark.

The plan also introduced the role of different types of hard surface (permeable/tarmac) as a biodiversity concern.

five: the larger the habitat blocks the greater the biodiversity capacity.

Tools

- Identify wildlife opportunities associated with urban design features, such as street corners and junctions, pocket parks, buffers, shelter belts, and sustainable drainage features.
- Combine resources: for example, combine balancing ponds from a number of developments, provide groups of large trees, use local parks.

Measure 4 Bio-enhance greenspace

Use a comprehensive approach to both public and private greenspace, including the smallest of areas such as grass verges and private gardens. Include biodiversity requirements in the design and management of this resource.

Tools

- Upgrade habitat – replacing some grass with native meadow or native shrubs/trees or relaxing moving regimes to encourage wildflowers.
- Use locally native shrubs and trees in landscape schemes.
- Provide residents with information about attracting wildlife to their gardens.

Figure 4.36
An approach for increasing local biodiversity

KEY
in addition to the townscape approach

*Measure 1
increased capacity*

*Measure 2
threads*

*Measure 3
local node*

*Measure 4
enhanced greenspace*

4.21 URBAN TREES

The first national study of urban trees in England 'Trees in town' (DETR 1993) found that *'most decisions on tree planting and management appear to address short-term needs only and take little or no account of the combined long-term effects on townscape'*. For aethetic, health and biodivestiy reasons this is an incredible indictment to the waste of a unique ingredient in the urban realm.

The health case for many more urban trees is strong. In terms of climate change, trees have value in both mitigation and adaptation. In addition to street trees, a matrix of stands of at least 12 trees plus small woods and copses can and should be provided in all but the densest urban centres. This 'urban forest' is part of preventative healthcare (NUFU 2000). There is also an urban design imperative for the use of trees: for outstanding specimen urban trees, for street trees, for avenues and for intimate groups of trees – bringing the scale and majesty of nature to town.

As a component for healthy neighbourhoods, trees:

- filter particulate from the air, including harmful PM10s
  – these fine particles are associated with mortality from cardiac and respiratory causes

- absorb pollutants such as ozone, nitrogen dioxide and sulphur dioxide – these gases can affect people with asthma and chronic lung disease

- absorb carbon dioxide and release oxygen

- give shade in the summer, from Sun Protection Factor (SPF) 6 or 10 for individual trees up to 100 in woodland – protection from the sun reduces incidence of skin cancer

- reduce stress levels (Ulrich 2000)

- can increase healthy longevity in the aged (Takano et al. 2002)

- can lead to reduced crime rates (Kuo and Sullivan 2001)

In terms of comfort and urban liveability, trees:

- attenuate noise

- slow wind speed

- reduce the heat island effect and provide a milder climate

- give character, soften hard urban form and provide landmarks

- provide habitats for birds and other wildlife

- add seasonal change and interest to streets

- can slow down urban water run-off after a storm, reducing likelihood of flooding.

'Tree planting is a crucial tool for creating new landscapes'

SOUIRCE: Space For Growth, English Partnerships

Plenty of room but acute absence of trees at this aestheticaly harsh nodal interchange in Kingston, London.

Trees adding softness and seasonality to a local shopping area in Bedford.

Figure 4.37
Tree species with berries and nuts for birds

Large trees	Small street trees and garden trees	
Birch		
Willow	Rowan	Elder
Oak	Bird cherry	Hazel
Ash	Yew	Holly
Beech	Hawthorn	Crab apple

4.21

Trees in Towns

The average density of urban trees and large shrubs in England is 58.4 per ha with approximately half of all urban areas having between 10 and 50 trees or shrubs per ha. 60% of all urban trees and shrubs in England are on private property (mainly gardens) or less accessible public land (e.g. schools, churchyards, allotments, etc.).

SOURCE: Trees in Towns II, Britt and Johnston 2008

An 'outstanding' local tree is one that plays a significant contribution to the aesthetic urban amenity. Urban designers – don't just plan buildings as landmarks – plant trees!

Celebrated local tree, Barcelona, Spain.

In addition, trees:

- increase property values

- can provide energy, firewood and timber products.

Trees have been shown to promote health both symbolically and literally, bringing nature into neighbourhoods – and on such a grand scale. The problems associated with trees (root damage to structures, for example) can usually be traced to poor understanding of their needs, poor or no proper planning and poor maintenance. With proper attention to planning and management, trees are part of the solution to healthy urban living.

TREES IN THE SPATIAL FRAMEWORK

Step 1 – Survey and research

Using a participatory process, explore people's perceptions and views on trees. Draw in professional support or local expertise.

- Are there important local trees or local associations with particular species?
- Is there a local authority urban tree strategy?

Step 2 – Plan tree cover as the spatial framework develops

We are used to urban areas that are denuded of trees. A participatory planning exercise can allow people to experiment with options and ideas for trees in an unthreatening way. Use it to help to generate support for a greater number and diversity of trees. Provide a wider understanding of the range of benefits from urban trees.

Trees are significant in good urban design:

- Street trees soften urban form

- Garden trees add seasonal interest

- 'Civic' trees articulate urban legibility

- Amenity trees on open space and recreation areas

- Outstanding trees in spaces where people congregate

- Community orchards for local festivities

- Avenues and pleached trees for boulevards, ramblas and squares

Plan deliberately for sites to accommodate the next generation of 'outstanding' urban trees. In a national survey of urban trees (DETR 1993) only 3 per cent of urban trees were recorded as providing an outstanding contribution to the visual amenity (often planes, oaks or pines).

Step 3 – Resolve technical issues and prepare management plan

Ensure close liaison between stakeholders and design team members. Potential problems – such as vandalism, tree root ingress and safety – can be handled by careful design. Early consultation ensured a close proximity between building and trees in Milton Keynes, UK through adapting building foundation design.

Step 4 – Plant, manage and monitor

Many planted trees die within the first 3 years of life. Newly planted trees require extra care during this time whilst they establish root systems. Involving local people can provide better results; for example, residents can help with:

■ street tree planting; choose from a selected species list

■ tree establishment; watering street trees outside their home and reporting broken stakes/ties

■ management of the small community woodlands in their neighbourhoods

■ setting-up a tree warden scheme to encourage involvement.

Participatory events such as tree dressing or planting days can encourage care and pride in local trees.

URBAN WOOD AND WOODLAND CYCLES

Urban wood and tree management needs facilities to support conversion from a largely linear process to the cyclical and systemic processes necessary for sustainability and health, whilst also dramatically increasing tree cover, in line with responses to global warming and urban health. A facility can bring together:

■ volunteers, skilled professionals and training opportunities

■ collection points for waste wood and tree surgery arisings with processing opportunities for woodchip biomass, wood storage, curing and re-use as sawn wood, charcoal production

■ local people with demonstrations and involvement in local tree, resource and biodiversity support

■ good practice in urban tree management and buy-in from residents for greater urban tree cover.

Bioregional have set up such a facility, called an 'urban tree station', together with the London Borough of Croydon. They estimate that it is diverting 10,000 tonnes of wood a year from landfill (FFI see www.bioregional.com).

Outstading tree commanding place in a public space, Copenhagen, Denmark.

Did this tree scheme look adequate in plan? Kingston, Surrey, UK.

Pleached trees in Bologne, France.

4.22

Nature conservation for developers

Developers should seek to optimise environmental opportunity by using this sequential approach.

1 Identify and seek to enhance, or protect, important environmental features.

2 Consider potential impacts on the environment of the development (direct, indirect and cumulative).

3 Seek to improve the environment.

4 Avoid adverse impacts, exploring all options, such as 'do nothing'.

5 Mitigate any residual adverse impacts caused by development.

6 As a last resort, always compensate for adverse impacts.

SOURCE: RSPB 2000a

4.22 BIODIVERSITY AND THE DEVELOPMENT PROJECT

Developers, designers, planners and the community should ensure that a number of specific actions are carried out as part of every significant development project.

1 HABITAT AND SPECIES AUDIT

As part of the twin-track approach, advocated in Section 5.2, biodiversity survey work must be undertaken. A habitat and species audit will indicate the occurrence of species or habitats of national or local importance. Local Biodiversity Action Plans should be consulted as part of this process. In an urban area (often deficient in wildlife), local importance or non-native species assemblages may rank highly. There are standard methods for conducting surveys – in the UK, a Phase 1 survey gives an assessment of basic nature conservation interest. Local wildlife groups may already hold data and can be contacted through the local wildlife trust. The local audit should clearly identify all relevant elements of the settlment wide wildlife network.

2 SAFEGUARDING, CREATING AND ENHANCING HABITATS

With the basic data to hand, the task now is to identify opportunities to enhance local habitats and species in the widest manner. Developers can provide varied, distinctive and attractive housing whilst enhancing wildlife value through:

- retention of existing habitat;
- creation of new habitats; and
- appropriate management of all landscape areas.

The schematic layout of development projects should be influenced by these goals. Once a robust framework of habitats has been provided, simple measures such as providing bat/bird sites and using locally native species in landscape schemes will prove effective at further increasing 'capacity'.

Making links and reversing habitat fragmentation

Linking habitats together both within the neighbourhood and to wildlife features surrounding the neighbourhood will strengthen the biodiversity value.

Brownfield sites

Increasing pressure for development on brownfield sites must be balanced with their merits in respect of wildlife and nature conservation. In some circumstances, the species assemblages can be especially important for urban biodiversity (Shirley and Box 1998). Each site must be judged on its merits. Specific areas of wildlife value do not necessarily preclude development on the site.

A renovation project providing opportunities to create new habitat, Ekostaden, Sweden.

Photo: John Dolecek

3 BIODIVERSITY MANAGEMENT DURING CONSTRUCTION

Biodiversity can all too often be unwittingly destroyed during construction work. A plan for habitat asset protection during the construction phase should be developed by a landscape architect. A site manager with lead responsibility for habitat protection should be identified on all development sites. There will be a need for training of contractors and sub-contractors.

Guidance for tree protection on development sites is often given by a national standard, in the UK this is BS 5837:2005 – Trees in relation to construction. Many local authorities also provide guidance for contractors on all aspects of habitat protection.

4 SUSTAINABLE MANAGEMENT

All too often greenspace does not live up to its biodiversity capacity due to a failure to adopt sustainable management practices. Partnerships with local wildlife groups formed during the survey stage may provide valuable links for developing a sensitive management approach.

Key principles are:

- *Managing for people and biodiversity* – Local involvement in the management of wildlife can be seen as part of the philosophy of sustainable resource management. It is a good way to influence the biodiversity of private land such as gardens. There are direct health benefits for people through activities and involvement in wildlife projects.

- *Choosing resource-efficient maintenance regimes* – Reductions in chemical inputs and labour are possible by working with natural processes. Plan for attractive swards of fine grasses with wildflowers, where possible avoiding the usual high pesticide/fertiliser/mowing types of turf. Use ground cover and mulch to keep weeds down not herbicides.

- *Recycling and closing loops* – Store grey water for landscape watering requirements. Chip or compost arisings including autumn leaves for re-use as mulches and soil conditioners.

Weed control in urban areas

In most urban areas weeds in gutters, the bases of walls and paving joints are controlled with regular application of pesticides. There is health value in reducing the use of these chemicals in neighbourhoods, some authorities in Europe are starting to pilot alternatives. In the town of Rennes, France, a member of the Healthy City network, as part of a programme to restore water quality alternatives to pesticides such as mechanical and thermic weed control techniques were assessed for efficiency and cost. Depending on location combinations of sweeping and steam weeding were found to be affordable and effective (Lefevre et al. 2001).

Linking with local biodiversity action plans

The UK Biodiversity Steering Group oversees the conservation of biodiversity in Britain. It recommends drawing up local Biodiversity Action Plans to complement the national action plan. Best practice for these is to address neighbourhood biodiversity resources such as back gardens, derelict land and habitats associated with urban buildings.

To enable a strong relationship between the local biodiversity action plan and development requires support. The South East England Development Agency (SEEDA) through its Building for Nature initiative has worked with development managers to create bat boxes, green walls, wildlife migration and other biodiversity support in both new build and renovation.

FFI: www.buildingfornature.com

Majestic mature tree successfully retained in difficult development circumstances by Islington Borough Council, London.

The touchstone for this innovative project has been to 'close all ecocycles at the smallest appropriate scale'. Sponsored by both the local authority and the utilities, it represents a significant way forward in terms of resource reduction in the city.

Urban eco cycling concept

This model for energy, waste and water management is known as the Hammarby model. It was developed jointly by Birka Energi, Stockholm Vatten and Skafab.

An integrated approach to resources underpins the design and planning of this new township in Stockholm, due to house 20,000 people.

The energy, water and waste utilities have worked together to formulate proposals based on resource cycle principles. Innovation has required new working methods with integrated collaboration between research, industry, national and local government organisations and environmental groups.

RESOURCES

The environment is at the heart of the development concept. The aim is to halve the negative environmental impact, compared with other modern developments. Although new technology and innovative design is seen as part of the solution, the commitment of the residents is also seen as essential. They will be provided with the ability to monitor their own energy and water consumption via an internal data network.

The three utilities leading the technical approach know it is in their companies' interests to be in the vanguard of the next generation of environmental-led solutions to urban resource needs.

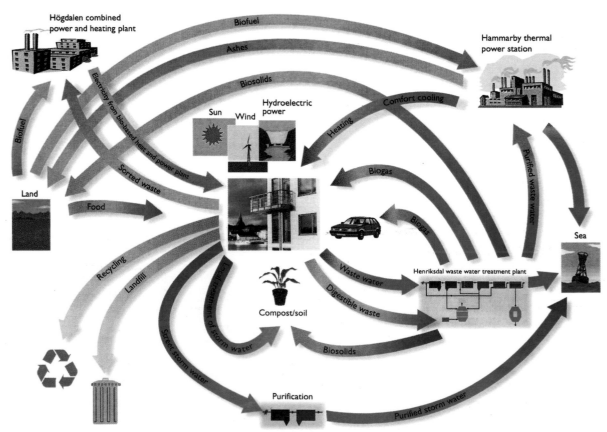

Energy

Demand is being reduced by efficiency in the choice of appliances and plant – lifts, fans, pumps, lights, etc. Technology will further reduce consumption: for example, lighting and ventilation are switched on only when someone enters the room.

District heating and cooling are provided. Energy is generated from solar panels, heat pumps, boilers burning biofuel and combustible waste.

Water

The local water cycle has been integrated into the 'ecocycle' model. As such, Hammarby Sjöstad will have its own sewage treatment plant, where waste water will be treated, the heat will be recovered and any nutrients will be recycled using new technology to enable them to be returned to agricultural land. Surface water is treated locally.

Food

There is provision for local food to be grown. Fertility is improved by the use of locally produced composts.

Waste

Household organic waste and sewage is used to produce biogas. Residual solids are used in agriculture: 80 per cent of nitrogen and phosphorus in waste is returned to the ground as fertiliser. Two leading-edge technologies are being piloted – urine separation for nitrogen recovery and vacuum system waste collection.

Biodiversity

The district is linked to the natural environment by an 'Ecoduct': a 50 m wide tree-adorned pathway that will be a conduit both for wildlife and for non-motorised movement.

PROVIDING FOR LOCAL NEED

Municipal and commercial services have been implemented in phases. These include a primary school, a nursery school, convenience stores, a health-care service and other local facilities will be provided once the neighbourhood reaches approximately 5,000 residents. A central library with meeting rooms is planned. In the larger neighbourhoods there are facilities for holding meetings, throwing parties, local clubs and hobbies.

Low traffic volumes and speeds in residential areas are combined with information technology to minimise the need for transport. Public transport takes priority, with a tram service and a boat service to the city centre.

URBAN DESIGN

Proximity, accessibility and resident integration are important design considerations. There will be the development of mixed use local centres for neighbourhoods in addition to a core nucleus – for the whole area. Development is based on a combination of densities from 4–6-storey inner city to more open 'outlying' layouts.

Mobilt sopsugsystem

Vacuum waste collection system.

Spatial plans for some of the neighbourhoods.

227

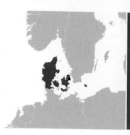
Lessons

Although there were huge invested sums in the district, urban renewal has been met with resentment and opposition in the beginning. One of early objections was that the efforts to counter the complex problems of a district were being tackled by purely physical urban renewal. As a solution, greater emphasis was placed on participation in subsequent stages.

In certain parts of Vesterbro the rent doubled over 5 years; thus residents with lower incomes were obliged to move out of the neighbourhood. The long time period required to complete urban renewal work caused residents to lose their interest to move back into their apartments after being decanted. It was concluded that refurbishment work of a block should not take longer than 3 years.

Photo: Cenergia Energy Consultants, Denmark

Different types of photovoltaic panels cladding the balcony extensions.

Photo: Cenergia Energy Consultants, Denmark

The communal courtyards and gardens.

Ambitions for healthy communities and carbon reductions will never be realised if we set tough objectives for new build alone. The urban fabric is in a state of constant renewal, this presents an enduring opportunity. In this case study the focus is placed on excellence in urban regeneration – the so called 'eco-renovation' approach found in Denmark and Sweden. In the UK, neighbourhood renewal initiatives 'deal' with social issues; however through ignoring the fundamental issues of over-consumption and waste this leaves communities still vulnerable in terms of over reliance on carbon intensive resource use, lacking any degree of self-reliance and lacking flexibility in an uncertain future.

Background

The Vesterbro area of Copenhagen was built between 1850 and 1920 and is located just outside the city centre. The district comprises some 23 five to six storey buildings (4,000 apartments) for 6,500 inhabitants as well as open spaces, offices, bars and enterprises. Surveys in the late 1980s indicated that the housing standard was very low: lack of central heating and warm water (64%), lack of toilets (11%) and of bathrooms (71%). The district had a high concentration of socio-culturally 'vulnerable' people. Most of the residents were on a low income and the unemployment rate was around 20%.

In 1990 Copenhagen municipality decided to refurbish Vesterbro, using an 'eco-renovation' model. A major urban renewal programme over some 10 years, underpinned by research and innovation.

Developing the approach

It was decided that the Vesterbro renewal would be based on ideas of urban ecology and that ecological technologies would be installed against the background of an experimental approach. There were three guiding principles:

* Thematic plans would analyse the available and appropriate technology for each resource issue.
* Pilot projects would be implemented as model projects in a first test period.
* An integrated planning process would be established to guarantee effective information sharing and involvement across different municipal departments and co-operation with all other interested parties, organisations, and companies involved in the urban renewal process.

In 1990 an Urban Renewal Centre was established as a place for meetings between the project management, tenants, municipal departments and trade associations. The centre had a library, a café and a permanent staff of four.

228

The eco-renovation approach covered:

- Low temperature district heating.
- Passive solar heating.
- Water, electricity and waste minimisation.
- Urban Ecology; Green areas green walls, climbing plants, inventory of local birds and vegetation.
- Traffic and active transport.
- Social management and resident engagement.

Piloting the approach

Early block renovation both employed best practice and piloted new approaches. In Tøndergade/Sundevsgade block, preliminary feasibility studies showed the potential for significant improvements in all resource areas. For example 50% energy reductions in room heating and domestic hot water. Façade insulation incorporated photo-voltaic capture with the addition of ventilation counter flow heat recovery behind the panels, making use of the heat captured by the dark panels. This system became an integral building component on re-clad facades and solar balconies, which also brought more light in to internal spaces. A solar collector on the roof heats up a communal water based heat store in the basement which, together with a connection to the district heating scheme, delivers both hot water and space heating through the same pipework to all dwellings. In the communal inner courtyard a SUDs system allows rainwater from the roofs to run around the garden in channels feeding both wildlife and water play areas before being collected for secondary use in WC flushing. The communal courtyard also houses bike parking shelters, attractive compost and recycling facilities and an earth sheltered community building with crèche, meeting and function rooms.

The soft infrastructure

It was acknowledged that success in eco-renovation depended on commitment from the residents. The Urban Renewal Centre was the focus for resident involvement. An Urban Renewal School was set up offering educational activities connected to the renewal project.

Funding

Funding streams have been various through different stages of the programme. It has been estimated that investment in this type of ecological neighbourhood has been 30% higher that in a traditional district. This can be partly offset by a return from the running costs (resource savings made and higher rent). Much of the pilot work was funded by EU programmes such as Thermiea and Energy, Environment and Sustainable Development (HQE2R project).

Entrance to the co-managed communal facility building. This earth sheltered building contains bookable function rooms and a creche.

The renovated rear elevations in the block's interior.

neighbourhood design | chapter 5

Overview

5.1 SCOPE OF THE CHAPTER

This chapter provides an integrated picture of planning and design at the local level, picking up the threads from the earlier chapters. The approach is radical. It demands time, co-operation, and huge creative effort on the part of local authorities, developers, service deliverers and communities in responding to health and environmental priorities.

The chapter is structured in seven main sections, each of which builds and develops on the previous one:

- The OVERVIEW introduces the key themes and more particularly sets out (in 5.2) a systematic process of township and neighbourhood design for sustainability which is very different from the road and site based approach which has dominated the recent past. It is essential reading.

- KEY SPATIAL ELEMENTS then explains the physical structure of settlements in terms of four aspects: land use, density, movement networks and greenspace. Analysis of these four can provide coherence to the design process.

- PROBLEMS AND OPPORTUNITIES draws together all the social, economic and environmental issues previously discussed in Chapters 3 and 4, then expands on specific spatial questions of location and the character of places.

- SHAPING SETTLEMENTS examines the spatial form of neighbourhoods and townships, integrating the four key elements. It offers ways of clearly distinguishing different forms, and of calculating the land needed for a new urban extension or new town.

- NEIGHBOURHOOD REGENERATION applies similar thinking to the renewal and restructuring of existing suburbs, recognising that most towns and cities need to evolve and change quite radically.

- DESIGNING PLACES then comes down to the urban design scale, showing how the blocks and streets make liveable areas and are the constituents of detailed masterplans.

- CASE STUDIES finally put it all together. The Freiburg case, in particular, demonstrates how city region planning, neighbourhood planning and street design are intimately connected: macro and micro are entwined.

CONTENTS

5.1

STRATEGIES FOR RENAAISSANCE

The 'quick strategy check' provides a summary picture of old and new spatial planning principles at the town/neighbourhood level.

Successful integrated spatial strategies – robust in the face of climate change, socially healthy and economically viable – are not rocket science. But they do require courageous leadership, honesty and sufficient powers at the local municipal level. Half-hearted attempts – green window dressing – will fail.

Figure 5.1
Quick strategy check

This chart aims to assist initial understanding of the differences between failed and successful strategies

		DON'T	*DO*
1	Overall approach	■ rely on a laissez-faire stance, with disjointed project-by-project decisions, and separate consideration of each policy area	■ work out an integrated spatial strategy for the town/township, aimed at health, equity, economic vitality and environmental sustainability
2	Timescale	■ shorten the plan period to avoid awkward decisions or political embarrassment	■ take a long-term inter-generational view, anticipating obvious problems and keeping options open where there is uncertainty
3	Housing	■ allocate new housing sites purely on the basis of minimising direct environmental impact and/or political expediency	■ allocate new housing sites on the basis of improving the function of the township and the life chances of residents, while protecting environmental assets
4	Density	■ plan use intensification on every brownfield site	■ encourage urban intensification within identified accessible zones, with valued open space protected
5	Commercial	■ permit low-density single use business parks or leisure parks premised on high car use	■ integrate office, retail and leisure activities into mixed-use town centres and high streets
6	Landscape	■ treat natural features as negative constraints on the freedom of development	■ recognise natural landscape features as the starting point for ecological planning
7	Transport	■ start with a road hierarchy and vehicle access	■ start with a strategy for public transport and pedestrian/cycling accessibility
8	Linkage	■ accept parcel-by-parcel land development with separate cul-de-sac access	■ link developments to create a permeable, accessible environment
9	Partnerships	■ work in compartmentalised boxes and respond too little too late	■ work together in cross-sectoral partnerships and **stay ahead of the game**
10	Robustness	■ hold down capital costs at the expense of maintenance charges and flexibility	■ design to minimise the need for maintenance and facilitate adaptation and personalisation

5.2 DEVISING THE SPATIAL FRAMEWORK

This section introduces the key elements of a local spatial framework and outlines the technical process for developing an effective spatial framework. Subsequent sections of the chapter then elaborate aspects of the process, the concepts and the techniques involved.

The context is provided by Chapter 2: the neighbourhood planning process. Looking at the seven stage cyclic process advocated there, Chapter 5 is concerned with 'understanding the locality', 'developing ideas' and 'agreeing a programme'.

2.2 The seven stage process

KEY MESSAGE

It is essential to have a clear picture of the evolving shape of the whole town/district before making decisions about specific neighbourhoods or development proposals. Understanding the dynamics which shape urban form is critically important. Every town or township should have a robust spatial framework which establishes the long-term pattern of land use, density, movement and greenspace, and reinforces the overall sustainability strategy for the city region as a whole. The framework and accompanying policies can provide the key focus for cross-sectoral debate and subsequent stakeholder commitments.

THE GENERAL PATTERN

The plan on the next page gives an idealised picture of local spatial policy. It is, effectively, a spatial framework for a township – one sector of a city – showing one possible pattern of public transport nodes, local high streets, graded densities and pedestrian accessibility.

For many reasons the urban district (or the whole small town) is the key scale for the provision of local services. It is large enough to offer a wide range of jobs and facilities and a fair degree of local autonomy, but small enough to be walked or cycled across and retain some sense of the locality. It also provides the interface between local people and residents or workers from other areas. The key organising principles are very important: the public transport network provides the rationale for residential and commercial patterns, while the watercourses and hills shape the greenspaces.

Inter-generational planning

The Spatial Framework should be designed to be the long term – i.e. for at least a generation (25 years) and probably several generations. It needs to provide a robust framework for economic activity, steering market pressures towards low carbon, community oriented patterns. It should be approved as part of the main town or city plan, with regular reviews. The long-term priorities and valid development trajectories should

Stakeholders review the structure of the whole settlement to build-up a picture of how to better support walking and cycling. Yeovil, SW England.

be clearly identified to allow effective assessment of incremental development proposals.

A positive planning tool

The framework is not akin to old-style land-use zoning maps. Rather, it is a key stage in a positive planning approach which moves from clarity over goals through to clarity about context and criteria for specific projects. Things to note about the plan are:

■ the very strong focus of urban activity on the main public transport/cycling spine routes

■ the grading of land use intensity in order to maximise accessibility to the spine

■ the lack of land use zones – rather uses are located according to the intensity of activity

■ the green network based on landscape features and giving continuity to open space provision

■ the centre at the main public transport mode

■ industry accessible from the railway and main roads

Figure 5.2
Principles of the twin-track model

The two networks are based on main public transport routes and greenspace respectively. Here they are illustrated following a linear town planning pattern.

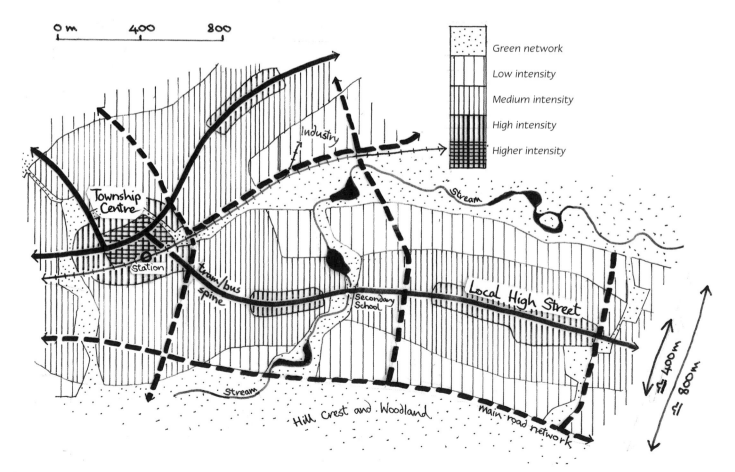

THE TWIN-TRACK MODEL

A useful starting point is the twin-track model of urban form. The two tracks are the public transport network and the greenspace/waterspace system. One provides the shaping for concentrations of human activity, while the other enables the ecology of the settlement to work effectively. The morphology of the settlement is then defined by pedestrian accessibility to the public transport system (and associated activity centres) on the one hand, and access to greenspace on the other. The pattern of streets and public spaces and buildings flow on from that.

The diagram below summarises an approach to working out this sustainable urban pattern. While current practice in defining development patterns often starts with the specific land release and the main roads, this approach starts with the public transport and greenspace systems, in line with the twin-network model. It is designed as much for existing urban areas as for urban extensions. The resulting spatial framework provides the big picture. It provides the context within which more detailed masterplans and development briefs for individual sites can be considered.

Figure 5.3
The twin-track design process

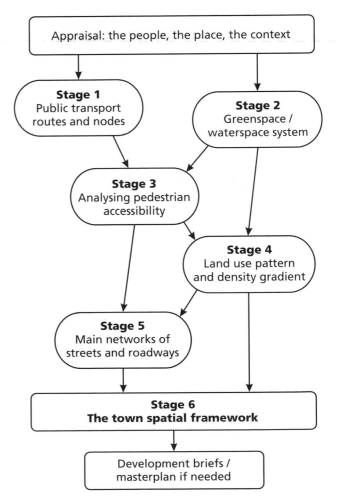

The next two pages illustrate this six-stage process in relation to a town expansion scheme.

5.2

Figure 5.4 **THE TWIN-TRACK DESIGN PROCESS IN DETAIL**
The following illustrates the application of the twin-track process to a town expansion scheme.

Stage 1
Public transport routes and nodes

Identify the main existing public transport routes, their effectiveness, viability, and the degree of flexibility in their routing (if any).

Consult and speculate on potential improvements (or threats) to the system: for example, could an old station be reopened or a new station offer better connections (see map)?

Identify existing/potential public transport nodes, graded

'A' intercity links and good local connections to all main areas
'B' good local connections to all main areas
'C' some regular connections but not comprehensive.

3.18 Public transport operation

Stage 2
The greenspace/waterspace system

■ Identify elements critical to local environmental capital in relation to biodiversity, landscape, water and energy/pollution management.

■ Identify currently valued or proposed recreational open spaces and routeways.

■ Consult/speculate on potential open-space corridors linking between existing facilities.

NB Much of this information is equally needed by the urban potential study, and should be available from the appraisal.

2.7 Understand the locality

4.8 Water planning

4.19 Biodiversity planning

5.8 Urban potential studies

Stage 3
Analysing pedestrian accessibility

■ Map existing pedestrian accessibility to public transport stops and local centres, identifying barriers and other deterrents to movement.

■ Analyse pedestrian accessibility to potential new routes or nodes/centres.

■ Evaluate the potential local catchments of alternative routes/nodes in the light of the prime greenspace/waterspace system.

NB The accessibility criteria applied here are critical to the emerging spatial framework. They must be robust and widely accepted.

3.9 Accessibility criteria

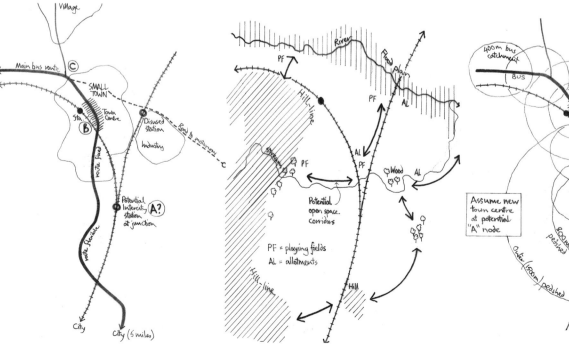

Stage 4
Land-use pattern and density gradient

Devise and evaluate patterns of land-use intensity, relating these patterns directly to the accessibility and open space analyses, and distinguish four levels of intensity.

1 Town-centre activities: retail, leisure, business, civic and high-density residential development.

2 Local high streets and environs: small-scale mixed uses (retail, etc.) with medium- to high-density residential development.

3 Local catchments: areas within easy reach of public transport services and nodes, mainly medium-density residential, with other uses as appropriate.

4 Greenspace system: areas dedicated to water/ecology/recreation/landscape, where new building is deterred.

3.10 Local shops and services

5.4 Graded density

Stage 5
Main networks of streets and routeways

1 Devise the network of distributor roads on a modified grid basis that responds to the contours, ensures permeability, and gives natural centrality to the town/township centre.

2 Plan the cycling/walking network on about a 200 m grid, using semi-car-free 'safe routes' as well as the distributor roads (20 mph), ensuring permeability and access to nodes, etc.

3 Identify neighbourhoods, based on historic associations when they exist, or the pattern of streets and catchment when they do not.

3.15 Neighbourhood movement strategy

Stage 6
The township spatial framework

The spatial framework is the combination of land-use pattern and the main networks. It should cover the whole town or township (existing/planned) and adjacent open space, showing how the settlement is linked to the wider area. It should specify:

1 the basic principles on which it is based – for example, criteria of pedestrian accessibility or of facility location

2 the density gradient, and specify the activities which are appropriate to each of use-intensity

3 the distributor network for walking/cycling, public transport and general traffic, but should not normally detail the minor access streets

4 specific sites for new development proposals (such as school, park, cinema) where they can be safely identified

5 spatial manifestations of policies for recreation, wildlife, water, energy/microclimate, food and cultural landscape

6 areas requiring a detailed masterplan and/or a development brief, with an indication of phasing where appropriate

7 neighbourhoods of function and/or character, existing and planned.

2.9 Agreeing a co-ordinated programme

4.5 Energy efficient layout and landscape

5.11 Designing neighbourhood cells

5.12 Linear districts and towns

5.3

Why mixed uses?

It is generally recognised that mixed uses will:

- *reinforce the viability of centres with overlapping uses, providing multiple reasons for people to go and stay in the centre*

- *allow people to make short walking trips between facilities rather than relying on longer car-based trips*

- *create vitality and character in a place; and*

- *provide the opportunity for individuals to live and work in close proximity.*

Health benefits

Mixed use neighbourhoods with walkable access to local facilities, are good for health. They promote physical activity and social capital (Leyden 2003; Frank et al. 2004; Calve Blanco 2009).

It is vital to be able to abstract the essential structure of settlements from the confused medley of activities and construction on the ground. The four elements presented here – land use, density, networks and greenspace – serve this purpose. They can be used to analyse the existing pattern as much as to help shape new. The relationship between them is the essence of local planning

5.3   A MIX OF USES

MESSAGE

With every urban district there should be a wide range of uses, including residential, educational, social, commercial, industrial and recreational activities. The diversity of use helps achieve the basic goal of increasing local autonomy (Chapter 1). However, the spatial pattern of mixing is not a casual matter. There are quite specific requirements which shape the appropriate locations. Mixed use local and district centres, rather than seperate zones for shops, offices, flats, social and health facilities, are critically important.

The need for guidance

The move towards fostering mixed-use development has become all pervading in recent urban planning policy. It is perceived as a method of reintegrating urban areas often sterilised by over

Figure 5.5
Mixed use considerations

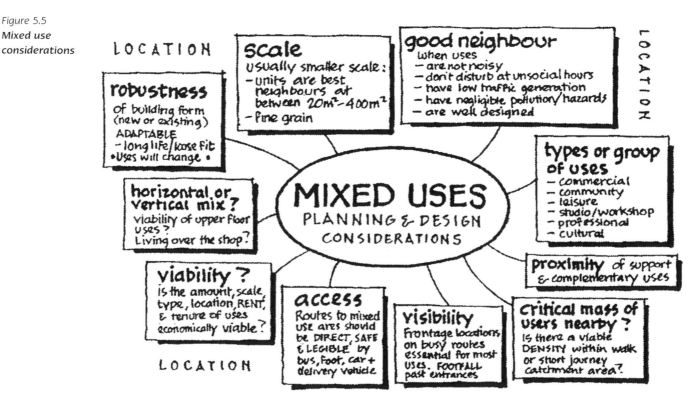

half a century of zoning policies. These policies have resulted in monoculture areas generating concentrated periods of interzone traffic movement and 'dead' periods where a zone is bereft of any activity (for example, shopping centres and industrial areas 'after hours', or residential estates during weekdays).

Whilst it is widely recognised that mixed uses are beneficial there is little guidance available on what constitutes appropriate mixed uses, the scale of mixed use, location and visibility of mixed uses, or critical mass of supporting population.

LOCATION AND SCALE

The phrase 'mixed use' covers a multitude of sins. It is vital to be clear about what it is appropriate to locate within a neighbourhood, an urban district or small town, and what it is not. Chapter 3 sets out guidelines for different activities in relation to catchments and accessibility. A distinction should be drawn between three settings for mixed use:

- people-intensive uses such as most shops, offices, pubs, cafes and service facilities which benefit from being clustered together in accessible local, district and town centres

- land hungry uses such as schools, parks, industrial estates which often do not fit within a centre and have their own locational logic within a town/district

- small scale uses such as workshops, hairdressers, nursery schools, corner shops which do not necessarily benefit from in-centre location and are compatible with primarily residential areas.

Subsidiarity

Activities should be pursued at the most local level appropriate to their nature and scale of operation. This means, for example, that there should be a primary school (or two) within or adjacent to every neighbourhood, and a secondary school in every country town or urban district. However, activities which rely on a wider hinterland for their clients – such as most larger-scale offices, or universities – should be located only where public transport provides that wider access.

Critical mass

Different retail and social uses will have different catchment populations needed to ensure continuing success. Chapter 3 set out possible catchments required. But the nature of the hinterland (concentrated or spread) varies widely according to the facility concerned, and also each facility may serve particular segments of a population. So the critical mass of clients needed to support a given use varies widely. The key factors are the nature and density of the population, the locational convenience and visibility in relation to networks and other uses, and the quality of the outlet and immediate environs.

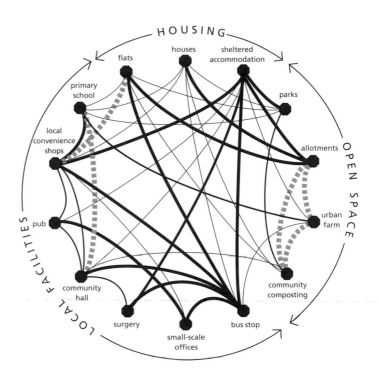

Figure 5.6

CONNECTIVITY BETWEEN LOCAL ACTIVITIES

▪▪▪ potential dual use or combined use of space
━━ important 200 metres close pedestrian connections
── important 400 metres connections
── other desirable 400 metres connections

3.8 Planning local accessibility

3.11 Town centre vitality

5.3

Whilst it might seem appropriate and convenient to locate the mixed use area in the centre of a neighbourhood ...

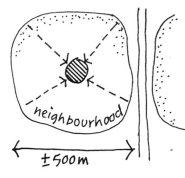

... it may be advisable to locate it at a more visible nodal point to attract more users ...

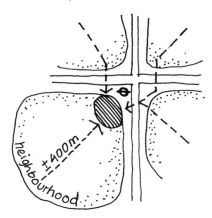

... or even better to acknowledge and design for the fuzzy reality of neighbourhoods

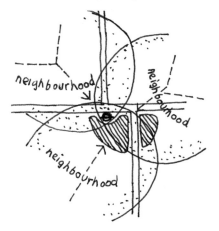

Figure 5.7
Location of mixed use areas and neighbourhood form

3.10 Local shops
and services

As a very rough guide it is possible to have a population of 10,000 people within 800 m actual (on the ground) distance of a local centre at an average density of 40 dwellings per hectare. This would allow not only for a resident population who would support many different uses but a wide variety of tenure-income groups adding to the diversity of uses.

It is unrealistic to expect a true diversity of mixed uses where the host population within walking distance is below, say, 4,000, unless there is strong reliance on passing trade.

Visibility of commercial and social uses

Commercial and social/cultural uses often thrive on a high level of footfall past their front doors and visibility from main routes. Therefore, whilst it might be considered wise to locate mixed uses in the centre of a neighbourhood, it may mean that these uses are only apparent to a relatively small number of people – out of sight, out of mind!

However, if the mixed uses are located on the edge of a neighbourhood, on a main route intersection and adjacent to another neighbourhood, the area is likely to attract a higher level of footfall and visibility. The high street, with bus routes along it acts as the 'uniting seam' between two neighbourhoods.

Time to take root

It is unlikely that a mixed-use area will be functioning fully at the commencement of a new development. This does not mean that the area will be unsuccessful in 5 years' time. A 'habit of use' must be established and also it may take some time before the critical population is fully in place.

Thus it may be wise to develop some buildings which are adaptable to a variety of small-scale mixed uses but which have ground floors devoted to residential use at the outset, which can be adapted at a later date.

CLUSTERING OF USES: SYMBIOSIS

The location, use mix and viability of local centres are interdependent. Small businesses, specialist shops, professional offices and restaurants are mutually supportive, with a high incidence of entrances and visibility through windows ('transparency'). Groupings of same uses reinforce trade: estate agencies, restaurants, shops, for example. A limited number of quite specific uses can thrive on first floors (hairdressers, photographers' studios, legal practices, and so on) if they are on a busy street and their presence is obvious at ground-floor level (but bear in mind the need for elderly/disabled access). Manufacturing or non-retail services can coexist if they are small scale, they have some element of transparency and do not interrupt retail frontages. Residential use in the form of flats and maisonettes can occur over other uses or in secondary frontage locations. Conversely any low population, large scale and dead frontage use such as warehousing is normally inappropriate. Generally a large range of uses can coexist together if they are:

- neighbourly in that they do not generate noise, fumes, vibration, undue traffic, or operate at anti-social hours

- smaller scale – say between 15 m2 and 500 m2.

Environmental quality – some activities are not such good neighbours: they may generate traffic which is undesirable in a living area (e.g. a recycling centre), or make noise late in the evening (a pub). However it is important not to over-segregate such activities. There may be some for example, who are quite happy to live conveniently close to the nighttime economy. And there may be ways of managing disturbance effectively.

Figure 5.9
Siting a new facility

Any new development project should be analysed in terms of appropriate connections with existing activity. This diagram could be used for consultation with interested parties, and subsequently for a site search and comparison

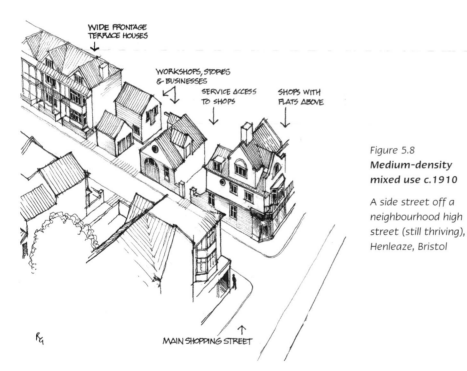

Figure 5.8
Medium-density mixed use c.1910

A side street off a neighbourhood high street (still thriving), Henleaze, Bristol

Mixed use neighbourhoods are good for health

Mixed use neighbourhoods have been found to encourage walking and promote social cohesion.

A study in Ireland, compared levels of social capital between mixed use, walkable neighbourhoods and more suburban car oriented neighbourhoods. Those living in mixed use, walkable neighbourhoods were found to have higher levels of social capital (Leyden, 2003).

People who live in mixed use developments have been found to walk more and be at a lower risk of obesity (NHF, 2007). Other benefits include availability of a fresh food and better access to parks and recreational facilities (Frank et al., 2004).

SPACE SHARING AND CO-LOCATION

Social opportunity and viability can be helped by the shared use of facilities. But clear lines of management responsibility and accountability are essential, with the legitimate needs of the partners recognised.

Connections between uses can be generated and implemented though using collaborative processes to solve common problems

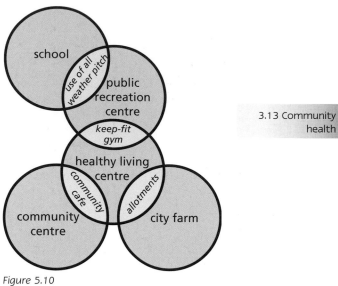

school

use of all weather pitch

public recreation centre

keep-fit gym

healthy living centre

community café

allotments

community centre

city farm

Figure 5.10

Clustering of facilities allows shared use and pooling of resources

3.13 Community health

4.13 Local food supply

4.8 Neighbourhood water planning

or achieve common objectives. A meeting of the 'providers' in the community – church, youth clubs, sports facilities, school, health centre, for example – would prove a fruitful starting place. Here are some examples of synergy:

- **Healthy Living Centre**
  The health centre can become a focus for community life, promote health and social inclusion, by forming a cluster with compatible social activities, sharing key facilities. The partnerships forged in the process of forming and managing the clusters can help build neighbourhood capacity and social capital.

- **Supermarket, street market and cinema**
  A common car park (small but still necessary) can serve the supermarket during the day, the cinema at night, and on occasion form a market square.

- **Community pubs**
  The pub in an isolated settlement can be the common base for post office and banking services, a consumer food co-op, a function room cum village hall and recycling facilities, as well as providing food and drink.

- **Community schools**
  Secondary schools can act as the focus of community life with shared use of recreational facilities, library and hall, together with adult education out of school hours.

- **Food parks**
  In higher density areas where gardens are small or non-existent, allotment provision could occur in the context of attractive 'food parks', with the opportunity of community composting, leisure plots and wildlife den, plus adjacent gardening/café facilities.

- **Sewage gardens**
  Local reed-bed sewage schemes, alongside SuDS (Sustainable Drainage Schemes) can offer the opportunity for community gardens, and wildlife habitats, based around water features.

5.4 GRADED DENSITY

BASIC PRINCIPLE

The planning of density is a key part of sustainable neighbourhood strategies. In the context of mixed land use, density policy relates not only to housing but to all other urban activities as well. Levels of 'use intensity' should vary in relation to the level of public transport accessibility and closeness to prime pedestrian nodes, grading from high-intensity uses near local high streets and bus stops, to low intensity near open country, open-space wedges or major roads. The overall average density should be higher than the current suburban average.

Reasons

- To minimise average trip lengths and maximise the level of accessibility.

- To increase the amount of active travel.

- To bulwark the viability of local shops, services and public transport.

- To permit diversity of residential character in every neighbourhood, and thus allow choice and encourage diversity of household types.

- To facilitate creation of the open space network and pedestrian access to open country.

- To facilitate the natural water cycle, biodiversity and local food and fuel.

- To support the viability of combined heat and power by linear concentration of demand.

- To allow a flexible response to the landscape and existing character of the area, contributing to visual coherence and legibility.

MEASURES OF USE INTENSITY

Use intensity is related to people and activities rather than buildings. It can be measured in terms of resident population per hectare, workers per hectare, or visitors/clients/shoppers per hectare, also in terms of flows of pedestrians ('footfall' in retail centres) or traffic. It is the level of use intensity, combined with sensitivity to specific needs, that should ideally determine appropriate location.

Different ways of calculating residential density

Residential density is usually expressed as dwellings per hectare (dph). Density can be either net or gross; gross can refer to either the locality or the whole of an urban area.

1 Town centre activities – (A and B centres)	high-density flats, offices of various sizes, superstores, comparison retailers, cinemas, library, colleges, hospital, etc.
2 Local high streets – along public transport routes	flats and town houses (3/4 storey), local shops and small offices (<200 m²) pubs, cafés, community facilities
3 inner accessible zone – close to public transport services and local high streets	mainly terraced housing, workshops and schools, playgrounds, small parks and allotments
4 outer accessible zone	mainly semi-detached housing, low-intensity industry/warehousing, schools, parks and allotments
5 greenspace system	parkland and playing fields, small-holdings and neighbourhood farms, woodland, ridges, rivers

Figure 5.11
Five levels of use intensity: relating density to mixed use

Application - This is a highly stylised breakdown. Section 5.14 illustrates its application to an existing urban township. Intensity zones cannot be applied in a mechanical way; they need to respond to local conditions and reflect the need for a varied and interesting aesthetic environment as well as a convenient, resource-efficient one.

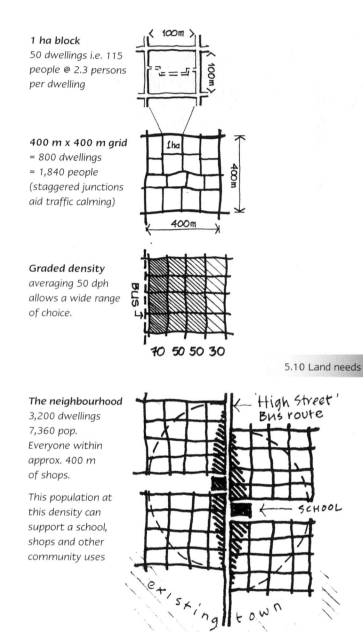

1 ha block
50 dwellings i.e. 115
people @ 2.3 persons
per dwelling

400 m x 400 m grid
= 800 dwellings
= 1,840 people
(staggered junctions
aid traffic calming)

Graded density
averaging 50 dph
allows a wide range
of choice.

5.10 Land needs

The neighbourhood
3,200 dwellings
7,360 pop.
Everyone within
approx. 400 m
of shops.

This population at
this density can
support a school,
shops and other
community uses

Figure 5.12
Block, grid and neighbourhood: relating density to form

- **Net residential density** reflects the character of the immediate housing environment (dwellings, gardens access streets and connected parking areas). The assumption behind 'dwellings per hectare', unless specifically stated otherwise, tends to be net density.

- **Gross neighbourhood density** embraces the whole of a neighbourhood, including the retail and social facilities, the schools, parks, playing fields, workshops, and distributor roads. It is important to be consistent where the boundary is drawn if comparing localities. For example, major areas of industry or open space would normally be excluded.

- **Gross urban density** includes the whole of a built up area, including major commercial and industrial areas, transport zones and major open spaces.

THE PITFALLS OF DENSITY STATEMENTS

The relationship between these three is not linear and can vary greatly between settlements. At low densities the difference between net and gross residential density may not be very great; but at high densities the difference can be startling. The gross urban density is invariably much lower than the residential densities. When working out what land is being used (perhaps if concerned about greenfield development), the net residential density is a very poor guide.

Dwellings per hectare is the usual measure of density because housing need is calculated in terms of households and dwellings. However, it can be misleading because of the variation in dwelling size between, say, an area of small flats and one of large houses. *Bedrooms per hectare* is a more accurate reflection of the residential environment, but does not necessarily reflect population levels. Many three-bedroom houses are occupied by one person.

Population per hectare is an appropriate measure when concerned about catchments or social need. In some situations, where employment and educational uses are significant, the residential population tells only part of the story. The week-day population could be equally important in order to work out the viability of, say, a convenience store.

WHICH DENSITY?

The pictures on the following pages illustrate a wide range of densities. The choice of density depends on location and demand. Some factors to consider :

- Variety of provision to satisfy different needs and markets is important: variety of tenure, size, price, storeys, garden size. The average density is therefore just that: an average.

■ Higher density does not necessarily equate with lower unit value. High density can be high status. It should always include generous balconies and/or roof gardens for those living off the ground.

■ The quality of residential development depends to a significant extent on how traffic, access and car parking are handled. Low car or car-free developments can achieve higher densities and create attractive, safe environments.

■ 50 dph (c. 100 –120 pph) is a fair average density to aim for: it can be achieved by 2–3 storey terraced development with some flats, gardens and normal levels of parking.

■ The land saving benefits of higher net densities beyond about 70 dph reduce progressively because the land needed for other uses such as schools and parks is proportional to population.

■ However, in town/city centres and much of inner London, where land values are high and public transport services good, much greater land savings (i.e. higher gross densities) are achieved through vertical mixed use, low levels of parking provision and compact design of schools etc.

Very high density and limited green space in Barcelona.

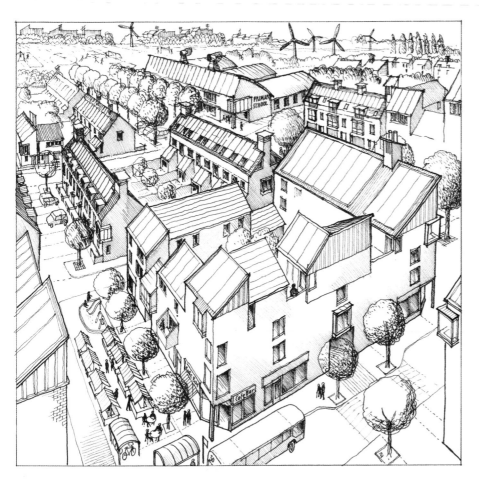

Figure 5.13
Variety is the spice of life

This drawing illustrates graded densities: high along the high street, where the bus runs; low close to the green space. Everyone can find accomodation to suit their needs. Cafe and market are close to the high street; the primary school close to the open space. Traffic is calmed. Photovoltaics and windmills provide locally sourced electricity. Street trees will in time provide shade in a hotter climate.

5.4

Figure 5.14
Neighbourhood samples – character, form and approximate net residential density
based on 200 m by 200 m samples from a range of typical residential developments

140 dph 1990s apartments.
Long straight streets producing rectangular grid forming perimeter blocks with large communal courtyard gardens. Four to six-storey aprtments with generous shared gardens and communal facilites within the courtyards. Mixed tenure and socio-economic groups. Limited parking.

90 dph 1900s terrace
Long straight streets producing rectangular grid with shallow plots between. Narrow fronted (approx 4 m). Two-storey terraces with short rear extensions, very short front gardens (approx 1 m).

90 dph tenements
Late nineteenth-century Scottish apartment blocks built from local red sandstone. Small one- and two-bedroom flats. The perimeter block layout surrounded courts or shared gardens. Buildings followed the regular grid of the street layout. Usually four to six storeys, types varied to suit a range of incomes.

75 dph mansions
Mid-nineteenth-century London apartments for the prosperous. Large flats. Set back from pavement by about 3 m to allow light to semi-basement floor. Often on irregular plots and usually ornate red-brick fronts.

65 dph 1950s estate flats
Immediate post-war mixed development of eight- to eleven-storey slab blocks and four-storey terraced maisonettes informally and loosely enclosing landscaped squares. Informal road layout serving the blocks. Some retail and community uses at ground level.

50 dph Georgian square
Georgian square. Formal square symmetrically approached by wide regular streets. Streets and square enclosed by four-storey terraces with basements. High rooms, vertically proportioned windows. Shallow rear areas with back alleys. Squares have landscaped central gardens.

based on 200 m by 200 m samples from a range of typical residential developments

50 dph 1900s terrace

Two-storey terrace houses approx 5m wide with front bay windows and deep rear extension wings. Short front gardens (approx 2 m), rear gardens of varying length due to converging street layout. Straight streets with angled corners approx 5.5 m wide, parking both sides.

40 dph 1990–2000 village

Cranked street pattern with hierarchy of streets, squares and alleys with mews-style parking courts in interior of perimeter blocks. Mainly two-storey cottages in informal terraces with some three- to four-storey formal terraces and buildings. Traffic calmed by built form. Vernacular appearance.

35 dph Traditional small town

Typical small market town. Medieval street pattern centred on informal market place. Continuous frontages on the back edge of pavements. Two- to three-storey properties on narrow, long plots, shops on ground floor in the centre.

35 dph 1980s estate

Typical 1980s residential area. Individual housing estates planned either side of a distributor road with few links between. The road is designed to carry relatively fast-moving traffic. Therefore, the housing is turned inwards on a cul de sac. Most housing is two-storey, detached or linked by garages.

30 dph 1930s estate

Inter-war uniform density local authority estate. Radial road layout with wide symmetrical bisecting avenues. Semi-detached villas on relatively wide, deep plots set back approx 5–6 m from back edge of footpath. Hipped roofs. Parks, recreation grounds and shops were also provided.

25 dph 1930s semi-detached

Owner-occupied housing often developed around arterial roads and bypasses. Basic house plan was given a variety of stylistic features, such as half-timber, bay windows, 'moderne' front doors. Some short culs de sac.

3.15 Neighbourhood
movement strategy

The manual for streets

*The new UK guidelines for street design
represent a radical departure from traditional
traffic engineering, stressing:*

- *priority for foot and pedal*
- *safety at junctions for pedestrians*
- *slow speeds, restricted sight lines*
- *connectivity*
- *multi-use streets*

SOURCE: DfT 2007

Filtered permeability

*Vehicle traffic is sometimes permitted along
all streets in a grid layout. This maximises
driver choice, spreads traffic so that no street
is too busy, avoids streets becoming dead at
night. But the advantages of restricting the
number of through streets (i.e. of filtered
permeability) are greater:*

- *facilitates play streets, with very low
  traffic levels and speeds*
- *keeps most streets quiet and non-
  polluted in relation to traffic*
- *gives cyclists and pedestrians safe routes
  through*
- *allows some streets to be more intimate
  and enclosed (e.g. mews)*
- *ensures some streets (local distributors)
  are wider and able to cope with bus
  services*

5.5   STREET NETWORKS

BASIC PRINCIPLE
The street framework is much more than a series of transport conduits. It is the most permanent feature of a neighbourhood, outlasting buildings. It defines the character of the public realm and the size of development plots as well as movement and access opportunities open to people. It should be planned so as to knit the neighbourhood together and tie into the wider urban realm. Permeability is vital. The principle of 'filtered permeability' means a denser network for non-motorised modes than for motorised.

ASSESSING THE STREET NETWORK

These tests can be applied to an existing locality undergoing change or to a proposed design for a new settlement.

1.   Connectivity by bus and bike
Does the network facilitate efficient longer distance trip-making by bike and public transport to main job and service centres in the town or city? Does it create attractive routes by bike and foot to adjacent localities and major greenspace?

It is all too easy to design a street pattern for a neighbourhood or estate that is inward-looking, restricting connectivity to adjoining areas, failing to maximise the viability and attractiveness of public transport. Most trips in most localities involve travelling between places, not within the neighbourhood or estate itself. So the efficiency of green modes for those longer trips is paramount.

2.   Local nodes
Does the network create natural transport nodes (as in a traditional town) where public transport services meet, walking/cycling routes coalesce, and vehicle routes pass through or by?

Transport nodes help to generate the critical level of activity to support local services. Bus/tram stops – preferably routes crossing – are vital. Local services and bus use reinforce each other. At the same time it is essential that car-users (currently, often the majority) see the facilities and pass them regularly, encouraging 'passing trade'.

3.   Foot and pedal permeability
Does the framework permit direct and convivial pedestrian and cycling routes from any part of the neighbourhoods to any other, and especially from homes to the centre and to bus-stops?

The density of the walking/cycling network can be much greater than the motorised network, giving pedestrians and cyclists a distance advantage and giving opportunity for car-free or car-low home-patches.

4. Block and site size

Does the framework offer some flexibility of block size – so that a variety of uses can be accommodated; and does it avoid over-large blocks that are likely to rely on long cul-de-sacs (over 100 m) in order to service the interior?

5. Public Realm

Is the framework designed with recognition of the opportunity for longer distance views and internal vistas, and some variety of shape (e.g. curved, straight, cranked) to help distinguish the character of different localities.

6. Traffic circulation

Does the nature of the layout ensure that traffic levels are low to moderate (e.g. less than 300 vehicles per hour at peak) on all except main roads? Does it ensure that freight traffic – to industrial estates or service zones) avoids residential areas where feasible? Does it encourage (or even demand) slow traffic speeds in residential streets and shopping streets (say 30kmph or 20mph), allowing a good proportion of 'home zones' – permeable only to pedestrians and cyclists?

NETWORK OPTIONS

Cul-de-sac patterns

Whole neighbourhoods of cul-de-sacs are not appropriate. They increase the distance that people have to travel to get to facilities – often doubling the distance to nearby services – and thus induce car dependence.

- If cul-de-sacs are necessary they should be short (max 100 m) and with good visibility from the end of the cul-de-sac to the main distributor to reduce crime.

- Where cul-de-sacs are interlinked by footpaths in order to increase pedestrian permeability, the vulnerability to crime (burglary and assault) is increased markedly – unless the footpaths are treated like minor streets, with fronting properties over-seeing them.

- The potential benefits of cul-de-sacs for play, sense of territoriality and social contact should be encouraged by home-zone design principles.

Grid patterns

Standard grids, with straight streets and consistent block size, have been used since the ancient Greek and Roman settlements. They are flexible, permeable and easy to design. Grid patterns are ideal for linear neighbourhood forms and satisfactory for compact cell neighbourhoods.

Impermeable environments - A cul-de-sac layout, combined with false health and safety principles along distributor roads, leads to the houses being cut off from the bus services which are intended for their convenience.

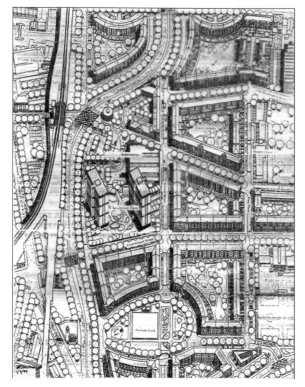

Figure 5.15

Street grid and perimeter blocks in the Crown Street reconstruction of the Gorbals, Glasgow.

Block size can vary widely; the normal minimum depth is about 50 m, with the maximum being 200 m.

- The 50 metre minimum is determined by the depth of two parallel terraces of dwellings, fronting directly onto the street and the need for gardens or space between them. This can equate to a net density of 60 dph.

- The maximum is determined by the need for pedestrian permeability, so that the maximum distance to reach a cross street is, say, 50 metres with the grain (i.e towards buses and local centre) or 100 metres against the grain. These standards (which are simply suggestions) lead to a maximum block size of 100 x 200 metres.

- Within that range there is huge flexibility. Section 5.17 illustrates how a medium sized block of nearly one hectare can be designed to give some communal facilities and good solar access.

Local distributors (vehicle streets) should still be sufficiently close to offer route choice, avoid congestion and provide options for buses: at least every 400 m in both directions, with a more frequent occurrence (e.g. 200 m x 300 m) being desirable in medium to high density areas.

Visual interest: the grid may be adapted to suit the circumstances and create attractive spaces. It may be cranked and off-set at junctions to reduce visibility and slow traffic. It should include elements of variety in more detailed design: varying street widths, circuses and squares at nodal points, central planted reservations, pinch points, buildings bridging at transition places, vistas towards views or landmark buildings.

Radial and web patterns

Radical street patterns are typical of many historic towns, where the radiating routes give access from the market centre to the agricultural hinterland.

- in order to achieve permeability and route choice radial patterns should take the form of a web – so that except at the very centre they are like a curved grid, with block size increasing the further from the centre, matching the density gradient

- web/radial patterns are good for cellular neighbourhoods with clearly defined centres – because they minimise the walking distance and maximise local catchment population

- in most other respects the principles elaborated for the grid street pattern apply equally to the web.

5.6 THE GREEN INFRASTRUCTURE

KEY PRINCIPLES

The green infrastructure or greenspace system is the essential backcloth to urban life, helping to maintain the neighbourhood ecosystem in equilibrium. The value of greenspaces is greatly enhanced if they are interlinked. Long-term planning and management policies must be incorporated in a Community Strategy (or equivalent) so as to:

- increase the level of provision in areas of open-space deficit and progressively establish corridors and pathways between existing green spaces

- identify specific parameters of the various functions to be fulfilled by the greenspace system and maximise potential synergy between functions

- integrate nature into the neighbourhood, including places where people can experience the natural in their everyday lives, enhancing health and well-being

- review the long-term management implications, minimising possible conflicts between functions and users; establishing partnerships and formal agreements where necessary.

The green infrastructure is the strategic mortar binding the settlement together. It provides essential services for human settlements in relation to air, water, food, energy, biodiversity and climate. It is also essential for healthy recreational activity and delight in nature. These functions need to be planned so that they mesh, promoting stability. Using the twin track process described earlier in this chapter, the greenspace system and accessibility issues need to be worked together to give spatial shape to sustainability in a settlement.

Climate adaption through the green infrastructure

In addition to providing carbon capture and climate mitigation functions, an increasing coverage of green infrastructure in urban areas can perform climate adaptive functions. In keeping with the terminology developed in the biodiversity section we can view the green infrastructure as consisting of: linear features such as corridors and links; patches such as reservoirs and stepping stones; and the overall matrix such as the finer grain links, threads and local nodes.

Living near even a small green space significantly lessons the risk of contracting fatal conditions such as heart disease and stroke. These conclusions can be drawn from a study of that matched data of the deaths of 366,000 people with the proximity of their homes to greenspace.

SOURCE: Mitchell and Popham 2008

'People with very good access to attractive and large Public Open Spaces were 50% more likely to have high levels of walking, defined as at least six walking sessions a week, totalling 108 miles.'

SOURCE: Forestry Commission, 2005.

1.4 Climate stability

4.20 Biodiversity framework

Safety versus wildness

The use of greenspaces by people, especially young, old and women alone, depends on their sense of security and relaxation. The interface between footpaths and shrubs/hedges should be designed and managed with this in mind, reducing opportunities for assault, but at the same time providing the secret and mysterious natural places that children love.

3.14 Recreational open space

3.5 Neighbourhood identity

1.5 Promoting healthy communities

4.4 Neighbourhood energy planning

4.8 Neighbourhood water planning

THE GREEN NETWORK IN NEIGHBOURHOOD LIFE

We cannot afford to leave the green network and its functions to chance but need to form partnerships to positively locate, design and manage it to perform the following vital functions.

Quality of life

- **Public health:** trees and greenery promote better public health. They can reduce stress measurably and also aid recovery and recuperation. Woodland can filter pollutants and so improve air quality; trees shade us from damaging UV radiation.

- **Recreation:** green spaces provide a vital resource for social recreation and relaxation that contribute to individual and community well-being. Both formally maintained parks/ playing fields and semi-natural spaces are needed to give us spaces for exercise and activities that increase fitness – provide a 'green gym'.

- **Livable places:** the green network and its elements form a key facet of urban amenity and can be used as part of the palette of urban design: giving outlook, providing a setting, contributing to distinctive local character, acting as a buffer between neighbourhoods or as a link to provide a connection.

- **Movement:** the greenspace network can increase the pleasure and choice of routes for non-motorised forms of transport, offering recreational round walks, links to open country and greenway connections to urban activities. Watercourses, hedgerows, shelter belts and playing field boundaries (among others) can offer connected linear corridors. Evidence indicates that people are more likely to walk in neighbourhoods which are greener.

- **Climate:** green spaces can provide cool air in the summer and warmth in the winter and thus moderate the extremes (especially of heat) to which cities are prone.

Resource management

- **Energy:** Greenspaces can provide shelter belts for wind moderation, reducing energy needs in settlements. More broadly, the growing trees 'fix' carbon and thus help to combat global warming.

- **Water cycle:** the green network provides the neighbourhood with the capacity to mimic the water systems of undeveloped land. It accommodates the storage, amelioration, percolation, surface conduit and discharge functions of a sustainable drainage system.

- **Air quality:** vegetation and soils absorb air-bourne pollutants and help to disperse pollution domes over cities, refreshing the air and acting like the green lungs of settlements.

■ **Biodiversity:** greenspaces are an essential habitat for the flora and fauna of urban spaces, and connect countryside and town for wildlife adaptability and migration.

4.19 Local biodiversity planning

Supporting local economy and community

■ **Woodland products:** trees and coppice can provide urban areas with local materials (for furniture, building and woodchip pallets). However, local products, markets and skills may need considerable development if the potential is to be realised.

4.16 Local materials management

■ **Waste:** the local composting and recycling plan can involve a community compost facility, with compost or re-use for energy of all 'waste' from greenspace management, including tree surgery arisings and autumn leaf litter.

■ **Local food:** the network can provide for a variety of facilities including neighbourhood farms, allotments, community orchards and community gardens.

4.14 Food growing

■ **Employment:** the integrated management of the green network provides a series of local job and training opportunities from strategic management to landscape maintenance. Ideally, the bulk of the work should be overseen, if not undertaken, by a locally based ranger service. This could also provide a degree of supervision and security so often lacking. The co-ordination of local volunteers and public events would also be part of the ranger's remit.

■ **Local participation:** the management of the greenspace network should involve local stakeholders such as amenity groups and sports clubs. Public events (apple day, tree dressing, etc.) and active participation with maintenance (tree planting, coppicing and hedgelaying) are also part of this territory.

> **Green infrastructure**
>
> *The green network includes existing or proposed designed space, permanently vegetated, and semi-natural and natural features. There may or may not be public access; the spaces in the network may or may not be contiguous.*
>
> *For example: hill crests, slopes too steep for development, hedgerows, watercourses and their margins, fields, avenues, shelterbeds, gardens and allotments, woods and parks.*

3.4 Developing social capital

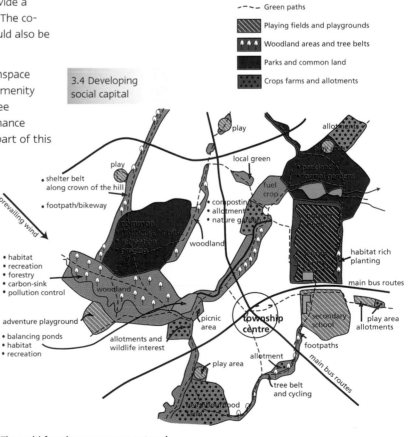

Figure 5.16
The multi-functional greenspace system showing the complex interweaving of natural and planned open space

The multi-function open space network

5.7

The Planning Process

Chapter 2 emphasised the process of **understanding the locality** as a stage in the cyclic process of neighbourhood planning. Neighbourhood appraisal was defined as a systematic overview of the attributes, problems and potential of an area, undertaken as an essential part of neighbourhood plan-making or a major development proposal. It was presented as a collaborative learning process. Here the emphasis is on content, not process.

2.7 Understanding the locality

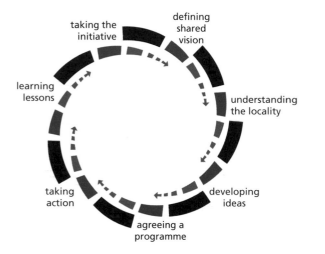

The scope of the appraisal reflects the settlement health map.

The determinants of health and well-being in our neighbourhoods

assessing problems and opportunities

5.7 THE SCOPE OF NEIGHBOURHOOD APPRAISAL

BASIC PRINCIPLES

The scope of the neighbourhood appraisal should be broad. Each part or aspect of the locality is likely to be affected by change, so an integrated understanding is vital. This does not have to imply onerous surveys and number crunching – but awareness. The Health Map provides an agenda for analysis. The over-arching questions are:

- **People:** who is living in the area, or adjacent to it? How is the population changing? How healthy and wealthy are they?

- **Lifestyle:** how physically active are the people – through active travel and recreational activity?

- **Community:** what are the main local concerns, and how are people locally addressing them? Are there supportive social networks? Where is social activity focused?

- **Economy:** is there much local economic activity? Is it economically and environmentally sustainable? What are the concerns of entrepreneur and employees?

- **Activities:** what facilities are there, and how successful are they? How do people use them and get to them? What is the pattern of movement?

- **Built environment:** what is the pattern of land use, buildings, densities, streets, spaces? What is the condition of them? What current plans and proposals?

- **Urban potential:** what is the potential of the area, and of specific sites? What locational and development options are there? Or are there issues of decay and under-use?

- **Character:** what are the distinctive features, most valued by local people? What is it important to enhance culturally?

- **Bio-physical context:** what are the characteristics of the landscape and ecology of the area? How is the neighbourhood and its activities impacting on the natural environment?

- **Global ecology:** what is the significance of the area in relation to climate change: mitigation and adaptation?

The next two pages expand the basic issues into a more comprehensive list of appraisal topics.

NEIGHBOURHOOD APPRAISAL – PEOPLE, COMMUNITY, ACTIVITIES

Topics | Units and sources

PEOPLE AND LIFESTYLE

Basic information
- population levels, structure and trends
- household characteristics and trends
- socio-economic, age and ethnic mix

- by ward/parish or defined neighbourhoods
- from census and special sample household survey

Quality of life
- health and social inclusion indicators
- economic and environmental indicators
- crime and safety indicators

- by ward/parish
- from local authority 'quality of life', 'state of the environment' or health profile report

Lifestyle
- active travel to work and facilities
- active recreational activity
- normal dietary habits

- by ward/parish/neighbourhood
- from census and special sample household survey

COMMUNITY AND ECONOMY

Community issues
- local issues raised by residents, workers, community groups, service providers, business people, councillors
- community involvement in local policy decisions
- stocktake of voluntary groups and activities
- social interaction and places where it happens

- by social group and specific interest
- from consultation and participatory process
- sample household survey

Economic activity
- job ratio and connecting patterns
- stocktake of local economic activity and employment opportunities
- LETS, credit unions and informal economic activity
- trends in home working

- by ward/parish/neighbourhood
- from consultation and participatory process
- from sample survey

ACTIVITIES

Local activities
- stocktake of all locally accessible facilities and services
- analysis of children's play: what and when?
- analysis of young people's activities
- analysis of old people's activities
- review of needs of any other particular group
- review of housing needs

- official databases
- from consultation and discussion with stakeholders
- from the sample survey

Local movement
- pedestrian and cycling flows, desire lines, barriers
- public transport services evaluated
- vehicle flows, speeds, accidents, parking

- data clearly mapped
- from operators, highway department, police
- from participant observation

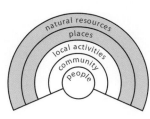

NEIGHBOURHOOD APPRAISAL – PLACE, NATURAL RESOURCES

Topics

Units and sources

PLACE

Basic information
- area, net residential and gross neighbourhood densities
- land-use pattern

- mapped/GIS data
- special surveys

Buildings and infrastructure
- condition of buildings, private and public spaces
- building stock, by tenure, type, size and use
- market trends, property prices and rents
- planning enquiries, applications and permissions
- infrastructure quality and spare capacity

- map at 1:2500 or 1:5000 scale
- information from land-use survey, agents and infrastructure providers (water, sewage, gas, electricity)
- planning authority records

Routeways and accessibility
- pedestrian routes classified by quality, safety and connectivity
- roads classified by traffic and environmental capacity
- accessibility to bus stops and tram/train halts
- accessibility to local facilities and open space

- mapping/GIS analysis at, say, 1:5000 scale
- special visual surveys

Urban capacity and potential
- potential use and density of vacant plots/fields
- potential for extra dwellings from conversion, upper storeys etc.
- potential for higher plot ratios
- environmental, access and aesthetic constraints

- analysis by land-use parcels and sampling of problematic areas – then mapped with constraints to give overall potential; should be part of local plan process

Aesthetic character
- local perceptions of the quality of public spaces
- townscape, and legibility analysis
- protected heritage (listed buildings, CAs, etc.)
- issues of noise, fumes, and visual intrusion

- annotated maps, relying on stakeholder/focus-group data and urban design analysis

THE NATURAL ENVIRONMENT

Local biophysical context
- landform and solar aspect
- microclimate conditions and air quality
- water catchment, drainage, flood plain
- wildlife habitats and corridors
- soil quality and contamination
- local sources of fuel or building materials

- map at 1:2500 or 1:5000 scale
- from the Local Plan or Environmental Capacity study
- supplemented by information from specialist interests (e.g. wildlife trusts, Environment Agency)

Global ecological footprint
- energy-efficiency in buildings, energy supply systems and transport
- water efficiency and opportunities for action
- materials recycling and re-use; opportunities
- local food production: opportunities
- tree cover and carbon sinks

- commentary, with maps, identifying current situation vis-à-vis best practice

5.8   URBAN POTENTIAL STUDIES

BASIC PRINCIPLE

It is vital to the achievement of coherent town planning that 'urban capacity' and land availability studies, undertaken by UK local authorities in order to find urban space for housing, are extended to encompass the potential for *all* urban uses and accessible *greenfield* sites as well as brownfield sites.

An urban potential study does just that. It provides a coherent assessment framework for the planning of a sustainable settlement, emphasizing assets as well as constraints, positives as well as negatives. The framework employs thresholds of impact similar to the SPECTRUM approach, and can be tied to a SPECTRUM stakeholder process.

Urban potential studies (though usually undertaken across a whole region, county or district) should involve local people in defining what is locally valued. In some situations a town, parish or neighbourhood council might itself choose to initiate a potential study to ensure local perspectives are given due weight in the wider planning game. The technique presented below is appropriate for either situation.

AN INTEGRATED APPROACH

- The Urban Potential Framework advocated here is appropriate at the level of the whole urban area.

- In common with other techniques, it estimates the capacity of specific sites and of land-use character zones. Each site or zone is categorised according to 30–40 land-use categories (typical urban areas – TUAs), allowing a sampling process within each category to reduce survey times if that is necessary.

- The Framework requires sites and zones to be assessed against twelve criteria of sustainable development, encompassing accessibility, environmental quality and resource management as well as the economic potential for urban intensification.

- The assessment is for mixed-use development as well as housing.

- The criteria act as constraints on development in some situations, but stress the potential for development in other situations. The Framework incorporates an adapted 'traffic light' system with weighting between criteria built into the assessment (see Figure 5.18).

Urban Potential Assessment

The Urban Potential Assessment technique, (also known as Sustainability Threshold Analysis (STA)), is derived from the method originally put forward in the UWE/LGMB Guide Sustainable Settlements (Barton et al. 1995). The Environment Agency revised the technique for application both at strategic and local levels. This involves a staged threshold approach which assesses environmental sustainability and offers options for development (Carroll et al. 2002).

STA was honed through a series of practitioner workshops from 1997 to 2000, and subsequently developed by Eufusion in partnership with South Hams D.C. (see South Hams 2009).

Quality of Life Capital

The Urban Potential Assessment technique is compatible with the Quality of Life (QOL) Capital approach advocated by English Heritage, the Environment Agency and Natural England (Threivel 2001).

The key to the QOL Capital approach is to ask: what are the benefits and services which are potentially affected by the planning process or the decision at issue? Evaluation of a specific site involves identifying:

- *the social, economic and environmental services that it offers*
- *who the services matter to, why, and at what spatial scale*
- *how important the services are*
- *whether we have enough of the services and*
- *whether the services are substitutable.*

The approach allows conclusions to be drawn about the future of each resource and enables management aims to be determined.

UK policy context

PPS3 for Housing, requires a Strategic Housing Land Availability Assessment, with a strong emphasis on the reuse of previously developed or 'brownfield' land (CLG 2006). There is a risk that such analysis is driven by the need to find more land for housing to the partial exclusion of other activities. Any valid method must enable the settlement to be considered in the round. It should guide decisions on sustainable development, planning for health and quality of life, not just satisfying new housing requirements.

5.8

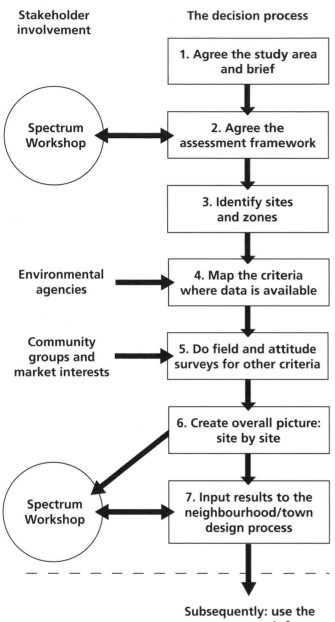

Stakeholder involvement

The decision process

Spectrum Workshop

1. Agree the study area and brief

2. Agree the assessment framework

3. Identify sites and zones

Environmental agencies

4. Map the criteria where data is available

Community groups and market interests

5. Do field and attitude surveys for other criteria

6. Create overall picture: site by site

Spectrum Workshop

7. Input results to the neighbourhood/town design process

Subsequently: use the assessment to inform site development briefs

Figure 5.17
**The process of assessing urban potential; the technical process is par
alled by a participatory process such as SPECTRUM.**

NOTES ON THE URBAN POTENTIAL PROCESS

1 **The study area** should include not only the existing built-up area, but also any neighbouring greenfield areas and assess them on a comparable basis with the brownfield sites.

2 **The Framework** is the key tool in this process that shapes later analysis. (See a sample framework on the next page.) Its criteria ascribe values to aspects of environment capital and to social/economic variables. It is therefore highly politically charged. The pressures from special interests could be intensive, but it is important to win their support at this stage. Involve them in the process.

3 **Identifying sites and zones** may be done initially by map and memory. A sample list of various 'typical urban area' (TUA) catergories is given overleaf. The list of different TUAs need adapting to local circumstances. Both sites/zones and TUA categories can be changed later if necessary.

4 **Mapping potential and constraints** can occur before the need for field surveys. State of Environment reports and statutory consultees can supply information on, for example, land liable to flood, nature conservation and cultural heritage. North-facing slopes, pedestrian accessibility and public transport access can be assessed by Geographical Information Systems (GIS), avoiding the need for time-consuming surveys. This process acts as a sieve to cut down the need for physical surveys.

5 **Field surveys** are undertaken for all areas where development is possible. The views of local people will be critical for some criteria, such as the value of open space, local cultural heritage, and noise levels. Parish/town councils and residents' groups must be involved. Assessing physical and market potential is highly skilled work relying on experienced planners with local knowledge, and effective consultation with market interests.

6 **Creating an overall picture**. This is the moment of truth. The process can be done using GIS software, applying a scoring or colour coding system to establish priorities, with a report setting the results in the context of housing estimates, etc. The process is likely to necessitate revisiting assumptions and judgements made previously.

7 **Using the study**. The urban potential analysis is not the be-all and end-all. Its results need to be used in a proper plan-making exercise that recognises the dynamics of change.

CRITERIA	POTENTIAL				
	Red – development **IMPOSSIBLE**	*Orange* – development **PROBLEMATIC**	*Yellow* – development **CONDITIONAL**	*Green* – development **OK**	*Blue* – development **PRIORITY**
1 Physical development potential		Contaminated land, buildings awkward to repair, steep slopes	Derelict land and buildings requiring treatment and/or rehabilitation		Previously developed land and vacant buildings capable of easy re-use
2 Market development potential	Land-locked site with no access possible	Zero/low-value site, lacking appeal or potential; owner unwilling to sell	Marketable site/ buildings depending on conditions and costs imposed	Likely to be viable irrespective of conditions or S106 costs	High-value sought-after location
3 Infrastructure capacity		Major threshold breached: shift in investment priorities required	Contribution needed to school/sewage treatment/roads/ station, etc.	No particular thresholds are breached	Spare capacity in local schools, p.t. services, road system, sewage treatment
4 Pedestrian accessibility to key local facilities	No facilities within 800 m	Few facilities available within 800 m	Legal agreement could fill key gaps in facilities	Most facilities within 800 m	Choice of facilities available, most within 400 m
5 Public transport accessibility to jobs/centres	No regular public transport services accessible or planned	Only poor services accessible or planned	Poor services, capable of improvement	Good-quality services within 400 m	Excellent-quality services within 300 m
6 Energy use and carbon-fixing	Very exposed sites	Shelter belts, woodland, coppices	North-facing slopes, tree-replacement conditions		Gentle south-facing slopes, spare CHP/CH capacity
7 Water	Areas liable to flood every 30 years or more	Marginal flood areas; high ground-water vulnerability	Areas of medium ground-water vulnerability	Supply, treatment, drainage OK; no flood risk	
8 Land, soils and local food production	Unstable land, areas prone to coastal erosion	Allotments, market gardens, organic farmland	High-quality soils; impact on farmland		Contaminated land
9 Biodiversity	SSSIs and other national designations	Locally defined valued habitats and wildlife corridors	Locally valued but common habitats, trees and hedgerows	No threat to assets	Potential to create new habitats in degraded areas
10 Air quality and noise	Areas prone to unacceptable level of pollution	Source of pollution capable of correction – but who will pay?	Mitigatable noise levels		
11 Open space value or impact	Valued and well-used public open-space (POS)	Common-land, valued public access land	Inadequate local open space, contribution needed	Ample supply of accessible open space locally	
12 Aesthetic and cultural heritage	Listed buildings; vulnerable landscapes of great value	Specific areas of valued landscape or great archaeological value	Conservation areas, AONBs, National Parks		Ugly or monotonous environment needing improvement

Figure 5.18

The urban potential assessment framework (illustrative)

Note: the specific criteria in each box need to be negotiated in the local context

- *modern estate housing*   42%
- *military sites*   7%
- *retail stores with carparking*   6%
- *safeguarded vacant land within settlement boundary*   5%
- *large terraces and semi-detached town houses*   4%
- *old industrial areas in poor condition*   4%
- *out-of-centre offices*   4%
- *old village cores and organic areas in towns*   3%
- *retail road frontages*   3%
- *derelict land*   3%
- *mansions*   2%
- *large/medium detached and semi-detached houses*   2%
- *city centre mixed uses*   2%
- *town centre mixed uses*   2%
- *utilities*   2%
- *community uses (not education)*   2%
- *open-site parking*   1%
- *purpose-built hotels*   1%
- *multi-storey former industrial buildings*   1%
- *all TUAs*   100%

Figure 5.19

Potential housing yield from different typical urban areas (TUAs) in south-west England

(TUAs yielding no gains are excluded)

Note: this is concerned with the re-use and intensification of sites or areas already urbanised. It excludes greenfield development.

SOURCE: Based on Baker Associates and UWE 1999

EVALUATING INDIVIDUAL SITES

The framework can be used to summarise the situation for a specific site and pinpoint what further work might need to be done to reduce the uncertainties or overcome barriers to development.

Site code no: Area in ha: Address	Grading				
		Red	Orange	Yellow	Green	Blue
Development potential	Physical			●		
	Market				●	
	Infrastructure				●	
Accessibility	Pedestrian			●		
	Public Transport		●			
Resources	Energy			●		
	Water				●	
	Land				●	
	Biodiversity					●
	Air and noise				●	
Place	Open space				●	
	Aesthetic quality					●

Figure 5.20

Illustrative chart for a derelict edge-of-town industrial site

In this example, poor public transport is the key factor. Unless that problem can be rectified – probably in the context of a wider plan for the area – development is inappropriate. The aesthetic and biodiversity benefits potentially achievable give urgency to the completion of an appropriate plan

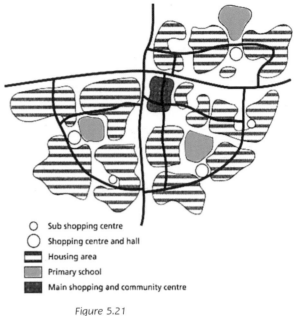

Sub shopping centre
Shopping centre and hall
Housing area
Primary school
Main shopping and community centre

Figure 5.21
Harlow: planned neighbourhoods

5.9 ANALYSING FORM AND FUNCTION

BASIC PRINCIPLE

It is vital to recognise and analyse existing patterns of development before planning their future. Neighbourhoods come in varied shapes and sizes. There is a key distinction to be drawn between neighbourhoods that are separate units and those that are interconnected parts of an urban continuum. Some areas of suburban sprawl do not coalesce into recognisable neighbourhoods at all.

This section provides an historic perspective on urban form, then suggests a typology to assist with analysis.

LEARNING FROM THE PAST

Older localities that grew up in response to pedestrian and public transport access to central business and industrial areas are normally interconnected and often mixed use. There are no clear boundaries between neighbourhoods, one area blending into another: fuzzy neighbourhoods. Often the local and district centres take the form of high streets, with facilities clustered along main distributors, creating a bustling but congested atmosphere. In higher density, socially mixed areas, the ideals of the compact city are sometimes realised, with catchment areas overlapping and facilities highly accessible by foot, providing excellent local choice. Conversely in areas where there is a concentration of disadvantaged households and the population has also fallen as households become smaller, the structure of neighbourhood provision has dissolved.

Planned neighbourhoods

In the post-war era the conscious planning of neighbourhoods led to a different pattern. Neighbourhoods were seen as units or 'cells'. Each had its own range of local facilities, often including a small industrial estate as well as retail, social, educational and recreational facilities. The ideal was noble, and in line with principles of decentralised provision in tune with sustainable development. But with increased mobility and falling population densities many such neighbourhoods are shadows of their former selves, cut off and isolated. Some classic town plans, however, avoided the pitfalls: neighbourhoods were linked into clusters and accessible on main distributors. Contemporary urban extensions often continue this tradition.

Car-based use segregation

In the late twentieth century the dominant pattern changed again. Driven by rising car reliance, the principle of integrated, mixed use neighbourhoods was often lost. Instead the pattern was of use-segregated dispersal, with each activity on a separate

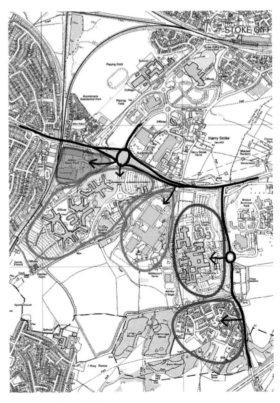

Figure 5.22
Land use segregation and cul-de-sac pods in Bristol's north fringe

Figure 5.23
Nodal point in high street

SOURCE: Barton, Davis and Guise 1995

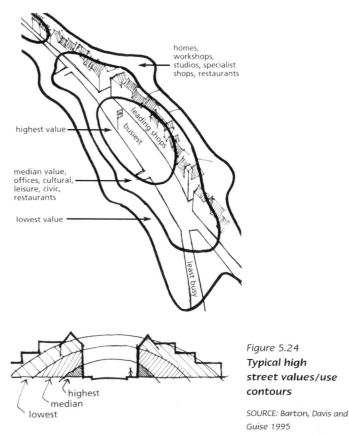

homes, workshops, studios, specialist shops, restaurants

highest value

median value, offices, cultural, leisure, civic, restaurants

lowest value

leading shops

busiest

least busy

highest
median
lowest

Figure 5.24
Typical high street values/use contours

SOURCE: Barton, Davis and Guise 1995

site with dedicated access off the main road system. We may call these single use enclaves 'pods' – like individual bean-pods hanging off the main roads stems. This pattern of activity disadvantages walking and cycling by increasing the distances, producing a pedestrian-unfriendly environment.

TRADITIONAL HIGH STREETS

The traditional high street provides a useful model to learn from. It typically provides the main social meeting places between residential neighbourhoods and the place for exchange of goods and services. It is also where the local meets the town and city – the place that gives a sense of identity to the locality. A high street is a series of interlinked activity generators – bus stops, supermarkets, community/religious buildings, cafés, shops and small offices. It is not uniform in use or level of activity, nor in property values. There are prime, secondary and tertiary locations. The latter provide a habitat for more marginal users – the low-key (often charitable) office, the garage workshop, recycling shops. Housing can fill the gaps between other uses, on upper floors and in the rear of plots with courtyard arrangements.

Variation in shape, form and use

In form, older high streets are rarely geometrically straight, but slightly irregular, changing direction gradually and opening out to places of congregation, typically former market places. This more organic form takes cues from the topography to give shelter and can take advantage of sunny settings for central locations. Most high streets are between three and five storeys high – at the limits of walk-up access. Living over the shop (LOTS) schemes – notable in Norwich, Ipswich, Cambridge and Stamford – show that residents can be encouraged to settle in upper floors, to their advantage and to that of the centre as a whole.

Adaptability

The high street is an organic structure which can absorb a considerable degree of adaptation over time: some areas improving, others declining, some being renewed. Plots remain surprisingly intact whilst buildings on them are often altered or rebuilt a number of times. The greatest threat to plots and the small-scale land uses that they accommodate, has been the comprehensive development area and the associated land assembly, such major developments have often proved to be less adaptable to changing economic climates than the smaller plots.

CLASSIFYING DESIGNED FORMS

Pods

- single use developments on individual sites
- car-reliant, land hungry, with ample car parking provision
- one (or sometimes two) access points onto the distributor road system, with limited pedestrian permeability to adjacent sites
- does not constitute a 'neighbourhood', though varied uses may coincide in one locality
- smaller pods may lie within a neighbourhood or town
- larger pods may be on a scale equivalent to a neighbourhood (e.g. a major business park)

Neighbourhood Cells

- mixed use neighbourhood 'units' with definite centres, or nuclei
- designed from the outset as local social entities, at a pedestrian scale
- normally separated from each other by open space, schools, industry or roads, with limited vehicle permeability
- often clustered together to support a shared district centre with higher level facilities
- may be 'off-line', like large mixed use pods, or on-line, like beads on a string

Compact Townships (or neighbourhood cluster)

- key planning level not the neighbourhood but the small town or urban township/district
- overlapping, 'fuzzy', mixed use neighbourhoods supporting township-level facilities within walking distance
- high density, and high pedestrian/cycle/vehicle permeability to maximise accessibility
- major open space kept to periphery of the township
- advocated by the Urban Task Force as part of a 'compact city' strategy

Linear Township

- overlapping, 'fuzzy' neighbourhoods clustered along a public transport spine
- neighbourhoods primarily residential identity zones, with facilities peripheral
- central spine provides a high street function with district and local facilities scattered along
- major greenspace in parallel linear form either side

Figure 5.24
Neighbourhood form archetypes

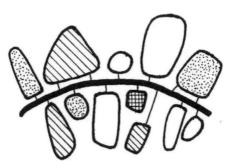

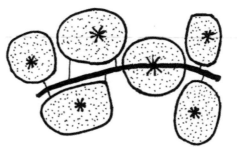

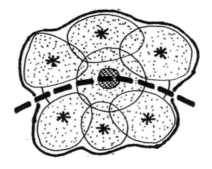

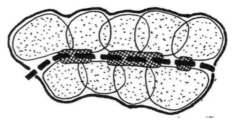

5.10

5.10   LAND NEEDS

This section describes a simplified method of working out the land budget (ie, the total land needs) for a new settlement or urban extension. It could also be applied to a major residential and mixed-use regeneration scheme – but that is more complex because of existing uses. The starting point for the method is assumed to be a target figure of dwellings for the settlement. It would be possible to re-orientate the start of the process if rather than dwellings there was a target for population. You could, indeed, reverse the whole process and start with a given site area, then work out how many people could live there.

Figure 5.25

Worked example: residential density and land-take. Note: all the figures given are purely illustrative

---

Starting point: Dwelling numbers

Assume a target figure for new dwellings in extension is 5000

↓

Working out population

Assume an average household size of 2.4:
5000 dwellings x 2.4 = 12,000 people

↓

Planning variety of density

• *1000 dwellings @ 100 dpha – flats in or close to mixed use centres and main public transport nodes: three and four storey development with roof gardens or large balconies; limited parking*

• *2000 dwellings @ 50 dpha average – houses, flats and maisonettes normally with small gardens or patios: two and three storey development*

• *2000 dwellings @ 33 dpha average – mainly 2 storey houses, some with larger gardens*

↓

Average net density

What, therefore is the average density?
1000 @ 100 dpha = 10 hectares
2000 @ 50 dpha = 40 hectares } > 110 ha for 5000 dwellings
2000 @ 33 dpha = 60 hectares   = 45 dpha

↓

DWELLINGS AND POPULATION

Let us assume, for the sake of argument, that the target figure for dwellings to be constructed in a new urban extension is 5,000.

This needs to be equated with population so that we can work out what else needs to be provided. Average household size varies according to culture, location and time. Who will be living in the new neighbourhood? A realistic view needs to be taken following consultation with relevant stakeholders (eg. market interests). Bearing in mind the structures in Chapter 4 (4.2 and 4.3) it is important to plan for an evolving and varied community. In the UK and NW Europe this is the normal range of average household size:

- 2.0 pph (persons per household) means a high proportion of 1 and 2 person households, many probably living in flats, and is typical of many inner city areas
- 2.5 pph means a higher proportion of families, often living in houses, and is typical of many outer city areas
- 2.25 pph is around the overall average, but this of course varies between cities and had been tending to fall gradually as society changes and people live longer.

Net residential density

Having worked out the eventual population, the next question is what kind of housing. Therefore what net residential density will they be living in? There is clearly a relationship between the expected average household size (including the varied households that go to make that average) and the kind of housing. In our example the average of 2.4 implies quite a number of families with children, but also a fair proportion of one and two person households. The exact mix of dwellings types will be decided by policy and market calculations (likely to vary over the growth phase of the settlement). For our initial land budget calculations we may assume graded densities (see section 6.4). We may also plan for some mixed use, where flats are provided over shops or offices.

Gross residential density

While net density gives a reasonable idea of the character of the housing, it does not tell us the land needs in a sustainable, mixed use development. Local shops and services, social facilities, schools, small scale workshops and offices, playgrounds, local parks and allotments all need space within what is primarily a residential area. These uses are not in proportion to net density. They are in proportion to population. So as net residential density rises so does the significance of these other uses in the land budget. Effectively the land-saving benefits of higher densities reduce sharply as net density rises.

Comparison of net and gross residential densities
Assumptions:
5000 dwellings @ 2.4 pp dwelling
12,000 population
4 ha per 1000 population non-residential land use

Net residential density (dpha)	Residential land take (ha)	Other uses land take (ha)	Total land take (ha)	Gross residential density (dpha)
20	250	48	298	17
30	167	48	215	23
40	125	48	173	29
50	100	48	148	34
60	83	48	131	38
70	71	48	119	42
80	63	48	111	45
100	50	48	98	51

In the example in the side column the land take for the neighbourhood is 110 ha for residential and 48 for other uses, giving a total of 158 ha. This equates to a gross residential density of 32 dpha or 76 ppha.

THE WIDER SETTING

In addition to the uses which are clearly part of the daily life of the neighbourhood, there are other more extensive green areas which are an essential part of the sustainable ecological whole. This green backcloth may overlap with the recreational uses listed above, but is essential to provide water management, local food, energy, biodiversity and pollution control systems, as well as an accessible landscape for wilder walks and cycle rides and deeper connection to nature. Some new settlement plans include almost as much land for the landscape setting as they do for the more clearly urban uses. The neighbourhood is part of a town or city. The illustration here does not include the land needed for major transport infrastructure, large industrial estates, central area development, stadium etc.

Figure 5.25 (continued)

Non residential uses

Working out land needs for non-residential uses for 5,000 dwellings, 12,000 population

OTHER USES	ASSUMPTIONS	Total ha
Recreation	Playing fields, local parks, playgrounds, allotments, leisure centre/swimming pool (2.4 ha per 1000)	29
Education	Primary Schools: 3 two class entry @ 2ha each.	6
	Secondary School: 1 six class entry, some shared p.f.	4
Social	Health centres, clubs, places of worship	2
Commerce	Retail centre with offices over	2
Industry	Small factories, garages, service industries	5
Total	Other uses	48

Calculating gross neighbourhood density

Mainly residential	110 ha
Other land uses	48 ha
Total area	158 ha

5000 dwellings divided by 158 equals just over 32 dpha gross

5.11

Sections 5.11 and 5.12 give guidance on two
classic neighbourhood or settlement forms
– cells and linear – which also happen to be
more adaptable to a variety of situations than
the cluster model. But many of the same
lessons apply whatever the form.

Figure 5.26
Closed cell pattern at Poundbury, Dorset

5.11 DESIGNING NEIGHBOURHOOD CELLS

Neighbourhoods are conventionally seen as distinct, identifiable
areas, so the default archetype of neighbourhood planning
is the neighbourhood unit or cell. This model is easier to
design and implement than the more complex, integrated
archetypes. But it carries risks of spatial and social segregation
that can compromise the health of residents and the level of
carbon emissions. There is no one simple recipe for success.
Neighbourhood cells come in a wide variety of sizes and forms,
depending on context. The design guidelines and examples
below show how they can be made to work.

BASICS: LOCATION, SIZE AND GROWTH

At the outset it is critical to know why and if a neighbourhood
cell, or group of cells, is the best answer in a given situation.
Because it is the default answer, enshrined in planning theory and
often suited to market preferences, it is all too easy to adopt
uncritically. So the questions to ask before any detailed planning
(see the six design principles in Chapter 1) are:

- is it a logical response to local needs and stakeholder views?

- is it potentially large enough to support local services? How
viable will services be before the cell is fully grown?

- is it well connected and accessible to nearby communities,
jobs and services?

- is it a coherent response to the physical setting and ecology?

- can it attract a good range of social groups and businesses?

- is there opportunity for continued adaptation and later
expansions?

Location

The cell should be closely tied into the mother settlement, so
residents can access a wide choice, jobs and facilities easily by
bus/tram, foot and pedal. If the location is more isolated then
the quality and comprehensiveness of the public transport
connections have to be exceptional. Otherwise car dependency will
result (see *Lessons from Cambourne* by Stephen Platt, Cambridge
Architectural Research Ltd, www.carltd.com).

Size

The minimum size for a neighbourhood cell is about 4,000 people
– normally sufficient to support a few shops and a primary school.
Larger sizes of up to 8,000 or 12,000 population are feasible,
depending on density and accessibility criteria. These may be able
to support a good range of convenience stores, some social and
leisure facilities, a 4-doctor surgery and a secondary school - i.e.
some district level facilities.

However, cells do not normally support the full range of local facilities, (e.g. including superstore, library, leisure centre and professional services). It is vital, therefore that they are seen as part of a greater settlement – which might be the town as a whole or might be a group of neighbourhoods supporting a district centre (as in Harlow – Figure 5.21).

Growth and decline

During the growth phase it is important to establish local services as soon as possible, so that residents get used to relying on walking/cycling access, not vehicle. These services include energy systems, public transport, shops and primary schools. It can be more effective from this perspective to expand an existing (maybe failing) neighbourhood rather than starting afresh.

Once a neighbourhood cell is 'complete' evolution does not stop. The population continues to change. If household size and population falls then local services may cease to be viable. This is a particular risk with offline cells. So opportunity for later growth and/or intensification is vital. In some cultures this may be thought of as 'second generation' space.

DESIGN GUIDANCE

The points below follow through the twin-track process of neighbourhood design (5.2)

5.2 Devising the spatial framework

Stage 1. Public transport routes and local centres

The neighbourhood should be very well served by existing or potential public transport routes that link to surrounding areas and major centres. The local centre must be directly served by the main p.t. route(s), and normally also visible to people passing by in their own vehicles.

3.18 Public transport

Stage 2. Greenspace and ecological potential

The disposition of the neighbourhood on the ground must ensure that valuable landscape features are conserved. They should be used positively to provide accessible greenspace and/or ecological services for the community. Creative planning of greenspace can give a unique quality to each neighbourhood.

5.6 Green infrastructure

Stage 3: Accessibility, density and population thresholds

The neighbourhood should be designed to maximise the number of people who are within easy walking distance of the centre, and of accessible greenspace. In some cultures easy cycling distance could be the criterion. The decisions on accessibility standards have to be taken in the context of the planned densities and population thresholds needed to support local services. NB. Actual, not straight line, distances.

3.9 Accessibility criteria

Cells for all seasons:-

Beads on a string

Greenfield land around a suburban metro line that leads from city to airport offers the possibility of stringing together a sequence of neighbourhood cells. Each one provides excellent regional access, good potential for local services near the station and access to high quality greenspace. Market potential in this location is high.

Converting out-of-town into in-town

An out-of-town shopping centre, well placed in relation to the whole municipality, is brought in-town by a new cell neighbourhood. The retail sheds and car parks are redeveloped at higher densities, with a mix of uses, and the extra custom justifies improved bus services. The new neighbourhood benefits from excellent local facilities

Peripheral expansion

An existing suburban neighbourhood with a limited range of facilities can be strengthened by judicious new development. The plan increases the population and viability of services while maintaining wedges of open land. The size of the neighbourhood is larger than usual but the local culture of walking and cycling helps to justify this.

Regenerating the fracture zone

A disjointed part of the inner city, with dead railway sidings, decaying industry and isolated housing pockets is given new life by a new station, new mixed density housing and progressive restructuring into a mixed use neighbourhood, including greenspace. A new local centre grows by the station.

Stage 4. Land use and density

The neighbourhood as a whole should be planned as mixed use, and in the centre in particular a wide variety of uses may coalesce: apartments, shops, pubs, cafés, social facilities, surgery, small-scale offices. Elsewhere zoning is important to safeguard community and low-rent activities such as schools, parks and industrial services, (vehicle repairs, builders yards, recycling centre, workshops).

Every neighbourhood should provide for a critical mass of population and a good range of households in terms of size, family status and income. This is vital to maintain local services. It implies planning a range of densities, house types and tenures.

Stage 5. Bus services and street networks

Every dwelling should be within 400 m of good bus service (or perhaps 600 m of a tram stop). To achieve this it is important that the main distributor roads (which normally double as bus routes) serve the whole neighbourhood effectively – i.e. they are embedded, not peripheral; and pedestrian access to those streets is direct and safe. The disposition of the development area should ensure that everywhere can access through but tram routes that give wider access, do not involve transfer, and have good frequency levels.

The bike network, doubling as main pedestrian network, needs careful planning from the outset, with a close grid or web of safe routes.

3.11 Town centre vitality

3.7 Resilient local economies

3.2 A diverse population

5.5 Street networks

3.17 Planning for the cyclist

Figure 5..27
A new neighbourhood cell

Closely tied into the existing urban area by bus and walking/cycling connections; graded density, mixed use centre, scruffy zone.

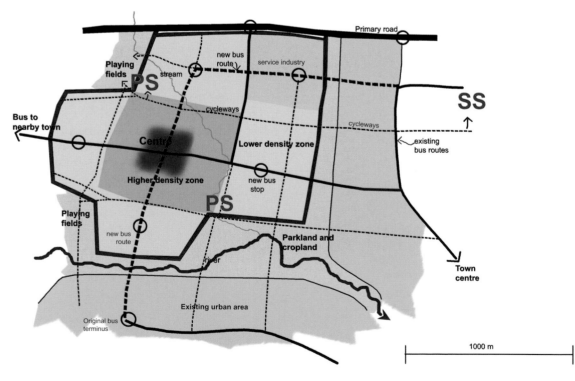

5.12 LINEAR DISTRICTS AND TOWNS

Linear settlements have occurred historically because of geographical constraint or public transport corridors. Linearity can apply equally to free-standing towns as to urban districts. It is often easier to implement than the nucleated archetype because it ties into traditional patterns and does not rely on high overall density. Its prime attraction is the viability of public transport. Its most evident problem is congestion along the spine route. While many variants exist in the literature the model advocated here is quite specific, aiming to provide market flexibility while maximising the proportion of non-motorised trips.

BASICS: LOCATION, SIZE AND SHAPE

Location: suburban

As with the cells model, the linear township must be closely tied into the main settlement by proximity, public transport links and road connections. If a completely new township is to be created, then the space needed is considerable say, 3–5 km2) which can be problematic. More possible in many situations is to absorb existing detached or sporadic development, integrating them into the form.

Also bear in mind the twin-track principle – the mixed use neighbourhoods clustered along the p.t. spine, parallel by linear parklands, often along rivers/streams, providing ecological and recreational services. The potential for excellent p.t. is critical. The potential of the greenspace to provide those services is also important.

Location: new settlement

The revived interest in new settlements and eco-towns gives urgency to the need to recognise locational realities. The points below apply equally to cell or compact town designs as to linear:

• simply stating that a proposed new town will be 'sustainable', with a good balance of homes, jobs and services, is no guarantee at all that it will be. Such a statement is often no more than spin, or wishful thinking

• any new or expanded settlement within the commuting hinterland of a city, or an urbanised sub-region, will share in the general pattern of commuting, normally to a wide range of employment locations, not just the city centre

• it is therefore a pre-requisite of any proposed new town location that it has good existing public transport links (rail and road) to main employment/service centres with the potential for up-grading and extending as the new population grows. It must, in other words, be a potential 'A' location. One good route into the city centre is not sufficient:

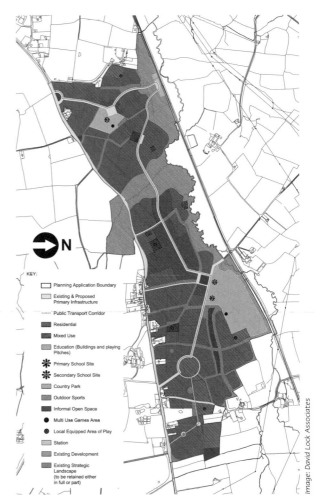

Image: David Lock Associates

Figure 5.28
Linear new settlement

Cranbrook in East Devon: all activities carefully planned, one spine bus route integrates the town, but it's seperation from Exeter, the mother city, may well compromise its transport sustainability.

3.18 Public transport

Linear concentration along a dedicated tram route: Vauban in Freiburg

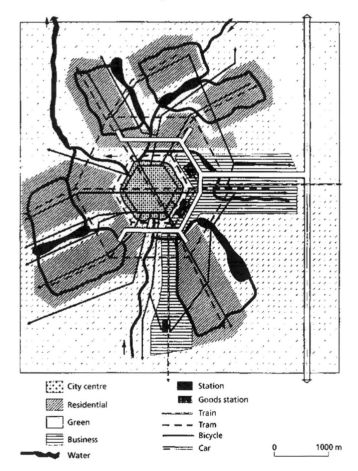

City centre
Residential
Green
Business
Water

Station
Goods station
Train
Tram
Bicycle
Car

0   1000 m

Figure 5.29
Linear districts and greenspace creating city form

SOURCE: Tjallingii 1995

- The location must also have the potential for economic development in scale with residential development, to hold a fair proportion of residents within the town for both employment and services. Allocating land and then just hoping is totally inadequate. What is the economic raison détre of the settlement? What potential is there for developing a 'market town' service role?

- All this means that completely new free-standing settlements are very unlikely to become sustainable. They may have carbon-neutral buildings, but their transport eco-footprint will be high. Car dependency and longer-than-average trip lengths will be the rule (see Lessons from Cambourne by Stephen Platt, Cambridge Architectural Research Ltd, www.carltd.com).

- Extending an existing settlement that already has some of the desired features is much more likely to succeed. It gives the town a head start, and it will achieve critical population thresholds more quickly (see below).

- The location of such a town should be selected so that it serves nearby villages effectively, and draws them closely into its orbit. The village and exurb population within easy cycling distance of 5 km of a good location can often be substantial – giving a massive potential filling to the viability of services, and reducing the distance residents have to travel.

Size

The key difference between the linear township and the neighbourhood cell model is scale. From the outset the linear form should be designed to support the full range of local facilities, including a 'district' centre and fair range of job opportunities. The target population is therefore 20–30,000 – sufficient to support facilities such as superstore, library, leisure centre, swimming pool, a good range of professional and health services, one or two secondary schools and a technical college.

Within the township, neighbourhoods are affinity areas rather than catchment areas: they may vary greatly in size, to reflect the progressive opportunities for development and unique site characteristics. The essence is that they are interconnected and permeable, not isolated.

Shape

Linearity does not have to mean the radial extension of a city. It can be adapted to a range of contexts. Free-standing linear settlements could be in the form of a cross, a circle, or a figure of eight. Urban extensions could be tangential, looped, or radial.

GETTING HIGH STREETS RIGHT

The most distinctive feature of the linear form advocated here is the high street. This is a new planned version of an old form. The high street is multi-modal, mixed use and ties neighbourhoods together. It is the focus of community life. In order to avoid the disadvantages of traditional high streets (congestion, noise, pollution) but at the same time attract people and business, it needs very careful placing within the street network.

Policy

■ Existing high streets should be maintained, extended and rejuvenated by encouraging intensification along their length, including higher density housing, where the market can support this.

■ New high streets rely for their viability on high connectivity with their immediate hinterland and excellent linkage to the rest of the town by bus and bike along its length, and by car across it.

■ The quality of the pedestrian and cycling environment is paramount, not just along the high street but in the streets that give access to it from adjacent areas.

■ Strict zoning should be avoided except for social provision of parks, schools etc. Rather there should be a flexible approach to change of use and rebuilding, allowing the market to adapt to changing social and economic conditions and thus maintain a higher level of service overall.

Traffic tamed but not forbidden

The drawback of the traditional high street has been its success. The combination of transport functions can range from street parking and bulk deliveries to main distributor road and public transport route. But in the same space cyclists and pedestrians want safe and convenient environments. The street acts as a series of casual meeting places, where the interests of conviviality should (but rarely do) take precedence. Pedestrianisation – even where feasible – is not necessarily the answer. The essence of the high street is that at times it is bustling with activity, the focus for residential areas that are placid by comparison. Vehicles contribute to that sense of bustle, provide access (this supporting local services) and assist the natural policing of the street after hours. Therefore:

■ Only exclude traffic where pedestrian activity is high and street space at a premium
■ Let buses and bikes right through if possible, with shared surface (colour coded) where appropriate
■ Widen pavements at important pedestrian nodes along the street
■ Allow on street parking where possible
■ Provide safe crossings at the places convenient to pedestrians
■ Traffic calmed to 20 mph through retail/social zones

Advantages of high streets

High streets can provide varied benefits by comparison with compact centres:

- *Better access from homes to local facilities*
- *Flexibility of hinterland size for facilities*
- *Flexibility of hinterland size over time as needs change*
- *Opportunity for maximising 'footfall' and business viability*
- *A wide range of property values, permitting marginal users frontage positions*
- *A clear source of local identity and sense of place*
- *A linear, mixed-use focus for possible district heating mains.*

Environmental capacity: Traffic flows

If feasible reduce traffic levels to 600 pcu per hour each way (this is the standard suggested by Buchanan in 1963 to allow easy road crossing and the ability to converse at normal volumes).

5.13

Renewal process

1 Observe
Keep a watching brief on healthy processes of gradual renewal

2 Contain
Protect vulnerable areas/groups from an over-enthusiastic market

3 Foster
Revive a flagging but not 'critical' local economy with judicious public investment and low-key partnerships that avoid 'labelling'

4 Revitalise
Regenerate (and maybe transform) with a major integrated regeneration programme

Density

1 Maintain
Deter intensification (e.g. in areas where current density levels match the accessibility status)

2 Gradually intensify
Encourage gradual and progressive intensification where high accessibility status warrants it

3 Greatly intensify
Radically increase densities (where public transport potential and the market will allow) to retrofit sustainability in low-density suburbs

4 Reduce
Gradually decrease densities and create open spaces in over-crowded zones, isolated urban enclaves, or greenspace priority areas

Aesthetic quality

1 Deregulate
Adopt a consciously laissez-faire aesthetic stance to encourage local taste and diversity

2 Conserve
Enhance the existing neighbourhood quality, protecting and reinforcing local distinctiveness

3 Enliven
Promote contrast and require higher standards in areas of tawdry or tedious character

4 Promote coherence
Require conformity to strict design codes to link up and coalesce a disjointed, disparate townscape

3.5 Neighbourhood identity

Land use

1 Stabilise
Attempt to maintain the current mix of activities in well-established neighbourhoods

2 Permit change
Allow uses to evolve in response to market pressures, encouraging adaptable building units and land use with minimal change

3 Guide change
Guide market pressures by criteria-based policies and clear spatial frameworks

4 Initiate change
Promote significant change through partnerships and development briefs and masterplans in areas of major growth or obsolescence

Figure 5.32
Dimensions of renewal strategy. *The renewal strategy needs to be complemented by clear policies for aesthetic quality, density and land use – together making a coherent package.*

RENEWAL STRATEGIES
Every neighbourhood (or part of a neighbourhood if appropriate) should have an identified strategy for renewal, reflecting in particular physical, social and economic characteristics. The renewal strategy should specify the policies needed for density, land use change and aesthetic quality, as well as for the renewal process itself.

1   **Observe:** where it is evident that there is steady, on-going investment in the area, with a healthy process of gradual renewal, no special policy is needed except for a watchful eye to avoid destabilisation.

2   **Contain:** in some areas, a very active land market may be forcing physical and social change in such a way as to threaten vulnerable groups or valued environments. This may occur, for example, in conservation areas, or in edge-of-centre areas where low-rent zones are being invaded by high rent commercial activity. Containment implies restrictions on land use change and redevelopment.

3   **Foster:** in other areas, the problem could be one of gradual but progressive decline, with inadequate levels of maintenance and renewal. Recognising these 'pre-critical' areas in time to take modest action to trigger a turn-around may avoid the need for drastic (and expensive) state action later. Initially intervention might simply mean that local authorities need to be responsive to residents concerns, reviewing management regimes (e.g. for local parks) and prepared to spend more. Beyond that intervention may take the form of policy change (freeing the market), and public/private/voluntary sector co-operation where the purpose is seen as 'enhancing quality' rather than 'rescue' (which risks prematurely labelling the area as a failure). Judicious new investment stemming from such a partnership can help revive confidence.

4   **Revitalise:** 'critical' areas are typified by little or no reinvestment and increasing levels of vacancy, often associated with trapped populations, declining service levels and/or failing industries. Government regeneration programmes are generally targeted at these areas. The keys to success are:

*   effective partnerships between public, private, voluntary and local community sectors
*   dynamic leadership (from any sector) and clarity of purpose
*   public investment designed to trigger private/voluntary sector activity
*   recognition of the needs of local people; and
*   recognition of the needs for (sometimes dramatic) social and economic restructuring

RETROFITTING SUSTAINABILITY

The process of renewal provides the opportunity to 'retrofit' sustainability. We can put that more strongly: given the unhealthy, unsustainable patterns of development in many settlements, there is an absolute obligation to ensure that the gradual process of renewal combats/adapts to climate change and promotes social inclusion/health.

'Ecological renewal' should ensure:

- all new buildings are as carbon-neutral as possible
- new buildings are adaptable (recognising life-cycle needs and the potential for change of use)
- new building/intensification occurs so as to reinforce the density gradient
- new development maintains or increases pedestrian/cycling permeability, creating new links if currently there are barriers
- new development enhances the aesthetic quality of the area, especially the attractiveness of pedestrian routes and meeting places
- land use change is in line with locational characteristics – enhancing accessibility by non-car means, ensuring access for all
- new hard surfaces are permeable, surface water is managed in line with sustainable drainage principles
- natural vegetation cover increases – through green roofs and balconies designed for planting as well as greenspace, soft gardens and street trees
- roofs/walls include solar collectors/photovoltaics or are designed for ease of later solar retrofit

5.14 INTENSIFICATION

STRATEGY 1:

REINFORCEMENT OF HISTORIC PATTERNS

Scenario

This is an inner suburb built up progressively between 1880 and 1960 around a historic tram route, which also functions as primary road, local distributor and linear shopping centre. Housing densities range from 50 dph for earlier development near the spine to 25–40 dph for the 'backlands' development later. Most surviving greenspace is in the backlands zone.

Appraisal

The population is relatively stable but with wide variations of wealth, class and household characteristics. There is gradual and progressive renewal of the physical structures signifying confidence in the economic future of the area. The quality of environment is humdrum but homely. Access to local facilities,

Two strategies for intensification

Section 5.11 demonstrated a spatial planning process for a major urban extension. The process is equally applicable to existing urban areas. The two basic strategies of reinforcement and restructuring are illustrated below. In both cases, the spatial framework should guide physical planning decisions in relation to

- *the use of brownfield sites*
- *regeneration of inner urban areas*
- *retrofit of outer suburban areas*
- *gradual renewal processes; and*
- *development control generally.*

5.14

Plan for gradual intensification when ...

- *The existing urban form is based on pre-car patterns that still have viability: for example, market towns with strong centres and pedestrian scale; city radials with linear centres, still focused on bus/ tram routes.*

- *The area is substantially built up, affords a satisfactory quality of environment, and has limited capacity for reshaping in the foreseeable future.*

and to city-wide facilities, is generally good. The existing urban form still mirrors the historic pattern of development and is for the most part well adapted to movement by foot and bus, albeit car use now dominates. The spine road acts as the main pedestrian, cycling, bus, car and service link; it is unsurprisingly both congested and polluted; however, there is no easy alternative. The greenspaces are well linked in the north but separated in the south.

Strategy

Reinforce the established pattern of development, concentrating higher intensity activities along the main spine while working towards reduced car reliance and greater continuity of greenspace. The numbers below refer to the map:

1 **Township centre**
  - Reinforce the main public transport node (e.g. reopen station).
  - Build on success – i.e. the existing retail 'hot-spot'.
  - Encourage/allow further intensification of 'B' centre activities.
  - Achieve improved pedestrian environment.

5.9 Analysing form and function

2 **Local high street**
  - Extend pedestrian, bike and bus priority measures, but not at the expense of on-street parking where it is important for passing trade.
  - Support innovation and diversity of shops and local facilities, with a flexible approach to the balance of retail and housing use along the frontage responding to changes in demand.
  - Allow redevelopment of all frontage plots where this increases plot ratios, encouraging a gradual change of character from two to three or four storeys, with adaptable building types.
  - Where the street narrows, apply a set-back building line to increase long-term capacity, compensating the owners/ developers with higher plot ratios.

5.4 Graded density

3 **Inner accessible zone**
  - Defined as areas within 200 m actual walking distance of the main street or 400 m of the township centre.
  - Encourage the gradual intensification of the area, requiring three storeys minimum for any new development, and modest parking/garden provision.
  - Flats and terraces predominating; aim for gross density of at least 50 dph, with average net densities of 60 or 70 dph.
  - Varied uses (e.g. workshops, primary schools, pocket parks).
  - Aim to extend zone by removing barriers to pedestrian access.

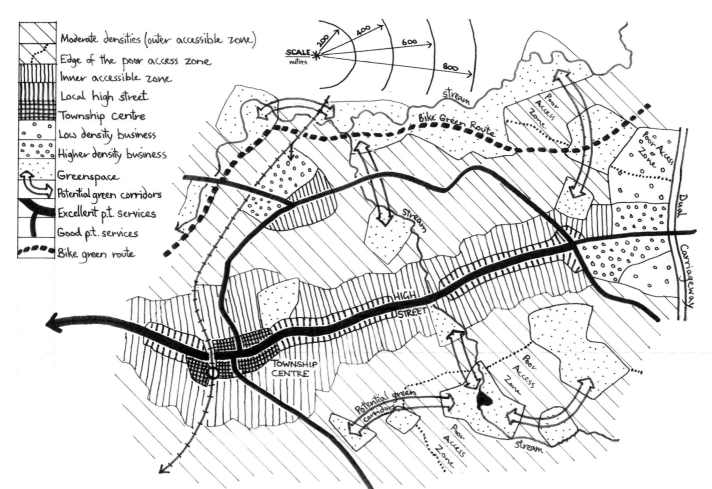

Key:
- Moderate densities (outer accessible zone)
- Edge of the poor access zone
- Inner accessible zone
- Local high street
- Township centre
- Low density business
- Higher density business
- Greenspace
- Potential green corridors
- Excellent p.t. services
- Good p.t. services
- Bike green route

Figure 5.33
Reinforcement strategy – urban radial sector

4 **Outer accessible zone**
- Defined as the built-up area between 200 and 400 m actual distance of a good bus route or 800 m of the township centre.
- Varied housing types, but aiming for at least 30 dph gross density, and at least 40 dph net density average. In some areas this implies gradual intensification.
- High-density housing not permitted.
- Industrial estates (but not office/business use) ideally form part of this zone.

5 **Poor access zone**
- Defined as built-up areas more than 400 m actual distance from a good bus route and over 800 m from the township centre.
- No intensification should be permitted, unless and until a strategy for improved accessibility is in place.
- Backland and 'infill' plots should be managed as allotments, woodland or biodiversity areas. Any development which *is* allowed should be at low density.
- Temporary low-intensity uses may be promoted pending

Figure 5.34
Intensification around tube station

Hypothetical scheme for intensification around a railway station in Barking, East London. Intensification is made easier because of local authority housing and ownership of land. New housing for sale pays for new social housing. The commercial attractiveness of the revitalised local centres around the stations is increased because of both higher catchment population and social diversity.

Use radical restructuring when ...

• *The existing urban form is largely low-density suburban 'sprawl', premised on high car reliance, and currently lacking adequate accessibility to jobs and services.*

• *There is some opportunity for judicious intensification and infill development.*

public transport investment.

6 **Greenspace system**
   • Includes all greenspaces including any 'waste' and linear zones of biodiversity/shelterbelt value.
   • Work to increase public access open space, where needed, in the outer accessible and poor access zones.
   • Increase the connectivity between greenspaces with wildlife/recreational corridors, linking through inner zones as well as the outer.

STRATEGY 2:

RADICAL RESTRUCTURING

This sceniario, is an outer urban area based around radial routes, including the railway, built up initially in the 1930s and expanded in the 1950s and 1960s. A business park is a more recent addition. Development is predominantly two-storey. Densities range from 20 dph to 40 dph. There is ample open space, though some of it is underused agricultural land with limited public access.

Appraisal

■ The population is stable but not particularly well off.

■ There is a paucity of young professionals and young single people.

■ The council estate is partially cut off from the rest of the area by the railway and open space, lacking any direct connection to the business park. It is a classic 'closed cell' design.

■ The estate is socially stigmatised, lacks viable services, and has inadequate public transport connections to the wider city. There are concentrations of poverty and unemployment.

■ The main residential area has better bus services (though only to limited destinations) and adequate local facilities. Car use is necessarily quite high.

■ The whole area lacks any township or district centre.

Strategy

The proposal to create a LRT (light rail transit) service with new stations along the existing railway offers the opportunity for restructuring urban form. The objectives are to:

■ increase the general quality and use of public transport

■ reduce the isolation of the council estate and the business park

■ provide a new township/district centre, with a good range of jobs and facilities

- increase population levels, particularly of under-represented groups.

The spatial framework could specify

- Use LRT stations as foci for development and bus services.

- Station location is critical to creating a viable overall strategy.

Promote a new township centre

- Estimate the critical level of accessible population that could be achieved over time, and thus the amount and quality of retail and other services that could be supported.

- Locate the new centre close to the isolated estate, acting as a functional link to adjacent neighbourhoods, drawing on wider spending power.

- Encourage quite high density commercial, retail, leisure and residential development, maximising pedestrian, cycling and public transport accessibility.

Intensify the inner accessible zone

- A priority for new sites close to the station and centre should be flats aimed at young singles and couples.

- New frontage development along potential local high streets should be three or four storeys, with use flexibility on the ground floor.

- Gradual renewal and intensification of the low-density housing estates, with three-storey development and terracing encouraged.

- The area of business park close to the station should be 'infilled' by developing on car parks and excess landscape areas, with three or four storeys permitted.

Promote gradual renewal elsewhere

- Encourage diversification of housing stock.

- Permit small-scale commercial development on main bus routes.

- Work to enliven and improve visual aesthetics.

Increase connectedness

- Create new pedestrian/cycling links between housing areas and the business park.

- Maintain/enhance green corridors between open spaces.

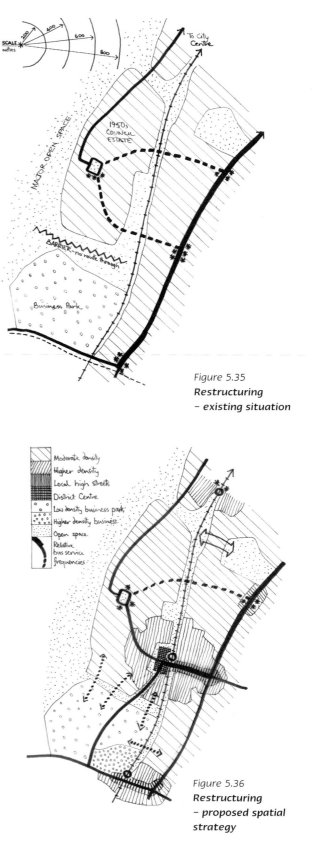

Figure 5.35
*Restructuring
– existing situation*

Figure 5.36
*Restructuring
– proposed spatial
strategy*

5.15

3.5 Neighbourhood
identity

Figure 5.34
Making a space into a place

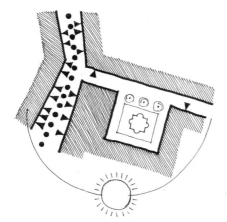

A space
An interesting composition to note but perhaps not to linger. Shady, off the beaten track

- ●●●●●● main pedestrian route
- urban art/play sculpture
- landmark seen from a distance
- sitting/eating/performing
- stalls
- active frontage (shopfronts, etc.)
- sun path
- major corners designed to define/ enclose the place

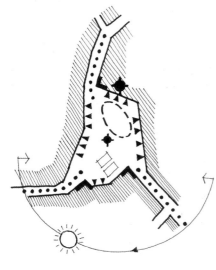

A place
Somewhere to sit, to observe, to be observed. Warm, active, lively, ever changing

designing places

5.15   DESIGN OF THE PUBLIC REALM

BASIC PRINCIPLES

The design of the spaces between buildings is akin to designing a complex of outdoor rooms, with different, sometimes overlapping, but well-defined functions. Good public realm design will result from a creative response to appraisals of context and site. It will be manifested in a network of sheltered, safe, accessible spaces with different functions and a clear definition between public, semi-public and private space. Existing landscape elements will be maintained to reinforce these aspects and will give the development a sense of place and local identity.

In order to achieve these principles public realm strategy must be an integral and guiding aspect of the spatial masterplan (see 3.11) and accompany design briefs for neighbourhood development, in terms of both regeneration and new build schemes.

AIMS OF A PUBLIC REALM STRATEGY

- **Aid the structuring, identity and legibility of the neighbourhood by setting out a network of linked open spaces, organised in a logical hierarchy**

Elements of this hierarchy include major access avenues or boulevards, tree-lined streets, nodal points (the focus of foot, cycle and bus routes), structure planting, formal and informal space from domestic to civic scale and function, landmark landscape elements. Water can also be used to create similar structuring effects. It should be clear from 'reading' the spaces whether we are approaching the centre of the neighbourhood or moving from one place with a particular identity to another. Linear landscape elements such as wildlife corridors (often utilising existing and new hedgerows) or linear parks/play spaces also give a shape and structure to a neighbourhood, possible demarcating one home-patch from another.

- **Provide spaces appropriate to their function, in terms of size, distribution, orientation/shelter boundaries and management regimes**

Too many public spaces created in the twentieth century are often too large or open, looking empty or lacking a comforting sense of enclosure. Note how small many successful traditional urban spaces can be. It is important that the design maximises the amount of sun penetration into the space during the most useful times of day, say between 10 am and 5 pm. A focal/nodal point requires legible routes following desire lines, generators of activity and appropriate levels of enclosure.

■ **Concentrate activities at nodal points**

It is activity and a particular mix of building or land uses that make spaces into places. Uses and activities thrive through concentration and overlaps. Increase footfall past shops, businesses and services through location on main routes to ensure high use and economic viability. Only use a zonal approach if land uses are un-neighbourly or large-scale single use.

■ **Ensure that non-private open spaces are accessible to all**

Accessibility to all residents and visitors regardless of age or levels of temporary or permanent disability underpins legislation at national and international level in many countries. The implications are fundamental to neighbourhood planning and involve directness and length of walking routes, gradients and changes of level and shelter, lighting and seating. Signage should be given particular consideration to give distance as well as direction. It is worth remembering that we are all susceptible to loss of full mobility at varying stages of our lives and thus what is accessible to people with disabilities is also helpful to very young children and those caring for them, and elderly people. Consideration should be given not only to wheelchair access, but also to the challenges faced by those with loss of vision or hearing, or limitations to manual dexterity.

■ **Increase the safety of the streets, paths, parks and squares, reducing the fear of crime**

Good lighting and the overlooking of public space is an essential ingredient in the process. This provision also helps accessibility and the attractiveness of a place, and it means that they are populated over a longer time period. Lighting can be provided in imaginative ways: appropriately scaled lamp posts can be alternated with 'wall washing' and lighting of trees and shrubbery. Foot routes, where not associated with roads/bus routes, should only be contemplated if they follow a strong desire line and are as short and direct as possible, avoiding obvious ambush points by allowing good lines of sight.

■ **Provide opportunity in particular for teenagers to meet and chat and lark about**

Whilst toddlers' and young children's needs can be catered for in well-designed play equipment, children over the age of about 10–11 years are often less well catered for. The recent concept of 'Teen-Village' may be useful in a main neighbourhood space. What is meant is the provision of open-sided shelters where youngsters can meet and chat. Siting, visibility and lighting are crucial and can perhaps best be done through community agreement, involving young people. Bikes and skateboards require more generous, often linear, provision. Skateboarding is a form of street theatre given appropriately robust, public settings,

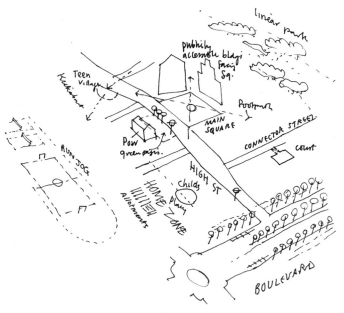

Figure 5.38
The varied elements of the public realm

Figure 5.39
Active frontages

Buildings facing the public realm should be designed to have active frontages, to contribute to the vitality and safety of neighbourhood streets. Active frontages (including gable ends) can comprise windows to habitable rooms, offices or shopfronts, and a high incidence of entrances. These create opportunities for 'passive surveillance' and activity. Blank walls facing the public realm should be avoided.

(from Guise 2009a)

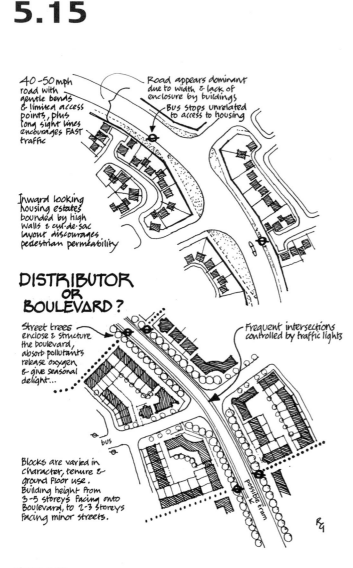

40-50 mph road with gentle bends & limited access points, plus long sight lines encourages FAST traffic

Road appears dominant due to width & lack of enclosure by buildings

Bus stops unrelated to access to housing

Inward looking housing estates bounded by high walls & cul-de-sac layout discourages pedestrian permeability

DISTRIBUTOR OR BOULEVARD?

Street trees enclose & structure the boulevard, absorb pollutants release oxygen & give seasonal delight...

Frequent intersections controlled by traffic lights

bus

Blocks are varied in character, tenure & ground floor use. Building height from 3-5 storeys facing onto Boulevard, to 2-3 storeys facing minor streets.

possible tram

RG

Figure 5.40
The main road as public realm

3.15 Neighbourhood movement strategy

as is basketball, which could also enliven a public arena-like space. An arc of generous steps with the wall of a building as a backdrop and the right orientation suggests a performance space, but when not used as such is just a change of level.

- **Foster stakeholder responsibility in the protection of the spaces immediately outside the dwelling**

The creation of zones of semi-private and semi-public space outside the dwelling overlooked by the dwelling and its neighbours can help the self-policing of groups of houses. The debate about the merits of cul-de-sac versus streets as to their relative safety and security has perhaps become too simplistic: neither layout is all good or all bad per se. If no one is at home in a cul-de-sac or a street, then the houses are vulnerable to break-in. Natural surveillance from a variety of potential and nearby sources is essential. Home-place streets can be as safe as a courtyard if there is a feeling of ownership of the street, conveyed by its length, enclosure, number of entrances and windows, etc.

- **Work with the grain of the locality to enhance biodiversity, habitat, shelter, and local distinctiveness**

The characteristics of the neighbourhood location and its setting should influence decisions regarding the layout and character of open spaces. If these characteristics are not taken into consideration in the design process, the outcome can involve wasteful site engineering works, unnecessary loss of habitats, increased run-off and poor microclimatic conditions. Furthermore, standardised and stereotyped layouts that have little relationship with the locality exacerbate the familiar criticism of 'anywhere' development. Instead, the size, shape and direction of plots, the frequency of streets and junctions should influence the layout of a new development.

- **The main road as public realm**

Inevitably, neighbourhoods will be bounded by or directly accessed by a relatively high-volume road. This road should be considered less as a conduit for fast-moving traffic and more as a connector, where public transport, cycling and pedestrian movement (both along and across it) can be incorporated. By introducing more frequent intersections, street trees and buildings with entrances and windows facing the street, it becomes the interface of the neighbourhood with the rest of the urban area, it becomes a boulevard – a place in its own right, where traffic is moderated by the overall environment. Generous tree planting (on either side of the road, plus the central reservation) is vital to improve air quality, provide shade in the summer and soften the effects of traffic.

Measures, standards and policies

The following modes of intervention are examples of those which might be appropriate within an Area of Neighbourhood Quality.

■ Design code. This would establish patterns of plot sizes, building set-back distances, heights, boundary conditions, and so on. This would guide new development and alterations.

■ Streetworks code: to inform utility agencies and highway authorities of standards on reinstatement, choice of materials, position and size of signage and street furniture.

■ Community agreement, where necessary, on limits to permitted development whether through restrictive covenants or Article 4 directions (in the UK), monitored by a residents' liaison group, working with the Local Authority, to ensure sensitive application.

5.16 PERIMETER BLOCK AND HOME PLACE

THE LIVEABLE REALM

The residential home-place integrates blocks, plots and streets to form the home environment. This section looks in detail at how block design influences plots and streets and so the quality of the home-place.

The home-place concept aims to integrate all the physical elements of the built environment that are likely to foster the conditions where residents can feel that they have a stake in their immediate locality outside the home. It is important to ensure that the sustainable home-place is:

2.11 Making a development proposal

■ **attractive** – the design should create surroundings that are aesthetically pleasing in terms of touch, hearing, smell, sight and history

■ **safe** – vehicular movement within the home-patch should be so controlled by the configuration of the street that vehicle speed is restricted to no more than about 15 mph (25 kmph). Personal safety should be assisted by 'natural surveillance' and a clear distinction between private and public space

■ **healthy** – the layout is such that walking to local facilities is the obvious option, and children can play outside in safe and attractive surroundings; access to these and greenspace lifts the spirit.

■ **sociable** – people can meet casually on the street and converse in sunny, informal spaces

■ **convenient** – where densities permit or require, the home-place can connect easily to playspace, allotments, corner shops and small office/workshop spaces

■ **identifiable** – a home-place has to have bounds where people can identify their own communal patch

Controlling the critical elements

A design code can enhance local distinctiveness.

- *Type and height of front of boundary hedge, railway or fence.*

- *Spacing and type of street trees and lights.*

- *Are semi-basements or attic storeys (with dormers) required?*

- *Placement of any extensions or projections in front of the main building line.*

A finer grain of local distinctiveness can be encoded in the building details:

- *Frequency and location where gables face the street.*

- *Importance of providing a gable end oriel window.*

- *Porches and/or verandas or other modelling elements.*

- *Range of building materials.*

- *Proportion of windows.*

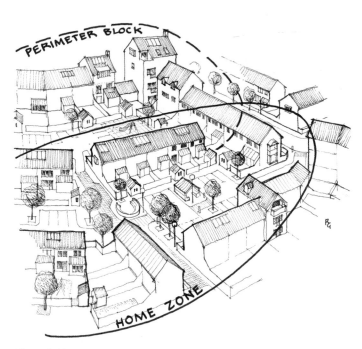

Figure 5.41
Designing for higher densities without loss of quality – the perimeter block

Homezones

The UK Government is now supporting the implementation and research of homezones. These are residential streets where pedestrians and cyclists take precedence across the whole carriageway. Communities are involved in deciding how best to achieve this, and the change in the hierarchy is signalled and consolidated through alterations to the street design. The goal is to provoke caution in the driver's mind, leading to a change in behaviour as the road becomes 'people' territory not 'car' territory.

The homezone is a concept that addresses some aspects of the home-place, but it is much more than just an exercise in traffic calming. It brings residents together and raises fundamental questions about their shared external space – the street. Both the processes required and resulting changes to residential streets can bring about shifts in communal understandings of territory, ownership and responsibility.

For further information, see: www.homezones.org

- **personalisable** – the design and layout of housing and gardens should permit individual expression and local communal choice where possible

- **adaptable** – the home-place must be capable of change and development, so that buildings may be renewed or uses can change without destroying the quality of the place

- **water-sensitive** – run-off should be minimised through SUDS, recharging ground water, and opportunities should be taken to harvest rainwater and re-use grey water

- **energy-efficient** – the design should maximise the value of passive solar heat while reducing heat loss through built form and wind shelter

- **biodiverse** – the design should provide small-scale wildlife habitats, with natural vegetation and birdlife contributing to quality.

DESIGNING FOR HIGHER DENSITIES: THE PERIMETER BLOCK

On most sites, the highest volume of accommodation at the lowest number of storeys can be achieved by locating development in a linear form around the periphery of the site. This layout also has the advantage of optimising use of external space and differentiating public and private external space. It is likely to fit into established neighbourhoods as it creates a network of streets.

Orientation of blocks

If poorly designed, the interiors of perimeter blocks can be shady and claustrophobic. Blocks must be shaped and orientated to allow maximum penetration of sunlight and maximise the number of southern elevations. Lower buildings on southern sides can also aid sun penetration.

Types of block

Perimeter blocks can (and should) have many variants to the basic pattern outlined above. For instance they can be cranked or deformed in alignment, to allow a more sympathetic relationship to site conditions (e.g. contours, existing building patterns) or to allow improved orientation to obtain increased sunlight. A cranked alignment can also be used to create chicanes in a street to reduce vehicular speeds. Variants in the basic pattern will also have the effect of creating variety in the street scene and give each block an identity.

Perimeter blocks, given a basic area usually ranging between 0.75 ha and 0.90 ha, have the flexibility to achieve a range of densities.

What are the advantages of perimeter blocks?

- They are very efficient in terms of land utilisation. Higher densities can be achieved with the minimum number of storeys.

- They allow high levels of direct and comprehensible accessibility from the street to each plot.

- They are safer: there is a sharp distinction between the public and private side of the development with consequent opportunities for surveillance and enclosure of private gardens. Any communal space at the rear can be accessed by residents only.

- They are flexible: a range of densities and tenures can be accommodated within and between each perimeter block. Additionally some mixed, non-residential uses can be accommodated.

THE HOME-PLACE STREET ENVIRONMENT

The home-place incorporates the concepts of the well-established Dutch woonerf (home street) with those espoused in the DfT *Manual for Streets* (2007). This concept should apply to all residential streets.

Basically, the proposal is that we should all consider the street outside our house as the public realm of our immediate neighbourhood – a place rather than a channel for cars. This place is where we feel we have some ownership or stake – it is 'our' space (belonging to us and our neighbours) – we can chat, play, park. The street is accessible by cars and delivery vehicles but it is so designed that it is only secondarily a route for vehicles. The home-place street should be a convenient route for bicycles and pedestrians. The main home-place street should not be designed as a cul-de-sac, although there may be courts and yards accessed from it.

1. Most parking to rear. The back door becomes main access.

2. Parking on street, with larger more private gardens but car dominated street.

Figure 5.42

Perimeter block development options

All these are family housing, mainly two storey terraces. A southerly orientation is a major layout consideration. Density ranges from about 40 dpha to about 65 dpha for the car-free option.

3. Car-free development with some single storey courtyard houses attractive to the elderly, frail or people with disabilities.

285

5.16

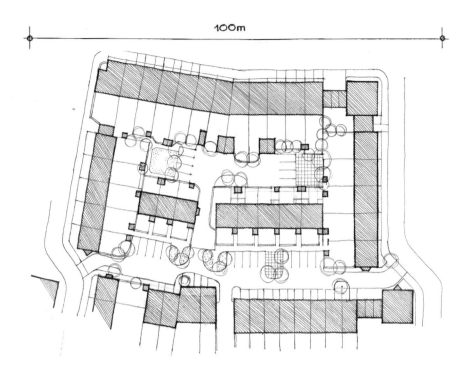

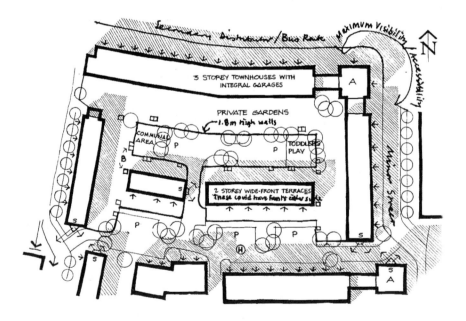

Figure 5.43

Indicative scheme for a neighbourhood block of 50 dph

The framework of this block allows for a variety of house sizes, types and tenure. Virtually the same footprint could be developed at 75 or 35 dph.

Design principles for the home-place

Extensive tree planting is an integral part of design – street trees and trees in the blocks absorb CO_2 and oxygenate the atmosphere as well as aiding privacy, shade and biodiversity; trees are also attractive!

Cranked blocks allow streets to follow contours and allow greater sunlight penetration to gardens.

The communal area and toddlers' play area would be subject to residents' choice as to appropriate function and management.

Street chicane every 50–60 m to calm traffic.

High proportion of wide-frontage terrace houses – allows extension and sunny, private gardens.

Most wide frontages face south or west to optimise passive solar gain.

KEY

A: *four-storey corner building – retail/service use on ground floor with three floors of flats above – highest building on the north-east of block reduces overshadowing*

B: *bicycle stores*

H: *home-place street – access only – calmed traffic on-street parking – meeting/sitting spaces*

S: *passive surveillance at gateways through oriel windows on gable ends*

> *house entrances*

FUTURE FLEXIBILITY

It is unlikely that a local centre will be functioning fully at the commencement of a new development. Thus, it may be wise to develop some buildings which are adaptable to a variety of small-scale mixed uses but which have ground floors devoted to residential use at the outset. This is particularly important along high streets or at the junctions of local distributors.

The diagram on this page shows a possible design for the three- or four-storey corner building in the block layout illustrated in Figure 5.43. It shows the ground floor and plot of the corner building. This has been designed as a flat and garden, but it might have an inbuilt permission to convert to, say, a shop, a workshop or a dentist's surgery with the garden plot convertible to a yard with some parking space or extra accommodation up to 50 per cent of the area of the garden plot.

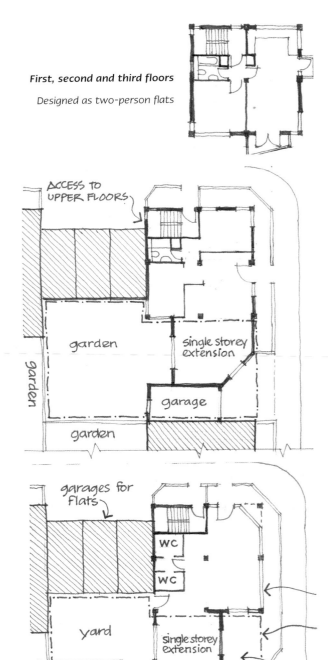

First, second and third floors

Designed as two-person flats

Ground floor – option 1

Four-person flat

Extension and WC area can easily be altered for later uses

An alternative to option 2 if commercial/service uses are not viable in the early years

Ground floor – option 2

Commercial/service use e.g. shop, bar, café, surgery, office, workshop, crèche

Approximately 8.5 m x 8.5 m shell

Total external area allocated to ground-floor unit. Integral permission for single-storey building/s on a maximum of 60 per cent of this area

Possible 'spill out' or conservatory area

Terrace housing

Figure 5.44
Three- or four-storey corner building designed for flexibility

The building design and planning consents ensure future adaptability for domestic, commercial or service uses

Whilst the term 'Masterplanning' is widely recognised in planning and development circles, its historic connotations of semi-autocratic control and end-state determinism should not be attributed to this process.

The process of masterplanning or developing an urban design framework, is one which consists of a number of stages and parallels the seven stage process of neighbourhood planning set out in Chapter 2. It involves a variety of participants; including local communities and politicians, planners, urban designers, landscape architects, transport and highway planners, utility agencies, funding agencies, the development industry architects and many other bodies.

ESTABLISHING A VISION

2.5 Defining a shared vision

The accompanying diagram shows some of the interrelated stages of the process. However, the development of a vision or the establishing of the character of a development is a critical first stage. From this, primary objectives can be defined. This capturing of the vision helps to give direction to the planning and design process, which can get diverted or 'bogged down' in the plethora of issues which have to be addressed or in the wide range of parties who need to be consulted.

The development of the vision should involve the stakeholders in the area. This vision may evolve through a number of methods of engaging people; often, but not exclusively through a 'charette', a workshop format event, sometimes extending over a number of days, where scenarios for the development of the area are posited and closely considered through working in groups on maps of the area. It is essential that the scenarios are based on the real constraints of the area.

Having agreed the overall vision and objectives, the masterplanning process can develop. This could be considered as a number of appraisals and plans which each concentrate on a topic area (see fig 5.45).

APPRAISAL

5.7 Scope of neighbourhood appraisal

The first stages might focus on the appraisal of the setting or context of the development. In some cases this appraisal may have been undertaken in sufficient detail as a basis for the previous 'envisioning' stage. Appraisal is essential in order to identify key links between the proposed neighbourhood and the existing locality. It will identify land uses, bus routes, facilities and catchment areas which will have an impact on the development, in terms of schools, employment etc. The positive aspects of scale and overall character of the adjacent settlement should be fully understood, to ensure the sensitive integration of the new with the existing, in terms of street patterns, edges, heights, relative densities, landmarks etc. Community aspirations, associations and sensitivities should also be included in the appraisal. Heritage and environmental designations, drainage patterns and general infrastructure will all help to shape the parameters of the proposal.

The appraisal of the site of the proposals will also be necessary. Given that the site is likely to have been developed previously, the history of the area should be understood, to identify previous uses, structures, street patterns, archaeological significance etc. This analysis should identify areas requiring remediation or avoidance (e.g. polluted areas, underground services etc.). Site appraisal will identify critical contours, drainage patterns, existing trees, hedgerows, habitats, views, existing structures and buildings which could be re-used, access points, critical boundaries and so on.

Masterplan topics

These appraisals will then influence the structuring of the scheme through a series of interacting layers or overlays of plans, each of which concentrate on the following topics (this sequence of examples is not necessarily in priority order).

■ **Hierarchy of streets, spaces and connections**

Identifying where connections are made with the existing street, path and bus routes are proposed and the internal hierarchy of major to minor streets, squares (if appropriate) and courtyards.

Figure 5.45
Appraisal, design elements and implementation

The sequence of overlapping considerations in developing an urban design framework for a neighbourhood. Design Codes provide guidance for smaller areas.

SOURCE: Guise 2009b

2.10 Taking action

This will also show the formal streets and informal (i.e. shared surface/homezone) streets. Overall this will delineate the extent of the public realm.

■ **Green infrastructure**

Indicates where (a) existing green features such as hedgerows, trees, watercourses or ponds will influence the layout, 'grain' and focal points of the development and (b) the structure of new planting to reinforce the existing and create greenspaces (large and small), allotments, shelterbelts and biomass should be and the approach to biodiversity. Reedbeds and sustainable urban drainage systems will also be shown.

■ **Active design infrastructure**

This will closely relate to the previous two plans, to indicate walk routes and their character (related to the full age and ability range), areas for children's play (younger and older), and areas for informal recreation and formal playing field provision.

■ **Uses, tenures and density**

Sets out type, amount and mix (horizontal and vertical) of uses, commercial, cultural and communal. Residential density and the mix of tenures will also be included.

■ **Key heights, frontages and landmarks**

Indicates the three dimensional character of the proposed neighbourhood through the identification of formal and informal (active) frontages, key groups, corners and terminating views; where development faces inward (to create privacy with existing development) or outward, key rooflines, heights and landmarks. Existing buildings, structures and materials to be rehabilitated should also be identified.

Figure 5.46

Using cross sections in urban design frameworks

The framework need not rely only on a street and block plan. In many situations the cross section is equally valuable.

SOURCE: Guise 2009b

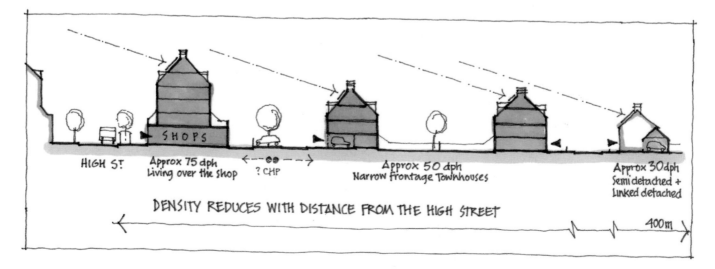

USING DESIGN CODES

Design codes are a method of street making: that is, the creation of a coherent set of streetscapes which addresses the three elements comprising the holistic 'street' (the street itself, the buildings on either side, and the plots on which the buildings sit).

In developing new neighbourhoods, or extending or infilling existing ones, we can first determine the appropriate character for particular types of streetscapes and then, by a combination of learning from the best examples of historical precedent and including best practice based on present-day requirements, we can identify key dimensions which are likely to produce the type of streetscapes that fulfil our aims.

This may seem rather too mechanical, but it was the way in which many of our Georgian streetscapes were developed. This method is more specific in its prescriptions than the rather vague statements on street character found in many planning briefs, and yet it provides the framework or envelope within which design freedom can operate.

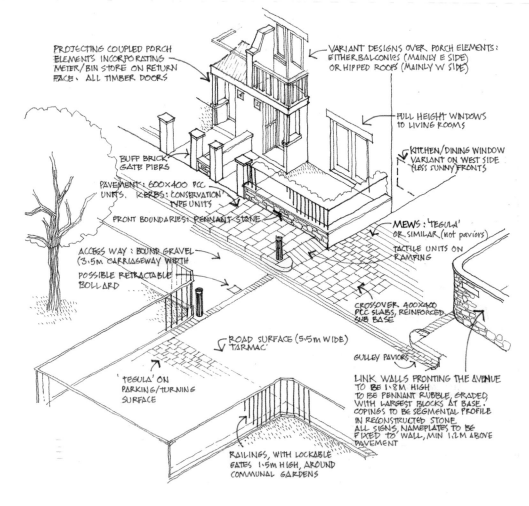

Figure 5.47

Detailed design code to establish a distinctive aesthetic character

Example of a Design Code for a neighbourhood street.

SOURCE: Guise 2009b

THE COMPACT NEIGHBOURHOOD CENTRE

This offers an example of the development of an urban design framework for a particular setting: the neighbourhood centre.

The concept sketch shows a neighbourhood centre that is the focus for a wide variety of uses and activities necessary for residents' immediate requirements. It is also intended to foster the sense of a lively and sociable place.

The main influences on the design and layout are:

- The centre is laid out to be at the convergence of foot, cycle and bus routes from residential streets – the point of maximum connectedness.

- It is anticipated that residents will use the centre as a single destination for all their basic requirements – making it convenient for them and economic for the enterprises and services as there will be maximum footfall across frontages.

- To ensure liveliness, sociability and safety (at night and day, weekdays and weekends) there are overlaps in the utilisation of space and time as much as possible. In particular, the school incorporates shared school/community

Figure 5.48
The neighbourhood centre

To be a place rather than just a space it has to be attractive and active. It must be a nodal point; it must be sheltered and sunny.

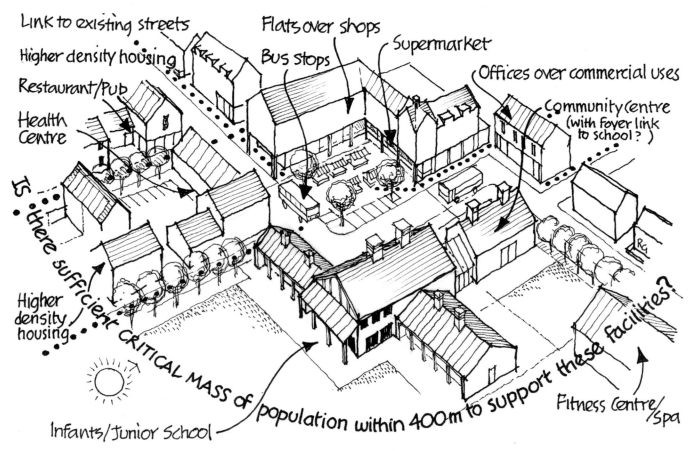

Link to existing streets
Higher density housing
Restaurant/Pub
Health Centre
Flats over shops
Bus stops
Supermarket
Offices over commercial uses
Community Centre (with foyer link to school?)
IS there sufficient
Higher density housing
CRITICAL MASS of population within 400m to support these facilities?
Infants/Junior School
Fitness Centre/Spa

use at its interface with the neighbourhood square. School security is ensured by using a controlled entrance in the common foyer. The cinema is located above the supermarket and shops have flats on upper floors.

- The car park is designed for maximum utilisation as it serves the cinema/supermarket, health centre and place of worship, which are located around the car park.

- The public realm is surrounded by 'active frontages' at street/square level. Thus, there is a high incidence of entrances, windows and publicly accessible uses at street level. Blank walls facing the major public spaces are kept to a minimum.

- The square is modest in size. This reduces redundant space, creates the feeling of an outdoor room and looks well peopled even when there are few people about. However, the square should be planned to accommodate bus shelters, bike-parking facilities, partially covered seating/youth hanging-out space, space for congregating, outside public venues, spill-out areas in front of shops and restaurants for display and sitting out and space for impromptu performances and market stalls.

- A neighbourhood centre will only be viable, long term, socially and economically if there is a critical mass of people living within walking distance, plus visability for passing trade.

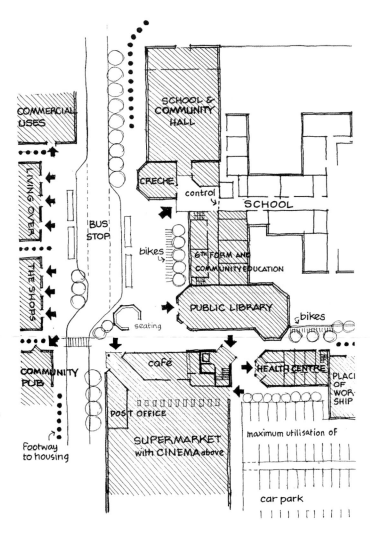

Figure 5.49
A neighbourhood centre in plan

A small park at the centre of the neighbourhood lies on the main footpath between the school (ahead) and the local shops (behind the camera). Recent measures have included the installation of boundary railings and symbolic gateway piers.

The sign reflects the original healthcare provision for the residents. The surgery no longer exists on site, although there is one nearby. The Community Forum and Community Support Forum and Community Support Officers operate from these premises instead.

The mixed nature of the development, with blocks of varying heights is apparent from this illustration. The modernist architectural style of the building is contrasted by the use of natural stone walls, imparting a sense of permanence and rootedness.

Neighbourhood planning concepts, pioneered in the interwar period, reached their high point in the UK in the first phase of the New Towns and in some city neighbourhoods dating from the late 1940s to early 1950s.

The Redcliffe flats scheme in Bristol built between the mid 1950s and early 1960s, is an example of this approach, illustrating how the neighbourhood concept has survived for 50 years despite adaptations.

Location and Origins

This development is located within 1 km and to the south east of the city centre, sandwiched between the magnificent church of St Mary Redcliffe, some 18th century housing on its northern fringe, and the canalised River Avon on its southern boundary. A bridge links it to the inner suburb of Bedminster. The scheme forms part of the major rebuilding programme following the extensive destruction of this mainly working class area during World War II.

The design, by the City Architects Department, followed neighbourhood planning principles of the time, where relatively high density residential blocks (approximately 75 dwellings per hectare), in mixed configuration of between 4 and 12 storeys, supplemented by some convenience shops, a pub (adding to two existing pubs nearby), a secondary school, nursery and a surgery. Each block has a laundry room and communal room on its ground floor.

The central park, on the site of a square destroyed in wartime, provides the main open space. Additionally each housing block encloses and defines areas of green space of different size and character.

Given its population profile, the assumption underpinning the scheme was that car ownership would be very low. Only limited space therefore is devoted to parking, allowing for generous open green space and a network of footpaths and access streets penetrating the whole scheme.

Recent Experience

The scheme remains popular with its residents, some of whom have lived there for many years. There are few signs of damage and graffiti. Car ownership remains low, therefore there is minimal erosion of the green spaces.

Facilities have shrunk somewhat; there are about 25% fewer shops, the surgery and one of the nearby pubs have closed. However, a Community Forum has been established, the nursery and school have expanded, and the laundries and communal rooms are still being used. Some of the open green spaces have been enclosed by railings to create ownership and defensible space, reinforced by the installation of entry-phone systems at entrances.

Bus routes still link the neighbourhood with the rest of the city, with stops on the road running along the west side of the scheme.

Conclusion

Whilst the architectural appearance of the scheme looks dated, its layout, almost the antithesis of the current orthodoxy of the perimeter block, has created some pleasant, sunny green spaces, and successful frontages. In places however, anonymous green spaces have had to be enclosed to create defensible space. The original investment in facilities is impressive, and its location and management have helped to maintain the scheme's popularity. The high level of connectivity with surrounding routes and facilities has contributed to its continuing viability.

The layout of the scheme is designed to maximise the penetration of sunlight, green spaces and pedestrian access. View from road on southern boundary of the scheme. The original modernist architectural design concept has been adapted through the retro fitting of low pitched roofs and uPVC 'Georgian' style front doors.

The Redcliffe Neighbourhood

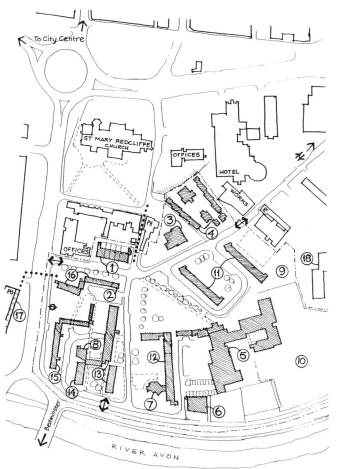

Key

1 Shops with 3 storey flats above (18 units)

2 Surgery on ground floor of flats

3 Church and church hall

4 Sheltered housing single storey (18 units)

5 Secondary school

6 Public house

7 Nursery school

8 Laundry

9 Playground

10 Playing fields

11 Blocks of 9 storey flats (2 x 54 units)

12 Block of 11 storey flats (88 units) with 3 storey wing (12 units)

13 Block of 3-5 storey maisonettes and flats (47 units)

14 Block of 5 storey maisonettes and flats (18 units)

15 Block of 3-5 storey maisonettes and flats (37 units)

16 Block of 5 storey maisonettes and flats (29 units)

17 L shaped block of 11-12 storey flats + 12 shops including post office - later phase?

18 One of 2 multi storey blocks of flats (2 x 108 units) – later phase

The Great Park has been a focus of planning policy for some years culminating in the 1998 planning permission. The current plan is for about 2,500 new homes, the vast majority for private sale – 6,000 people in all – plus a large business park, a local centre and primary school. The original hope of the planners was that there would be investment in a high quality public transport route linking the development to the Metro system and the city centre.

Context

Newcastle Great Park lies on the A1 trunk road immediately to the north, and slightly west, of the built up area of Newcastle, about 8 km from the city centre. The airport is a few kilometres to the west. The area is part of a peripheral ring around the city of market and population growth. The site is still (2009) mostly green fields, but development of commerce and housing is progressing.

The SOLUTIONS analysis

The Great Park was used as one of a number of test cases for research into the sustainability of outer city areas (SOLUTIONS 2009). The research involved experimenting with different possible local urban forms and assessing their relative sustainability – particularly from the viewpoint of potential accessibility to facilities and the likelihood of reduced car dependence. The survey of residents in the affluent suburbs adjacent to the Great Park showed that at present car dependence is very high, and the level of active travel low (see comparative statistics in Section 3.8). Is it likely that the new development would do better?

The existing plan

The first map shows the general disposition of land uses as proposed. The density of the housing is relatively high for outer suburban situation. Following the typology of neighbourhood form earlier in the chapter, the pattern is classified as essentially a series of pods – separate land uses in distinct enclaves, with limited interconnection. The analysis of accessibility suggested, for example:

* Only a quarter of residents within 800 metres of the local centre.
* Just under half within 400 metres of the likely bus route – and some doubts as to whether a good service would be viable.
* Less than 20% within easy walk of the primary school
  The conclusion was, comparing this with other places, car ownership and use would be high, and active travel low. Local facilities and bus services would struggle to succeed unless they attracted custom from elsewhere.

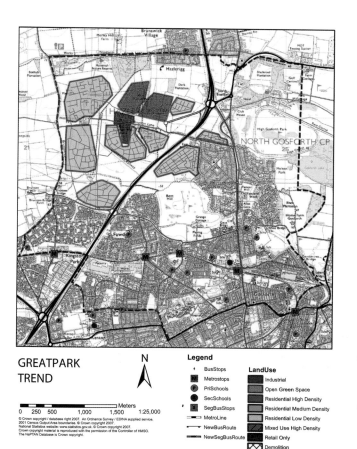

GREATPARK
TREND

N

Meters
0 250 500   1,000   1,500   1:25,000

© Crown copyright / database right 2007. An Ordnance Survey / EDINA supplied service.
2001 Census Output Area boundaries. © Crown copyright 2007.
National Statistics website: www.statistics.gov.uk. © Crown copyright 2007.
Crown copyright material is reproduced with the permission of the Controller of HMSO.
The NaPTAN Database is Crown copyright.

Legend

| BusStops |
| Metrostops |
| PriSchools |
| SecSchools |
| SegBusStops |
| MetroLine |
| NewBusRoute |
| NewSegBusRoute |

LandUse

| Industrial |
| Open Green Space |
| Residential High Density |
| Residential Medium Density |
| Residential Low Density |
| Mixed Use High Density |
| Retail Only |
| Demolition |
| Leisure Use |
| Zone Boundary |

The linear plan

The best alternative form tested was linear development, eventually with a much higher population, around a high street spine that was the main bus and bike route and focus for local facilities. This option could potentially achieve a very different outcome:

- Almost 100% within 800 metres of a local centre.
- Two thirds being within 400 m of a bus stop, with much more chance that the bus service would be viable.
- Two thirds of households within easy walking distance of a primary school.

The conclusion was, again looking at other places for comparison, behaviour could be less car based, more active travel, offering more chance of local community networks developing, and much more robust in the face of possible climate change carbon tax or travel restrictions

The alternative location

However, the linear scheme depended for its attractiveness on investment in high quality public transport along the spine. There is no guarantee of this being forthcoming. It also required commuters and shoppers to change onto the Metro to reach the city centre and other regional attractions. The alternative was to suggest a different location for development altogether. Existing stations on the Metro out towards the airport provided the opportunity. The public transport already is there. No transfers are needed for regional access. There is space near the stations for development, and programming would be simpler than the linear scheme on the original site. The proposal on the map is for a series of cells around stations, which provide comparable local accessibility to the linear scheme.

Ironically the option had been excluded early in the planning process because it invades the green belt. This points up a critical conclusion. Sites for development should not be allocated on the basis of land ownership or fewest environmental constraints, but also taking account of the most efficient development pattern for the city.

Source

A full report on this case study and other parts of the SOLUTIONS project are on www.suburbansolutions.ac.uk

The project ran from 2004-09, was funded by EPSRC, and the acronym stands for 'the sustainability of land use and transport in outer city neighbourhoods'.

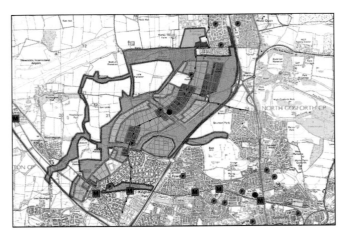

GREATPARK PLUS+ LINEAR EAST

1:35,000

0 250 500 1,000 1,500 2,000 2,500 Meters

© Crown copyright / database right 2007. An Ordnance Survey / EDINA supplied service.
2001 Census Output Area boundaries. © Crown copyright 2007.
National Statistics website: www.statistics.gov.uk. © Crown copyright 2007.
Crown copyright material is reproduced with the permission of the Controller of HMSO.
The NaPTAN Database is Crown copyright.

Legend

BusStops
Metrostops
PriSchools
SecSchools
SegBusStops
MetroLine
NewBusRoute
NewSegBusRoute

LandUse
Industrial
Open Green Space
Residential High Density
Residential Medium Density
Residential Low Density
Mixed Use High Density
Retail Only
Demolition
Leisure Use
Zone Boundary

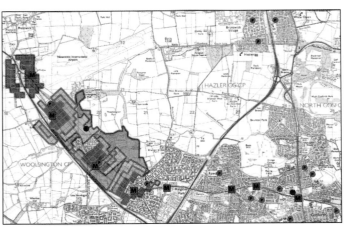

GREATPARK PLUS+ CELLS WEST

1:35,000

0 250 500 1,000 1,500 2,000 2,500 Meters

© Crown copyright / database right 2007. An Ordnance Survey / EDINA supplied service.
2001 Census Output Area boundaries. © Crown copyright 2007.
National Statistics website: www.statistics.gov.uk. © Crown copyright 2007.
Crown copyright material is reproduced with the permission of the Controller of HMSO.
The NaPTAN Database is Crown copyright.

Legend

BusStops
Metrostops
PriSchools
SecSchools
SegBusStops
MetroLine
NewBusRoute
NewSegBusRoute

LandUse
Industrial
Open Green Space
Residential High Density
Residential Medium Density
Residential Low Density
Mixed Use High Density
Retail Only
Demolition
Leisure Use
Zone Boundary

neighbourhood checklists | chapter 6

community checklist

This checklist is concerned with the health and sustainability of a neighbourhood, urban district or small town. The first section deals with the neighbourhood decision-making process that might be appropriate for the preparation of a local community strategy or spatial framework. Subsequent sections then work through the substantive issues, generally following the ordering of the guide, starting with people and community and ending with design.

The community checklist is intended for:

■ community groups evaluating the current situation in their town or neighbourhood

■ local councillors concerned with establishing partnerships and appropriate policy frameworks

■ local planners trying to set a neighbourhood agenda, or compare different localities, or prepare a spatial framework

■ community alliances wishing themselves to promote and be involved in a neighbourhood plan.

Note: cross references to earlier parts of the book are given at the start of each section.

Chapter 6 acts as a summary of the guide in the form of two complementary checklists. The community checklist provides a quick test of the overall health of a neighbourhood, while the development checklist provides criteria for judging the local impact of development proposal.

CONTENTS

6.1

6.1 NEIGHBOURHOOD DECISION-MAKING

Local communities are not masters of their own fate. Most development decisions within a locality are taken by private, public or voluntary sector organisations based outside the locality. The community interest is represented by the local planning authority through Development Plans and development management decisions, following consultation with parish or town councils.

However, there is potential for more active community involvement. This guide recommends the creation of neighbourhood plans at the level of the urban district or the country town. These can offer a sense of local identity while being at a practical scale for local provision and spatial planning. Plans could take the form of neighbourhood 'community strategies', contributing to district-wide Community Strategies that have to be produced by every local authority. Or they could take the form of Supplementary Planning Guidance adopted by the local authority.

Community ownership of the process is very important. While in some areas local interests may be co-ordinated by parish or town councils, in others it will be necessary to establish new community forums. Community development trusts provide a possible model.

CHECKLIST

This checklist starts from the assumption that local community groups, working with town/parish councils, are interested in developing neighbourhood (or 'township') level of policy-making for sustainable development.

Starting up 2.4

■ Is there an identifiable need for a town, district or neighbourhood strategy?

■ Is there already some form of sub-local-authority policy-making (e.g. within the Development Plan) that could provide the starting point for community planning?

■ Is there a sufficient initial community of interest amongst a range of political/voluntary/public/

private sector groups to warrant launching an initiative?

■ Are there widely recognised problems, opportunities and aspirations which can act as a motivator for other groups and interests to get involved?

■ Is the suggested area on a scale large enough to address the problems, and defined so as to avoid, on the one hand, the premature exclusion of interested parties, and on the other, loss of focus by including too much?

■ Is there a lead organisation (maybe the local authority itself, or a formal public/private/voluntary partnership) which has a clear and accepted idea about what needs to be done, and in what way?

Getting going 2.5

■ Is there a project brief, agreed by all the main stakeholders, which defines:
• the remit and the scope of the project
• the way decisions are to be taken
• how people are to be involved
• programme of work
• the intended outputs?

■ Does the stakeholder group include all the relevant 'movers and shakers' in the public, private and voluntary sectors, together with effective representation of the interests of residents, vulnerable/marginal groups and the wider (global) public interest?

■ Is there an inclusive and effective mechanism of public involvement (e.g. a citizens' forum or a focus group) that offers real participation without raising unrealistic expectations?

■ Has a 'neighbourhood appraisal' been undertaken encompassing social, economic and environmental issues in a format appropriate for policy-making?

■ Have major policy options been clearly identified and evaluated by stakeholders against fundamental health and sustainability criteria?

Making it happen 2.9

■ Has a long-term spatial framework been approved which can work towards a healthier and more sustainable environment, providing an effective context for short-term decision-making?

■ Have influential agencies (such as the health authority the education authority, county highways, or major local firms) committed themselves to fulfilling their part in the overall strategy?

■ Are both the local authority planning department and the planning committee (or equivalent) fully on board?

■ Where there are major development sites, urban extensions or regeneration areas, have development briefs and masterplans been prepared as appropriate?

■ Are specific development proposals coming forward, and being evaluated, in the context of the spatial framework and other policy guidance?

■ Is the implementation, and subsequent management, of projects occurring on a sustainable basis?

6.2 PEOPLE AND COMMUNITY

The starting point for any evaluation of the health of a neighbourhood or small town is the people of the area: their quality of life, living conditions, social networks, and the issues that concern them. Even when the prime motives for a local strategy are environmental or economic it is vital to put people centre stage. The benefits are awareness of all the different interests (including those of future generations), a holistic, human-orientated view, and legitimacy.

This section illustrates the kind of questions that need asking. They may be answered in a variety of ways, according to context:

• *through professional appraisal of statistics, such as those in state-of-the-environment reports or equivalent*

• *through social surveys*

• *through public consultation*

• *through collaborative policy-making processes.*

CHECKLIST

People   3.2

■ Who lives in the area, especially in terms of social and racial groups, types of household, age groups, and income levels? Is there a diverse, reasonably balanced community, or is it dominated by one group?

■ How is the population changing? Is there much in and out migration? If so, of what kind? And what factors (within or outwith) are causing it?

■ What 'quality of life' is enjoyed (or endured) by residents? Key indicators include:
  • mortality rates (by ward and age group)
  • the population of working-age people in work
  • unemployment claimants
  • the proportion of income-support residents
  • recorded crime per 1,000 population
  • families becoming homeless
  • school education results
  • car ownership rates.

■ What perceptions do residents have about the quality of their area? What do they like? What do they dislike? What priorities for urgent action?

■ Who else (besides residents) rely on the facilities of the neighbourhood (for example, entrepreneurs, workers, shop-keepers, people regularly socialising or playing in the area, visitors who value it)?

Community and housing   3.3, 3.4

■ Is there a thriving local community, especially in terms of the networks of association, mutual support and friendship that are vital for mental health and for groups such as children and retired people?

■ Are there specific places – facilities or external spaces – which are important for maintaining/building the sense of community?

■ Is there civic engagement on the part of local people? How does that manifest itself, or what seeds are there for future growth?

■ Is there a good mix of different types of housing in terms of tenure, size and affordability which can promote social inclusion and allow people to choose the location that maximises their own convenience and minimises the need to travel?

- Are specific housing needs, identified by local surveys and Housing Authority lists, being provided for in such a way as to avoid the creation of ghettos and to recognise locational needs (such as sheltered housing close to a local centre)?

6.3 ACCESS TO LOCAL FACILITIES AND JOBS

Good local accessibility to retail, leisure, health and education facilities is critical to establishing healthy neighbourhoods. It means that people without access to a car have convenient options (often now denied). In addition it means that a higher proportion of trips will be on foot or bike – active travel that combats obesity – and those who do use cars can choose not to travel so far. This cuts pollution and energy use. Having more people on the street also increases safety and the opportunity for casual meetings, facilitating friendship networks and a sense of community.

The possibility of local work opens up choices for residents and is important for those wanting part-time employment. It also reduces the average length of the (normally motorised) journey to work and increases the number gaining healthy exercise.

Planning can support (or restrict) local work by attitudes to homeworking, small workshops and the provision of local facilities. More broadly, planning policy can be re-oriented away from the injudicious support of dispersed business parks (which are car/lorry reliant, energy intensive, land-hungry and socially exclusive) towards the development of mixed-use district and town centres.

CHECKLIST

Local accessibility   3.8

- What range of facilities (retail, civic, leisure, social, religious, healthcare, educational, etc.) are available within or close to the neighbourhood?

- How accessible (in terms of the propensity of residents to walk or cycle) are different parts of the neighbourhood to key local facilities such as local shopping centres, superstores, schools, health centres, and parks/playgrounds?

- What are the perceptions of local people about what new facilities are needed?

- Is there a good range of jobs and training opportunities locally available, matching the needs of the population?

Retail and business centres   3.11

- Can existing district/town centres or local high streets compete effectively with out-of-centre stores and/or regional shopping centres and provide a social hub for the community?

- Can potential entrepreneurs find appropriate locations for their business in the context of mixed-use centres at public transport nodes rather than edge-of-town business parks?

- Is there a strategy in place to encourage innovative and environmentally benign entrepreneurial activity – through business networks and training programmes?

- Is there a clear official planning strategy, in partnership with local stakeholders, to enhance the attractiveness and viability of local retail centres?

- Are new stores (especially supermarkets) being located so as to reinforce the quality and use of existing or planned mixed-use centres?

- Are local retail outlets (especially in low-density suburbs and villages) being actively supported by market, voluntary and local authority action?

Schools and health centres   3.12, 3.13

- Does the Education Authority give a high priority to local access to nursery, primary and secondary schools, with appropriate standards and procedures in place?

- Are schools run as community facilities with opportunities for a range of activities, or treated as exclusive fortress schools?

- Does the Health Authority support, or plan to achieve, a good range of accessible local health services?

Recreation   3.14

- Does the local authority have a strategy for local play, and a programme for rectifying gaps in provision where residents support this?

- Does the Local Plan have policies protecting/ enhancing open space provision (parks, playing fields, allotments, informal greenspace) so that accessibility and continuity are improved?

- Is the maintenance and management of open space successful in offering quality and freedom with a sense of safety, thus inviting use by everybody?

6.4 PLANNING FOR MOVEMENT

The aim of movement is not only to get to places but, at the level of the neighbourhood, it is also about enjoying the process of moving.

Objectives for local movement planning are:

- *encouraging healthier life-styles – more walking and cycling*

- *improving access to local facilities and to public transport, especially for those who do not use a car and for less-mobile people*

- *enhancing the viability of local facilities and employment opportunities*

- *reducing accidents, street crime and fear of crime*

- *reducing energy use, air pollution and CO$_2$ emissions.*

Key to these objectives is getting people from all sectors of society to walk. Research shows that people's propensity to walk is directly related to distance, and significantly affected by how safe, convenient and pleasurable the experience of walking is. Safety is also a key factor in encouraging cycling, especially for children and older people. Public transport use is profoundly affected by distance to stops, reliability and the speed and comfort of service as well as frequency. Achieving these objectives requires close co-operation between transport providers, together with effective land-use planning.

CHECKLIST

General issues   3.15, 5.5

- What is the current balance of different types ('modes') of movement – walking, cycling, bus, car – for particular purposes: for example, to the local shops, schools, work places?

- Which streets are dangerous, or perceived to be dangerous, in terms of accidents and assaults and what has been done to reduce the dangers?

- What are the views of local people about the problems of and priorities for movement within the town/district and to the wider area?

- Is the district/town part of a sub-regional area, with a coherant, integrated plan for sustainable transport, which could improve the overall level of accessibility? If not, how could it be prompted?

Walking and cycling   3.16, 3.17

- Does the local authority have a strategy for the incremental improvement of conditions for pedestrians, for example through pavement widening, crossings, new connections, safe routes to school?

- Has a safe cycle network (on and off street) been identified, together with a programme for implementation?

Public transport   3.18

- What are the pattern and quality of public transport services, and how accessible are homes to good-quality services?

- Is there any plan for the improvement of public transport services, with key interests involved?

- Are new developments (housing, commercial, institutional) being closely linked to existing or new public transport routes and nodes?

Traffic reduction   3.19

- Are the levels of traffic and of congestion rising or falling?

- Is there a coherent strategy, area-wide, for traffic reduction, with a programme of investment in traffic management and the promotion of alternatives?

- Is new development being classified (by relative accessibility) as car-free, car-limited or traffic calmed?

6.5/6

Neighbourhoods, and urban areas generally, are not divorced from the landscape within which they sit, but part of it. They rely on the land for management of water, pollution and energy, and for local food production. The quality of the greenspaces in and around the neighbourhood is central to the quality of life for the residents. That quality is measured in terms of natural beauty, wildlife diversity, cultural heritage and recreational value. The effectiveness and quality of greenspaces is greatly enhanced if they are interconnected to form a system. For example, linear parks along streams can benefit wildlife, ease problems of water run-off, provide air-cleansing woodland and attractive walks. Yet in some urban areas where the amount of open space is well below official standards, some spaces are being sold off for development.

CHECKLIST   4.8, 4.12, 4.19, 4.21, 5.6

■ Is there a long-term strategy for creating, enhancing and linking multifunctional greenspaces as part of an ecosystem approach to the area?

■ Are water courses, drainage systems and balancing ponds being planned as accessible aesthetic and biodiverse amenities?

■ Have flood-plains been identified and plans for their protection/improvement been incorporated in Development Plans?

■ Are urban trees being planted and protected as part of a healthy neighbourhood strategy, with particular concern for their energy and pollution functions (e.g. windbreaks, carbon absorption, particulate cleansing) as well as visual, biodiversity and recreational functions?

■ Are wildlife havens and corridors being planned/enhanced as part of an overall biodiversity strategy?

■ Is there potential to increase community composting and food production through partnerships and management of allotments, city farms and local parks?

A basic principle of sustainable development is that buildings and settlements should use resources at sustainable rates and avoid polluting their own or the global backyard. Key resources in this respect are energy, water, food, air, minerals, biodiversity and climate. Processes of urban development and renewal should ensure that assets are properly valued, used and re-used efficiently, with levels of wastes and emissions that can be satisfactorily absorbed by the environment.

It is difficult to exaggerate the central importance of buildings in achieving sustainable development. Taking energy as an example, the energy used in buildings equals that consumed by transport and industry combined. Indeed, because of the dominance of housing in most neighbourhoods, it is likely that the heating, lighting and appliances of homes constitute the majority of local energy demand, with knock-on effects on the exploitation of non-renewable reserves, on air quality and CO_2 emissions.

There are important social, health and economic issues as well as environmental. An effective energy efficiency programme can, in time, eradicate fuel poverty and premature winter deaths, while reducing costs for householders and businesses.

The checklist below may paint an over-ambitious picture of what can be achieved at the neighbourhood level. But in fact many aspects are technically and behaviourally much easier to achieve than reduced transport energy use/emissions.

CHECKLIST

Energy   4.4, 4.6

■ Does the local authority have an energy strategy in place, for all users and suppliers, working in concert with key energy agencies?

■ Are there policies in place (in Local Plan or Supplementary Planning Guidance) which ensure that new developments are sited and laid out so as to reduce heat loss and maximise solar gain?

■ Is there an effective programme of action for increasing the energy efficiency of the neighbourhood's older housing stock, particularly that occupied by low-income households?

■ Are there any innovative energy schemes in the locality: for example, Community Heating with Combined Heat and Power (CHP), local sourcing of renewable energy, very low-energy solar buildings?

■ Are buildings being constructed out of low-energy and/or locally sourced materials?

Water   4.8

■ Is there available information about local water resources and a strategy (agreed between the water authority and the local authority) for their management?

■ Are building renovations and new developments as a matter of course incorporating water demand reduction, grey water recycling and sustainable drainage systems (SUDS)?

■ Is there a long-term strategy to enable the town/district to become self-sufficient in water supply and treatment?

Food   4.12

■ Is the potential for households to grow their own food at or very close to their dwelling being maintained, and enhanced through new allotment provision?

■ Are new dwellings being planned with (for the most part) south-facing gardens?

■ Are there opportunities and encouragement for farmers' markets and fresh greengrocer stalls in attractive locations?

Waste   4.17

■ Are kerbside recycling collections available and any new developments/renovations constructed with space for household recycling?

■ Is there a policy context that encourages local reuse, repair and recycling initiatives?

6.7	URBAN FORM

The most significant scale for the planning of local facilities, jobs and community development is not normally the neighbourhood (with a population of 2,000–10,000), but the urban township or district (12,000– 40,000). This level of population is sufficient to support a good range of retail, cultural, leisure and employment facilities, including for example superstore(s), technical college, library, leisure centre. It is roughly equivalent to a rural town of 8,000– 20,000, plus its hinterland.

Yet many such areas are not well served, or are experiencing progressive decline as facilities migrate to bigger centres and dispersed car-based locations, with consequent impacts on accessibility, social inclusion, health, congestion, energy use and emissions.

We recommend developing a robust spatial framework for each urban township or country town. The purpose of such a framework is to revitalise, reshape, and provide a context within which individual development decisions can be properly taken. The framework also acts as focus for debate and partnership between private, public and voluntary-sector stakeholders, working with the local planning authority.

The social and economic health of a neighbourhood may be judged indirectly by the incremental process of renewal – from ongoing maintenance of home and garden through to piecemeal redevelopment. This is mainly reliant on private householders and businesses, who will only reinvest if they and their bankers have confidence in the future of the area.

CHECKLIST

Spatial framework   5.2, 5.11

■ Is there a spatial framework for the district/ town, based on the principles of health, equity, environmental quality and resource efficiency?

■ Does the framework have accessibility to public transport services (existing and planned) as its starting point, and the basis for land-use planning?

■ Does the framework incorporate an open space

6.8

strategy geared to recreational access and sustainable resource management?

- Is mixed-use development encouraged at appropriate locations, with good pedestrian connections between uses, and space-sharing where possible?

- Does density guidance (not only for residential development) reflect the level and quality of pedestrian accessibility?

Urban regeneration   5.13

- Is there a gradual process of housing and business renewal and reinvestment across the area?

- Is the potential for brownfield development and urban intensification properly assessed in relation to accessibility and environmental capital (or quality)?

- Does the strategy identify 'critical' areas where major intervention through urban regeneration projects is justified, and provide the policy context for those projects?

- Does the strategy also identify what might be called 'pre-critical' areas, where judicious investment by the local authority, housing associations, private sector or voluntary partnerships might assist revival?

6.8   URBAN DESIGN

People identify with the 'neighbourhood' in the sense of a familiar distinctive locality, often with its own name. They also gain a sense of security (or insecurity) by the feeling of the street, square or block where they live (the 'home-patch'). If people feel safe and secure on their street then the chance of mental well-being is significantly increased. Equivalently, if traffic is calmed and non-intrusive, then the street can become the forum for conversation, play, and the development of local social networks. The design of home-places is also key to solar access and the adaptability of the area to small-scale work and retail facilities.

The streets, squares and courts knit together to create the public realm. The attractiveness of the

public realm, its variety and local distinctiveness are central to the principle of a walkable neighbourhood.

CHECKLIST   **3.5, 5.15, 5.16**

- Is there a strategy for maintaining and enhancing (or improving where necessary) the distinctive character and identity of each neighbourhood, with appropriate participation in the process by residents and/or residents' groups?

- Has a townscape survey of the locality been undertaken, preferably with the involvement of residents, which identifies distinctive local character?

- Is there a programme for home-place enhancement, particularly through traffic management, provision of local play facilities and landscaping (as in the UK's 'homezone')?

- Where new or infill development is proposed, is this guided by the principles of facing and overlooking the street ('perimeter block development') so as to safeguard the aesthetic quality and the natural surveillance of the street?

- Is new/infill development geared to maximising passive solar gain and sunny back gardens while at the same time minimising materials use and heat loss by wall sharing?

- Do new blocks or streets incorporate a variety of built forms allowing for some diversity of user and adaptability between users (e.g. from house to corner shop or office)?

development checklist

6.9	**INTRODUCTION**

This checklist develops the principles of healthy neighbourhoods at the level of a specific site or project within the neighbourhood – for example a mixed-use renewal scheme, a new retail outlet or a new housing development. The checklist is intended to assist people making decisions about developments, assessing the extent to which a specific project fulfils health and sustainability criteria.

The checklist is indicative rather than comprehensive. It focuses on factors relevant at the neighbourhood level and does not deal, for example, with detailed building design. The first section works through the process of consultation and establishing partnerships with relevant agencies and the local community. The subsequent sections address the key substantive issues of need, location, context, site appraisal and design.

Who should use this checklist?

The checklist should be used by socially responsible developers and by anyone else evaluating the local impact of a development. It does not include economic viability criteria. It is potentially useful to:

- major landowners who wish to consider the future use of a site or influence a detailed local plan for an area in order to sell land

- the local authority as land owner and/or developer, who have to balance social/environmental responsibility with getting good financial return

- other investing organisations, public, private or non-profit, who wish to evaluate alternative investment options or refine a specific proposal

- project managers and designers charged with developing and implementing a project, negotiating with other interests and ensuring compliance with official policy

- development control officers, in pre-application discussions with developers and in evaluating planning applications

- local councillors charged with making decisions about new development proposals and networking with potential future investors

- community groups, responding to and commenting on proposals that affect their neighbourhood.

Origins of the checklist

This checklist is based on that in the WHO publication Healthy Urban Planning *(Barton and Tsourou 2000), adapted to reflect the neighbourhood emphasis.*

Other assessment tools

In Britain there are official methods for assessing the sustainability of projects.

- BREEAM for commercial/institutional developments

- The Code for Sustainable Homes for residential development

- Environment Impact Analysis (EIA) for very major proposals

The checklist presented here is broader in scope and more alligned with neighbourhood impacts than building design.

See also the SPECTRUM approach advocated in Chapter 2, especially the Houndwood case study.

6.10	THE PROCESS OF DECISION-MAKING

Consultation is a necessary part of the decision-making process even for small house-holder development applications, but with larger projects it is often necessary to go beyond consultation if a co-ordinated and healthy scheme is to result. Other interests will be at stake. Action by a range of agencies (such as infrastructure agencies, service providers) is likely to be critical to the quality of the outcome.

CHECKLIST

Establishing the need for the project   2.4

- Is the purpose of the project clear?

- Is the project responding to needs identified in the development plan or community strategy for the town/district?

- Is there backing from the wider community for the principle of such a project?

- Is the project tied to the site by reason of its specific characteristics, or is it footloose?

- If footloose, then have alternative locations been properly investigated?

Working with the relevant agencies   2.5

- Is there a clear framework agreement at the outset between the project developer and the local planning authority which establishes who should be partners or consultees in the decision process, and how they should be involved, given the particular scale and nature of the project?

- Are the specific project development interests appropriately involved:
  - land owners?
  - developers?
  - any current tenants in or users of the site?
  - potential end users?

- Are relevant infrastructure providers involved:
  - providers of transport infrastructure?
  - operators of public transport?
  - agencies for water supply, sewage treatment and drainage?
  - companies providing gas, electricity and district heating companies?
  - education, leisure, health, police and fire services?

- Is the community actively involved:
  - neighbours?
  - local community groups?
  - urban social/environment/civic/economic lobbies?

Mechanisms for co-operation   2.5, 2.6, 2.9

- Has an effective working partnership been established between all key stakeholders, with a co-operative attitude established so that issues and possible solutions can be properly recognised and evaluated?

- Are there close working relationships with organisations with whom potential joint development and operation could be desirable?

- Are community interests being effectively recognised through public meetings, focus groups, Planning for Real, citizens' juries or other appropriate means, on a practical time-scale and with participation of the key players, so that the results can be properly incorporated in the development proposals?

- Is the professional and technical work being staged in such a way that decisions are not reached prematurely and the health, social, environmental and economic context of the project and the site is fully taken into account?

The project programme   2.5, 2.7, 2.8

- Is there a project brief which sets out the stages of planning and implementation in a logical manner?

- Is there a full appraisal of the site and its context, including identification of any statuary or legal constraints?

- Have the opportunities afforded by the site, and the potential relationship to the surrounding area, been taken account of in the development brief?

- Have options been considered properly, with stakeholders involved, before decisions are made?

- Is there a clear design framework or masterplan which shapes and contextualises individual buildings to achieve overall coherence?

■ Does the detailed design, and subsequent construction programme, recognise the priorities and frameworks established earlier?

■ In the wake of construction, is there user/resident involvement in the on-going management of the development, and in monitoring outcomes to ensure objectives are achieved without undesirable side-effects?

6.11 CHOOSING THE RIGHT LOCATION

This section looks at the question as to whether a given site is appropriate for development. The check-list could also be used to compare and evaluate alternative sites. The main issues raised are about the quality of the environment, safeguarding of resource quality, and the level of accessibility.

The criteria here relate to those used in the development potential framework in Section 5.8 and the SPECTRUM approach detailed in the Houndwood case study, Chapter 2.

A possible site can be evaluated, for each question below, as being:

- *a priority for development, helping to solve wider problems and create quality*
- *satisfactory for development, with no particular impacts*
- *possible, subject to negotiated agreement to mitigate problems*
- *difficult, requiring fundamental shifts in approach or policy*
- *impossible, because essential local social/ environmental capital is destroyed.*

CHECKLIST

Social and economic dynamics 3.3, 3.4, 3.7

■ Is the proposed site of the development appropriate in terms of impact on any retained uses on site? Where there are existing tenants (often with tenure but low ability to pay) could the transition be managed in an equitable way so their situation is improved not undermined?

■ Would the development, if it were to happen on the proposed site, be compatible with neighbouring activities – bearing in mind scale, shading, pollution, noise, traffic generation?

■ If a residential development, does the proposed site mean that the new dwellings complement existing provision to ensure a good diversity of housing opportunities within the area (as opposed to creating one-class or one-age ghettos)?

■ Would the proposal threaten or disrupt existing social networks and capital, or conversely could it help heal a currently socially fragmented, atomised community?

■ If a commercial proposal, would the location facilitate access to possible support services, employees, clients, and have a beneficial effect on local rent levels and longer run viability of the area?

Movement networks 3.15

■ Is the site well served by existing or potential walking and cycling routes that offer safe and convenient routes to local facilities and by public transport services?

■ Could the development of the site help to justify the improvement of public transport services? Could it contribute financially?

■ Is there reasonable road access to the site without exceeding the physical capacity of the network or causing environmental damage or increased danger?

■ Is the site a barrier? Are there 'desire lines' accross it which should be realised by providing a permeable development?

Accessibility 3.6, 3.8

■ Would potential residents have good access to a wide range of jobs both locally and regionally without being obliged to rely on car use?

■ Would residents be within easy walking or cycling distance of a good range of local facilities, social, health, leisure, shopping, education and open space?

■ Would commercial uses be embedded within an urban area so that a good proportion of employees or clients could be within walking or cycling distance?

- Would the development help reinforce the viability and vitality of local service centres by increasing their catchment population and/or by complementary commercial or social activities?

- Do employment or social facilities have an appropriate degree of public transport accessibility to afford easy access from the surrounding area to:
  - local facilities on a main local bus or tram route?
  - district facilities at a nodal point for local public transport services?
  - city-wide facilities at the hub of services, including close to main-line rail services?

Biodiversity and carbon fixing   4.20, 4.21

- Would development on the site affect a protected wildlife conservation area or valued wildlife habitat?

- Are woods and copses conserved and potentially enhanced by the development and brought into productive use?

- Is there potential on the site for increasing carbon capture through new planting, and moderating temperature extremes through general 'greening'?

Pollution and hazard

- Is the site, or part of the site, subject to excessive levels of air pollution, noise, vibration, ground contamination or industrial hazard, beyond that which can be solved by good design?

- Is the development liable to cause excessive levels of pollution, noise or danger for people in the vicinity, either directly through the nature of its activity or indirectly because of traffic generated? This applies most obviously to industrial or extractive activities in residential areas.

Water resources   4.9, 4.10

- Does the proposed site avoid areas susceptible to flooding, and avoid exacerbating problems of excessive surface run-off?

- Is it located where there is space capacity in the water supply system (or on-site catchment potential), avoiding areas where groundwater abstraction rates are not sustainable?

- Is it located where there is spare capacity in the surface and wastewater drainage systems, or on-site potential to deal with these?

Minerals, land and soil   4.11

- Does it avoid high-grade soils, areas of organic farming and with intensive local food production (such as allotments)?

- Does it safeguard potentially useable virgin or recyclable mineral resources?

- Does it re-use or reclaim derelict urban land and thus reduce pressure on greenfields sites?

Energy use   4.5, 4.6

- Is the site in a sheltered position? Does the proposal avoid exposed hill crests?

- Is the site level or gently sloping towards the sun, avoiding north-facing zones, so as to maximise the potential for solar gain?

- Is the site in a position to benefit from the introduction of district heating and combined heating and power in the wider area, or to help justify the extension to the network which would benefit others?

Built environment   3.5, 5.13

- Could the site potentially provide an attractive environment for people living, working and playing: safe streets, pure air, pleasing aesthetic (sound, sight, smell and touch)?

- Would it have the capacity to enhance the environmental quality of the neighbourhood preserving what is valued, including history, townscape and landscape, while regenerating dead, hazardous or ugly elements?

- Would development enable existing structures on site to be rehabitated or, failing that, their materials re-used?

6.12   **SITE AND CONTEXT APPRAISAL**

Good analysis of the site and its context are necessary if the principles of sustainable development are to be converted into practice in the development scheme. It is critical that the developers (and their designers) engage with this appraisal and understand its significance. To encourage this, the local authority could oblige developers to submit a site appraisal in support of their development application. Such a submission could take the form of annotated maps and short statement of stakeholder consultations. In the UK it might equate with the Design and Access Statement.

CHECKLIST

Land use and character   5.7, 5.15

- What are the surrounding uses? Is there potential complementarity with proposed uses on the site, especially in terms of pedestrian movement?

- Can development on the site be used to trigger renewal or revitalisation on neighbourhood sites (thus enhancing the land values of both)?

- What is the prevailing scale and character of surrounding development? Should the new development seek to reinforce this?

- What locally distinctive architecture or townscape, reflecting the traditional materials and culture of the area, could be used as a starting-point for design?

Movement and accessibility   3.9, 3.15

- What existing/proposed pedestrian or cycling routes, desire lines (routes people instinctively take through an open space) and rights of way could be affected (positively or negatively) by the project?

- Where are the nearest bus, tram or rail stops, and how could access be gained most directly and safely to them from the site?

- Where are the nearest schools, surgeries, shops, cafés, pubs, children's play areas, parks and playing fields in relation to the site?

- How does the distance or the time taken to reach these facilities compare with approved standards?

- Do existing or possible pedestrian and cycling routes offer good quality in terms of
  - road traffic safety?
  - perceived personal safety?
  - gradients and surface?

- ease of use by the less mobile?
- attractiveness?
- directness?

- Do any specific new links need to be made to avoid a land-locked site and improve permeability?

- Are the relative merits of different possible vehicle access points identified in terms of noise and danger (on and off site) and a permeable road network?

Ground conditions and topography

- Has the condition of the soil and ground been investigated to determine stability and bearing capacity?

- Are there past (potential) mineral workings, subterranean structures or areas of landfill on or adjacent to the site that might cause hazard?

- Is the ground contaminated with any hazardous materials, and have radon levels been checked?

- Have slopes been analysed in terms of gradient and aspect to guide design decisions so as to:
  - minimise cut and fill and retaining walls?
  - minimise disruption of natural drainage?
  - maximise solar gain or shade (according to climate)?
  - avoid undue exposure?

Microclimate, air and noise   4.5

- Have the implications of prevailing insulation levels, wind patterns, diurnal air flows and frost risk been considered?

- Have sheltered positions been identified, especially in relation to neighbouring buildings and tree shelter belts?

- Is the site affected by sources of air pollution or noise, especially major roads or factories?

- Is there potential on-site or by agreement with neighbours for mitigating or reducing levels of pollution or noise?

Water, wildlife and landscape   4.9/4.22

- Has the amount and quality of rainwater and its potential for use on-site been assessed?

- Has information been gathered on infiltration, groundwater, watercourses (flow, pollution and wildlife interest)?

■ Has the potential for on-site treatment of grey and black wastewater been evaluated?

■ Is there potential treatment of polluted watercourses to enhance on-site health and biodiversity?

■ Has a wildlife survey been conducted, identifying habitats (often associated with watercourses) that are inherently valuable and could contribute distinctive character to development?

■ Have locally significant landscape features been identified (on or near the site) such as tree groups, hedgerows, streams or crests of hills?

■ Does the site contribute (now or potentially) to a green corridor important for recreation, wildlife or landscape?

Re-use of buildings and local materials

■ Have existing unused/derelict buildings on sites been assessed for their historic/townscape value, their value as an embodied energy resource, and the viability of retaining them?

■ If demolition is unavoidable, is there potential for re-using the materials either reclaimed for building or for hardcore?

6.13	NEIGHBOURHOOD HEALTH AND SUSTAINABILITY IMPACT

This section provides a checklist for evaluating the project brief, masterplan or concept stage of a development project. It is a form of project appraisal. Depending on the scale of the development, the questions have a different significance. On very major sites with a range of uses and perhaps 1,000 dwellings, the questions relate more to the internal arrangements. For smaller sites, the question is how they fit into the wider neighbourhood.

CHECKLIST

The mix of activities 5.3

■ What measures have been taken to ensure that the development contributes to a broad pattern of mixed use, with a rough balance of homes, jobs and services in any given locality, township or

small settlement?

■ Does the development complement (rather than reproduce) the neighbouring activities, and link to them by easy, direct access so as to enhance viability and attractiveness?

■ If employment or services: does it avoid the creation of single-use or isolated facilities, instead contributing to clusters of mixed uses in local centres or high streets?

■ If housing: does it provide options for home-based work or subsequent change of use to local services?

Housing balance 3.3

■ Does the development contribute to ensuring there is a wide variety of types of housing (especially tenure and price) within a given neighbourhood or small town?

■ If a large development (varies with the context: the normal UK threshold is 15–25 dwellings), does it include a proportion of social housing?

■ Again, if a larger project, does it provide variation on site in relation to garden provision, built form and character, in order to offer options to people with different needs?

Public transport access 3.18

■ Is the land close to public transport used at an appropriately high intensity to facilitate access to public transport?

■ If this is a major development: are the main magnets of pedestrian activity located close to tram or bus routes and every part of the development within striking distance (for example, 400 m) of a stop?

■ Are any stops financed by the development conveniently located by principal users, well served by pedestrian routes, sheltered, visible and safe?

Cycling 3.17

■ Is the level of design appropriate to encourage potential cyclists?

■ Do any cycle routes provided by the development link effectively with desire lines for the wider area?

■ Are the cycle routes as direct as possible, with

gradients, bends, kerbs and junctions designed correctly?

- Have potential areas of conflict between cyclists and vehicles or pedestrians been identified and effectively resolved?

- Has provision been made (if appropriate) for secure cycle parking and changing/shower facilities?

Pedestrian environment   3.16

- Do pedestrian routes create a continuous and coherent network and hierachy of routes ensuring a permeable environment with ease of access to all neighbouring areas?

- Are gradients and the use of kerbs minimised to facilitate use by those with impaired mobility such as the frail elderly, people with hearing or sight impairments and wheelchair users, also by parents with pushchairs and children with skateboards or tricycles?

- Are the road-crossing points designed to give pedestrians effective protection from traffic, and the right of way wherever possible?

- Are the footpaths designed to give visually attractive and varied routes while ensuring good visibility and minimal risk of ambush?

- Are the public faces of buildings (entrances, windows) aligned towards footpaths and squares so that they provide informal surveillance?

Traffic and parking   3.19

- Is there a legible road hierarchy that allows ease of access for vehicles and reasonably direct routes (to minimise noise and pollution within and around the development)?

- Are streets in residential, shopping and central areas designed for 'natural' traffic calming, with 30 kmph design speed and priority for pedestrians, cyclists and buses clearly established?

- Is the level of parking provision as low as is realistic, given the use and the location of the development?

- Is there a travel plan which aims to reduce car reliance, promote walking, cycling and public transport use, and encourage/initiate a car club or car share scheme?

Public greenspace   3.14, 5.6

- Is provision made for accessible and appropriate open spaces particularly satisfying local needs for meeting-places, children's play for a range of ages, kick-around, sport, allotments and recreational walks?

- Are green spaces designed with both beauty and a sense of safety, both shelter and sunlight in mind?

- Does greenspace in the development link into a wider network:
  - encouraging circular walks and cycle rides?
  - providing a variety of wildlife habitats?
  - managing water resource sustainably?
  - managing the microclimate?
  - helping to improve air quality?

Privacy, security and gardens   5.16, 5.17

- Does the layout of external spaces around homes provide an appropriate level of surveillance and sense of user control, clearly distinguishing between public and private access?

- In areas with lower density, are gardens shaped and orientated to assist home growing and composting?

- In areas with higher density, are there balconies, roof gardens or patios, or communal gardens or allotments next to the buildings?

Energy strategy   4.4

- Is the development designed to minimise the need for artificial heating or cooling, with appropriate solar orientation and natural ventilation?

- Has the landscape around the buildings been designed to reduce wind speed, provide summer shade and allow winter sun?

- Is the heating/cooling system (if needed) the most environmentally economical available: for example, in northern climes, combined heat and power using renewable fuels?

- Has the potential for renewable energy capture been realised?
  - biomass boilers
  - ground source heat pumps
  - solar water heating

6.13

- photovoltaics
- wind energy
- water power

Water strategy   4.8

■ Does the proposed development harvest rainwater to provide for at least some uses on site?

■ Are systems to be installed which encourage re-use of grey water?

■ If the existing capacity in centralised sewage systems is limited or none is accessible, does the development deal with its own sewage?

■ Will a SUDS system be in place to allow all surface water to percolate into the ground or reach local streams, with pollutants removed?

Biodiversity strategy   4.19

■ Does the development preserve and enhance the value of any special on-site habitats (for example, stream banks, trees and hedgerows)?

■ Does the layout provide green corridors or 'stepping stones' across the site, increasing the potential for wildlife infiltration?

■ In higher-density schemes has thought been given to providing nooks and crannies for wildlife colonisation?

Noise and pollution

■ Are the buildings laid out and constructed so as to minimise problems of noise between neighbours on and off site?

■ Have problems of airborne pollution (from neighbouring areas), on-site ground contamination, or watercourse pollution been identified and managed so as to reduce health risks to an acceptable level?

Buildings and local materials   4.17

■ Have existing buildings on site been incorporated in the development scheme?

■ Have local sources of traditional building materials (normally associated with low energy use) been identified and used where appropriate, to give more of a sense of place and continuity with the past?

■ Are buildings designed for long-term adaptability in use, especially in terms of ground floor space and extensions?

■ Are dwellings designed as lifetime homes, able to offer a good environment for elderly and infirm occupants as well as able-bodied?

bibliography

Acheson, D. (1998) Inequalities in health. The stationery office, London

Addenbrooke, P., Bruce, D., Courtney, I., Heliwell, S., Nisbett, A. and Young, T. (1981) Urban Planning and Design for Road Public Transport, Confederation of British Road Passenger Transport, London.

Aldous, T. (1992) Urban Villages, Urban Village Group, London.

Aldrige, J. and Sempik, J. (2002) Allotments article in Social and Therapeutic Horticulture, Centre for Child and Family Research, Evidence Issue 6.

Allen, T. (2000) Housing renewal – doesn't it make you sick? Housing Studies. Vol 15, No 3, pp. 443–416.

Arnstein, S. (1969) 'A ladder of citizen participation', JAIP, XXX:4, pp. 216–24.

Atkinson, R. and Kintea, K. (1998) Reconnecting Excluded Communities: the Neighbourhood Impacts on Owner Occupation, Scottish Homes, Research Report 61, Glasgow.

Baker Associates and UWE (1999) Strategic Study of Urban Housing Potential in the South West Region: Final Report, South West Regional Planning Conference, Bristol.

Barton H. et al. (2000) Sustainable Communities: The Potential for Eco-neighbourhoods, Earthscan, London.

Barton, H. (1990) 'Local global planning', The Planner, 76:42 (26 October), pp. 12–15.

Barton, H. (2001) Towards a Theory of Sustainable Settlements: Integrating Health and Ecosystem Approach, paper given to the Housing Studies Association, April 2001.

Barton, H. and Grant, M. (2006) 'A health map for the local human habitat', The Journal of the Royal Society for the Promotion of Health, November 2006, Vol. 126, No 6, pp. 252-253.

Barton, H. and Kleiner, D (1998). Eco-neighbourhoods: a review and typology in Local Environment, June 1998

Barton, H. and Tsourou, C. (2000) Healthy Urban Planning, Spon, London.

Barton, H. andHorswell, M. (2009). Active travel patterns and facility use in outer city neighbourhoods – part of the report on the SOLUTIONS project (Sustainability of Land Use and Transport in Outer City Heighbourhoods). www.suburbansolutions.ac.uk

Barton, H. Davis, G. and Guise, R. (1995) Sustainable Settlements: A guide for Planners, Designers and Developers, UWE and LGMB, Bristol.

Barton, H., Grant, M., and Guise, R. (2003) Shaping Neighbourhoods; a guide for Health, Sustainability and Vitality, Spon Press, London.

BDOR (2006). An exciting future for community plans. Market and Coastal Towns Association, and SW ACRE Network of Rural Community Councils (SWAN). www.swan-network.org.uk/uplands/documents/community_plans_report.pdf

Beeson (2000) The Effectiveness of the 'Safe Routes to School' Programme, Unpublished MA dissertation, University of the West of England, Bristol.

Benson, J. and Roe, M. (Eds.) (2007) Landscape and Sustainability, Routledge, London.

Bently I. et al. (1985) Responsive Environments: A Manual for Designers, Architectural Press, Oxford.

Berry, T. 1991, (Ecozoic Era), Schumacher memorial lecture October 1991, E. F. Schumacher Society, Bristol.

Birmingham City Council (2001) Places for Living: Residential Design Guide for Birmingham, Department of Planning and Architecture, Birmingham.

Blackledge, D., May, A. and Wegener, M. (2007) 'Lessons for Policy', In Marshall, S. and Bannister, D. Land Use and Transport: Planning: European Perspectives on Integrated Policies. Elsevier, London

Bowyer, S., Caraher, M., Eilbert, K. and Carr-Hill R. (2009). Shopping for Food; Lessons from a London Borough. British Food Journal, vol 111, issue 5, pp 452-474.

Bowyer. S., Caraher, M., Duane. T. and Carr-Hill, R. (2006) Shopping for Food: Accessing healthy affordable food in three areas of Hackney. Centre for Food Policy, City University; London.

Breheny M., Gent, T. and Lock, D. (1993) Alternative Development Patterns: New Settlements, Department of the Environment, Planning Research Programme, HMSO, London.

Brenneisen, S. (2006) Space for Urban Wildlife: Designing Green Roofs as Habitats in Switzerland, Urban Habitats, Vol. 4, No. 1, pp. 27-36.

BRESCU (1998) Building a Sustainable Future: Homes for an Autonomous Community, General Information Report 53, BRESCU, Garstang.

Brighton & Hove Council (1998) Wildlife for People: A Wildlife Strategy for Brighton and Hove, Brighton & Hove Council, Brighton.

Bristow, H. (1999) 'A Fresh Approach to Local Food Supply', Urban Environment Today, 22 July 1999.

Britt, C. and Johnston, M. (2008) Trees in Towns II: A new survey of urban trees in England and their condition and management, Department of Communities and Local Government, London.

Buchanan, C. (1963) Traffic in Towns, HMSO, London.

Burgess, G. (2008), Planning and the Gender Equality Duty – why does gender matter?

Burns, D., Hambleton, R. and Hoggett, P. (1994) The Policies of Decentralisation, London, Macmillan.

Butland, B., Jebb, S., Kopelman, P., McPherson, K., Thomas, S., Mardell, J. and Parry, V. (2007) Foresight Tackling Obesities: Future Choices—Project Report, Government Office for Science, London.

Calthorpe, P. (1993) The Next American Metropolis: Ecology, Community and the American Dream, Princeton Architectural Press, New York.

Calve-Blanco, T. (2009) Neighbourhood accessibility, social capital and mental well-being. Draft PhD, UWE, Bristol.

Campbell, C. (1999) Social Capital and Health, Health Education Authority, London.

Carley, M. (1996) Sustainable Transport and Retail Vitality: State of the Art for Towns and Cities, Historic Burghs Association of Scotland, Edinburgh.

Carmona, M. (2001) Housing Design Quality: Through Policy, Guidance and Review, Spon, London.

Carroll, B., Barton, H., Turpin, M. (2002). Sustainability Threshold Analysis: report submitted to the Environment Agency, Bristol

Cervero, R. (1993) America's Suburban Centres: The Land Use–Transportation Link, Unwin-Hyman, London.

City of York Council (2000) School Organisation Plan 2000–2005, City of York Council, York.

Civic Trust and Ove Arup Partners (2001) Sustainable Suburbs: Developing the Tools, Civic Trust, London.

Cooper, A. (2009). pers. comm.. Some initial findings from the PEACH project

Croucher, K., Myers, L., Jones, R., Ellaway, A. and Beck, S. (2007) Health and the Physical Characteristics of Urban Neighbourhoods: A Critical Literature Review, Final Report, Glasgow Centre for Population Health, Glasgow.

Crowther, R., Rolfe, L., Hill, A., Morgan, S., Rutter, H. and Watson, J. (2004) Indications of Public Health in the English Regions 3: Lifestyle and its impact, Association of Public Heath Observatories, Stockton on Tees.

Dauny, A. and Plater-Zybeck, E. (1991) Towns and Town-Making Principles, Howard University, New York.

Davis, A., Valsecchi, C. and Fergusson, M. (2007) Unfit for Purpose: How Car Use Fuels Climate Change and Obesity, Institute for European Environmental Policy, London.

DCLG (2005) Planning Policy Statement 1: Delivering Sustainable Development, Department of Communities and Local Government, London.

DCLG (2006a) Planning Policy Statement 3 (PP53) on Housing CLG, London

DCLG (2006b) Strong and prosperous communities. Local Government White Paper Cm 6939-1

DCLG (2007a) Planning Policy Statement: Planning and Climate Change, A Supplement to Planning Policy Statement 1, Department of Communities and Local Government, London.

DCLG (2007b) Planning for a sustainable future. Cm 7120, T80

DCLG (2008) Code for Sustainable Homes: Technical guide, Department of Communities and Local Government, London.

De Knegt (1996) Design for Lower Car Use in Residential Areas, Planning and Transport Research and Computation International Association (PTRC) European Transport Forum: Proceedings of Seminar C, Planning for Sustainability, Brunel University, London.

de Vries, S., Verheij, R., Grenewegen, P. and Spreeuwenberg, P. (2003) Natural environments – healthy relationships? An exploratory analysis of the relationship between and health. Environment and planning A, 35, pp. 1717-1731 Green space

Dean, M. (2003), Growing Older in the 21st Century, Economic and Social Research Council, Swindon.

DEFRA, 2009. Shared UK principles of sustainable development, available online at http://www.defra.gov.uk/sustainable/government/what/principles.htm [accessed 15 November 2009]

Dennis, N. (1968) 'The Popularity of the Neighbourhood Community Idea', in Pahl, R. (ed.), Readings in Urban Sociology, Pergamon Press, Oxford.

Department for Education and Employment (1999) Organisation of School Places, DfEE Circular 9/99, HMSO, London.

DETR (1993) Trees in Towns, Department of the Environment, Transport and the Regions, HMSO, London.

DETR (1996) Planning Policy Guidance Notes PPG6: Town Centres and Retail Development, Department of the Environment, Transport and the Regions, HMSO, London.

DETR (1997a) Passive Solar Estate Design, Energy efficiency programme, Best practice programme 27, Department of the Environment, Transport and the Regions, HMSO, London.

DETR (1997b) Planning Policy Guidance Notes PPG1: General Policy and Principles, Department of the Environment, Transport and the Regions, HMSO, London.

DETR (1997c) Planning Policy Guidance Notes PPG7: The Countryside: Environmental Quality and Economic and Social Development, Department of the Environment, Transport and the Regions, HMSO, London.

DETR (1998a) A New Deal for Transport Better for Everyone, The Government's White Paper on the Future of Transport, The Stationery Office, London.

DETR (1998b) National Sustainability Strategy, Department of the Environment, Transport and the Regions, HMSO, London.

DETR (1998c) Planning for Sustainable Development: Towards Better Practice, Department of the Environment, Transport and the Regions, HMSO, London.

DETR (1998d) Places, Streets and Movement, A Companion Guide to Design Bulletin 32 (Residential Roads and Footpaths), Department of the Environment, Transport and the Regions, HMSO, London.

DETR (1998e) Planning for the Communities of the Future, Department of the Environment, Transport and the Regions, HMSO, London.

DETR (1998f) The Use of Density in Urban Planning, Planning research programme, Department of the Environment, Transport and the Regions, HMSO, London.

DETR (1998g) Guide to Community Heating and CHP: Commercial, Public and Domestic Applications, Energy efficiency, Best practice programme, Good Practice Guide 234, BRESCU, Garstang.

DETR (1999a) Local Government Act (Best Value), Department of the Environment, Transport and the Regions, HMSO, London.

DETR (1999b) Community Heating – A Guide for Housing Professionals, Energy efficiency programme, Good practice guide 240, BRESCU, Garstang.

DETR (1999c) Selling CHP Electricity to Tenants – Opportunities for Social Housing Landlords, Energy efficiency programme, New practice report 113, Department of the Environment, Transport and the Regions, HMSO, London.

DETR (1999d) New Deal for Communities, Department of the Environment, Transport and the Regions, HMSO, London.

DETR (1999e) Opportunities for Change, Department of the Environment, Transport and the Regions, HMSO, London.

DETR (1999f) Quality of Life Counts: Indicators for a Strategy for Sustainable Development for the UK: A Baseline Assessment, Government Statistical Service, London.

DETR (1999g) School Travel Strategies and Plans: A Best Practice Guide for Local Authorities, Department of the Environment, Transport and the Regions, HMSO, London.

DETR (1999h) From Workhorse to Thoroughbred: A Better Role for Bus Travel, Department of the Environment, Transport and the Regions, HMSO, London.

DETR (1999i) Towards an Urban Renaissance, E&FN Spon, London.

DETR (1999j) Planning Policy Guidance Notes PPG12: Development Plans, Department of the Environment, Transport and the Regions, HMSO, London.

DETR (2000a) Local Government Act, Department of the Environment, Transport and the Regions. The Stationery Office, London.

DETR (2000b) Our Countryside:The Future – A Fair Deal for Rural England (The 'Rural White Paper'), Department of the Environment, Transport and the Regions, The Stationery Office, London.

DETR (2000c) Our Towns and Cities: The Future – Delivering an Urban

Renaissance (The 'Urban White Paper'), Department of the Environment, Transport and the Regions, The Stationery Office, London.

DETR (2000d) Planning Policy Guidance Note 13: Transport, Department of the Environment, Transport and the Regions. The Stationery Office, London.

DETR (2000e) Planning Policy Guidance Note 3: Housing, Department of the Environment, Transport and the Regions. The Stationery Office, London.

DETR (2000f) Preparing Community Strategies, draft guidance, Department of the Environment, Transport and the Regions, The Stationery Office, London.

DETR (2000g) Transport Statistics Travel to School, Department of the Environment, Transport and the Regions, The Stationery Office, London.

DETR (2000h) Encouraging Walking: Advice to Local Authorities, Department of the Environment, Transport and the Regions. The Stationery Office, London.

DETR (2000i) Building a better quality of life: A strategy fro sustainable construction. Department of the Environment, Transport and the Regions, The Stationery Office, London.

DETR (2000j) Waste Strategy 2000, Department of the Environment, Transport and the Regions, The Stationery Office, London.

DETR and CABE (2000) By Design: Urban Design in the Planning System, Thomas Telford Publishing, London.

DETR and DTI (1999) Planning for Passive Solar Design, Building Research Establishment, Garstang.

DfT (2007a) Manual for streets, Department for Transport, Communities and Local Government, Thomas Telford Publishing, London.

DfT (2007b) National Travel Survey 2006. Transport statistics, London

DfT (2008) Building sustainable transport into new developments: a menu of options for growth points and Eco-towns. DfT, London

Dittmar, H. (2006) Can Traditional Urbanism and Architecture Be Green? Presentation to the Prince's Foundation, November 2006, accessed on-line 16 April 2009 at www.princes-foundation.org/files/conferencetraditional.pdf

Dodd, J. (1988) Energy Saving through Landscape Planning, Property Services Agency, London.

DoE (1973) Circular 82/73, Department of the Environment, HMSO, London.

DoE (1993) Reducing Transport Emissions Through Planning, Department of the Environment, HMSO, London.

DoE (1994) Urban Tree Strategies, HMSO, London. DoE (1996) Greening the City: A Guide to Good Practice, HMSO, London.

DoH (1998) Our Healthier Nation, Department of Health, The Stationery Office, London.

DoH (1999) Saving Lives: Our Healthier Nation, The Stationery Office, London.

DoH (2002) Securing our future health: taking a long-term view - the Wanless Report, HM Treasury, London.

DoH (2004) Accessibility Planning: An Introduction for the NHS, Department of Health, London.

DoH (2007) Draft guidance on health in strategic environmental assessment, Consultation document, Department of Health Publications, London.

Drax (2005) Environmental performance review 2004. Drax Power Limited.

DTI (2007). Meeting the Energy Challenge: a white paper on energy. HMSO, London

Duany, A. and Plater-Zybeck, E. (1991) Towns and Town-making principles. Howard University Graduate school of Design, Rizzoli, New York

Dwelly, T. (2000) Living at Work: A New Policy Framework for Modern Home Workers, Joseph Rowntree Foundation, York.

Early, D. (1994) 'The National Playing Fields Association', in Planning Practice and Research, 9:1, pp. 71–7.

ECOTEC (1993) Reducing Transport Emissions Through Planning, DoE/HMSO, London.

English Nature (1995) Accessible natural greenspce in towns and cities – a review of appropriate size and distance criteria. English Nature Research Report No. 153

English Partnerships (n.d.) Space for Growth, EP, London.

English Partnerships and the Housing Corporation (2000) Urban Design Compendium, EP, London.

Environment Agency (2000) A Study of Domestic Greywater Recycling, EA, Bristol.

Environment Agency and South Gloucester Council (1999) Sustainable Drainage Systems: A Guide to Developers, Interim advice note C10, South Gloucester Council, Thornbury.

Environmental Associations with Children's Health. Department of Exercise and Health Sciences, Bristol University

EST (2001) Energy Services: A Review of the EST Residential Pilot Projects 1996–2000, Energy Saving Trust, London.

EST (2007) Green Barometer: Measuring Environmental Attitude, April, Energy Saving Trust, London.

EU Expert Group on the Urban Environment (1995) European Sustainable Cities Report: Part Two.

Fairlie, S. (1996) Low Impact Development, Jon Carpenter, Oxfordshire.

Forest of Dean District Council (1998) Residential Design Guide, Forest of Dean District Council, Coleford, Gloucestershire.

Forestry Commission (2005). Economic benefits of accessible green spaces for physical and mental health. Scoping study, CJC Consulting, Oxford. Available online at http://www. Forestry.gov.uk/pdf/fchealth10-2final. pdf/$file [accessed 15 November 2009]

Frank, L., Andersen, M. and Schmid T. (2004) Obesity relationships with community design, physical activity and time spent in cars. American Journal of Preventative Medicine, 27(2), pp. 87-96

Frey, H. (1999) Designing the City Towards a More Sustainable Urban Form, E&FN Spon, London.

Garnett, T. (1999) City Harvest: The Feasibility of Growing more Food in London, Sustain, London.

Garnett, T. (1996) Harvesting the cities; The Ashram Acres project, Birmingham, Town and Country Planning, 65 (9), 264-265.

Gartland, L. (2008) Heat islands: Understanding and mitigating heat in urban areas, London: Earthscan.

GCC (2008). East End Local development Strategy, Glasgow City Council.

Available online at http://www.glasgow.gov.uk/en/YourCouncil/PolicyPlanning_Strategy/ServiceDepartments/Development_Regeneration/eelds.htm [accessed 15 November 2009]

Gilchrist, A. (2000) 'Design for Living: the Challenge of Sustainable Communities', in Barton, H. et al. Sustainable Communities, Earthscan, London.

Girardet, H. (1999) Creating Sustainable Cities, Green Books, London.

GLA (2007) Health Issues in Planning, Best Practice Guidance, Greater London Authority, London.

GLC (1965) The Planning of a New Town (The 'Hook Book'), Greater London Council, London.

Gloucestershire Market Towns (2000) Market Towns Health Check 2000, Gloucestershire County Council, Gloucester.

Goodacre, C., Sharples, S. and Smith, P. (2000) Integrating Energy Efficiency with the Social Agenda in Sustainability, paper presented at the Second Sustainable Cities Network Conference, 12–13 September, Manchester.

Green, G. and Tsourous, A. (eds.) (2008) City leadership for health: Summary evaluation of Phase IV of the WHO European Healthy Cities Network, WHO Europe, Copenhagen.

Greenspace Scotland (2008) Health Impact Assessment of greenspace: A Guide. Greenspace Scotland, Stirling

Guise, R. (2009a). Building Futures. Hertfordshire County Council, Hertford.

Guise, R. (2009b). Design Guide for Central Bedfordshire. Bedfordshire County Council, Bedford.

Guy, C. (2008) No more food deserts? Town and Country Planning, April 2008, p.162–3.

Hall, P. and Ward, C. (1998) Sociable Cities, John Wiley, Chichester.

Halpern, D. (1995) Mental Health and the Built Environment, Taylor and Francis, London.

Hanlin, P. Walsh, D. and Whyte, B. (2006) Let Glasgow Flourish, Glasgow Centre for Population Health, Glasgow.

Harris, R. and Larkham, P. (1999) Changing Suburbs: Foundation, Form and Function, E&FN Spon, London.

Hartig, T. Evans, G. Jamner, L. Davis, D. and Garling, T. (2003) Tracking restoration in natural and urban field settings, Journal of Environmental Psychology, 23, 109–123

Hartig, T, Mang, M & Evans, G. (1991) Restorative Effects of Natural Environmental Experiences, Environment and Behaviour, 23, 3–26.

Hass-Klau, C. et al. (1992) Civilised Streets: A Guide to Traffic Calming, Environment and Transport Planning, Brighton.

Haughton, G. and Hunuter, C. (1994) Sustainable Cities, Regional Studies Association, London.

HCN/DACRSPNE (2004) Nature and Health: The influence of nature on social, psychological and physical well-being, Health Council of the Netherlands and Dutch Advisory Council for Research on Spatial Planning, Nature and the Environment. The Hague: Health Council of the Netherlands and RMNO, 2004; publication no. 2004/09E; RMNO publication nr A02ae.

HEA (1999a) Deprived Neighbourhoods and Access to Retail Services, Health Education Authority, London.

HEA (1999b) Promoting Community Health – Developing the Role of Local Government, Health Education Authority, London.

HEA (2000a) Beacon Community Regeneration Partnership – The Beacon Energy Action Area, Health Education Authority, London.

HEA (2000b) Safely to School Pilot Project, Health Education Authority, London.

HEA (2000c) Town Centre 2000 Regeneration Scheme, Health Education Authority, London.

HEA (2000d) Walking for Health – Specific Benefits, Health Education Authority, London.

Hertfordshire County Council (1995) Accessibility isochromes, Hertfordshire County Council, Hertford.

Hillier Parker (1998) The Impact of Large Food Stores on Market Towns and District Centres, HMSO, London.

Hillman, M. and Whalley, A. (1983) Energy and Personal Travel: Obstacle to Conservation, Policy Studies Institute, London.

Hillman, M., Adams, J. and Whitelegg, J. (1991) One False Move, Policy Studies Institute, London.

Hoggart, P. and Kimberlee, R. (2001) Going Local? Area and Neighbourhood Governance. Centre for Local Democracy: Occasional paper no.1, UWE, Bristol.

Hopkins, R. (2000) 'The Food Producing Neighbourhood', in Barton, H. (ed.), Sustainable Communities, E&FN Spon, London.

Hou, F. and Myles, J. (2004) Neighbourhood inequality, neighbourhood affluence and population health. Social Science & Medicine, vol.60, issue 7, April 2005, pp 1557-1569

Hough, M. (1995) Cities and Natural Processes, Routledge, London.

Howard, E. (1902) Garden Cities of Tomorrow, Faber, London.

Howe, J. and Wheeler, P. (1999) Urban food growing; the experience of two UK cities, Sustainable Development, 7 (1), pp. 13–25.

Hulme Regeneration Limited (1994) Rebuilding the City: A Guide to Development in Hulme, Hulme Regeneration Ltd, Manchester.

IAIA, Quigley, R., L. den Broeder, P. Furu, A. Bond, B. Cave and R. Bos (2006) Health Impact Assessment International Best Practice Principles. Special Publication Series No. 5. Fargo, USA: International Association for Impact Assessment.

ICE (2000) Returning Roads to Residents, Institute of Civil Engineers, Thomas Telford, London.

IDEA (1998) Local Agenda 21 Roundtable Guidance No. 15 'Sustainable Agriculture and Food', IDEA, London.

IHT (2001) Guidance for Providing for Journeys on Foot, Institution of Highways and Transportation, London.

IPCC (2007) IPCC Fourth Assessment Report: Climate Change 2007, Intergovernmental Panel on Climate Change, Geneva.

Ison, E. (2007) Health impact assessment (HIA) of the drqaft East End Local Development Strategy: 'Changing Places: Changing Lives'. The Glasgow Centre for Population Health, Glasgow.

Jackson R. J. and Kochitzky, C. (2001) Creating a healthy environment: the impact of the built environment on public health. Sprawl Watch Clearing house. Washington DC

Jenks, M., et al. (1996) The Compact City: A Sustainable Urban Form? E&FN Spon, London.

Johnston, J. and Newton, J. (n.d.) Building Green, London Ecology Unit, London.

Joseph Rowntree Foundation (1995) Made to Last: Creating Sustainable Neighbourhoods and Estate Regeneration, Joseph Rowntree Foundation, York.

Kalache, A. and Kickbusch, I. (1997). A global strategy for healthy ageing. World Health 50(4):4-5

Kennedy, M. and Kennedy, D. (Eds.) (1997) Designing Ecological Settlements, EA.UE, Dietrich Reimer Verlag, Berlin.

Kuhl, D. and Cooper, C. (1992) 'Physical Activity at 36 Years: patterns and children predictors in a longitudinal study', Journal of Epidemiology and Community Health, 46, pp. 114-19.

Kuo, F. (2001). Coping with poverty – impacts of environment and attention in the inner city. Environment and Behaviour, 33, pp. 5-33.

Kuo, F. and Sullivan, W. (2001) Environment and Crime in the Inner city: Does Vegetation Reduce Crime? Environment and Behaviour 33(3)

Larkin, M. (2003) Can cities be designed to fight obesity? Lancet 362, pp. 1046-1047.

Larsen, Helwg-Larsen, T. and Bull, J. (2007) Zero Carbon Britain: an alternative energy strategy. CAT Publications, Machynlleth, Wales

Lavin, T. Higgins, C. Metcalfe, O. and Jordan, A. (2006) Health impacts of the built environment – a review, Institute of Public Health in Ireland, Dublin.

LDA (2006) Healthy and Sustainable Food for London: The Mayor's Food Strategy, London Development Agency, London.

Leach, Gerald. (1975), Energy and food production, Food Policy, vol. 1(1), pp. 62-73.

Lefevre, L., Blanchet, P. Angoujard, G., (2001) Non-chemical weed control in urban areas. The BCPC Conference: Weeds, 2001, Volume 1 and Volume 2. Proceedings of an international conference held at the Brighton Hilton Metropole Hotel, Brighton, UK, 12-15 November 2001, British Crop Protection Council.

Leyden, K. (2003) Social Capital and the Built Environment: The importance of walkable neighbourhoods. American Journal of Public Health, 9(9).

LGA (1998) Energy Services for Sustainable Communities: The Local Government Position, Local Government Association, London.

LGA (2000a) A New Future for Allotments, LGA, London.

LGA (2000b) Local Spatial Development Strategies, LGA, London.

LGA (2000c) Reforming Local Planning: Planning for Communities, LGA, London.

LGA (2001) Growing in the Community: Good Practice Guide to the Management of Allotments, LGA, London.

LGA and LGMB (1998) Energy Services for Sustainable Communities: The Local Government Position, LGA, London.

Living Streets (2008) Backseat Children: how our car dependent culture compromises safety on our streets. Living Streets, London

Llewelyn Davies (1998) Sustainable Residential Quality – New Approaches to Urban Living, LPAC, London.

Lovasi, G., Quinn, J., Neckerman, K., Perzanowski, M. Rundle, A. (2008)

Children living in areas with more street trees have lower prevalence of asthma, Journal of Epidemiology and Community Health, July, 62(7), pp. 647-9.

LUC and CAG (2001) Quality of Life Capital, English Nature, English Heritage, the Environment Agency and the Countryside Agency, London.

Lynch, K. (1981) A Theory of Good City Form, MIT Press, Cambridge, MA.

Maas, J. et. al (2006) Green space, urbanity, and health: how strong is the relation? Journal of Epidemiology and Community Health, 60, pp. 587-592.

Macfarlane, S. (1950) 'Peckam', Plan 7 – Journal of the Architectural Student's Association, pp. 22-7.

Making Cities Liveable (1996) Making Cities Liveable Newsletter, MCI.

Maller, C., Townsend, M., Ptyor, A., Brown, P. and St Leger, L. (2005) Healthy nature healthy people: Contact with nature as an upstream health promotion intervention for populations, Oxford University Press, Oxford.

Marmot, M. and Wilkinson, R. (Eds.) (1999) The Social Detriments of Health, Oxford University Press, Oxford.

Marvin, S. and Guy, S. (1997) Creating Myths rather than Sustainability: The Transition Fallacies of the New Localism, Local Environment, 2:3, pp. 311-18.

McDonough, W. and Braungart, M. (2002) Cradle to Cradle: Remaking the way we make things. North Point Press, New York.

McGill, J. (2001) Planning for Efficient Natural Resource Use in the Housing Sector, unpublished thesis, Faculty of the Built Environment, University of the West of England, Bristol.

McLoughlin, B. (1968) Urban and Regional Planning: a Systems Approach, Faber, London.

MEA (2005) Millennium Ecosystem Assessment reports:Ecosystems and Human Well-being. Island Press, Washington DC

Melia, S. (2009) The potential for car-free development in the UK. Draft PhD, UWE, Bristol

Milton Keynes Development Corporation (1992) The Milton Keynes Planning Manual, Chesterton Consulting, Milton Keynes.

Mitchell, R. Popham, F. (2008), Effect of exposure to natural environment on health inequalities: an observational population study, The Lancet, Volume 372, Issue 9650, pp. 1655-1660.

Mollison, B. (1998) Permaculture: A Designers Manual, Togari Publications, Australia.

Morris, W. and Kaufman, J. (1997) Mixed Use Development: New Designs for New Livelihoods, Queensland Department of Tourism, Small Business and Industry, Brisbane.

NAHB (1999) Smart Growth: Building Better Places to Live, Work and Play, National Association of Home Builders, USA.

National Consumer Council (2004) Why do the Poor pay more, and get less? National Consumer Council, London.

National Heart Forum (2007) Building health: Creating and enhancing places for healthy, active lives, National Heart Forum, London.

NCH (2004) Going hungry: The struggle to eat healthily on a low income, National Children's Home, London.

NEF (n.d.) Participation Works! 21 Techniques of Community Participation for the 21st Century, New Economics Foundation, London.

index and key terms

In the following index, page numbers in bold indicate a definition and in italics indicate a figure